Schriftenreihe Zentrum und Peripherie

Band 13

Dorothea Alewell | Wenzel Matiaske [Hrsg.]

Standards guter Arbeit

Disziplinäre Positionen und interdisziplinäre Perspektiven

Unter Mitarbeit von Ortrud Leßmann

Nomos

Die Deutsche Nationalbibliothek verzeichnet diese Publikation in der Deutschen Nationalbibliografie; detaillierte bibliografische Daten sind im Internet über http://dnb.d-nb.de abrufbar.

ISBN 978-3-8487-5814-2 (Print)

ISBN 978-3-8452-9931-0 (ePDF)

Die Schriftenreihe ist bis Band 8 bei Rainer Hampp Verlag, Mering, erschienen.

1. Auflage 2019

Inhaltsverzeichnis

Teil III: Standards Guter Arbeit und der Einfluss des rechtlichen Rahmens

Einleitung

Dorothea Alewell und Wenzel Matiaske

Mitte 2017 hat sich in Hamburg der interdisziplinäre und hochschulübergreifende Forschungsverbund »Standards Guter Arbeit und ihre Wirkungen auf die Nachhaltigkeit der Erwerbs- und Leistungsfähigkeit« konstituiert. Ziel des Verbundes ist es, Standards »Guter Arbeit« und ihre Entwicklung und Genese unter aktuellen Bedingungen zu untersuchen, sowie deren Wirkungen auf die Nachhaltigkeit der Erwerbsfähigkeit und -willigkeit von Arbeitnehmern und Selbständigen zu beschreiben und zu analysieren. Sozialethische und juristische Normen sowie die organisationssoziologische, personalwirtschaftliche und psychologische Forschung orientieren sich immer noch häufig am sog. Normalarbeitsverhältnis, während sich im realen Arbeitsleben bereits sehr heterogene Entwicklungen vollzogen haben und auch weiterhin stattfinden. Forschungsergebnisse aus verschiedenen Disziplinen – ökonomischer Arbeitsmarktforschung, personalwirtschaftlicher, psychologischer und soziologischer Forschung sowie juristischer Analysen – deuten auf eine Erosion dieses Standards des Normalarbeitsverhältnisses zugunsten anderer Arten von Vertragsbeziehungen und Beschäftigungsformen hin. Vom Normalarbeitsverhältnis abweichende Beschäftigungsformen machen mittlerweile rund ein Drittel der Gesamtbeschäftigung aus und bilden in manchen Beschäftigungsbereichen bereits den neuen empirischen Standard. Parallel dazu ist die Entwicklung der grenzenlosen Unternehmung und hybrider Organisationen entlang der nationalen und internationalen Wertschöpfungsketten in Organisationstheorie, Theorie der Unternehmung und strategischem Management seit mehreren Jahrzehnten ein viel diskutiertes Thema. Das Feld der Arbeit hat sich im Kontext dieser Entwicklungen durch neue Vertragsformen, durch projektförmige, räumlich und zeitlich entgrenzte Formen der Organisation (z. B. in Crowd- und Click-Work) und das Entstehen neuer Akteure (wie Anbieter von Plattformmärkten) teilweise schon radikal gewandelt. Aber auch dort, wo wir noch traditionelle Arbeitsverhältnisse beobachten, entstehen als Konsequenz der Internationalisierung, der Individualisierung und der Digitalisierung neue Anforderungen an (Mit-)Arbeitende – in qualifikatorischer Hinsicht, aber auch auf der Ebene individueller sozialer, psychologischer und seelischer Ressourcen und Belastungen. Neue Problemlagen und Anforderungen entstehen auch mit Blick auf die kollektiven Systeme der Arbeitnehmervertretung und der Sozialversicherung. Bisherige typische Lösungen oder empirische Standards der Ausformung von Arbeitsbeziehungen beginnen sich zu verändern oder haben sich schon deutlich verändert. Arbeitnehmer werden durch Leih-Arbeitnehmer, durch Werkauftragsnehmer oder (Solo-)Selbständige ersetzt, Arbeitgeber mit klar definierten rechtlichen Aufgaben auch im Arbeitsschutz werden Entleiher oder Auftraggeber. Wo bisher Arbeitnehmer in begrenzten Mitgliedschaftsrollen in Organisationen eingebunden waren, sind jetzt Arbeitskraftunternehmer in hoch autonomen und entgrenzten, zugleich aber möglicherweise auch prekären Beziehungen tätig. Es stellt sich also auf mehreren Ebenen die Frage, welche Standards von Arbeit sich im Geflecht dieser Veränderungen auf den Arbeitsmärkten und in den Organisationen und Wertschöpfungsketten herausbilden, und welche Wirkungen auf die Interessenlagen und die Wohlfahrt der betroffenen Parteien diese haben werden. Welche der sich neu entwickelnden Standards werden für welche Akteure »gut« sein?

Hinsichtlich der Frage, welche Maßstäbe der normativen Bewertung für die Einstufung von Arbeit oder Arbeitsbedingungen zukünftig als »gut« verwendet werden können oder sollen, erscheint uns angesichts der hohen Heterogenität der verschiedenen Akteure, ihrer Nutzen- und Wohlfahrtsvorstellungen und ihrer Handlungs- und Lebenssituationen, kein konkreter einheitlicher übergreifender Maßstab verfügbar. Vielmehr entwickeln wir die Vorstellung von »Guter Arbeit« mit Bezug auf die individuelle Wohlfahrt der Arbeitnehmer, Arbeitskräfte und Arbeitskraftunternehmer und den Interessen der jeweils betroffenen Gruppen. Gut ist aus der Perspektive der jeweiligen Gruppen das, was ihre individuelle Wohlfahrt erhöht. Damit ist inkludiert, dass es Interessenkonflikte und Bewertungsdivergenzen hinsichtlich der Frage gibt, was gut ist und was die Standards guter Arbeit sind und dass es eine interessante empirische Frage ist, welche Standards – im Sinne empirischer Üblichkeiten – sich bilden und durchsetzen, und von wem sie als gut betrachtet werden.

Neben der empirischen Bestandsaufnahme dieser Entwicklung neuer Standards in den Beschäftigungsverhältnissen und -bedingungen sowie den damit einhergehenden Verschiebungen in den Anforderungen, Gefährdungen und Belastungen, benötigten Ressourcen und möglichen Reaktionsweisen und Instrumenten sowie der Wohlfahrt und den Nutzen der beteiligten Gruppen und Akteure sind möglicherweise auch die tradierten Standards der beteiligten Forschungsdisziplinen selbst kritisch zu hinterfragen. So stellen sich beispielsweise Fragen danach, ob wir – wie bisher – Autonomie in erster Linie als eine wohlfahrtssteigernde Ressource der Arbeitskräfte interpretieren dürfen, oder ob ein Zuviel an Autonomie auch zu einer neuen Anforderung, einem neuen Stressor oder zu einer Belastung werden kann. Wir müssen fragen, ob wir – wie bisher, uns weiterhin auf das Normalarbeitsverhältnis und das Leitbild des Arbeitnehmers als zentralem Bezugspunkt unserer Forschung konzentrieren können, oder ob nicht gerade die Beschäftigten in den vom Normalarbeitsverhältnis abweichenden Beschäftigungsformen, Arbeitskräfte unter ganz verschiedenen Vertragsformen und Arbeitskraftunternehmer und ihre jeweiligen Arbeitsbedingungen unsere zentrale Aufmerksamkeit gewinnen sollten.

Diese Neubestimmung von Standards guter Arbeit kann nur auf mehreren Ebenen und unter Beteiligung verschiedener empirischer und sozial- und geisteswissenschaftlicher Disziplinen gelingen. Denn angesprochen sind damit

- das kulturelle System mit normativen Leitbildern zu Arbeit und ihrer Rolle für die individuelle Lebensführung,
- das soziale System mit der Entwicklung neuer Arbeits- und Lebensformen, und neuen Varianten von sozialer Ungleichheit,
- das ökonomische System mit zahlreichen Wirkungen auf dem Arbeitsmarkt, in den Organisationen, in Personalmanagement und Arbeitsorganisation, und
- das rechtliche System mit dem Individual- und Kollektivarbeitsrecht und dem Sozialrecht, wo sich neue Problemlagen der Herstellung von Schutz und materieller Absicherung für Arbeitende unter verschiedenen Vertragsformen stellen.

Die Beiträge in diesem Sammelband, deren Autorinnen und Autoren alle Mitglieder des Hamburger Forschungsverbundes »Standards Guter Arbeit« sind, spiegeln diese breite thematische und fachliche Palette der neuen Fragestellungen rund um Standards guter Arbeit und ihre derzeitigen Veränderungen wieder. Neben einer Vergewisserung über den Stand der Forschung zu den jeweiligen Fragestellungen skizzieren die Autorinnen und Autoren auch jeweils ausführlich die sich ergebenden noch offenen Forschungsfragen und mögliche Schritte, um diese zu beantworten.

Individuelles Wohlbefinden, Gesundheit und Persönlichkeitsförderlichkeit sind – aus Sicht der Arbeitspsychologie – auf der Ebene der Individuen verankerte Bewertungsmaßstäbe dafür, ob eine Arbeit eine »gute Arbeit« ist. Zwei der Beiträge in diesem Sammelband setzen an diesen Bewertungsmaßstäben an:

Jörg Felfe und *Katharina Klug* eruieren aus arbeitspsychologischer Perspektive den Stand der Forschung zur gesundheitsorientierten Führung und entwickeln hierzu eine Forschungsagenda. Die psychologische Forschung zur gesundheitsförderlichen Personalführung identifiziert einen deutlichen Einfluss des Verhaltens der Führungskräfte auf die Gesundheit ihrer Mitarbeiter – aber auch auf die Gesundheit der Führungskräfte selbst. Dabei wurden bereits idealtypisch positiv und negativ auf die Gesundheit wirkende Führungsstile identifiziert. Die Autoren gehen jedoch davon aus, dass nicht alle Vorgesetzten einheitlich nur einen der beiden Idealtypen von positiven oder negativen Führungsstilen anwenden, sondern dass in der Realität immer positive und negative Elemente von Führung gemischt auftreten können und werden. Daher skizzieren sie eine Forschungsagenda zu der Frage, welche Inkonsistenzen und Wechselwirkungen auf die Gesundheit von Mitarbeitern und Führungskräften es gibt, wenn Führungskräfte ein solcherart gemischtes Führungsprofil aufweisen. Zudem stellen die Autoren die Frage, welche Veränderungen für die Personalführung und ihre Wirkungen auf die Gesundheit unter den veränderten Bedingungen von Digitalisierung und atypischer Beschäftigung auftreten. Der Maßstab guter Arbeit liegt in dieser Untersuchung eindeutig in individueller Gesundheit und dem Wohlergehen der einzelnen Führungskräfte und Mitarbeiter.

Christine Busch und *Tim Vahle-Hinz* setzen ebenfalls am individuellen Wohlergehen, an der Gesundheit und der Persönlichkeitsentwicklung von Beschäftigten an. Gefährdungsbeurteilungen interpretieren die Autoren als ein Verfahren, um die Erfüllung und/oder Gefährdung dieser Zielvorstellungen an konkreten Arbeitsplätzen festzustellen. Die Arbeitswelt verändert sich durch Digitalisierung, Globalisierung und den demografischen Wandel. Der Gesetzgeber hat im Bereich der Gefährdungsbeurteilungen bereits auf solche Veränderungen reagiert – im Kontext der Digitalisierung müssen seit Ende 2013 neben physischen auch psychische Gefährdungen mit beurteilt werden. Die Autoren setzen sich daher als Ziel zu untersuchen, ob und wie Wohlbefinden, Gesundheit und Persönlichkeitsförderlichkeit als Standards guter Arbeit auch unter den aktuellen Bedingungen in der Arbeitswelt gesichert werden können. Hierbei stellen sie mehrere Fragen: Welche Veränderungen in der Arbeitswelt sind für die Standards einer guten Arbeit und die Feststellung dieser Standards in Deutschland von Bedeutung? Welche gesundheitlichen Folgen gehen mit diesen Veränderungen einher? Sind die bisherigen Faktoren zur Beschreibung von psychischen Belastungsfaktoren im Kontext dieser Veränderungen anwendbar? Gibt es neue oder zusätzliche Belastungsfaktoren, die zu berücksichtigen sind? Und wenn ja, wie sind diese anhand der Klassifizierung von Stressoren und Ressourcen zu beschreiben? Wie sollte eine Beurteilung von Gefährdung unter diesen veränderten Bedingungen aussehen? Welche Schwierigkeiten ergeben sich? Sie leuchten insbesondere die großen Herausforderungen aus, die multikulturelle Belegschaften und flexible Arbeitsformen für Gefährdungsbeurteilungen mit sich bringen. Denn wirken nach dem jetzigen Stand der Forschung schon aufgabenbezogene Ressourcen und Belastungen bei Beschäftigtengruppen mit und ohne Migrationshintergrund sehr unterschiedlich, so gilt das erst recht für beschäftigungsbezogene Ressourcen und Belastungen in Abhängigkeit von der Beschäftigungsform. Deutlich wird, dass uniforme Standards im Bereich der psychischen Gefährdungsbeurteilung vermutlich wenig Aussagekraft für das individuelle Wohlergehen von Personen aus unterschiedlichen kulturellen Hintergründen und unter unterschiedlichen Beschäftigungsformen entfalten werden. So lässt sich der Beitrag auch als ein deutliches Plädoyer für differenzierte Standards psychischer Gefährdungsbeurteilungen lesen.

Auch weitere Beiträge wenden sich dieser Frage nach der Differenzierung oder Uniformität von Standards guter Arbeit, der Personalarbeit und/oder der Beschäftigtengruppen zu.

Sven Hauff diskutiert aus personalwirtschaftlicher Sicht Vor- und Nachteile differenzierender oder uniformer Gestaltung von Beschäftigungssystemen am Beispiel der High-Performance-Work-Systems in Unternehmen. Er geht von dem Befund aus, dass mit den Empfehlungen der Best-Practice-Strategien eine universalistische Ausrichtung des strategischen Human-Resource-Managements (HRM) angelegt wird, über die dann faktisch universale Standards von Arbeitsbedingungen für alle Beschäftigtengruppen innerhalb eines Unternehmens geformt würden. Demgegenüber werden mit einer differenzierenden Gestaltung pluraler Beschäftigungssysteme innerhalb eines Betriebs auch die Standards der Arbeitsbedingungen für verschiedene Beschäftigtengruppen ausdifferenziert. Auf diesem Hintergrund diskutiert er auf ökonomischer Ebene sowohl die Vor- und Nachteile einer differenzierenden Ausgestaltung verschiedener Beschäftigungssysteme als auch die möglichen Rückwirkungen differenzierter

Standards auf das Verhalten und die Einstellung der Beschäftigten. Um diese Frage auch empirisch zu untersuchen, muss neben den von den Personalverantwortlichen intendierten und implementierten HRM-Strategien auch in den Blick genommen werden, welche HRM-Maßnahmen von den Beschäftigten wahrgenommen werden und Verhaltensrelevanz entfalten.

Daniela Rastetter setzt an der Diversität von Belegschaften und dem darauf bezogenen Diversity-Management an. Sie geht davon aus, dass die Herstellung gerechter, nichtdiskriminierender Arbeit aus Sicht der kritischen Arbeitsforschung, der Geschlechter- und der Ungleichheitsforschung sowie der Gewerkschaften und weiterer Institutionen, die sich um Arbeitnehmerrechte und Arbeitnehmerschutz kümmern, ein zentraler Standard guter Arbeit ist. Bei steigender Heterogenität der Beschäftigungsformen und Arbeitsbedingungen werden jedoch, so ihr Ausgangspunkt, die Herausforderungen bezüglich Nichtdiskriminierung komplexer. Dies gilt sowohl für die Steuerungsformen gesetzlicher und betrieblicher Art als auch in Bezug auf die Ansprüche und Erwartungen der Beschäftigten selbst. Auf organisationaler Ebene treffen Arbeitsgesetze, betriebliche Gleichbehandlungsstrategien sowie Interessen verschiedener Beschäftigtengruppen und deren Vertretungen zusammen und konstituieren das mikropolitische Feld, in dem Gleichbehandlung und Nichtdiskriminierung ausgehandelt werden. Unter den betrieblichen Strategien ist der Ansatz des Diversity Managements besonders interessant, da dessen Anspruch gerade im Managen der Heterogenität besteht. In der von Daniela Rastetter skizzierten Forschungsagenda »Antidiskriminierung und Gleichstellung bei digitalisierter Arbeit« soll daher untersucht werden, wie Gleichstellung im Rahmen fortschreitender Digitalisierung verhandelt wird und welche Rolle dabei Rechtsnormen, z. B. Antidiskriminierungsgesetze, auf der einen Seite und Diversity Management auf der anderen Seite spielen. Welche Interessen bezüglich Vielfalt und Nicht-Diskriminierung treffen in der Organisation aufeinander und welche Einflussmöglichkeiten haben verschiedene Akteursgruppen auf dieses Feld? Welche Gleichstellungsstandards resultieren daraus und welche Empfehlungen lassen sich für die Gestaltung diskriminierungsfreier(er) digitalisierter Arbeit ableiten? Erfüllt die betriebliche Strategie des Diversity Managements ihre eigenen Ziele, nämlich Vielfalt vorteilhaft zu gestalten, auch im Hinblick auf die Heterogenität digitalisierter Arbeit? Welche Wahrnehmungen und normativen Erwartungen haben die Beschäftigten selbst bezüglich Fairness und Nichtdiskriminierung? Inwieweit sind Antidiskriminierungsgesetze wirksam, wenn es einerseits immer weniger eindeutige (Minderheiten-

)Interessen gibt und damit die Interessenvertretungen zum Teil ihre Legitimation verlieren, andererseits jedoch mangels des Standards des rechtlichen und sozialen »Normalarbeitnehmers« auf verschiedene Gruppierungen mehr Rücksicht genommen werden muss? Welche alten und neuen AkteurInnen handeln mit wie viel Durchsetzungsmacht in diesem Feld? Welche Rolle spielen Interessenvertretungen, Gleichstellungsakteurinnen, die Politik, Gewerkschaften?

Auch *Dorothea Alewell* und *Tobias Moll* setzen an der zunehmenden Diversität von Belegschaften an, jedoch hinsichtlich eines speziellen Kriteriums – der Religion und Spiritualität. Sie vermuten, dass sich eine zunehmende Diversität nicht nur nach den häufig untersuchten Merkmalen von Alter, Geschlecht und ethnischer Zugehörigkeit, sondern auch nach den Merkmalen Spiritualität, Religionszugehörigkeit und Religiosität entwickeln kann und wird. Diese religionsbezogene und spirituelle Diversität könnte besonders dann betrieblich relevant werden, wenn, wie von Teilen der Managementforschung erwartet, in Zukunft nach der physischen, psychischen und kognitiven Energie nun auch die seelische Energie von Arbeitnehmern als vierte große Quelle von Arbeitsmotivation und -einsatz relevant wird, und zugleich größere Teile der Erwerbstätigen als bisher nach dem Sinn ihrer Tätigkeit als einem Teilaspekt der Spiritualität fragen. Denn dann sollten Spiritualität, Religion und Religiosität eine höhere Relevanz für das personalwirtschaftliche Handeln gewinnen als bisher. Daher gehen Alewell und Moll der Frage nach, ob und welche Relevanz Spiritualität, Religion und Religiosität von Arbeitnehmern an den Arbeitsplätzen in Deutschland haben könnten, bereits haben und ggf. auch haben sollten. Dabei leuchten sie die zahlreichen Verbindungslinien zwischen bisherigen Managementdiskursen und Fragen der Religion im Unternehmen sowie die – bisher eher spärlichen – Bestände empirischer Befunde aus, die zum Umgang mit Religion in deutschen Unternehmen vorliegen.

Barbara Müller, Christoph Seibert und *Oliver Vornfeld* greifen ebenfalls spirituelle Aspekte der Erwerbstätigkeit auf, nämlich die Herstellung von Sinn. Sie leuchten das Spannungsfeld zwischen Arbeit und Sinn aus anthropologischer, historischer und soziologischer Perspektive aus. Sie fragen nach der Bedeutung, welche Arbeit für die menschliche Suche nach dem Lebenssinn hat, und nach der Gestaltung von Strukturen, die es ermöglichen, konkrete Arbeitsabläufe als ein sinnhaftes Tun zu erfahren. Bei dieser Analyse gerät der Zusammenhang zwischen Lebensformen und den darin eingelassenen Verständnissen des Verhältnisses von Arbeit und Sinn in den Blick. Die historische Analyse verschiedener Lebensformen zeigt u. a., dass die Kopplungsverhältnisse zwischen Lebensform, Arbeit und Sinn nicht nur *in sich* komplex sind, sondern darüber hinaus auch *unter einander* erheblich variieren. Daran hat sich nach Ansicht der Autoren bis heute nichts geändert, sondern sie vermuten im Kontext moderner Gesellschaftsformationen eher einen Komplexitätszuwachs als einen Komplexitätsabbau. Damit konfrontiert die historische Analyse exemplarisch mit einer Problemkonstellation, die traditionalen Gesellschaften zwar nicht unbekannt ist, aber erst in posttraditionalen Gesellschaften zu einem sozialen Konstitutionsmerkmal par excellence wird. Gemeint ist das sogenannte »Faktum des [u. U. vernünftigen] Pluralismus«[1] verschiedener Lebensformen, mitsamt den damit einher gehenden unterschiedlichen Ausgestaltungen des Verhältnisses von Arbeit und Sinn. Dieses Faktum wirft die Frage nach den für posttraditionale Gesellschaften wirksamen *Mechanismen sozialer Integration* auf. Im Ergebnis zeigen die Autoren, wie wichtig eine qualitativ sinnvolle Arbeit bzw. Sinnstiftung durch Arbeit als Maßstab für das Gelingen oder Nicht-Gelingen von sozialer Integration und Gesellschaft überhaupt ist. Die Neubestimmung von Standards Guter Arbeit muss daher, so ihre zentrale These, die Sinnhaftigkeit von Arbeit und die Bedingungen, unter denen Sinn empfunden wird und hergestellt werden kann, deutlich mit in den Blick nehmen.

Drei weitere Beiträge setzen sich mit dem Recht und seiner Bedeutung für bzw. Interaktion und Wechselwirkung mit den Standards guter Arbeit auseinander.

Florian Schramm und *Ines Kannengießer* wenden sich dem Recht als Rahmen für Standards Guter Arbeit zu, und zwar zunächst dem Arbeitszeitrecht. Sie diskutieren das Ineinandergreifen von nationalen und europäischen Normen im Arbeitszeitrecht mit den Interessen der verschiedenen Akteure, die diese Normen mit Leben füllen. Sie leuchten dabei das dynamische Ineinander-Verwobensein von Law in the Books und Law in Practice aus – und präsentieren damit ein Beispiel, welches sehr anschaulich macht, wie auch das Recht zur Erosion einheitlicher Standards beitragen kann und die Entstehung einer heterogenen Regelungslandschaft unterstützt: Für die Arbeitszeit ist neben dem deutschen Arbeitszeitgesetz auf der europäischen Ebene die Arbeitszeitrichtlinie 2003/88/EC relevant. Diese räumt den Mitgliedsstaaten auf Ebene der Sozialpartner einen ge-

1 Vgl. John Rawls, Politischer Liberalismus (1993), Frankfurt a. M. 1998, S. 106.

wissen Spielraum zur weiteren Ausgestaltung des Arbeitszeitrechts ein, konkret einen verhandelbaren Ausgleichszeitraum, welcher zur Ermittlung der durchschnittlichen wöchentlichen Höchstarbeitszeit der Arbeitnehmer dient. Mit einer Ausweitung dieses Ausgleichszeitraums ist ggf. auch ein Unterschreiten des vorgesehenen Mindeststandards möglich. In der qualitativen empirischen Analyse zeigt sich, dass der Ausgleichszeitraum bei Tarifverträgen häufig abweichend geregelt wird, von dem Flexibilitätsspielraum also kräftig Gebrauch gemacht wird. Die konkrete Ausgestaltung der tariflichen Bestimmungen im Hinblick auf die Flexibilisierungsoptionen durch die Ausgleichszeiträume obliegt überwiegend der Betriebsebene. In diesem Kontext wird die wichtige Rolle der Arbeitgeber und Betriebs- und Personalräte für Standards Guter Arbeit deutlich. Denn dem Verständnis der Experten folgend müssen diese verstärkt als Hüter der rechtmäßigen Umsetzung der Arbeitszeitregelungen fungieren.

Margarete Schuler-Harms und *Katharina Goldberg* untersuchen die soziale Absicherung von »alten« und »neuen« Selbständigen als Herausforderung für das Sozialrecht. Ausgehend von dem digitalisierungsbedingten Befund der partiellen Verdrängung des Normalarbeitsverhältnisses zugunsten verschiedener Formen der Selbständigkeit über Crowd- und Gig-Work bzw. plattformbasierter Arbeit konstatieren sie zunächst die fehlende Systematik der Einbindung Selbständiger in die Sozialversicherung – und zeigen diese anhand einer ausführlichen Bestandsaufnahme der derzeitigen Sicherung Selbständiger in der Sozialversicherung auf. Dieser Zustand der Sozialversicherung wird in der Literatur begründet über die Vielfalt und Wandelbarkeit der Selbständigkeit und den mit ihr einhergehenden Sicherungsbedürfnissen. Zugleich werden aber Stimmen, die eine systematischere Einbindung Selbständiger in die sozialen Sicherungssysteme fordern, gerade gegenwärtig wieder deutlich lauter. Anlass genug, auch über die Bestandsaufnahme hinaus ein Forschungsprogramm zu skizzieren, welches diese Herausforderungen an die Sozialversicherung in den Blick nimmt und u. a. auf folgende Fragen fokussiert: War und ist selbständige Erwerbstätigkeit (noch) »gute Arbeit«? Greift die deutsche Sozialversicherung in Bezug auf selbständige Erwerbstätigkeit und neue Arbeitsformen hinreichend weit oder droht sie ihre Zwecke zu verfehlen und ihre Funktionen zu verlieren?

Hans Hanau und *Wenzel Matiaske* fokussieren mit der betrieblichen Mitbestimmung eine zentrale Institution der Arbeitsbeziehungen der sozialen Marktwirtschaft. Ausgehend von einer Skizze der Entwicklung vom Betrieb hin zur flexibler Organisation arbeiten die Autoren heraus, dass die Umstellung von betrieblicher Produktion auf die Leistungserstellung in Wertschöpfungsketten, Allianzen und Netzwerken mit einer Entgrenzung der Arbeitsverhältnisse einherging. Diese Entwicklung beförderte zugleich die »Verbetrieblichung« der Arbeitsbeziehungen und wurde durch die Verlagerung von Kompetenzen von den überbetrieblichen Tarifbeziehungen auf die betriebliche Mitbestimmung ermöglicht und verstärkt. In jüngster Zeit ist allerdings nicht mehr nur eine Erosion der Tarifbeziehungen zu beobachten, sondern es mehren sich die Hinweise auch auf eine Schwächung der betrieblichen Mitbestimmung. Empirisch wie theoretisch ist jedoch bislang unklar, welche Determinanten die Ausdünnung der betrieblichen Mitbestimmung verursachen. Dies wäre einerseits zu erhellen, um andererseits Hinweise auf die Konstruktion neuer Standards der Mitbestimmung im entgrenzten Betrieb zu gewinnen. Darüber wäre auch mit Blick auf die Implementierung funktionaler Äquivalente zur Funktion der Mitbestimmung zu erurieren, welche Randbedingungen erfüllt sein müssen, um die Akzeptanz und damit die Nachhaltigkeit alternativer Institutionen von »voice« im entgrenzten Betrieb zu gewährleisten.

Der Forschungsverbund ist dankbar für die finanzielle Unterstützung seiner Arbeit insgesamt durch die Landesforschungsförderung Hamburg. Ferner gilt unser Dank Jan Dumkow und Simon Weingärtner für das kritische Gegenlesen der Beiträge, Lena Bultmann für die Formatierung und das sorgfältige Lektorat sowie Ortrud Leßmann für das Lektorat und die Koordinierung des gesamten Bandes von der Idee bis zum fertigen Produkt.

Der Hamburger Forschungsverbund »Standards Guter Arbeit und ihre Auswirkungen auf die Nachhaltigkeit der Erwerbs- und Leistungsfähigkeit« wird an den hier skizzierten Themen und Forschungsprogrammen in den nächsten Jahren intensiv weiterarbeiten. Wir wünschen allen Beteiligten Forscherinnen und Forschern viel Erfolg und gute Ergebnisse dabei!

Hamburg, im November 2018 Dorothea Alewell und Wenzel Matiaske

Teil I

Standards Guter Arbeit und die Gesundheit

A Person-oriented Approach to Health-oriented Leadership – State of the Art and a Research Agenda

Katharina Klug and Jörg Felfe

1. Introduction

Working conditions are essential determinants of health: Whereas having work is beneficial for health, being healthy is also an important precondition to maintain employment (Jahoda, 1982; Ross, & Mirowsky, 1995). Given the amount of time people spend at work, physical and psychosocial working conditions have a significant impact on health. Work is therefore closely intertwined with individual health as a central functional capability (Nussbaum, 2000). Aside from health in terms of physical, mental and social well-being (WHO, 1948), working conditions also affect people's subjective well-being in terms of satisfaction with work and with life in general (Drobnič, Beham, & Präg, 2010; Hauff & Kirchner, 2013). Subjective well-being, in turn, can be construed as a correlate of health (Diener & Chan, 2011; Schimmack, Diener, & Oishi, 2002). Standards to define »decent« work should therefore include worker health and well-being as criteria, as well as aspects that contribute to health and to the prevention of stress, occupational injuries and diseases. Defining health-related labor standards requires investigating conditions which support or hinder employees in maintaining good health as a central functional capability.

Many modern economies, including Germany, are witnessing intensifying working conditions and rising sickness absence due to stress-related diseases (BAuA, 2012). Against this background, prevention at the workplace is becoming increasingly relevant. Leadership plays a critical role for a sustainable implementation of workplace health promotion, as leaders both represent and shape organizational structures. Recent developments, such as the growth of atypical employment and the digitalization of the workforce, pose new challenges to legislators, employers and employees: Blurred boundaries in new organizational structures and employment arrangements, such as platform-based clickwork, network organizations and temporary agency work may undermine standards of employee protection and participation on the collective level (see Kirchner & Beyer 2016, as well as Hanau & Matiaske in this volume). In this chapter, we consider the additional challenges faced by leaders and followers on the inter-individual level in their everyday work, such as the absence of face-to-face interaction in virtual teams or increased job insecurity in employment relationships which deviate from the standard of permanent, full-time employment with a single organization (Bell & Kozlowski, 2002; Eichhorst & Buhlmann, 2015; Maier, Viete, & Ody, 2017). Research findings on these individual-level stressors can in turn define standards on the collective level in terms of provisions for health-related risk assessments (see Busch & Vahle-Hinz in this volume).

The concept of Health-oriented Leadership emphasizes that direct supervisors affect employee health both directly through their behavior towards followers, but also indirectly by influencing tasks and working conditions (Franke & Felfe, 2011a; Franke, Felfe, & Pundt, 2014). In the worst case, leaders create stress for their followers through hostility or avoidance of leadership (Schyns & Schilling, 2013; Skogstad, Einarsen, Torsheim, Aasland, & Hetland, 2007). Last but not least, leaders are not only organizational actors, but their own health and behavior is subject to prevailing working conditions and their subordinates' influence (Franke et al., 2014; Wirtz, Rigotti, Otto, & Loeb, 2017).

So far, different leadership styles have been identified as generally beneficial or harmful for follower health (Montano, Reeske, Franke, & Hüffmeier, 2017). In the literature, these »styles« are mostly considered as consistent and exclusive within leaders. However, moderate correlations between different styles indicate that there may be leaders displaying both positive and negative behaviors, that is, inconsistent or mixed behavior. Therefore, an open question is how leaders combine different and even potentially contradicting leadership behaviors and, in turn, how this mixed leadership behavior affects health and well-being. The aim of this chapter is to discuss Health-oriented Leadership in the context of standards of decent work, as well as the question if and how Health-oriented Leadership can be applied in the digital workforce.

In the following, we briefly review the literature on the association between leadership and health and propose to conceptualize profiles of »mixed leadership« in order to account for inter-relations and inconsistencies between Health-oriented Leadership and other established leadership concepts pertinent to health and well-being. We then develop a research agenda to investigate the antecedents and consequences of mixed leadership profiles for both leaders' and followers' health and well-being: first, in the context of »traditional« work, and second, in the context of flexible employment in a digitalizing economy.

2. Leadership and health: state of the art

Leadership has a significant impact on health and well-being in several ways (Ducki & Felfe, 2011; Franke, Ducki, & Felfe, 2015): First, a leader's behavior and communication have a direct effect on follower health. For example, supervisors' consideration and social support has been associated with lower stress, burnout and health complaints among employees (Dormann & Zapf, 1999; Rowold & Heinitz, 2008; Vincent, 2012). Second, leaders indirectly affect health by shaping their followers' tasks and working conditions (Nielsen, Randall, Yarker, & Brenner, 2008). Employees whose supervisors provide them with autonomy, task variety and participation in decisions tend to report less stress and exhaustion (Vincent, 2012). Third, leaders themselves are affected by several stressors, such as a high workload, time pressure, interruptions or multitasking, which can affect not only their own health, but also increase the risk that supervisor stress spills over to employees (Price & Weiss, 2000; Steinmetz, 2011). These findings suggest that, because leaders are partly responsible for their followers' psychosocial working conditions but are also subject to considerable psychosocial stressors themselves, leadership behavior as well as leaders' working conditions may play an important role in health-related risk assessments (see Busch & Vahle-Hinz in this volume). Finally, leaders serve as role models for their followers. Supervisors who take care of their own health while successfully accomplishing their tasks are likely to motivate their employees to show positive health behavior as well (Franke et al., 2015).

As for leader behavior, current psychological research distinguishes prototypical leadership »styles« which are generally beneficial (e.g., transformational or Health-oriented Leadership) or harmful (e.g., laissez-faire) for employee health and well-being (Montano et al., 2017). Leaders may also practice elements of different styles which may compensate, neutralize or reinforce one another, but combinations of different leadership behaviors have not been studied yet. These combinations may result in specific profiles of mixed leadership with differing consequences for health and well-being.

2.1. Positive leadership »styles«

Perhaps the most prominent concept of positive leadership behavior in the literature is transformational leadership (Bass, 1999; Bass & Avolio, 1994). Transformational leaders inspire and support their followers, which is associated with lower employee strain and better well-being (Felfe, 2006; Nielsen et al., 2008; Rowold & Heinitz, 2008). However, transformational leaders also set high standards and challenge their employees, which may not always be healthy, if not stressful (Franke & Felfe, 2011b).

Aside from leadership behavior that is generally deemed effective, such as transformational leadership, understanding the associoation between leadership and health requires a framework that specifically conceptualizes health-relevant leadership behavior (Rigotti, Emmerich, & Holstad, 2015). The concept of Health-oriented Leadership was developed to fulfil this requirement (Franke et al., 2014; Franke & Felfe, 2011a). This concept proposes three factors that contribute to healthy working conditions: 1) leaders' SelfCare, that is, how leaders treat their own health, is an important precondition for 2) StaffCare, that is, leaders' concern for their followers' health in terms of concrete behavior. In turn, StaffCare promotes health and well-being, by 3) enabling followers to practice SelfCare. Figure 1 illustrates the components of Health-oriented Leadership and their respective inter-relationships.

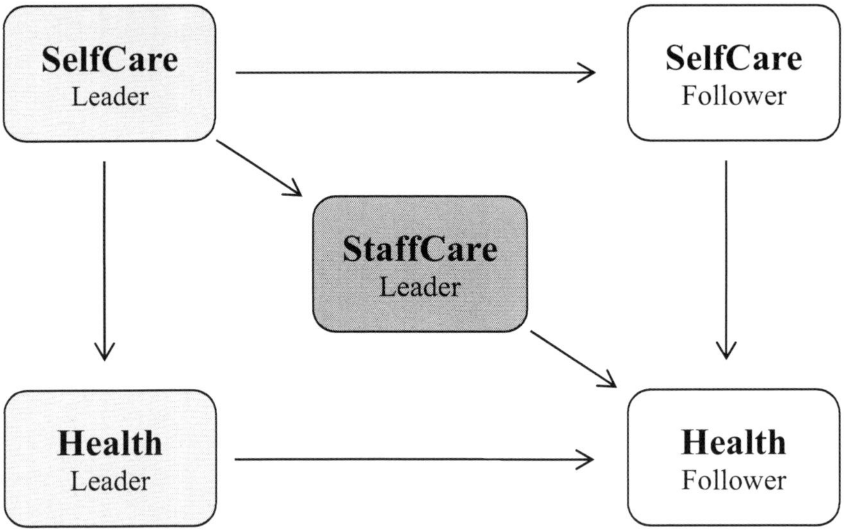

Figure 1: Conceptual model guiding research on profiles of mixed leadership and health.

In turn, each of these three factors consists of three dimensions. The behavior dimension refers to personal health-related activities and behaviors. The value dimension reflects the significance assigned to leaders' and followers' health, as well as the extent to which leaders and followers value actively creating healthy working conditions. The awareness dimension refers to followers' perception of their own health and stress symptoms (follower SelfCare), as well as the leader's ability to observe and adequately assess followers' stress (Franke et al., 2015). Previous validation studies have confirmed that followers whose leaders behave in a health-oriented way report more SelfCare, and consequently, better health and less strain (Franke et al., 2014; Pundt & Felfe, 2017).

2.2. Negative leadership styles

Certain leadership behaviors are not only counter-productive for efficiency, but can also harm follower health. For example, laissez-faire leadership is characterized by passiveness, delaying decisions and the absence of involvement. Laissez-faire leaders avoid active leadership, which creates conflict, task ambiguity and, in turn, distress for followers (Skogstad et al., 2007). In the most extreme form of negative leadership, abusive leaders show aggressive and hostile behavior toward their followers (e.g., ridiculing, insulting, threatening), which is obviously stressful and impairs follower health (Schyns & Schilling, 2013; Tepper, Moss, Lockhart, & Carr, 2007).

2.3. Leadership in the digital age

In the context of deregulated employment and digitalization, leaders may have to supervise dispersed followers with whom they may not interact face-to-face (Bell & Kozlowski, 2002). Employees may experience task ambiguity and uncertainty about the continuance of their jobs or the demand for their skills (Bell & Kozlowski, 2002; Eichhorst & Buhlmann, 2015; Loebbecke & Picot, 2015). Moreover, leaders and followers may not be able to build a long-term relationship when tasks are outsourced to freelancers or clickworkers (Peinl & Bildat, 2017; Valerio, 2016). Digital workers, often solo-self-employed and less integrated in organizational structures or social security schemes (see Schuler-Harms & Goldberg in this volume) may enjoy high autonomy, but also have to rely on SelfCare to maintain good health. In this context, clickwork represents a new phenomenon and special case of digital work. As of now, clickwork concerns only a small group of workers and serves as a sidejob for most (Maier et al., 2017). However, existing evidence about the working conditions of clickworkers suggests some specific health risks: Carrying out »microtasks«, clickworkers face working conditions characterized by fragmented and repetitive, simple tasks offering little opportunity for challenge and personal development. The absence of organizational affiliation, poor social support, and restricted access to organizational resources may cause social isolation due to the absence of teams and cooperation (Peinl & Bildat, 2017). It thus seems that clickwork is associated with an increased risk of hazardous psychosocial working conditions. Moreover, the lack of organizational integration raises the question of responsibility of organizations and leaders for the risk assessment of clickworkers (Busch & Vahle-Hinz in this volume). These developments raise the question if and how Health-oriented Leadership can be applied in the digital workforce.

3. Research agenda: A person-oriented approach to Health-oriented Leadership

The different leadership styles discussed in the literature represent ideal prototypes. Most likely, not all leaders practice any of these styles in pure form. It is for example conceivable that some leaders show concern for their employees' health, but also tend to delay decisions, and show abusive behavior when they are stressed themselves. Moderate correlations between different styles indicate that there may be a considerable number of leaders displaying both positive and negative behaviors, for example transformational but also sometimes abusive. Considering Health-oriented Leadership, both leader behavior (SelfCare and StaffCare) and follower behavior (SelfCare) can contribute to unique profiles of mixed leadership.

Considered separately, different leadership styles can be positively or negatively associated with health and well-being, but it is so far unknown which mixed profiles occur. From a different perspective, research on co-leadership has shown that differing and potentially contradicting behavior by two or more leaders can have both additive and interactive effects on follower well-being (Sharma & Pearsall, 2016; Vidyarthi, Erdogan, Anand, Liden, & Chaudhry, 2014).

As for health consequences, it is easy to imagine that, for instance, a combination of high leader SelfCare, high StaffCare and absence of abusive leadership is particularly beneficial for follower health, whereas the opposite is particularly harmful. However, it is less clear how inconsistent profiles associate with follower health. Can high follower SelfCare compensate low leader StaffCare, or does this discrepancy cause more stress than the reversed pattern? These open questions can be addressed with a person-oriented analysis, which allows to uncover configurations of leadership and investigate their associations with health (Bergman & Lundh, 2015).

Moreover, whereas follower health has been widely researched, leader health is rarely considered. First, it is conceivable that certain profiles of leadership are more or less beneficial not only for followers, but for leaders as well: For example, transformational leadership may improve leaders' satisfaction as they observe personal growth in their followers. Laissez-faire leadership may be convenient in the short-term, but ultimately create stress as problems remain unresolved. A combination of low leader SelfCare and high StaffCare may be beneficial for followers, but unhealthy for leaders. Specific profiles of mixed leadership may thus differ in their consequences not only for followers, but also for leader health.

Figure 2 illustrates prototypical combinations leader Self- and StaffCare with differing implications for leaders' and followers' health. It can be expected that a combination of both high leader SelfCare and high StaffCare would be most desirable for everyone's health, whereas, for example, low leader SelfCare in combination with high StaffCare (termed »leader sacrifice«) could a) result in good follower health, but poor leader health, or b) poor health for both followers and leaders, because the leader's negative role model behavior in terms of SelfCare offsets the benefits of StaffCare. The typology can be extended by other pertinent leadership behaviors (e.g., laissez-faire, transformational), as well as follower SelfCare to account for more differentiated leadership constellations.

		Leader SelfCare	
		Low	*High*
StaffCare	*Low*	»Low care«	»Follower sacrifice«
	High	»Leader sacrifice«	»High care«

Figure 2: Example combinations of leader SelfCare and StaffCare, illustrating profiles of Health-oriented Leadership

To sum up, we propose that a considerable number of leaders combine elements of leadership behaviors into inconsistent, mixed profiles that have so far been neglected in the literature. Different profiles of mixed leadership may have specific antecedents and consequences for both leaders' and their followers' health. Moreover, it is an open question whether such inconsistent profiles represent stable dispositions or change over time. In the following, we outline a general framework and specific research questions to guide empirical investigations of mixed leadership profiles and health.

3.1. Research framework and conceptual model

Figure 3 illustrates the conceptual model which summarizes the hypothesized relationship between profiles of mixed leadership, employment and working conditions, and health. We assume that leadership profiles affect outcomes of health and well-being both directly and indirectly by shaping demands and resources at work, as well as by buffering or exacerbating associations between demands, resources and health (Bakker & Demerouti, 2007; Demerouti, Bakker, Nachreiner, & Schaufeli, 2001). At the same time, we propose that prevailing demands and resources at the workplace, as well as follower health and behavior, bring about different leadership profiles and affect leaders' health. The hypothesized relationships may further differ in different employment contexts, such as platformbased work, remote work or virtual teams, and depend on practices of human resource management (see Hauff in this volume).

The following sections present research questions and study designs to address different aspects of the framework in four separate steps, such as the content and stability of mixed leadership profiles, their antecedents and consequences.

3.2. Identifying profiles of mixed leadership

The first step is to identify profiles of mixed leadership and to establish a relationship with health and well-being. We propose the following research questions:

- Which profiles of mixed leadership can be identified?
- How do leadership profiles associate with followers' health?

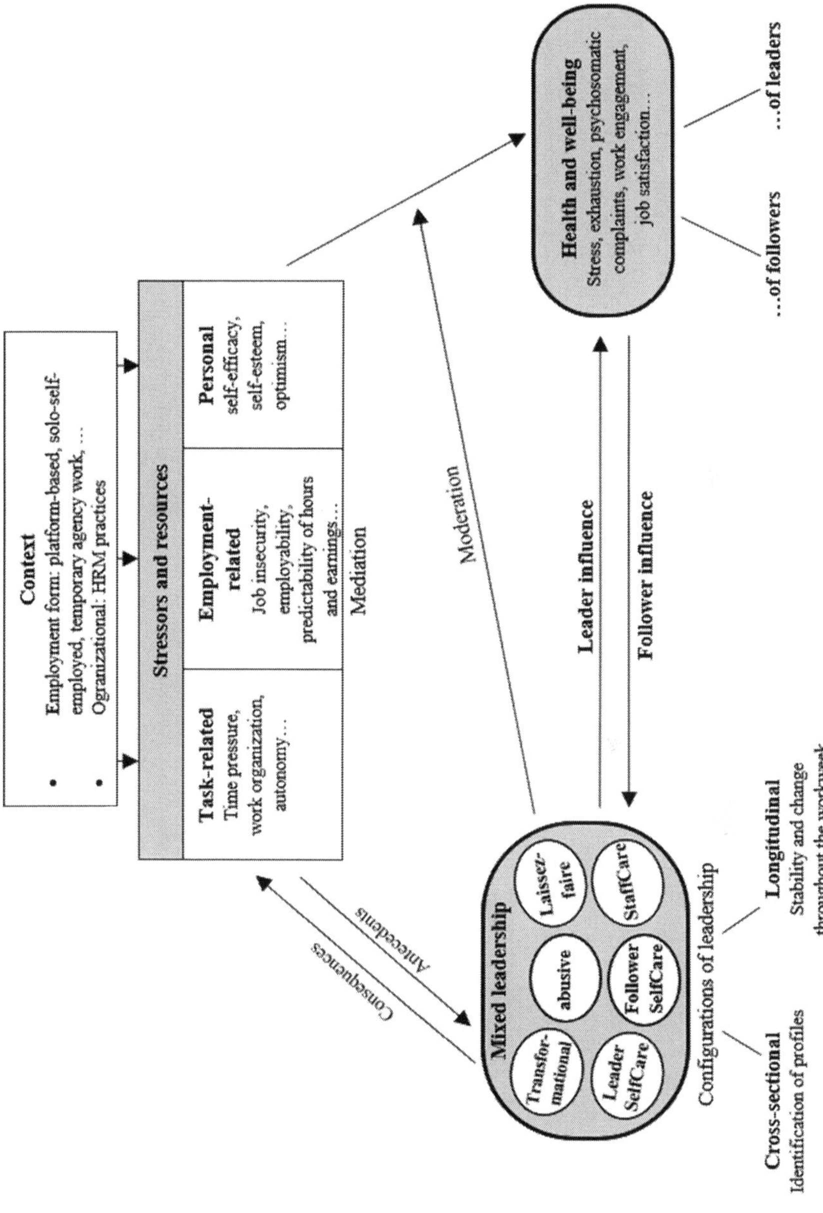

Figure 3: Conceptual model guiding research on profiles of mixed leadership and health.

The objective is to identify configurations of different leadership behaviors such as leader SelfCare, StaffCare, follower SelfCare, abusive or laissez-faire leadership, as well as to explore the profiles' relationships with pertinent outcomes of health and well-being at work, such as stress, exhaustion, psychosomatic symptoms, commitment or work engagement.

Identifying profiles in terms of configurations of different leadership behaviors requires person-oriented analytical methods, which focus on patterns and inter-relations of concepts rather than effects of isolated variables (Bergman & Lundh, 2015). Whereas classic variable-oriented methods (e.g., moderated regression techniques) analyze how constructs function separately across individuals, person-oriented methods such as latent profile analysis (LPA) show how constructs combine within individuals. LPA thus allows uncovering relevant subpopulations in heterogeneous samples, characterized by similar constellations of different variables (Bergman & Lundh, 2015; Wang & Hanges, 2010). LPA enables us to model the complex interplay of different leadership behaviors, their predictors and consequences for health and well-being. Person-oriented and variable-oriented methods of analysis can also be combined. For example, profiles detected with LPA may be used as a grouping variable in subsequent variable-oriented anylyses that investigate predictors and outcomes of different profiles (Wang & Hanges, 2011).

The reserch question can be addressed in a cross-sectional survey design. Ideally, both followers and their direct supervisors provide data on leadership behavior, health and well-being in a multi-level design, in order to compare and cross-validate results based on follower ratings with those based on leaders' self-rating. We expect 1) to identify distinct profiles of mixed leadership, including consistent and inconsistent profiles, and 2) specific relationships with health and well-being. For example, positive outcomes for followers, but negative effects for leaders can be expected in a combination of low leader SelfCare, high StaffCare and high follower SelfCare. High follower SelfCare may compensate negative effects of low StaffCare, or create conflict and more stress than both low StaffCare and low follower SelfCare, etc.

The purpose of this first step is to explore whether meaningful profiles exist at all, and to investigate their respective relationships with followers' and leaders' health and well-being. By taking follower SelfCare into account, we can further account for followers' influence on leaders' health.

3.3. Stability, antecedents and consequences of leadership profiles over time

Once profiles of mixed leadership have been identified, the next step is to investigate their stability and susceptibility to change over time. Leadership behaviors vary, for example over the course of a workweek (Zacher & Wilden, 2014). For instance, one leader's StaffCare may decline and abusive behavior increase as the workload increases, whereas another reacts with declining SelfCare and withdrawal from leadership in terms of laissez-faire, but maintains high StaffCare. Average leadership behavior may be driven by personality traits, whereas daily working conditions and interactions with followers predict short-term fluctuations. Changes in leader behavior over time and their causes and consequences for health have rarely been investigated and not at all for inconsistent behavior (Ohly & Gochmann, 2015). We therefore propose to address the following research questions:

- Are profiles stable or subject to change over time?
- Do personal and contextual factors predict daily fluctuations in leadership behavior?

The objective is to investigate stability and change in leadership profiles, their antecedents and consequences across the workweek. This objective can be realized in a diary design, in which daily observations of leadership behavior, working conditions, health and well-being are collected from both followers and their teams throughout the workweek. Additionally, a baseline survey should assess relevant stable predictors, such as leaders' and followers' personality, self-efficacy or self-esteem (see Figure 2). We expect for example that 1) stable factors, such as leader personality and overall team climate, predict general profiles of leadership behavior (e.g., averaged across the week), 2) daily stressors predict fluctuations in leadership behavior, and 3) changes in leadership behavior (e.g., decreasing StaffCare and increasing abusive behavior) will predict changes in daily well-being (e.g., decrease in mood, increase in exhaustion or distress).

Building on the cross-sectional analysis, a diary study will strengthen empirical evidence by investigating antecedents and consequences of mixed leadership profiles for leader and follower health in a repeated measures design. The diary design allows to shed more light on underlying mechanisms by taking daily fluctuations and processes over time into account. Moreover, the stability of leadership profiles can be examined (see Figure 2).

3.4. A closer look at antecedents: Followers' influence

Another pertinent question is how different leadership profiles can be explained and predicted by followers. Leadership research has predominantly focused on the leader's personality to predict leadership behavior, although working conditions such as task content and job control may also play an important role (Judge, Bono, Ilies, & Gerhardt, 2002). However, leaders are subject to their followers' influence. For example, leaders may find it easier to display positive behaviors when followers perform well. Followers' behavior and well-being may also influence the leader. For example, follower work engagement has been shown to spill over to leaders' engagement (Wirtz et al., 2017). Moreover, the team stress level may influence a leader's StaffCare behavior (Martinko, Harvey, Sikora, & Douglas, 2011; Wirtz et al., 2017). Accordingly, Health-oriented Leadership may depend on followers' behavior. For example, follower SelfCare may affect a leader's capacity to practice StaffCare. Overall, previous research has rarely examined the reverse influence of followers on leaders. We therefore propose the following research questions:

- How does followers' behavior predict different leadership profiles?
- What is the relative impact of the leader's personality or prevailing working conditions, compared to followers' behavior and stress?

The objective is to investigate the antecedents of leadership profiles in more detail. This can be accomplished with an experimental design, where respondents are asked to rate how they would react to different scenarios. Variables which emerge as significant predictors of leadership behavior in step 2 (e.g. leader's workload, team stress, distance between follower and leader) will be systematically varied across the scenarios. It can be expected 1) that followers' behavior as well as working conditions (workload, time pressure) predict leadership profiles, and 2) that leaders' personality moderates the relationship between working conditions and leadership behavior (e.g., a leader with low self-efficacy may react to team-level stress with withdrawal and laissez-faire, whereas someone with high self-efficacy increases StaffCare).

An experimental study will strengthen causal evidence by manipulating predictors of leadership profiles, and thus contribute to explaining how leadership profiles come about.

3.5. Outlook: Mixed leadership in the digital age

The research framework described above serves to investigate profiles of mixed leadership and health in the context of »traditional« employment relationships. Leadership likely has a substantial influence on health in this context, because leaders and followers interact face-to-face on a daily basis, are embedded in organizational structures and build long-term relationships. After deepening the understanding in the context of tradititional work, this may serve as a reference for switching to digital work. In the context of digital work, personal interactions and relationships may be less pronounced or even absent (Peinl & Bildat, 2017). Moreover, digital work is often realized in atypical employment relationships (e.g., remote work as a solo-self-employed freelancer). These employment relationships are often accompanied by specific demands and resources, such as task ambiguity, uncertainty about hours and earnings, personal flexibility and variety in jobs and tasks (Vahle-Hinz, 2016).

These developments raise the question to what extent existing insights from the traditional context can be transferred, and whether findings can be replicated in the context of digitalized work. For example, some profiles may occur more or less frequent, or their respective consequences may differ. Therefore, research within traditional employment relations needs to be complemented with an analysis of profiles of mixed leadership, their antecedents and consequences among digital workers. We propose to address the following research questions:

- What is the role of leadership behavior in digital employment relations, characterized by virtual collaboration between team members and leaders?
- Can leadership alter specific stressors of »digital« jobs, such as task ambiguity, or do working conditions in the digital age require different leadership strategies to maintain health?

The objective is to investigate leadership and health in the context of digital work with its specific characteristics (e.g., remote work and virtual communication).

This objective could be realized in complementary cross-sectional and diary studies in order to analyze the role of relevant characteristics of digital work in the relationship between leadership profiles and health. Relevant variables include e.g., the form of employment and team composition (see Figure 2), ambiguity and autonomy, physical distance and the degree of communication between leaders and followers. Potential study populations could be project teams consisting of both traditional employees and freelancers or clickworkers, or employees working partly on site and partly in remote work or virtual teams. Such populations would allow to compare digital work with »traditional« employment both within, and between persons. A diary design allows investigating variations of these variables within persons over time, for example by comparing remote work or home office days with days on site. We expect that the relationship between leadership profiles and health will differ between work contexts: For example, the relationship between leadership behavior and health may be stronger or weaker in remote virtual work compared to work on site. Follower SelfCare may be more salient in remote work, as digital workers have less personal contact with their leaders and have to rely on strategies of self-leadership. Moreover, specific stressors and resources such as task ambiguity and autonomy can be expected to be more salient in remote work compared to work on site. Finally, the frequency and quality of communication between leader and follower in remote work can be expected to influence stressors such as task ambiguity.

In addition to examining the general relationship between leadership profiles, stressors and health in the traditional context, a complementary research perspective with a focus on »new« forms of work allows testing the applicability and consequences of mixed leadership in the context of digital work.

4. Conclusion: Health-oriented Leadership and standards of decent work

Existing research has established that within »traditional« work arrangements of dependent employment, leadership has a substantial impact on health and well-being. Supervisors have a considerable influence on their employees by means of direct communication, but also by allocating tasks and shaping the working conditions within their teams. Still, there are a number of blind spots that need to be addressed in order to include issues of leadership in the discussion about standards of decent work. Most importantly, inter-relations and inconsistencies between different leader behaviors should be considered in a person-oriented analysis. With the research agenda presented in this chapter, we aim to identify and investigate profiles of mixed leadership, in order to provide a more differentiated picture of what constitutes »good« leadership with regards to both leaders' and followers' health. Furthermore, we aim to identify factors which facilitate or hinder the implementation of good leadership in practice. Standards in terms of guidelines for good leadership behavior and how to foster it may be developed based on the findings. Such guidelines, especially when incorporated in provisions regarding risk assessments, can help to protect both leaders' and employees' health as a central functional capability (Nussbaum, 2000).

Changing employment relations in the context of digitalization, likely accompanied by changing interpersonal relationships between leaders and followers, raise the question what leadership means to both followers and leaders in the digital workforce: Do leaders lose influence over a self-organized and dispersed workforce? Can we apply established concepts of Health-oriented leadership or do we need to develop new concepts in order to define standards of good leadership and, in consequence, standards of decent work in the digital economy? Rather than giving answers, the research agenda proposed in this chapter serves to stimulate a discussion and to suggest questions to guide the empirical investigation of these issues.

References

Bakker, A. B. & Demerouti, E. (2007). The Job Demands-Resources model: State of the art. *Journal of Managerial Psychology*, *22*(3), 309–328. https://doi.org/10.1108/02683940710733115.

Bass, B. M. (1999). Two decades of research and development in transformational leadership. *European Journal of Work and Organizational Psychology*, *8*(1), 9–32. https://doi.org/10.1080/135943299398410.

Bass, B. M. & Avolio, B. J. (1994). *Improving Organizational Effectiveness Through Transformational Leadership*. Thousand Oaks, CA: SAGE.

BAuA. (2012). *Stressreport Deutschland 2012: Psychische Anforderungen, Ressourcen und Befinden*. Dortmund: Bundesanstalt für Arbeitsschutz und Arbeitsmedizin.

website: http://www.baua.de/de/Publikationen/Fachbeitraege/Gd68.pdf?__blob=publicationFile&v=5.

Bell, B. S. & Kozlowski, S. W. J. (2002). A typology of virtual teams. Implications for effective leadership. *Group & Organization Management*, *27*(1), 14–49. https://doi.org/10.1177/1059601102027001003.

Bergman, L. R. & Lundh, L.-G. (2015). Introduction: The Person-oriented approach: Roots and roads to the future. *Journal for Person-Oriented Research*, *1*(1–2), 1–6. https://doi.org/10.17505/jpor.2015.01.

Busch, C. & Vahle-Hinz, T. (2019). Gesundheit und Wohlbefinden in einer Arbeitswelt im Wandel: Aufrechterhaltung von Standards guter Arbeit bei multikulturellen Belegschaften und flexibler Arbeit. In D. Alewell und W. Matiaske (Eds.), *Standards Guter Arbeit – disziplinäre Positionen und interdisziplinäre Perspektiven*, Baden-Baden: Nomos, 39–61.

Demerouti, E., Bakker, A. B., Nachreiner, F., & Schaufeli, W. B. (2001). The Job Demands-Resources Model of Burnout. *Journal of Applied Psychology*, *86*(3), 499–512.

Diener, E. & Chan, M. Y. (2011). Happy People Live Longer: Subjective Well-Being Contributes to Health and Longevity. *Applied Psychology: Health and Well-Being*, *3*(1), 1–43. https://doi.org/10.1111/j.1758-0854.2010.01045.x.

Dormann, C. & Zapf, D. (1999). Social support, social stressors at work, and depressive symptoms: Testing for main and moderating effects with structural equations in a three-wave longitudinal study. *Journal of Applied Psychology*, *84*(6), 874–884.

Drobnič, S., Beham, B., & Präg, P. (2010). Good job, good life? Working conditions and quality of life in Europe. *Social Indicators Research*, *99*(2), 205–225. https://doi. org/10.1007/s11205-010-9586-7.

Ducki, A., & Felfe, J. (2011). Führung und Gesundheit: Überblick. In B. Badura, A. Ducki, H. Schröder, J. Klose & K. Macco (Eds.), *Fehlzeitenreport 2011. Führung und Gesundheit* (pp. 7–12). Berlin: Springer.

Eichhorst, W. & Buhlmann, F. (2015). *Die Zukunft der Arbeit und der Wandel der Arbeitswelt* (IZA Standpunkte No. 77). Bonn: Forschungsinstitut zur Zukunft der Arbeit.

Felfe, J. (2006). Validierung einer deutschen Version des »Multifactor Leadership Questionnaire« (MLQ Form 5 x Short) von Bass und Avolio (1995). *Zeitschrift für Arbeits- und Organisationspsychologie A&O*, *50*(2), 61–78. https://doi.org/10.1026/0932-4089.50.2.61.

Franke, F., Ducki, A., & Felfe, J. (2015). Gesundheitsförderliche Führung. J. Felfe (Ed.), *Trends der psychologischen Führungsforschung: Neue Konzepte, Methoden und Erkenntnisse*, Göttingen: Hogrefe, 253–263.

Franke, F., & Felfe, J. (2011a). Diagnose gesundheitsförderlicher Führung – Das Instrument »Health-oriented Leadership«. In B. Badura, A. Ducki, H. Schröder, J. Klose & K. Macco (Eds.), *Fehlzeiten-Report 2011* (pp. 3–13). Berlin, Heidelberg: Springer.

Franke, F. & Felfe, J. (2011b). How does transformational leadership impact employees' psychological strain? Examining differentiated effects and the moderating role of affective organizational commitment. *Leadership*, *7*(3), 295–316. https://doi.org/10. 1177/1742715011407387.

Franke, F., Felfe, J., & Pundt, A. (2014). The impact of health-oriented leadership on follower health: Development and test of a new instrument measuring health-promoting leadership. *Zeitschrift für Personalforschung*, *28*(1–2), 139–161.

Hanau, H. & Matiaske, W. (2019). Mitbestimmung im entgrenzten Betrieb – Arbeitsrechtliche und personalwirtschaftliche Perspektiven. In D. Alewell und W. Matiaske (Eds.), *Standards Guter Arbeit – disziplinäre Positionen und interdisziplinäre Perspektiven*, Baden-Baden: Nomos, 213–242.

Hauff, S. (2019). Human Resource Management zwischen Uniformität und Differenzierung. In D. Alewell und W. Matiaske (Eds.), *Standards Guter Arbeit – disziplinäre Positionen und interdisziplinäre Perspektiven*, Baden-Baden: Nomos, 65–80.

Hauff, S. & Kirchner, S. (2013). Wandel der Arbeitsqualität. Arbeits- und Beschäftigungsbedingungen zwischen 1989 und 2006 in einer evaluativ-relationalen Perspektive. *Zeitschrift für Soziologie*, *42*(4), 337–355.

Jahoda, M. (1982). *Employment and Unemployment: A Social-Psychological Analysis*. Cambridge: Cambridge University Press.

Judge, T. A., Bono, J. E., Ilies, R., & Gerhardt, M. W. (2002). Personality and leadership: A qualitative and quantitative review. *Journal of Applied Psychology*, *87*(4), 765–780. https://doi.org/10.1037//0021-9010.87.4.765.

Kirchner, S. & Beyer, J. (2016). Die Plattformlogik als digitale Marktordnung. *Zeitschrift für Soziologie*, *45*(5), 324–339. https://doi.org/10.1515/zfsoz-2015-1019.

Loebbecke, C. & Picot, A. (2015). Reflections on societal and business model transformation arising from digitization and big data analytics: A research agenda. *The Journal of Strategic Information Systems*, *24*(3), 149–157. https://doi.org/10.1016/j.jsis.2015.08.002.

Maier, M. F., Viete, S., & Ody, M. (2017). *Plattformbasierte Erwerbsarbeit: Stand der empirischen Forschung* (IZA Research Report No. 81). Bonn: Forschungsinstitut zur Zukunft der Arbeit.

Martinko, M. J., Harvey, P., Sikora, D., & Douglas, S. C. (2011). Perceptions of abusive supervision: The role of subordinates' attribution styles. *The Leadership Quarterly*, *22*(4), 751–764. https://doi.org/10.1016/j.leaqua.2011.05.013.

Montano, D., Reeske, A., Franke, F., & Hüffmeier, J. (2017). Leadership, followers' mental health and job performance in organizations: A comprehensive meta-analysis from an occupational health perspective. *Journal of Organizational Behavior*, *38*(3), 327–350. https://doi.org/10.1002/job.2124.

Nielsen, K., Randall, R., Yarker, J., & Brenner, S.-O. (2008). The effects of transformational leadership on followers' perceived work characteristics and psychological well-being: A longitudinal study. *Work & Stress*, *22*(1), 16–32. https://doi.org/10. 1080/02678370801979430.

Nussbaum, M. C. (2000). *Women and Human Development: The Capabilities Approach*. Cambridge: Cambridge University Press.

Ohly, S., & Gochmann, V. (2015). Tagebuchstudien in der Führungsforschung. In J. Felfe (Ed.), *Trends der psychologischen Führungsforschung: Neue Konzepte, Methoden und Erkenntnisse* (pp. 567–576). Göttingen: Hogrefe.

Peinl, I. & Bildat, L. (2017). *Forschungsdesiderate: Bezahlte repetitive Crowdarbeit und Gesundheit.* Kiel, Hamburg: ZBW – Deutsche Zentralbibliothek für Wirtschaftswissenschaften, Leibniz-Informationszentrum Wirtschaft. http://dx.doi.org/10.1314 0/RG.2.2.10139.46886.

Price, M. S. & Weiss, M. R. (2000). Relationships among coach burnout, coach behaviors, and athletes' psychological responses. *The Sport Psychologist*, *14*(4), 391–409.

Pundt, F. & Felfe, J. (2017). *Health-oriented Leadership. Instrument zur Erfassung gesundheitsförderlicher Führung*. Göttingen: Hogrefe.

Rigotti, T., Emmerich, A., & Holstad, T. (2015). Zukünftige Forschung zum Zusammenhang von Führung und Gesundheit. In J. Felfe (Ed.), *Trends der psychologischen Führungsforschung: Neue Konzepte, Methoden und Erkenntnisse* (pp. 265–276). Göttingen: Hogrefe.

Ross, C. E. & Mirowsky, J. (1995). Does employment affect health? *Journal of Health and Social Behavior*, *36*(3), 230–243.

Rowold, J. & Heinitz, K. (2008). Führungsstile als Stressbarrieren: Zum Zusammenhang zwischen transformationaler, transaktionaler, mitarbeiter- und aufgabenorientierter Führung und Indikatoren von Stress bei Mitarbeitern. *Zeitschrift für Personalpsychologie*, *7*(3), 129–140. https://doi.org/10.1026/1617-6391.7.3.129.

Schimmack, U., Diener, E., & Oishi, S. (2002). Life-satisfaction is a momentary judgment and a stable personality characteristic: The use of chronically accessible and stable sources. *Journal of Personality*, *70*(3), 345–384. https://doi.org/10.1111/1467-6494.05008.

Schuler-Harms, M. & Goldberg, K. (2019). Soziale Absicherung von alter und neuer Selbständigkeit als Herausforderung für das Sozialrecht. In D. Alewell und W. Matiaske (Eds.), *Standards Guter Arbeit – disziplinäre Positionen und interdisziplinäre Perspektiven*, Baden-Baden: Nomos, 189–212.

Schyns, B. & Schilling, J. (2013). How bad are the effects of bad leaders? A meta-analysis of destructive leadership and its outcomes. *The Leadership Quarterly*, *24*(1), 138–158. https://doi.org/10.1016/j.leaqua.2012.09.001.

Sharma, P. N. & Pearsall, M. J. (2016). Leading under adversity: Interactive effects of acute stressors and upper-level supportive leadership climate on lower-level supportive leadership climate. *The Leadership Quarterly*, *27*(6), 856–868. https://doi.org/ 10.1016/j.leaqua.2016.08.003.

Skogstad, A., Einarsen, S., Torsheim, T., Aasland, M. S., & Hetland, H. (2007). The destructiveness of laissez-faire leadership behavior. *Journal of occupational health psychology*, *12*(1), 80–92. https://doi.org/10.1037/1076-8998.12.1.80.

Steinmetz, B. (2011). Gesundheitsförderung für Führungskräfte. In E. Bamberg, A. Ducki, & A.-M. Metz (Eds.), *Gesundheitsförderung und Gesundheitsmanagement in der Arbeitswelt. Ein Handbuch* (pp. 537–559). Göttingen: Hogrefe.

Tepper, B. J., Moss, S. E., Lockhart, D. E., & Carr, J. C. (2007). Abusive supervision, upward maintenance communication, and subordinates' psychological distress. *The Academy of Management Journal*, *50*(5), 1169–1180.

Vahle-Hinz, T. (2016). Stress in nonregular work arrangements: A longitudinal study of task- and employment-related aspects of stress. *Journal of occupational health psychology*, *21*(4), 415–431.

Valerio, S. de. (2016). The rise of the »just-in-time workforce«: On-demand work, crowdwork, and labor protection in the »gig economy«. *Comparative Labor Law & Policy*, *37*.

Vidyarthi, P. R., Erdogan, B., Anand, S., Liden, R. C., & Chaudhry, A. (2014). One member, two leaders: Extending leader-member exchange theory to a dual leadership context. *The Journal of applied psychology*, *99*(3), 468–483. https://doi.org/10.1037/a0035466.

Vincent, S. (2012). Analyseinstrument für gesundheits- und entwicklungsförderliches Führungsverhalten: eine Validierungsstudie. *Zeitschrift für Arbeitswissenschaft*, *66*(1), 38–57.

Wang, M. & Hanges, P. J. (2010). Latent class procedures: Applications to organizational research. *Organizational Research Methods*, *14*(1), 24–31. https://doi.org/10.1177/1094428110383988.

WHO (1948). *Constitution of the World Health Organization*. New York: World Health Organization. Retreived from: http://www.who.int/about/mission/en/.

Wirtz, N., Rigotti, T., Otto, K., & Loeb, C. (2017). What about the leader? Crossover of emotional exhaustion and work engagement from followers to leaders. *Journal of occupational health psychology*, *22*(1), 86–97. https://doi.org/10.1037/ocp0000024.

Zacher, H., & Wilden, R. G. (2014). A daily diary study on ambidextrous leadership and self-reported employee innovation. *Journal of Occupational and Organizational Psychology*, *87*(4), 813–820. https://doi.org/10.1111/joop.12070.

Gesundheit und Wohlbefinden in einer Arbeitswelt im Wandel: Aufrechterhaltung von Standards guter Arbeit bei multikulturellen Belegschaften und flexibler Arbeit

Christine Busch und Tim Vahle-Hinz

Aus arbeitspsychologischer Perspektive ergeben sich Standards guter Arbeit vor dem Hintergrund human gestalteter Arbeit. Zentral sind hierbei die Humankriterien der Arbeit: Ausführbarkeit, Schädigungslosigkeit, Beeinträchtigungsfreiheit und Persönlichkeitsförderlichkeit (Hacker & Richter, 2013). In jüngerer Zeit wurde außerdem Zumutbarkeit hinzugefügt (Ulich, 2005). Ausführbarkeit, Schädigungslosigkeit und Beeinträchtigungsfreiheit machen sehr deutlich, dass human gestaltete Arbeit ohne physische und psychische Schädigungen oder Beeinträchtigungen dauerhaft durchführbar sein muss. Im Wesentlichen geht es hier um den Schutz der Gesundheit und des Wohlbefindens von Beschäftigten. Das Kriterium der Persönlichkeitsförderlichkeit geht über den Gesundheitsschutz hinaus und postuliert eher eine Gesundheitsförderlichkeit von Arbeit (vgl. auch Felfe & Klug, 2019). Hintergrund ist, dass Arbeit die Möglichkeit zur Entfaltung und Entwicklung der Persönlichkeit bieten sollte, was auf Grundlage von handlungstheoretischen Modellen (Hacker, 2003) förderlich für Gesundheit und Wohlbefinden ist. Anzumerken ist, dass es bei der Persönlichkeitsförderlichkeit nicht darum geht, einen Zwang zur Selbstentfaltung aufzubauen, vielmehr steht im Mittelpunkt, Arbeit so zu gestalten, dass eine Entwicklung möglich ist.

Gesundheitsschutz und Gesundheitsförderlichkeit sind damit zentrale Anliegen der arbeitspsychologischen Tätigkeit (vgl. z. B. Metz, 2011). In der Forschung ist die Identifizierung von psychischen Belastungsfaktoren zentral. Faktoren, die aus arbeitspsychologischer Perspektive wichtig für eine gut gestaltete Arbeit sind, werden zumeist als Stressoren und Ressourcen klassifiziert (Bakker & Demerouti, 2007). Während Stressoren Merkmale der Arbeitstätigkeit sind, die die Wahrscheinlichkeit einer Stressreaktion erhöhen (Zapf & Semmer, 2004), beschreiben Ressourcen Merkmale der Arbeitstätigkeit, die die Wirkung von Stressoren reduzieren können. Gleichzeitig tragen Ressourcen zur Erfüllung von Arbeitsaufgaben bei und/oder haben eine positive Wirkung auf Gesundheit und Persönlichkeitsförderlichkeit der Beschäftigten (Bakker & Demerouti, 2007). Die negativen gesundheitlichen Auswirkungen von Stressoren sowie die positiven Effekte von Ressourcen wurden vielfach untersucht (Bakker & Demerouti, 2016; Nixon, Mazzola, Bauer, Krueger & Spector, 2011; Rau & Buyken, 2015; Zapf & Semmer, 2004). Oftmals werden die psychischen Belastungsfaktoren hinsichtlich der Merkmale der Arbeitsaufgabe (z. B. Handlungsspielraum), der Arbeitsorganisation (z. B. Arbeitszeit), der sozialen Beziehungen (z. B. soziale Unterstützung) und der Arbeitsumgebung (z. B. Arbeitsmittel), klassifiziert (BAuA, 2014). Ein Verfahren zur Beurteilung der Gefahren eines Arbeitsplatzes ist die im Arbeitsschutzgesetz vorgesehene Gefährdungsbeurteilung (§5 ArbSchG). Seit 2013 wird hierbei auch explizit die Berücksichtigung von psychischen Belastungsfaktoren genannt.

Zusammenfassend kann festgestellt werden, dass Wohlbefinden, Gesundheit und Persönlichkeitsförderlichkeit – aus Sicht der Arbeitspsychologie – Standards einer guten Arbeit sind. Stressoren und Ressourcen helfen dabei, zu beschreiben, inwiefern diese Standards eingehalten werden. Gefährdungsbeurteilungen sind ein Verfahren zur Feststellung der Einhaltung dieser Standards. Die Arbeitswelt verändert sich rasant. Digitalisierung, Globalisierung und der demografische Wandel spielen neben anderen Themen eine wichtige Rolle (vgl. Bundesministerium für Arbeit und Soziales, 2017; Bundesministerium für Wirtschaft und Energie, 2014; Deutsche gesetzliche Unfallversicherung e.V., 2016; European Foundation for the Improvement of Living and Working Conditions, 2015). Es gilt zu untersuchen, ob und wie Wohlbefinden, Gesundheit und Persönlichkeitsförderlichkeit als Standards guter Arbeit gesichert werden können. Hierbei ergeben sich mehrere wichtige Fragen:

- Welche Veränderungen in der Arbeitswelt sind für die Standards einer guten Arbeit und die Feststellung dieser Standards in Deutschland von Bedeutung?
- Welche gesundheitlichen Folgen gehen mit diesen Veränderungen einher?
- Sind die bisherigen Faktoren zur Beschreibung von psychischen Belastungsfaktoren im Kontext dieser Veränderungen anwendbar?
- Gibt es neue oder zusätzliche Belastungsfaktoren, die zu berücksichtigen sind? Und wenn ja, wie sind diese anhand der Klassifizierung von Stressoren und Ressourcen zu beschreiben?

- Wie sollte eine Beurteilung von Gefährdung unter diesen veränderten Bedingungen aussehen? Welche Schwierigkeiten ergeben sich?

Im Folgenden wird zunächst auf die Gefährdungsbeurteilung psychischer Belastungen eingegangen. Anschließend liegt der Fokus auf multikulturellen Belegschaften und flexiblen Beschäftigungsverhältnissen in Deutschland, da dies bedeutsame Veränderungen in der Arbeitswelt sind, die sich auf Standards guter Arbeit auswirken können. Abschließend werden Handlungsfelder formuliert. Diese ergeben sich aus dem Verfahren der Gefährdungsbeurteilung und den dargestellten Veränderungen der Arbeitswelt.

1. Gefährdungsbeurteilung psychischer Belastungen

Die Förderung der Gesundheit und der Persönlichkeit sowie des Wohlbefindens bestimmen aus Sicht der Arbeitspsychologie die Standards einer guten Erwerbsarbeit. Das Verfahren der Gefährdungsbeurteilung (GBU) dient der Überprüfung, ob an konkreten Arbeitsplätzen diese Standards eingehalten werden und nimmt im Arbeitsschutzhandeln eine zentrale Rolle ein. Sie ist gesetzlich vorgeschrieben und insbesondere im Arbeitsschutzgesetz geregelt. Rechtliche Grundlagen finden sich aber auch in anderen Gesetzen, wie u. a. dem Arbeitssicherheitsgesetz, dem Jugendarbeitsschutzgesetz und der Arbeitsstättenverordnung.

Der § 5 Abs. 1 ArbSchG verpflichtet den Arbeitgeber zur Durchführung einer Gefährdungsbeurteilung, d. h. der Arbeitgeber muss durch eine Beurteilung die für die Beschäftigten mit ihrer Arbeit verbundenen Gefährdungen ermitteln – gemeinsam mit den erforderlichen Maßnahmen, um diese abzuwenden. Seit 2013 wird explizit die Berücksichtigung von psychischen Belastungen in Gefährdungsbeurteilungen rechtlich verlangt (§ 5 ArbSchG Abs. 3). Eine Gefährdung durch psychische Belastungen wird damit gleichrangig gesehen zur Gefährdung durch die Gestaltung und die Einrichtung der Arbeitsstätte und des Arbeitsplatzes (1), zur Gefährdung durch physikalische, chemische und biologische Einwirkungen (2), zur Gefährdung durch die Gestaltung, die Auswahl und den Einsatz von Arbeitsmitteln, insbesondere von Arbeitsstoffen, Maschinen, Geräten und Anlagen sowie den Umgang damit (3), zur Gefährdung durch die Gestaltung von Arbeits- und Fertigungsverfahren, Arbeitsabläufen und Arbeitszeit und deren Zusammenwirken (4) und zur Gefährdung durch unzureichende Qualifikation und Unterweisung der Beschäftigten (5). Darüber hinaus verpflichtet der § 6 ArbSchG zur Dokumentation und der § 3 zur Kontrolle der Einhaltung und Wirksamkeit der Maßnahmen und Wiederholung bei Veränderungen.

Die ebenfalls im ArbSchG verankerte Nationale Arbeitsschutzkonferenz (NAK) hat methodische Vorgehensweisen in Leitlinien zusammengefasst. Diese Leitlinien zur Gefährdungsbeurteilung dienen dem übergeordneten Ziel, die Sicherheit und Gesundheit der Beschäftigten durch einen effizienten und systematischen Arbeitsschutz zu erhalten, zu verbessern und zu fördern. Der Arbeitsschutz wird hierbei durch Maßnahmen der betrieblichen Gesundheitsförderung ergänzt. Dieses übergeordnete Ziel entspringt der Gemeinsamen Deutschen Arbeitsstrategie (GDA) nach § 20a ArbSchG, welche von Bund, Ländern und Unfallversicherungsträgern gemeinsam entwickelt wurde. Konkretes Ziel der Leitlinien ist ein abgestimmtes Vorgehen der für den Arbeitsschutz zuständigen Landesbehörden und der Unfallversicherungsträger bei der Beratung und Überwachung der Betriebe. So existiert auch eine Leitlinie zur Gefährdungsbeurteilung psychischer Belastungen (Geschäftsstelle der Nationalen Arbeitsschutzkonferenz, 2015). Für die Träger der GDA stehen die verhältnispräventiven Ansätze im Vordergrund. Das Hauptaugenmerk richtet sich auf die gute, das heißt menschengerechte Gestaltung der Arbeitsplätze und Arbeitsabläufe (ebda, 2015, S. 6). Die GBU hat auf Tätigkeits- und Arbeitsplatzebene stattzufinden. Bei gleichartigen Arbeitsbedingungen ist die Beurteilung eines Arbeitsplatzes oder einer Tätigkeit ausreichend (§ 5 ArbSchG). Alle Tätigkeiten und Arbeitsabläufe im Betrieb sollen beurteilt werden, wie z. B. Wartung, Instandhaltung oder Reparatur.

Die Leitlinie geht sowohl auf Prozesse als auch auf Inhalte der Gefährdungsbeurteilung psychischer Belastungen ein. Gemäß der Leitlinie sind die folgenden sieben Prozessschritte zu berücksichtigen:

1. Festlegen von Arbeitsbereichen und Tätigkeiten
2. Ermitteln der Gefährdungen
3. Beurteilen der Gefährdungen
4. Festlegen konkreter Arbeitsschutzmaßnahmen nach dem Stand der Technik (bei diesem Schritt ist die Rangfolge der Schutzmaßnahmen nach § 4 ArbSchG zu beachten)
5. Durchführen der Maßnahmen
6. Überprüfen der Wirksamkeit der Maßnahmen

7. Fortschreiben der Gefährdungsbeurteilung (insbesondere Anpassung im Falle geänderter betrieblicher Gegebenheiten nach § 3 ArbSchG)

In der Leitlinie zur Gefährdungsbeurteilung psychischer Belastungen werden inhaltliche Schwerpunkte der Gefährdungsbeurteilung psychischer Belastungen genannt. Dazu gehören Arbeitsinhalte und -aufgaben (z. B. fehlender Handlungsspielraum), Arbeitsorganisation (z. B. Zeitdruck, wechselnde und/oder lange Arbeitszeiten, häufige Nachtarbeit), soziale Bedingungen (z. B. fehlende soziale Kontakte, ungünstiges Führungsverhalten), Arbeitsumgebung (z. B. räumliche Enge, unzureichende Softwaregestaltung) und neue Arbeitsformen (z. B. räumliche Mobilität, atypische Arbeitsverhältnisse, diskontinuierliche Berufsverläufe, zeitliche Flexibilisierung, reduzierte Abgrenzung zwischen Arbeit und Privatleben). Im Folgenden wird auf Veränderungen in der Arbeitswelt eingegangen, die Einfluss auf Standards guter Arbeit haben und in der GBU Berücksichtigung finden sollten.

2. Veränderungen in der Arbeitswelt: Multikulturelle Belegschaften

Entgegen aller früheren Prognosen wird nach einer aktuellen Studie des Instituts der Deutschen Wirtschaft (IW, 2017) die Bevölkerung in Deutschland bis zum Jahr 2035 auf mehr als 83,1 Mio. Menschen anwachsen. Das wäre rund eine Million Menschen mehr als im Jahr 2015. Als Gründe hierfür werden die Migration, insbesondere die Rekordzuwanderung im Jahr 2015 und die hohe Nettomigration in den Folgejahren sowie die steigende Geburtenrate genannt. Entsprechend wird sich die Struktur der Erwerbstätigen in Deutschland verändern. Neben einem Zuwachs an Älteren und Frauen werden vor allem Menschen mit Migrationshintergrund die Belegschaften in Deutschland prägen.

Auf Basis des Mikrozensus hatten im Jahr 2016 18,6 Mio. Menschen bzw. 22,5 % der Gesamtbevölkerung in Deutschland einen Migrationshintergrund – fast 1,5 Mio. mehr als 2015. Bei den unter 5-Jährigen stellten Menschen mit Migrationshintergrund 38,1 % der Bevölkerung in 2016. Eine Person hat einen Migrationshintergrund, wenn sie selbst oder mindestens ein Elternteil nicht mit deutscher Staatsangehörigkeit geboren wurde. Mit 12,7 Mio. haben zwei Drittel der Personen mit Migrationshintergrund eigene Migrationserfahrung. Sie werden auch Zugewanderte genannt. 1,6 Millionen Schutzsuchende lebten 2016 in Deutschland. Das sind Ausländerinnen und Ausländer, die sich unter Berufung auf humanitäre Gründe in Deutschland aufhalten. Die meisten Personen mit Migrationshintergrund stammten 2016 aus Europa, insbesondere aus der Türkei (15,1 %), gefolgt von Polen (10,1 %) und der Russischen Föderation (6,6 %) (Statistisches Bundesamt, 2017a).

Multikulturell steht jedoch nur im engeren Sinne für nationale bzw. ethnisch-kulturelle Diversität (vgl. auch Alewell & Moll, 2019). Multikulturell im weiteren Sinne schließt auch andere »besondere« Merkmale wie Alter, Geschlecht, Behinderung, soziale Benachteiligung oder sexuelle Orientierung ein. Im betrieblichen Kontext taucht in diesem Zusammenhang der Begriff Diversity Management auf (Rastetter, 2019). Er steht dafür, diese »besonderen« Merkmale nicht als defizitär zu betrachten, sondern als gegeben wahrzunehmen, zur Empathie anzuregen, Diskriminierungen abzuschaffen und Vielfalt als Chance zu betrachten (Krell, 2010). Diversity Management zielt auf die Wertschätzung von Vielfalt ab. Maßnahmen des Diversity Managements sind neben der Bedarfsanalyse Trainings, Coachings, Teamentwicklungsmaßnahmen und Mentoring Programme sowie eine Umgestaltung der Personalpolitik. Diversity Management ist in vielen Großbetrieben bereits institutionalisiert und gelebte Realität, wobei bisher das Genderthema die Praxis dominierte; aktuell wird jedoch Diversität im engeren Sinne zunehmend wichtiger für die betriebliche Praxis und das Diversity Management.

Daten des Sozioökonomischen Panels zeigen, dass Personen mit Migrationshintergrund häufiger in ihrer Gesundheit beeinträchtigt sind als Personen ohne Migrationshintergrund (Lampert, Ryl, Saß, Starker & Ziese, 2010). Erstere erleben häufiger muskuloskelettale Erkrankungen bzw. Schmerzen und psychische oder psychosomatische Beschwerden (Oldenburg, Siefer & Beermann, 2010). Herz-Kreislauf-Erkrankungen treten jedoch seltener auf (Razum et al., 1998). Da Personen mit Migrationshintergrund eine höchst heterogene Gruppe darstellen, variieren die Krankheitsrisiken mit Sozialstatus, Herkunftsland, Geschlecht, Alter, Aufenthaltsdauer und Einwanderergeneration (Schenk, Ellert & Neuhauser, 2008). Deshalb bleibt unklar, inwiefern die auf Basis repräsentativer Statistiken berichteten Unterschiede zwischen Menschen mit Migrationshintergrund und Menschen ohne Migrationshintergrund auf den Migrationshintergrund oder den Sozialstatus, insbesondere die berufliche Tätigkeit zurückzuführen sind.

Menschen mit und ohne Migrationshintergrund in Deutschland unterscheiden sich in vielerlei Hinsicht, u. a. hinsichtlich des Bildungsstandes;

13,5 % der Personen mit Migrationshintergrund haben keinen allgemeinen Schulabschluss und 38,8 % keinen berufsqualifizierenden Abschluss (Personen ohne Migrationserfahrung: 1,8 % bzw. 14 %) (Statistisches Bundesamt, 2017a). Neben dem Bildungsstand wirken Sprachhindernisse, fehlende Anerkennung von Bildungsabschlüssen und Diskriminierung von Personen mit Migrationshintergrund als Zugangsbarrieren zu qualifizierten Erwerbstätigkeiten (Brinkmann et al., 2006; Kirkcaldy et al., 2006). Menschen mit Migrationshintergrund im Alter von 25 bis 65 sind häufiger erwerbslos als jene ohne oder gehen ausschließlich einer geringfügigen Beschäftigung nach. Im Vergleich zu Erwerbstätigen ohne Migrationshintergrund sind Erwerbstätige mit Migrationshintergrund fast doppelt so häufig als Arbeiterinnen und Arbeiter tätig. Sie finden vor allem im produzierenden Gewerbe, im Handel und im Gastgewerbe eine Beschäftigung (Statistisches Bundesamt, 2017a).

In unseren Studien, in denen Wohlbefinden und Gesundheit von Menschen mit Migrationshintergrund und Menschen ohne Migrationshintergrund in multikulturellen, gering qualifizierten Belegschaften untersucht wurden, zeigte sich, dass diese gleichermaßen psychisch beeinträchtigt waren (Clasen, Busch, Vowinkel & Winkler, 2013; Vowinkel, Busch & Cao, 2013): Jeder Zweite litt an Erschöpfung und jeder Vierte war von psychosomatischen Beschwerden betroffen. Die Menschen mit Migrationshintergrund berichteten jedoch in Übereinstimmung mit anderen Studien (Hoppe, Heaney & Fujishiro, 2010) bei gleichen Arbeitsbedingungen ein höheres psychisches Wohlbefinden als ihre einheimischen Kollegen.

Sozial ungleich verteilte Gesundheitschancen beruhen im Besonderen auf psychosozialen Stressprozessen (Lampert et al., 2010; Steptoe & Marmot, 2002; Wege et al., 2008). Diese entstehen durch arbeitsbezogene Probleme und ungünstige Arbeitsbedingungen (Borrell et al., 2004; Kawachi & Marmot, 1998; Marmot, Bosma, Hemingway, Brunner & Stansfeld, 1997). Geringqualifizierte haben häufiger als qualifizierte Beschäftigte befristete Arbeitsverträge und erfahren eine größere Arbeitsplatzunsicherheit (Borrell et al., 2004; Lyly-Yrjänäinen, 2008). Sie sind häufiger als andere von körperlichen Belastungen (Hanebuth, Meinel & Fischer, 2006; Lyly-Yrjänäinen 2008; Niedhammer et al., 2008), Umgebungsbelastungen (Borrell et al., 2004; Lyly-Yrjänäinen, 2008) oder chemischen Belastungen betroffen (Lyly-Yrjänäinen, 2008; Niedhammer et al., 2008). Dazu kommen hohe Konzentrationsanforderungen und Zeitdruck sowie ein durch Maschinen vorgegebener Arbeitstakt (Lyly-Yrjänäinen, 2008). Diese Belastungen treten meist in Kombination mit geringen Ressourcen wie fehlende Kontrolle, mangelhafte soziale Unterstützung oder geringe Gratifikationen durch die Arbeit auf (Borrell et al., 2004; Niedhammer et al., 2008; Rydstedt, Devereux & Sverke, 2007). In unseren qualitativen Studien mit Un- und Angelernten konnten wir zeigen, dass es den Beschäftigten an Wertschätzung durch den Vorgesetzten und Gelegenheiten zur Partizipation fehlte. Gleichzeitig benannten sie und ihre Vorgesetzten aufgabenbezogene Kommunikation durch den Vorgesetzten, die Präsenz und das Interesse des Vorgesetzten und wertschätzendes Feedback durch den Vorgesetzten als bedeutsame, gesundheitsförderliche Verhaltensweisen (Winkler, Busch & Duresso, 2013). Wir führten eine Längsschnittuntersuchung über sechs Monate in un- und angelernten, multikulturellen Belegschaften (N = 225) durch, wobei 48 % der untersuchten Personen einen Migrationshintergrund aufwiesen. Ziel der Untersuchung war, den angenommenen Einfluss von Vorgesetztenverhalten auf das Wohlbefinden der Beschäftigten zu überprüfen. Es zeigte sich, dass eine Veränderung des wertschätzenden Feedbacks durch die direkte Führungskraft, eine Veränderung der Unterstützung und der aufgabenbezogenen Kommunikation durch den Vorgesetzten, Einfluss auf Veränderungen im Wohlbefinden der Mitarbeiter über einen Zeitraum von sechs Monaten hatten (Winkler, Busch, Clasen & Vowinkel, 2015).

In weiteren Studien mit Un- und Angelernten (N = 474, 50 % der Personen mit Migrationshintergrund) untersuchten wir die wichtige Kulturdimension »Machtdistanzorientierung« bei den Beschäftigten und ihren direkten Vorgesetzten. Machtdistanzorientierung beschreibt das Ausmaß, inwiefern eine ungleiche Machtverteilung in einer Organisation oder einer Institution akzeptiert und erwartet wird. Untergebene mit einer hohen Machtdistanzorientierung stellen die Autorität des Vorgesetzten nicht in Frage und akzeptieren eine aufgabenorientierte Führung, wogegen Beschäftigte mit einer geringen Machtdistanzorientierung die Meinungen und Aussagen von Vorgesetzten als gleichwertig zu ihren eigenen ansehen und eine mitarbeiterorientierte Führung erwarten. Sie erwarten von ihren Vorgesetzten bei Veränderungsprozessen informiert und beteiligt zu werden sowie eine persönliche Beziehung zu ihrem Vorgesetzten aufzubauen (Bochner & Hesketh, 1994). Von Vorgesetzten mit einer hohen Machtdistanzorientierung wird dagegen erwartet, dass sie wenig partizipativ führen sowie persönliche Beziehungen zu ihren Untergebenen scheuen (House, Hanges, Javidan, Dorfman & Gupta, 2004). Von Vorgesetzten mit einer hohen Machtdistanzorientierung wird daher auch gesundheitsförderliches Verhalten, wie soziale Unterstützung und wertschätzendes Feedback, nicht erwartet und von den Untergebenen als unauthentisch wahrgenommen. Un- und angelernte Beschäftigte mit Migrationshintergrund zeigten in unseren Studien eine höhere mittlere Machtdistanzorientierung als Un- und Angelernte ohne Migrationshintergrund. Weiterhin zeigte sich, dass die Machtdistanzorientierung der unteren Vorgesetzten einen wesentlichen Einfluss auf den Zusammenhang von wertschätzendem Feedback des Vorgesetzen und Wohlbefinden sowie Gesundheit der Beschäftigten in dem Sinne hatte, dass wahrgenommenes wertschätzendes Feedback des Vorgesetzten nur dann in hohem positiven Zusammenhang mit der Gesundheit der Beschäftigten steht, wenn der Vorgesetzte eine geringe Machtdistanzorientierung aufweist. Gesundheitsförderliches Führungsverhalten hat nur dann die gewünschten positiven Auswirkungen, wenn der Vorgesetzte selbst eine geringe Machtdistanzorientierung hat und authentisch in seinem Verhalten ist (Winkler, Busch, Clasen & Vowinkel, 2014).

Multigruppenanalysen mit Strukturgleichungsmodellen zeigen auf, dass sich Standards guter Arbeit bei un- und angelernten Beschäftigten ohne Migrationshintergrund und Beschäftigten mit Migrationshintergrund unterscheiden. Erstere profitieren stärker von der sozialen Unterstützung durch Vorgesetzte als Beschäftigte mit Migrationshintergrund hinsichtlich Gesundheit und Wohlbefinden. Handlungsspielraum muss dagegen bei Un- und Angelernten als Ressource kritisch gesehen werden: Bei Beschäftigten ohne Migrationshintergrund konnten wir keinen Zusammenhang zu Gesundheit und Wohlbefinden feststellen. Er war bei Beschäftigten mit Migrationshintergrund sogar negativ. Autonomie hinsichtlich der Art und Weise, wie die Arbeit bewältigt wird, hatte in unseren Studien keinen oder sogar einen negativen Zusammenhang zu Gesundheit und Wohlbefinden der un- und angelernten Beschäftigten (Vowinkel, Busch, Clasen & Winkler, 2017a).

Eine besondere Situation erleben Zugewanderte. Zugewanderte sind aufgrund der oben beschriebenen Zugangsbarrieren zum Arbeitsmarkt häufig überqualifiziert für ihre Tätigkeiten, was eine psychische Belastung darstellt (Eurofound, 2007). Darüber hinaus wirken auch das Ereignis der Migration selbst und der migrationsbedingte Akkulturationsprozess als Belastung (Berry, 2006; Carta et al., 2005). Unterschiedliche Wertesysteme, Sprachbarrieren und Diskriminierung stellen weitere Belastungen dar (Brzoska, Reiss & Razum, 2010). So zeigen Studien, dass Beschäftigte mit Migrationshintergrund einer höheren Gefahr ausgesetzt sind, Opfer von Diskriminierung am Arbeitsplatz durch Kollegen, aber auch durch Vorgesetzte, zu werden als einheimische Beschäftigte (De Castro et al.,

2006; Wadsworth et al., 2007). Auch berichten Beschäftigte mit Migrationshintergrund häufiger von psychosozialen Belastungen durch das Verhalten ihrer Vorgesetzten (Grofmeyer, 2010) bzw. mehr sozialen Stressoren (Hoppe, 2011). Die besondere Bedeutung sozialer Belastungen für Beschäftigte mit Migrationshintergrund konnten wir auch in unseren Studien bestätigen: Wir stellten in Längsschnittstudien nicht nur fest, dass soziale Stressoren ausschließlich bei Beschäftigten mit Migrationshintergrund über die Zeit zunahmen, sondern dass ausschließlich diese in ihrem Wohlbefinden und ihrer Gesundheit durch soziale Stressoren beeinträchtigt waren (Vowinkel, Busch, Clasen & Winkler, 2017b). Geringqualifizierte mit Migrationshintergrund können in zweifacher Hinsicht als benachteiligt gelten – als Angehörige einer gesellschaftlichen Minderheit und als Angehörige einer sozial benachteiligten Gruppe.

Trotz dieser Erkenntnisse wird der überwiegende Teil der Maßnahmen zur Gesundheitsförderung in der Arbeitswelt mit qualifizierten, d. h. auch überwiegend einheimischen, Beschäftigten durchgeführt (Bamberg & Busch, 2006; Richardson & Rothstein, 2008). Es fehlte sicherlich bis vor wenigen Jahren noch an Angeboten, die Un- und Angelernte und Menschen mit Migrationshintergrund sowie betriebliche Entscheidungsträger ansprechen und die die Besonderheiten multikultureller Belegschaften berücksichtigen (Busch, 2017). Denn die eigentlichen Herausforderungen für den Erfolg des Arbeitsschutzes und der betrieblichen Gesundheitsförderung bestehen darin, die Teilnehmer zu erreichen bzw. hohe Teilnehmerquoten zu erzielen und die intendierten Verhaltensänderungen im Unternehmen dauerhaft sicherzustellen (Elke, Gurt, Möltner & Externbrink (2015). Genau diesen Herausforderungen hatten wir uns in mehrjährigen Projekten gestellt und betriebliche Gesundheitsförderungsprogramme entwickelt, die gezielt und nachhaltig multikulturelle Belegschaften und Menschen mit Migrationshintergrund sowie betriebliche Entscheidungsträger ansprechen. Es wurden Programme sowohl für kleine und mittelständische als auch für Großbetriebe in Kooperation mit Krankenkassen, wie der AOK und der IKK classic, entwickelt und in zahlreichen Betrieben erfolgreich erprobt. Selbst Leiharbeiter konnten wir mit den Programmen nachhaltig erreichen. Detaillierte Programmmanuale und Evaluationsstudien dieser Programme liegen vor (Busch, 2014, 2015; Busch & Clasen, 2014; Busch, Cao, Clasen & Deci, 2013; Busch, Koch, Clasen, Vowinkel & Winkler, 2017; Busch et al., 2015).

Zusammenfassend zeigt sich, dass Belegschaften in Deutschland zunehmend kulturell diverser werden. Aktuell sind multikulturelle Belegschaften in Deutschland überwiegend in un- und angelernten Tätigkeiten zu finden. Studien verweisen auf Arbeitsbedingungen in multikulturellen Belegschaften, die über die in den Leitlinien zur Gefährdungsbeurteilung psychischer Belastung genannten hinausgehen, z. B. Machtdistanzorientierung des Vorgesetzten oder Diskriminierung, bzw. eine andere Qualität haben, z. B. soziale Unterstützung und Handlungsspielraum. Sie zeigen auch die besonderen Anforderungen an den Prozess der Gefährdungsbeurteilung bei multikulturellen Belegschaften auf. So ist die Annahme von gleichartigen Arbeitsbedingungen selbst bei nahezu identischen, an Maschinen gebundenen Tätigkeiten kritisch zu sehen (siehe auch Mohr & Korek, 2017). Die kulturelle Diversität der Belegschaft und einhergehende unterschiedliche Wertesysteme der Beschäftigtengruppen und der Vorgesetzten, das individuell wahrgenommene Vorgesetztenverhalten, aber auch voneinander abweichende Arbeitszeitregelungen und Beschäftigungsverhältnisse stellen sehr unterschiedliche Arbeitsbedingungen dar, die für Standards guter Arbeit von Bedeutung sind und in einer Gefährdungsbeurteilung berücksichtigt werden müssen. Des Weiteren muss Handlungsspielraum als Ressource kritisch gesehen werden. Soziale Belastungen spielen eine besondere Rolle.

3. Veränderungen in der Arbeitswelt: Flexible Arbeit und flexible Beschäftigungsverhältnisse

Tregaskis, Brewster, Mayne, und Hegewisch (1998) beschreiben sehr treffend die Probleme bei der wissenschaftlichen Betrachtung von flexibler Arbeit: »Despite the extent of the discussion of flexible working, the concept itself remains unclear. Different, but overlapping, terminology is used: and nearly all of it is arguably inaccurate in that it fails to describe exactly the area that is discussed…« (Tregaskis et al., 1998, S. 62). Unter dem Überbegriff flexible Arbeit subsumieren sich gesamtgesellschaftliche Veränderungen (z. B. die Flexibilisierung des Arbeitsmarktes), betriebsspezifische Veränderungen (z. B. die Flexibilisierung von Produktionsprozessen) und individuelle Veränderungen (z. B. die Forderung zur verstärkten Vereinbarung von Familie und Beruf). Aus einer systemtheoretischen Betrachtungsweise (Willke, 2000) kann flexible Arbeit als eine Reaktion des Unternehmens auf veränderte Umweltbedingungen (z. B. steigender Wettbewerb aufgrund von Globalisierungsprozessen oder erhöhte Anforderung der Beschäftigten Familie und Beruf besser miteinander vereinbaren zu können) verstanden werden. Da flexible Arbeit eine Reaktion auf Anforderungen von Beschäftigten oder Anforderungen des Wettbewerbs ist, kann sie konsequenterweise entweder beschäftigtenorientiert oder unternehmensorientiert sein (Kattenbach, Demerouti & Nachreiner, 2010).

Atypische Beschäftigungsformen (z. B. befristete Beschäftigung, Leiharbeit, geringfügige Beschäftigung) können als eine unternehmensorientierte Strategie der Flexibilisierung verstanden werden (Alewell & Hauff, 2014, Hauff 2019). Beispielsweise ermöglicht Zeitarbeit numerische Flexibilität (die Anzahl der Beschäftigten variiert in Abhängigkeit vom Bedarf des Unternehmens) (vgl. Reilly, 1998). Befristete Beschäftigung erlaubt dem Unternehmen Anpassungsfähigkeit hinsichtlich der zukünftigen Beschäftigungsstruktur.

Das Statistische Bundesamt definiert atypische Beschäftigung in Abgrenzung zu Normalarbeitsverhältnissen (Statistisches Bundesamt, 2008):

> Das Normalarbeitsverhältnis gilt als Norm der Beschäftigung und ist gekennzeichnet durch unbefristete Vollzeit- oder Teilzeittätigkeit, die in die sozialen Sicherungssysteme eingebunden ist. Des Weiteren besteht eine Identität zwischen Arbeits- und Beschäftigungsverhältnis (Statistisches Bundesamt, 2008, S. 6).

Atypisch sind Beschäftigungsverhältnisse, die von dieser Norm abweichen. Anhand dieser Definition sind Beschäftigungsformen wie Zeitarbeit, befristete oder geringfügige Beschäftigung als atypische Beschäftigungsformen anzusehen. Die Definition des Statistischen Bundesamtes (2008) bezieht sich allerdings nur auf abhängige Beschäftigung. Solo-Selbständigkeit wird nicht berücksichtigt. Aber auch diese Beschäftigungsform kann aus unternehmensorientierter Perspektive als flexibles Beschäftigungsverhältnis angesehen werden (vgl. Hanau & Matiaske, 2019; Schuler-Harms & Goldberg, 2019). So ermöglicht die Auftragsvergabe an Selbständige dem Unternehmen Flexibilität durch das Outsourcing nicht kernrelevanter Beschäftigungsfelder.

Das Normalarbeitsverhältnis ist weiterhin am stärksten auf dem deutschen Arbeitsmarkt vertreten. Allerdings ist der Anteil atypisch Beschäftigter in den letzten Jahrzehnten gestiegen (Vahle-Hinz & Plachta, 2014) und liegt nun relativ konstant bei ca. 20 % der abhängig Beschäftigten (Statistisches Bundesamt, 2017b). Wird dazu noch der Anteil von 5,5 % Solo-Selbständigen an allen Erwerbstätigen in Deutschland betrachtet (Statistisches Bundesamt, 2017b), kann festgestellt werden, dass ein nicht unerheblicher Teil der Erwerbstätigen in Deutschland in flexiblen Beschäftigungsformen arbeitet. Auf europäischer Ebene ist von ca. 25 % flexibel Beschäftigten auszugehen (Europäische Kommission, 2006, zitiert nach Eurofound, 2010, S. 1). Für den deutschen Arbeitsmarkt gehen Eichhorst und Tobsch (2013) auch für die Zukunft von dieser zweiteiligen Beschäftigungsstruktur aus. Mit Blick auf Wohlbefinden, Gesundheit und Persönlichkeitsförderlichkeit als Standards guter Arbeit stellen sich durch diesen Wandel der Beschäftigungsformen folgende Fragen: Wie sehen die Arbeitsbedingungen dieser Beschäftigungsformen aus? Welche gesundheitlichen Folgen sind davon zu erwarten? Können die bisherigen gesundheitsbezogenen Beschreibungen von Arbeitsbedingungen als Standards guter Arbeit auch in diesen Formen der Beschäftigung Anwendung finden?

Einige Studien beschäftigen sich mit Unterschieden in Arbeitscharakteristiken zwischen Festangestellten und flexibel Beschäftigten (Nienhüser & Matiaske, 2006). So berichten Goudswaard und Andries (2002), basierend auf Umfragedaten der European Fundation for the Improvement of Living and Working Conditions, dass flexibel Beschäftige weniger anspruchsvolle Tätigkeiten ausüben und geringere Autonomie über die Ausführung ihrer Arbeitstätigkeit aufweisen als Festangestellte. Auf der anderen Seite sind Festangestellte höheren Arbeitsbelastungen ausgesetzt. Diese Ergebnisse werden in anderen Studien bestätigt (De Cuyper et al., 2008). Gracia, Ramos, Peiró, Caballer, und Sora (2011) zeigen z. B. in einer multinationalen Studie, dass Festangestellte höheren Arbeitsbelastungen ausgesetzt sind und länger arbeiten als flexibel Beschäftigte. Auch Guest, Oakley, Clinton, und Budjanovcanin (2006) berichten von höheren Arbeitsbelastungen für Festangestellte. Wagenaar et al. (2012) berichten ebenfalls von höheren Arbeitsbelastungen für Festangestellte und geringerer Autonomie für flexibel Beschäftigte. Des Weiteren befinden sich Festangestellte vermehrt entwicklungsförderlichen Tätigkeiten, wogegen flexibel Beschäftigte häufiger in gesundheitlich belastenden Tätigkeiten zu finden sind (Wagenaar et al., 2012).

Während in den Studien zu Arbeitsbedingungen flexibel Beschäftigter eine vorsichtige Tendenz zu schlechteren Arbeitsbedingungen vorhanden ist, zeigte sich in Studien, die den Zusammenhang von flexiblen Beschäftigungsverhältnissen mit Indikatoren für Wohlbefinden und Gesundheit untersuchen, eine deutlich heterogene Befundlage. Es werden sowohl keine Zusammenhänge, positive Zusammenhänge als auch negative Zusammenhänge berichtet. So zeigt sich z. B. in der Studie von Bernhard-Oettel, De Cuyper, Berntson, und Isaksson (2008) kein Zusammenhang von befristeter Beschäftigung mit allgemeinem Wohlbefinden und Lebenszufriedenheit. Ebenso bestätigen Bernhard-Oettel, Sverke, und De Witte (2005) keine Unterschiede zwischen Festangestellten und befristet Beschäftigten hinsichtlich allgemeinem Wohlbefinden oder arbeitsbezogener Anspannung. Demgegenüber finden sich in der Literatur auch positive Zusammenhänge von befristeter Beschäftigung und Zeitarbeit mit Indikatoren für Wohlbefinden (vgl. Guest, Isaksson & De Witte, 2010; Mauno, Kinnunen, Mäkikangas & Nätti, 2005). Mauno et al. (2005) verweisen z. B. auf höhere Arbeitszufriedenheit von befristet Beschäftigten im Vergleich mit Festangestellten. Benavides, Benach, Diez-Roux, & Roman (2000) berichten hingegen negative Zusammenhänge bezüglich Arbeitszufriedenheit für Selbständige, befristet Beschäftigte und Zeitarbeiter. Außerdem stellen die Autoren höhere Werte in Müdigkeit und vermehrte Berichte über Muskel- und Rückenschmerzen fest. Gehäufte gesundheitliche Beschwerden flexibel Beschäftigter werden auch bei Martens, Nijhuis, Van Boxtel, und Knottnerus (1999) und Aronsson, Gustafsson, und Dallner (2002) nachgewiesen. Die Studie von Kivikäki et al. (2003) berichtet sogar von einem erhöhten Mortalitätsrisiko bei flexibel Beschäftigten.

Zusammenfassend kann festgestellt werden, dass die bisherige Forschung zu den gesundheitlichen Auswirkungen flexibler Beschäftigungsverhältnisse insgesamt inkonsistente Forschungsergebnisse hervorgebracht hat (De Cuyper et al., 2008; Imhof & Andresen, 2017). Hierfür werden verschiedene Gründe diskutiert. Zum einen zeigen Forschungsergebnisse, dass klassische Stressoren und Ressourcen in Stichproben von flexibel Beschäftigten andere Wirkungen zeigen können, als in Stichproben mit Beschäftigten in Normalarbeitsverhältnissen. De Cuyper und De Witte (2006) zeigen beispielsweise, dass hohe Autonomie bei Festangestellten mit einer starken Erhöhung der Arbeitszufriedenheit in Verbindung steht, dieser Effekt für befristet Beschäftigte aber nur sehr schwach erkennbar ist. Zum anderen wird ausführlich diskutiert, dass die Kategorien zur Beschreibung von flexiblen Beschäftigungsverhältnissen zu unklar differenzieren und inkonsistente Ergebnisse damit auf die Heterogenität der untersuchten Stichprobe zurückgeführt werden können (Imhof & Andresen, 2017; Marler, Woodard Barringer & Milkovich, 2002). Oft werden auch globale Konzepte, wie atypische Beschäftigung oder contingent work, als Untersuchungskategorien verwendet (Tregaskis et al., 1998), ohne dass die Zusammensetzung dieser Kategorien erläutert wird.

Mit einem dritten Erklärungsweg für die inkonsistente Befundlage haben wir uns in vorheriger Forschung intensiv beschäftigt. Die Grundannahme dieses Erklärungswegs ist es, dass neben den klassischerweise untersuchten Stressoren und Ressourcen der Arbeitsaufgabe, Stressoren und

Ressourcen, die aus der Beschäftigungssituation resultieren, zu berücksichtigen sind (Lewchuk, De Wolff, King & Polanyi, 2005; Vahle-Hinz, 2017). In einer initialen Arbeit konnten wir vier beschäftigungsbezogene Stressoren (effort to maintain employment, uncertainty about the work environment, uncertainty about future employment, constant evaluation effort) und vier beschäftigungsbezogene Ressourcen (employment control, earnings control, security when unemployed, complexity due to employment) identifizieren (Vahle-Hinz, Kirschner & Thomson, 2013). Des Weiteren konnten wir feststellen, dass beschäftigungsbezogene Stressoren und Ressourcen, über aufgabenbezogene Stressoren und Ressourcen, Varianz in Wohlbefindens- und Motivationsindikatoren aufklären können (Vahle-Hinz, 2016) sowie eine stresspuffernde Wirkung von Autonomie als aufgabenbezogene Ressource, auf den Zusammenhang zwischen beschäftigungsbezogenen Stressoren und Wohlbefinden, besteht (Vahle-Hinz et al., 2013).

4. Multikulturelle Belegschaften und flexible Arbeit als Herausforderung für Gefährdungsbeurteilungen

Die bisherige Forschung weist einige Schwachstellen auf, die eine Nutzung der Erkenntnisse für GBU erschweren. In einem aktuellen Review der Literatur über Studien zu Wohlbefinden in flexiblen Beschäftigungsverhältnissen beschreiben Imhof und Andresen (2017) einige dieser Problemfelder, die insbesondere auch für multikulturelle Belegschaften von Interesse sind. Die Autoren verweisen darauf, dass erstens oftmals unklar ist, welches Beschäftigungsverhältnis konkret in der jeweiligen Studie untersucht wird. Zweitens stellen sie fest, dass, obwohl es länderspezifische Rahmenbedingungen für flexible Beschäftigungsverhältnisse gibt, diese in den Studien nicht berücksichtigt werden. Drittens zeige sich eine sehr heterogene Operationalisierung von Wohlbefinden, wodurch eine Vergleichbarkeit der Studien gefährdet sei. Dies betrifft multikulturelle Belegschaften im Besonderen. Viertens wurden bisher nur vereinzelt spezifische beschäftigungsbezogene und individuelle Faktoren untersucht, die relevant für Gesundheit und Wohlbefinden in flexiblen Beschäftigungsverhältnissen sein könnten. Fünftens werden methodische Limitationen bemängelt, die es vor allem nicht erlauben Veränderungen in Gesundheit und Wohlbefinden zu analysieren.

Diese Einschätzungen decken sich mit unseren eigenen Beobachtungen (vgl. Busch, 2017; Vahle-Hinz, 2013 und die vorangegangenen Abschnitte). Um fundierte Kenntnisse für GBU bei flexiblen Beschäftigungsverhältnissen und in multikulturellen Belegschaften zu schaffen, sollten die genannten Kritikpunkte in zukünftigen Forschungen Berücksichtigung finden. Wie können wir Gesundheit und Wohlbefinden sowie Arbeitsbedingungen in flexiblen Beschäftigungsverhältnissen und bei multikulturellen Belegschaften für GBU valide erfassen? Sind die in den oben beschriebenen Leitlinien zur GBU genannten Arbeitsbedingungen auch in flexiblen Beschäftigungsverhältnissen und in multikulturellen Belegschaften Belastungen oder welche andere Qualität haben sie in flexiblen Beschäftigungsverhältnissen und in multikulturellen Belegschaften? (siehe auch Hauff in diesem Band) Kann es sein, dass Ressourcen, wie Handlungsspielraum oder Autonomie zu Belastungen werden und damit das theoretische Modell gekippt wird? Welche Belastungen sind zu ergänzen? Ist der in den Leitlinien beschriebene Prozess der GBU für flexible Beschäftigungsverhältnisse und multikulturelle Belegschaften gültig?

Das bereits erarbeitete Konzept der beschäftigungsbezogenen Stressoren und Ressourcen adressiert sehr gut den vierten Kritikpunkt von Imhof und Andresen (2017). Daher erscheint es lohnenswert dieses Konzept weiter zu erforschen und beispielsweise, bezugnehmend auf den ersten Kritikpunkt, in klar spezifizierten Subgruppen, wie z. B. befristete Beschäftigung in multikulturellen Belegschaften, zu testen. Die für GBU so zentralen rechtlichen Grundlagen und länderspezifischen Rahmenbedingungen für flexible Beschäftigungsverhältnisse lassen sich besonders gut interdisziplinär adressieren.

Literaturverzeichnis

Alewell, D. & Hauff, S. (2014). Teilzeit, Befristung, Freelancer & Co. – Eine systemische Betrachtung. In: *Personal Quarterly*, 4, 9–15.

Alewell, D. & Moll, T. (2019). Religion, Religiosität und Spiritualität am Arbeitsplatz in deutschen Unternehmen. In: D. Alewell & W. Matiaske (Hrgs.), *Standards Guter Arbeit – disziplinäre Positionen und interdisziplinäre Perspektiven*, Baden-Baden: Nomos, 107–137.

Aronsson, G., Gustafsson, K. & Dallner, M. (2002). Work environment and health in different types of temporary jobs. In: *European journal of work and organizational psychology*, 11(2), 151–175. Doi: 10.1080/13594320143000898.

Bakker, A. B. & Demerouti, E. (2007). The job demands-resources model: State of the art. In: *Journal of Managerial Psychology*, 22(3), 309–328. Doi: 10.1108/026839407 10733115.

Bakker, A. B. & Demerouti, E. (2016). Job demands – resources theory: Taking stock and looking forward. In: *Journal of Occupational Health Psychology*, 22(3), 273–285. Doi: 10.1037/ocp0000056.

Bamberg, E. & Busch, C. (2006). Stressbezogene Interventionen in der Arbeitswelt. In: *Zeitschrift für Arbeits- und Organisationspsychologie*, 50(4), 215–226.

Benavides, F. G., Benach, J., Diez-Roux, A. V. & Roman, C. (2000). How do types of employment relate to health indicators? Findings from the Second European Survey on Working Conditions. In: *Journal Epidemiol Community Health*, 54, 494–501.

Bernhard-Oettel, C., De Cuyper, N., Berntson, E. & Isaksson, K. (2008). Well-being and organizational attitudes in alternative employment: The role of contract and job Preferences. In: *International Journal of Stress Management*, 15(4), 345–363.

Bernhard-Oettel, C., Sverke, M. & De Witte, H. (2005). Comparing three alternative types of employment with permanent full-time work: How do employment contract and perceived job conditions relate to health complaints? In: *Work & Stress*, 19(4), 301–318. Doi: 10.1080/02678370500408723.

Berry, J.W. (2006). Acculturative Stress. In: Wong P.T.P. & Wong L.C.J. (Hrsg.), *Handbook of multicultural perspectives on stress and coping*. New York: Springer, 287–298.

Bochner, S. & Hesketh, B. (1994). Power distance, individualism/collectivism, and job-related attitudes in a culturally diverse work group. In: *Journal of Cross-Cultural Psychology*, 25(2), 233–257. Doi: 10.1177/0022022194252005.

Borrell, C., Muntaner, C., Benach, J., et al. (2004). Social class and self-reported health status among men and women: what is the role of work organisation, household material standards and household labour? In: *Social Science & Medicine*, 58(10), 1869–87.

Brinkmann, U., Dörre, K., Röbenack, S., et al. (2006) *Prekäre Arbeit.* Bonn: Friedrich-Ebert-Stiftung.

Brzoska, P., Reiss, K. & Razum, O. (2010). Arbeit, Migration und Gesundheit. In: B. Badura, H. Schröder, J. Klose & K. Macco (Hrsg.), *Fehlzeiten-Report 2010: Vielfalt managen, Gesundheit fördern – Potenziale nutzen.* Berlin: Springer, 129–139.

Bundesanstalt für Arbeitsschutz und Arbeitsmedizin (BAuA) (2014). *Gefährdungsbeurteilung psychischer Belastung. Erfahrungen und Empfehlungen.* Berlin: Erich Schmidt Verlag.

Bundesministerium für Arbeit und Soziales (BMAS) (2017). *Weissbuch Arbeiten 4.0.* https://www.bmas.de/SharedDocs/Downloads/DE/PDF-Publikationen/a883-weiss buch.pdf?__blob=publicationFile.

Bundesministerium für Wirtschaft und Energie (BMWi) (2014). *Zukunft der Arbeit in Industrie 4.0.* https://www.bmwi.de/Redaktion/DE/Publikationen/Digitale-Welt/zukunft-der-arbeit-in-industrie-4-0.pdf?__blob=publicationFile&v=3.

Busch, C. (2014). Gesundheitslernen in betrieblichen Maßnahmen der Prävention. In: *Die Zeitschrift für Erwachsenenbildung*, 1, 38–40.

Busch, C. (2015). Neue Wege – ausgewählte Beschäftigtengruppen: Geringqualifizierte. In: B. Badura, A. Ducki, H. Schröder, J. Klose & M. Meyer (Hrsg.), *Fehlzeiten-Report 2015. Neue Wege für mehr Gesundheit – Qualitätsstandards für ein zielgruppenspezifisches Gesundheitsmanagement*. Heidelberg: Springer.

Busch, C. (2017). Wertegebundene Interventionen zur Gesundheitsförderung in der Arbeitswelt. In: C. Busch, A. Ducki, J. Dettmers & H. Witt (Hrsg.), *Der Wert der Arbeit. Festschrift zur Verabschiedung von Eva Bamberg*. Augsburg: Rainer Hampp Verlag, 173–186.

Busch, C., Cao, P., Clasen, J. & Deci, N. (2013). *Betriebliches Gesundheitsmanagement bei kultureller Vielfalt: Ein Stressmanagement-Programm für Service, Gewerbe und Produktion*. Springer-Verlag.

Busch, C. & Clasen, J. (2014). Multikulturelle Belegschaften. In: In B. Badura et al. (Hrsg.), *Fehlzeitenreport 2014. Erfolgreiche Unternehmen von morgen – gesunde Zukunft heute gestalten*. Heidelberg: Springer, 93–102.

Busch, C., Clasen, J., Deci, N., Keller-Landvogt, K., Maßholder, F., Vowinkel, J. & Winkler, E. (2015). Arbeitswelt als Zugang – ein Multiplikatorenprogramm zur Gesundheitsförderung von Un- und Angelernten mit hohem Migrantenanteil: ReSuDi. In: *Das Gesundheitswesen*, 77(1), 35–36.

Busch, C., Ducki, A., Bamberg, E., Roscher, S., Clasen, J., Kalytta, T., Liedtke, G. & Gloede, D. (2015). Entwicklung und Evaluation eines Gesundheitsförderungsprogramms für Un- und Angelernte unter besonderer Berücksichtigung der Transfersicherung. In: *Das Gesundheitswesen*, 77(1), 129–130.

Busch, C., Koch, T., Clasen, J, Vowinkel, J., & Winkler, E. (2017). Evaluation of an Organizational Health Intervention for Low-Skilled Workers and Immigrants. In: *Human Relations*, 70(8), 994–1016. Doi: 10.1177/0018726716682308.

Carta, M.G., Bernal, M., Hardoy, M.C., et al. (2005). Migration and mental health in Europe (the state of the mental health in Europe working group, appendix 1). In: *Clinical practice and epidemiology in mental health*, 1(13). Doi: 10.1186/1745-0179-1-13.

Clasen, J., Busch, C., Vowinkel, J. & Winkler, E. (2013). Arbeitssituation und Gesundheit von geringqualifizierten Beschäftigten in kulturell diversen Belegschaften. In: *Gruppendynamik und Organisationsentwicklung*, 44(2), 91–110. Doi: 10.1007/s11 612-013-0212-4.

De Castro, A. B., Fujishiro, K., Sweitzer, E., et al. (2006). How immigrant workers experience workplace problems: a qualitative study. In: *Archives of Environmental and Occupational Health*, 61 (6), 249–258.

De Cuyper, N., De Jong, J., De Witte, H., Isaksson, K., Rigotti, T. & Schalk, R. (2008). Literature review of theory and research on the psychological impact of temporary employment: Towards a conceptual model. In: *International Journal of Management Reviews*, 10(1), 25–51. Doi: 10.1111/j.1468-2370.2007.00221.x.

De Cuyper, N. & De Witte, H. (2006). Autonomy and workload among temporary workers: Their effects on job satisfaction, organizational commitment, life satisfaction, and self-rated performance. In: *International Journal of Stress Management*, 13(4), 441–459. Doi: 10.1037/1072-5245.13.4.441.

Deschermeier, P. (2017). Bevölkerungsentwicklung in den deutschen Bundesländern bis 2035. In: *IW-Trends*, 3, 2017. https://www.iwkoeln.de/fileadmin/publikationen/2017/357919/IW-Trends_2017-03-04_Deschermeier.pdf.

Deutsche Gesetzliche Unfallversicherung e. V. (DGUV) (2016). *Neue Formen der Arbeit. Neue Formen der Prävention. Arbeitswelt 4.0: Chancen und Herausforderungen.* http://publikationen.dguv.de/dguv/pdf/10002/dguv-nfda_de_barrierefrei.pdf.

Eichhorst, W. & Tobsch, V. (2013). *Has atypical work become typical in Germany? Country case study on labour market segmentation (Emplyoment).* Genf: International Labour Office (ILO).

Elke, G., Gurt, J. Möltner, H., & Externbrink, K. (2015). *Arbeitsschutz und betriebliche Gesundheitsförderung – vergleichende Analyse der Prädiktoren und Moderatoren guter Praxis.* Dortmund: BAuA. https://www.baua.de/DE/Angebote/Publikationen/Berichte/Gd82.html.

European Foundation for the Improvement of Living and Working Conditions (Eurofound) (2007) Employment and working conditions of migrant workers. Publications Office of the European Union, Luxembourg Europäische Kommission (2006) Modernising labour law to meet the challenges of the 21st century, Green Paper, COM (2006) 708 final, Brüssel.

European Foundation for the Improvement of Living and Working Conditions (Eurofound) (2010) Flexible forms of work: 'very atypical' contractual arrangements. Dublin.

European Foundation for the Improvement of Living and Working Conditions (Eurofound) (2015) New forms of employment. Publications Office of the European Union, Luxembourg.

Geschäftsstelle der Nationalen Arbeitsschutzkonferenz (2015). *Leitlinie Beratung und Überwachung bei psychischer Belastung am Arbeitsplatz.*

Geschäftsstelle der Nationalen Arbeitsschutzkonferenz (2017). *Leitlinie Gefährdungsbeurteilung und Dokumentation.*

Goudswaard, A. & Andries, F. (2002). *Employment status and working conditions. Work.* Dublin: European Fundation for the Improvement of Living and Working Conditions.

Gracia, F. J., Ramos, J., Peiró, J. M., Caballer, A. & Sora, B. (2011). Job attitudes, behaviours and well-being among different types of temporary workers in Europe and Israel. In: *International Labour Review*, 150(3), 235–254.

Grofmeyer, E. (2010) Anforderungen und Lösungen kultureller Diversifizierung. In: B. Badura, H. Schröder, J. Klose, K. Macco (Hrsg.), *Fehlzeiten-Report 2010. Vielfalt managen: Gesundheit fördern – Potenziale nutzen.* Berlin: Berlin, 253–262.

Guest, D. E., Isaksson, K. & De Witte, H. (Hrsg.) (2010). *Employment contracts, psychological contracts, and employee well-being: an international study*. Oxford University Press.

Guest, D. E., Oakley, P., Clinton, M. & Budjanovcanin, A. (2006). Free or precarious? A comparison of the attitudes of workers in flexible and traditional employment contracts. In: *Human Resource Management Review*, 16(2), 107–124. Doi: 10.1016/j. hrmr.2006.03.005.

Hacker, W. (2003). Action regulation theory: A practical tool for the design of modern work processes? In: *European Journal of work and organizational psychology*, 12(2), 105–130.

Hacker, W. & Richter, P. (2013). *Psychische Fehlbeanspruchung: Psychische Ermüdung, Monotonie, Sättigung und Stress* (Vol. 2). Berlin: Springer-Verlag.

Hanebuth, D., Meinel, M. & Fischer, J. E. (2006). Health-related quality of life, psychosocial work conditions, and absenteeism in an industrial sample of blue- and white-collar employees: a comparison of potential predictors. In: *Journal of Occupational and Environmental Medicine*, 48(1), 28–37.

Hoppe, A. (2011). Psychosocial working conditions and well-being among immigrant and German low-wage workers. In: *Journal of Occupational Health Psychology*, 16(2), 187–201. Doi: 10.1037/a0021728.

Hoppe, A., Heaney, C. A. & Fujishiro, K. (2010). Stressors, resources, and well-being among Latino and White warehouse workers in the United States. In: *American Journal of Industrial Medicine*, 53(3), 252–263. Doi: 10.1002/ajim.20752.

House, R. J., Hanges, P. J., Javidan, M., Dorfman, P. W. & Gupta, V. (2004). *Culture, leadership, and organizations – The GLOBE Study of 62 societies*. London: Sage Publications Ltd.

Imhof, S. & Andresen, M. (2017). Unhappy with well-being research in the temporary work context: mapping review and research agenda. In: *The International Journal of Human Resource Management*, 1–37.

Kattenbach, R., Demerouti, E. & Nachreiner, F. (2010). Flexible working times: Effects on employees' exhaustion, work-nonwork conflict and job performance. In: *Career Development International*, 15(3), 279–295. Doi: 10.1108/13620431011053749.

Kawachi, I. & Marmot, M. G. (1998). Commentary: What can we learn from studies of occupational class and cardiovascular disease? In: *American Journal of Epidemiology*, 148(2), 160–163.

Kirkcaldy, B., Wittig, U., Furnham, A., Merbach, M. & Siefen, R. G. (2006). Migration und Gesundheit. In: *Bundesgesundheitsblatt – Gesundheitsforschung – Gesundheitsschutz*, 49(9), 873–883.

Kivikäki, M., Vahtera, J., Virtanen, M., Elovainio, M., Pentti, J. & Ferrie, J. E. (2003). Temporary Employment and Risk of Overall and Cause-specific Mortality. In: *American Journal of Epidemiology*, 158(7), 663–668.

Krell, G. (2010). Personelle Vielfalt in Organisationen und deren Management. In: B. Badura, H. Schröder, J. Klose, K. Macco (Hrsg.), *Fehlzeiten-Report 2010. Vielfalt managen: Gesundheit fördern – Potenziale nutzen*. Berlin: Springer, 3–10.

Lampert, T., Ryl, L., Saß, A. C., Starker, A. & Ziese, T. (2010). Gesundheitliche Lage und Gesundheitsverhalten der Bevölkerung im Erwerbsalter in Deutschland. In: *Fehlzeiten-Report 2010*, 69–81.

Lewchuk, W., De Wolff, A., King, A. & Polanyi, M. (2005). Beyond job strain: Employment strain and the health effects of precarious employment. In: *Working in a Global Society Working Papers, 2005–1*. Hamilton: Labour Studies Programme, McMaster University.

Lyly-Yrjänäinen, M. (2008). *Who needs up-skilling? Low-skilled and low-qualified workers in the European Union*. http://www.eurofound.europa.eu/sites/default/files/ef_publication/field_ef_document/ef0897en.pdf.

Marler, J. H., Woodard Barringer, M. & Milkovich, G. T. (2002). Boundaryless and traditional contingent employees: worlds apart. In: *Journal of Organizational Behavior*, 23(4), 425–453. Doi: 10.1002/job.148.

Marmot, M. G., Bosma, H., Hemingway, H., Brunner, E. & Stansfeld, S. (1997). Contribution of job control and other risk factors to social variations in coronary heart disease incidence. In: *The lancet*, 350(9073), 235–239.

Martens, M. F. J., Nijhuis, F. J. N., Van Boxtel, M. P. J. & Knottnerus, J. A. (1999). Flexible work schedules and mental and physical health. A study of a working population with non-traditional working hours. In: *Journal of Organizational Behavior*, 35–46.

Mauno, S., Kinnunen, U., Mäkikangas, A. & Nätti, J. (2005). Psychological consequences of fixed-term employment and perceived job insecurity among health care staff. In: *European Journal of Work and Organizational Psychology*, 14(3), 209–237.

Metz, A. M. (2011). Intervention. In: E. Bamberg, A. Ducki & A.-M. Metz (Hrsg.), *Gesundheitsförderung und Gesundheitsmanagement in der Arbeitswelt*. Göttingen: Hogrefe, 185–220.

Mohr, G. & Korek, S. (2017). Psychische Gefährdungsbeurteilung: Praxisprobleme jenseits von Lehrbuchwissen und Leitfäden. In: C. Busch, A. Ducki, J. Dettmers & H. Witt (Hrsg.), *Der Wert der Arbeit. Festschrift zur Verabschiedung von Eva Bamberg*. Augsburg: Rainer Hampp.

Niedhammer, I., Chastang, J.F., David, S. et al. (2008). The contribution of occupational factors to social inequalities in health: findings from the national French SUMER survey. In: *Social science & medicine*, 67(11), 1870–81. Doi: 10.1016/j.socscimed. 2008.09.007.

Nienhüser, W. & Matiaske, W. (2006). Effects of the »principle of non-discrimination« on temporary agency work: compensation and working conditions of temporary agency workers in 15 European countries. In: *Industrial Relations Journal*, 37(1), 64–77. http://doi.org/10.1111/j.1468-2338.2006.00390.x.

Nixon, A. E., Mazzola, J. J., Bauer, J., Krueger, J. R. & Spector, P. E. (2011). Can work make you sick? A meta-analysis of the relationships between job stressors and physical symptoms. In: *Work & Stress*, 25(1), 1–22. Doi: 10.1080/02678373.2011.569175.

Oldenburg, C., Siefer, A. & Beermann, B. (2010). Migration als Prädiktor für Belastung und Beanspruchung? In: *Fehlzeiten-Report 2010*. Berlin: Springer-Verlag, 141–151.

Rastetter, D. (2019). Vielfalt gleichstellen? Gleichstellung, Antidiskriminierung und Diversity Management im Kontext von digitalisierter Arbeit. In: D. Alewell & W. Matiaske (Hrsg.), *Standards Guter Arbeit – disziplinäre Positionen und interdisziplinäre Perspektiven*, Baden-Baden: Nomos, 81–105.

Rau, R., & Buyken, D. (2015). Der aktuelle Kenntnisstand über Erkrankungsrisiken durch psychische Arbeitsbelastungen. In: *Zeitschrift für Arbeits- & Organisationspsychologie*, 59(3), 113–129. Doi: 10.1026/0932-4089/a000186.

Razum, O., Zeeb, H., Akgün, H. S. & Yilmaz, S. (1998). Low overall mortality of Turkish residents in Germany persists and extends into a second generation: merely a healthy migrant effect? In: *Tropical Medicine & International Health*, 3(4), 297–303.

Reilly, P. A. (1998). Balancing flexibility-meeting the interests of employer and employee. In: *European Journal of Work and Organizational Psychology*, 7(1), 7–22.

Richardson, K. M. & Rothstein, H. R. (2008). Effects of occupational stress management intervention programs: a meta-analysis. In: *Journal of Occupational Health Psychology*, 13(1), 69–93.

Rydstedt, L. W., Devereux, J. & Sverke, M. (2007). Comparing and combining the demand-control-support model and the effort reward imbalance model to predict long-term mental strain. In: *European Journal of Work and Organizational Psychology*, 16(3), 261–278.

Schenk, L. Ellert, U. & Neuhauser, H. (2008). Migration und gesundheitliche Ungleichheit. In: *Public Health Forum*, 16 (59), 18–19.

Statistisches Bundesamt (2008). *Atypische Beschäftigung auf dem deutschen Arbeitsmarkt. Begleitmaterial zum Pressegespräch am 9. September 2008 in Frankfurt am Main.*

Statistisches Bundesamt (2017a). *Bevölkerung mit Migrationshintergrund – Ergebnisse des Mikrozensus 2016.* https://www.destatis.de/DE/Publikationen/Thematisch/Bevoelkerung/ MigrationIntegration/Migrationshintergrund.html.

Statistisches Bundesamt (2017b). *Anteil atypischer Beschäftigung unverändert bei 21 %. Pressemitteilung vom 16. August 2017 – 281/17.*

Steptoe, A. & Marmot, M. (2002). The role of psychobiological pathways in socio-economic inequalities in cardiovascular disease risk. In: *European Heart Journal*, 23, 13–25.

Tregaskis, O., Brewster, C., Mayne, L. & Hegewisch, A. (1998). Flexible working in Europe: The evidence and the implications. In: *European Journal of Work and Organizational Psychology*, 7(1), 61–78. Doi: 10.1080/135943298398961.

Ulich, E. (2005). *Arbeitspsyschologie* (6. Auflage). Stuttgart: Schäffer-Poeschel Verlag.

Vahle-Hinz, T. (2013). *Psychologische und psychophysiologische Studien zu Arbeit und Gesundheit – Mit besonderer Berücksichtigung von flexiblen Beschäftigungsverhältnissen, Stressspezifität und Schlaf* (Dissertation). Hamburg: Universtät Hamburg.

Vahle-Hinz, T. (2016). Stress in nonregular work arrangements: A longitudinal study of task- and employment-related aspects of stress. In: *Journal of Occupational Health Psychology*, 21(4), 415–431. doi.org/10.1037/a0039967.

Vahle-Hinz, T. (2017). Atypische Beschäftigung und Standards guter Arbeit. In: C. Busch, A. Ducki, J. Dettmers & H. Witt (Hrsg.), *Der Wert der Arbeit. Festschrift zur Verabschiedung von Eva Bamberg*. Augsburg: Rainer Hampp Verlag, 203–216.

Vahle-Hinz, T., Kirschner, K. & Thomson, M. (2013). Employment-related demands and resources. New ways of researching stress in flexible work arrangements. In: *Management Revue*, 24(3), 199–221.

Vahle-Hinz, T. & Plachta, A. (2014). Flexible Beschäftigungsverhältnisse. In: B. Badura, A. Ducki, H. Schröder, J. Klose & M. Meyer (Hrsg.), *Fehlzeitenreport 2014. Erfolgreiche Unternehmen von morgen – gesunde Zukunft heute gestalten*. Heidelberg: Springer, 103–112.

Vowinkel, J., Busch, C. & Cao, P. (2013). Subjektive arbeitsbezogene Gesundheit in un- und angelernten, kulturell diversen Belegschaften. In: *Gruppendynamik und Organisationsentwicklung*, 44(2), 111–132. Doi: 10.1007/s11612-013-0208-0.

Vowinkel, J., Busch, C., Clasen, J. & Winkler, E. (2017a). Job characteristics, well-being, and power distance: Comparing low-skilled immigrants and German workers. (submitted).

Vowinkel, J., Busch, C., Clasen, J. & Winkler, E. (2017b). Social stressors and well-being among low-skilled multicultural coworkers. (submitted).

Wadsworth, E., Dhillon, K., Shaw, C., et al. (2007) Racial discrimination, ethnicity, and work stress. In: *Occupational Medicine*, 57(1), 18–24. Doi: 10.1093/occmed/kql088.

Wagenaar, A. F., Kompier, M. A. J., Houtman, I. L. D., van den Bossche, S., Smulders, P. & Taris, T. W. (2012). Can labour contract differences in health and work-related attitudes be explained by quality of working life and job insecurity? In: *Int Arch Occup Environ Health*, 85, 763–773. Doi: 10.1007/s00420-011-0718-4.

Wege, N., Dragano, N., Erbel, R., Jockel, K. H., Moebus, S., Stang, A. & Siegrist, J. (2008). When does work stress hurt? Testing the interaction with socioeconomic position in the Heinz Nixdorf Recall Study. In: *Journal of Epidemiology & Community Health*, 62(4), 338–341.

Willke, H. (2000). *Systemtheorie I: Grundlagen* (6. überarb. Auflage). Stuttgart: Lucius & Lucius.

Winkler, E., Busch, C., Clasen, J. & Vowinkel, J. (2014). Leadership behavior as a health-promoting resource for workers in low-skilled jobs and the moderating role of power distance orientation. In: *German Journal of Research in Human Resource Management*, 28(1–2), 96–116. Doi: 10.1688/ZfP-2014-0.

Winkler, E., Busch, C., Clasen, J. & Vowinkel, J. (2015). Change in leadership behavior predicts change in job satisfaction and well-being: A longitudinal investigation of low-skilled workforces. In: *Journal of Leadership & Organizational Studies*, 22(1), 72–87. Doi: 10.1177/1548051814527771.

Winkler, E., Busch, C. & Duresso, R. (2013) Gesundheitsförderliches Führungsverhalten bei un- und angelernten, kulturell diversen Belegschaften. In: *Gruppendynamik und Organisationsentwicklung*, 44(2), 153–169. Doi: 10.1007/s11612-013-0206-2.

Zapf, D. & Semmer, N. K. (2004). Stress und Gesundheit in Organisationen. In: H. Schuler (Hrsg.), *Enzyklopädie der Psychologie, Themenbereich D, Serie III, Band 3 Organisationspsychologie* (2. Auflage). Göttingen: Hogrefe, 1007–1112.

Teil II

Diversität, Differenzierung, Uniformität und Sinn

Human Resource Management zwischen Uniformität und Differenzierung

Sven Hauff

Ein Leitgedanke der strategischen Human Resource Management (HRM) Forschung besagt, dass die Wirkungen des HRM auf die Beschäftigten und/oder den Unternehmenserfolg nur dann verstanden werden können, wenn die Wechselwirkungen verschiedener HRM-Aktivitäten in Betracht gezogen werden (Jackson et al. 2014). Der Fokus liegt daher auf der Analyse von HRM-Systemen als spezifische Bündel bzw. Konfigurationen von HRM-Praktiken. Bei der Frage, welche HRM-Systeme in der Lage sind die Unternehmensleistung zu erhöhen, scheiden sich allerdings die Geister. Auf der einen Seite wird argumentiert, dass es ein ideales Set an HRM-Praktiken gibt, welches unabhängig vom Unternehmenskontext zur Steigerung der individuellen Leistung und damit auch zur Erhöhung der organisationalen Performance beiträgt. Prominente Beispiele dieser universalistischen Perspektive sind sogenannte High-Performance Work Practices (Appelbaum et al. 2000; Huselid 1995), High-Commitment HRM Systems (Walton 1985) oder High-Involvement HRM Systems (Lawler 1986), die zunehmend als Best-Practice-Strategien im Umgang mit Personal gelten. Auf der anderen Seite vertreten viele Forscher die Ansicht, dass je nach Kontext unterschiedliche HRM-Strategien angemessen sind (Jackson et al. 2014). Demnach sollten Unternehmen in Abhängigkeit von internen (z. B. Unternehmensstrategie, Größe, verwendete Technologie, Qualifikationen der Mitarbeiter) und externen (z. B. Branche, Arbeitsmarksituation, nationale Institutionen, Kultur) Bedingungen verschiedene HRM-Systeme verwenden, um erfolgreich zu sein.

Die Kontingenzperspektive impliziert unter anderem, dass für verschiedene Beschäftigtengruppen unterschiedliche HRM-Systeme angewendet werden. Diese Differenzierung der HRM-Strategie wird meist damit begründet, dass nicht alle Mitarbeiterinnen und Mitarbeiter eines Unternehmens einen gleich hohen strategischen Wert für das Unternehmen haben, wodurch unterschiedlich hohe Investitionen gerechtfertigt sind (Huselid/Becker 2011; Lepak/Snell 1999, 2002). Die genannten Best-Practice-Strategien werden entsprechend nicht für alle Beschäftigten angewendet, sondern nur für diejenigen, die einen hohen strategischen Wert für das Unternehmen besitzen. Problematisch hierbei ist allerdings, dass eine HRM-Differenzierung eine Ungleichbehandlung der Beschäftigten impliziert, die potenziell negative Folgewirkungen haben kann. Best-Practice-Strategien gehen in der Regel mit Arbeits- und Beschäftigungsbedingungen (z. B. hoher Autonomie und Beteiligung, Weiterbildung und Beschäftigungssicherheit) einher, die aus der Perspektive der Beschäftigten durchaus positiv zu bewerten sind.[1] Somit schaffen sie nicht nur neue Standards eines effizienten und erfolgversprechenden Umgangs mit Personal, sondern zugleich auch neue *Standards guter Arbeit.* Diese Standards können von allen Beschäftigten als Referenzpunkt zur Bewertung der eigenen Arbeitsqualität (im Sinne der Arbeits- und Beschäftigungsbedingungen) herangezogen werden. Fällt der Vergleich negativ aus bzw. wird die Verteilung als ungerecht wahrgenommen, können verringerte Motivation und erhöhte Fluktuation der benachteiligten Beschäftigtengruppen die Folge sein, wodurch mögliche Effizienzgewinne einer HRM-Differenzierung verringert oder zunichte gemacht werden (Krausert 2017; O'Connor/Crowley-Henry 2017).

Eine HRM-Differenzierung kann sich somit als ein zweischneidiges Schwert erweisen: Einerseits kann sie ökonomisch sinnvoll sein, da hohe Investitionen nur für besonders wertvolle Mitarbeiterinnen und Mitarbeiter getätigt und somit Kosten gespart werden; andererseits könnte sie negative Folgen hervorrufen, so dass eine Uniformität im Sinne der Best-Practice-Strategien angemessener wäre. Ziel des vorliegenden Beitrags ist es, sich dieser Problematik konzeptionell zu nähern. Hierzu werden zunächst die Positionen für eine stärkere Uniformität im HRM erläutert. Darauf aufbauend wird auf die Hintergründe und Notwendigkeit einer differenzierten HRM-Strategie eingegangen. Abschließend wird diskutiert, welche Auswirkungen ein HRM im Spannungsfeld zwischen Uniformität und Differenzierung haben kann.

---

1 Autonomie, Beteiligung, Weiterbildung und Beschäftigungssicherheit werden dabei als Ressourcen verstanden, die zum Wohlbefinden der Beschäftigten beitragen. Eine derartige Sichtweise ist nicht unumstritten. Z. B. kann eine erhöhte Autonomie auch zu höheren Belastungen am Arbeitsplatz führen. Vgl. hierzu auch Busch/Vahle-Hinz in diesem Band.

1. Plädoyer für mehr Uniformität

Vertreter der universalistischen Perspektive im strategischen HRM argumentieren, dass ein bestimmtes Set an HRM-Praktiken unabhängig vom spezifischen organisationalen Kontext zur Steigerung der individuellen und damit auch der organisationalen Leistung beiträgt. Einer der prominentesten Ansätze stellt hierbei das Konzept der sogenannten *High-Performance Work Practices (HPWP)* (Appelbaum et al. 2000; Huselid 1995) dar. Auch wenn bislang kein allgemein akzeptiertes Verständnis dazu vorliegt, welche HRM-Praktiken als HPWP gelten (Posthuma et al. 2013), nutzen die meisten Forscher das Ability, Motivation, Opportunity Modell (Appelbaum et al. 2000), nach dem HRM-Praktiken dazu beitragen sollten, dass die Beschäftigten die nötigen Fähigkeiten haben, hoch motiviert sind und auch die Gelegenheit haben, ihre Fähigkeiten und ihre Motivation entsprechend einzusetzen. Zentrale HRM-Praktiken sind intensive Rekrutierung und regelmäßige Weiterbildung zur Steigerung der Fähigkeiten; Leistungsbeurteilung, Gewinnbeteiligung, Karriereperspektiven und Arbeitsplatzsicherheit zur Steigerung der Motivation sowie abwechslungsreiche Tätigkeiten, Autonomie und Partizipation als Mittel zur Steigerung der Gelegenheiten (Jiang et al. 2012). Fähigkeiten, Motivation und Gelegenheit stellen hierbei Grundprobleme des Personalmanagements dar, die unabhängig vom Kontext gelöst werden müssen. Daher sind Unternehmen angehalten, HPWP uneingeschränkt einzusetzen, um die Leistungsfähigkeit aller Beschäftigten zu steigern. Tun sie dies nicht, müssen sie mit Wettbewerbsnachteilen rechnen.

Während HPWP ein sehr breites Spektrum an HRM-Praktiken beinhalten, haben High-Commitment HRM Systems (Walton 1985) und High-Involvement HRM Systems (Lawler 1986) einen etwas engeren Fokus (Lepak et al. 2006). *High-Commitment HRM Systems* zielen darauf, dass sich die Beschäftigten stärker mit den Unternehmenszielen identifizieren und sich somit in hohem Maße für diese Ziele engagieren. Hierfür erhalten Beschäftigte z. B. intensive Trainings- und Weiterbildungsmöglichkeiten, interne Aufstiegsmöglichkeiten, eine gute Bezahlung sowie Beschäftigungssicherheit. Im Austausch sollen die Beschäftigten eine hohe Bindung zu Unternehmen und deren Zielen aufbauen. *High-Involvement HRM Systems* konzentrieren sich dagegen stärker auf die Frage der Beteiligung der Mitarbeiter – u. a. durch größere Autonomie und Mitspracherechte, Job Rotation oder Qualitätszirkel – wodurch ebenfalls eine höhere Leistung erreicht werden soll. Sowohl High-Commitment als auch High-

Involvement HRM Systems werden dabei als Best-Practice-Strategien im Umgang mit Personal gesehen, da Wettbewerbsvorteile eben nur dann erwartet werden, wenn sich alle Beschäftigten mit den Unternehmenszielen identifizieren bzw. wenn alle Beschäftigten eine höhere Leistung auf Basis von Vertrauen und Freiräumen erbringen.

Das Argument der Gleichbehandlung aller Mitarbeiter wird aus einer eher prozessorientierten Perspektive zusätzlich gestärkt.[2] Bowen und Ostroff (2004) nehmen beispielsweise an, dass Unternehmen nur dann erfolgreich sind, wenn sie über ein *starkes HRM-System* verfügen. Die Idee hierbei ist, dass HRM-Praktiken eine Form der Kommunikation zwischen Arbeitgebern und Arbeitnehmern darstellen. Die Stärke eines HRM-Systems beschreibt dabei das Maß an Kongruenz bzw. Konformität innerhalb eines HRM-Systems. Ein starkes HRM-System liegt dann vor, wenn die Beschäftigten eine geteilte Interpretation der organisationalen Politiken, Praktiken, Vorgehensweisen und Ziele haben und somit eine einheitliche Wahrnehmung davon existiert, welche Verhaltensweisen erwartet und honoriert werden.

Die Stärke eines HRM-Systems wird in Anlehnung an die Attributionstheorie über die Kritierien Distinkheit, Konsistenz und Konsens konzeptualisiert. Distinktheit beschreibt allgemein, inwieweit eine Person, ein Objekt oder eine Sache in einer bestimmten Situation hervorsteht und Aufmerksamkeit auf sich zieht. Die Distinkheit von HRM-Praktiken kann u. a. durch das Ausmaß, indem HRM-Praktiken salient und leicht beobachtbar sind (Visibilität) und durch die Eindeutigkeit und Klarheit der HRM-Praktiken (Verständlichkeit) beeinflusst werden. Konsistenz bezieht sich allgemein auf den zeitlichen Bestand. Dieser kann erreicht werden, wenn eindeutige Ursache-Wirkungsbeziehungen zwischen gewünschtem Verhalten und den assoziierten Konsequenzen bestehen (Instrumentalität), wenn HRM-Praktiken als gültig wahrgenommen werden (Validität) und wenn stabile Signale durch HRM-Praktiken ausgesendet werden (konsistente Botschaften). Konsens beschreibt schließlich das Maß an personeller und situativer Übereinstimmung, was laut Bowen und Ostroff (2004) nur durch eine einheitliche Linie in der Personalarbeit (Übereinstimmung zwi-

2 Ein weiteres Argument zur Gleichbehandlung aller Mitarbeiter stellt das Gebot der Chancengleichheit und Nichtdiskriminierung dar. Vgl. hierzu Rastetter (2019) in diesem Band.

schen HR Entscheidern) und durch ein hohes Maß an distributiver, prozeduraler und interaktiver Gerechtigkeit (Fairness) gewährleistet werden kann. Insbesondere die Kritierien der Konsistenz und des Konsensus verweisen auf eine Gleichbehandlung aller Mitarbeiter. Eine unterschiedliche Behandlung von Beschäftigtengruppen würde unterschiedliche Signale in Bezug auf die Arbeitgebererwartungen und den damit verbundenen Verpflichtungen senden, was einen negativen Effekt auf die Unternehmensleistung zur Folge hätte.

2. HRM-Differenzierung als ökonomische Notwendigkeit

Im HRM werden in der Regel plurale Ziele verfolgt, wobei nicht nur Qualifikation, Einstellungen und Verhalten der Beschäftigten eine Rolle spielen, sondern auch Aspekte wie Flexibilität und Kosten (Hauff et al. 2017). Bei näherer Betrachtung fällt auf, dass die universalistischen Ansätze letzteres i. d. R. vernachlässigen. Beispielsweise wird im Kontext der Diskussion um HPWP meist nicht berücksichtigt, dass das Angebot an Beschäftigungssicherheit eine Einschränkung der Flexibilität mit sich bringt oder dass umfassende Personalentwicklungsmaßnahmen und Gewinnbeteiligung der Beschäftigten höhere Kosten implizieren (Godard 2004; Kaufman 2015). Vor diesem Hintergrund finden sich in der Literatur verschiedene Überlegungen dahingehend, dass eine Differenzierung des HRM durchaus ökonomisch sinnvoll sein könnte (für einen Überblick vgl. auch Krausert 2017; Marescaux et al. 2013).

Einen der prominentesten Ansätze zur HRM-Differenzierung stellt der *HR-Architektur-Ansatz* von Lepak und Snell (1999, 2002) dar. Der zentrale Gedanke des Ansatzes besagt, dass Unternehmen die HRM-Strategie von der Einzigartigkeit des Humankapitals und dessen strategischem Wert abhängig machen. Mit dem Kriterium der *Einzigartigkeit* beziehen sich Lepak und Snell in Anlehnung an transaktionskosten- und humankapitaltheoretische Überlegungen auf die Frage, wie spezifisch das Humankapital ist. Eine hohe Spezifität liegt dabei dann vor, wenn benötigtes Humankapital nicht frei auf dem Arbeitsmarkt zur Verfügung steht, sondern nur firmenintern aufgebaut und im Extremfall auch nur firmenintern verwendet werden kann. Der *strategische Wert des Humankapitals* bezieht sich dagegen, in Anlehnung an den Resource-based View, auf den Beitrag des Humankapitals zum Unternehmenserfolg.

Durch die Kombination dieser beiden Dimensionen ergeben sich vier verschiedene HRM-Strategien (vgl. Abbildung 1). Die *commitmentorientierte Personalstrategie* wird für Beschäftigte eingesetzt, deren Humankapital einzigartig und sehr wertvoll ist. Diese Beschäftigten können nicht ohne weiteres auf dem externen Arbeitsmarkt beschafft werden, daher sind umfassende Investitionen in Weiterbildung erforderlich. Damit diese Investitionen nicht verloren gehen, wird das Commitment der Beschäftigten durch langfristige Perspektiven, Karriereoptionen, Bonussysteme etc. gesteigert. Bei der *produktivitätsorientieren Personalstrategie* ist das Humankapital wertvoll, kann aber auf dem externen Arbeitsmarkt beschafft werden. Der Fokus im HRM liegt daher weniger auf der Entwicklung und dem Training der Mitarbeiterinnen und Mitarbeiter, sondern vielmehr im Bereich der Rekrutierung sowie der Festlegung der Vergütung. Die *kontroll-orientierte Personalstrategie* bezieht sich auf Beschäftigte mit allgemeinem Humankapital, welche aus Unternehmenssicht keinen besonderen strategischen Wert haben. Typische Beschäftigungsverhältnisse sind daher befristete Verträge oder Leiharbeit. Der Fokus im HRM liegt dabei meist auf Standardisierung und Kostenkontrolle. Die *kooperationsorientierte Personalstrategie* zielt schließlich auf Humankapital, das zwar einzigartig, aber nur von begrenztem Wert für das Unternehmen ist. Die Folge sind Allianzen und Partnerschaften, z. B. im Bereich von Forschung- und Entwicklung, Finanzdienstleistungen oder

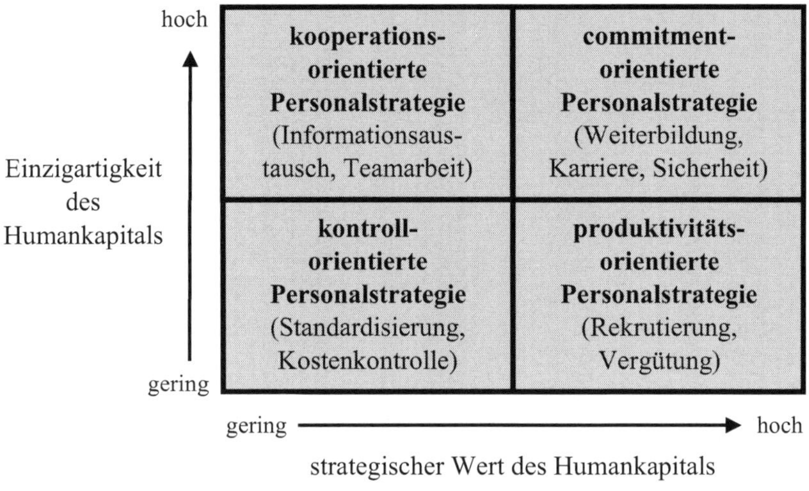

Abbildung 1: HR-Architektur

Quelle: in Anlehnung an Lepak/Snell (2002: 520)

Rechtsberatung. Das HRM konzentriert sich entsprechend auf die Sicherstellung des Informationsaustausches und die Zusammenarbeit in gemeinsamen Teams.

Auch andere Autoren sind der Ansicht, dass die strategische Bedeutung der Beschäftigten eine Ungleichbehandlung legitimiert. So heben beispielsweise Huslied und Becker (2011: 424) hervor: »some jobs are more valuable (strategic) than others, and they should be managed accordingly. This means that disproportionate investments must be made in strategic roles, ensuring that the organization places top talent in these positions. [...] Attracting, selecting, developing, and retaining world-class talent represents a very significant investment for most organizations, and the harsh reality is that most organizations simply do not have the time or resources to do this for all organizational roles. This means that a decision about where and how to invest must be made.« Im Gegensatz zu Lepak und Snell (1999, 2002) wird hier weniger das Humankapital, sondern die strategische Bedeutung von bestimmten Positionen innerhalb des Unternehmens betont. Der Ausgangspunkt der HRM-Differenzierung sind somit weniger die Beschäftigten als vielmehr die Positionen innerhalb eines Unternehmens. Als »strategic jobs« gelten dabei all diejenigen Positionen, die entscheidend zur Wettbewerbsfähigkeit und dem Unternehmenserfolg beitragen.

Ähnlich wird auch im Rahmen des *Talentmanagements* argumentiert (Gallardo-Gallardo et al. 2013). Eine weit verbreitete Definition von Talentmanagement stammt von Collings und Mellahi (2009: 304), die Talentmanagement definieren als »activities and processes that involve the systematic identification of key positions which differentially contribute to the organisation's sustainable competitive advantage, the development of a talent pool of high potential and high performing incumbents to fill these roles, and the development of a differentiated human resource architecture to facilitate filling these positions with competent incumbents and to ensure their continued commitment to the organization.« Die Differenzierung der HRM-Strategie stellt somit einen zentralen Bestandteil des Talentmanagements dar. Vor dem Hintergrund der Konkurrenz um Spitzenkräfte und den zunehmenden Fach- und Führungskräftemangel wird dabei immer wieder betont, dass Talente bzw. High-Potentials besonders beworben und umsorgt werden müssen, da sie nur so gewonnen und an das Unternehmen gebunden werden können. Dabei erhalten sogenannte idiosynkratische Abmachungen bzw. I-Deals (Rousseau 2005) eine zunehmende Bedeutung. Diese stellen individuelle Aushandlungen zwischen

Arbeitgebern und Arbeitnehmern dar, in deren Folge die Arbeits- und Beschäftigungsbedingungen zunehmend entstandardisiert werden und die Unterschiede zwischen verschiedenen Beschäftigtengruppen zunehmen.

3. HRM im Spannungsfeld zwischen Uniformität und Differenzierung

Die Frage, inwieweit eine universelle HRM-Strategie im Sinne der Best-Practice-Ansätze oder doch ein differenziertes HRM erfolgversprechender ist, lässt sich heute nicht eindeutig beantworten. Dies liegt vor allem darin begründet, dass der Gedanke der Differenzierung bislang kaum in empirischen Forschungsarbeiten aufgegriffen wird. So zeigen Bainbridge et al. (2017), dass 93 % der Studien zu HRM-Systemen entweder mit Skalen oder Indizes arbeiten, wodurch HRM-Systeme nur in Form eines Kontinuums zwischen »mehr oder weniger« abgebildet werden. Dies entspricht nicht der Idee der HRM-Systeme und den Erfahrungen aus der Praxis, dass für unterschiedliche Beschäftigtengruppen unterschiedliche Sets an HRM-Praktiken verwendet werden (Hauff et al. 2014 sowie Busch/Vahle-Hinz 2019 in diesem Band).

Dieses Forschungsdefizit ist aus mehreren Perspektiven heraus problematisch. Erstens liegt kaum Wissen hinsichtlich der Frage vor, wie verbreitet bestimmte HRM-Strategien sind. Eine Annäherung an diese Frage wäre insbesondere für die Einschätzung der Arbeitsqualität verschiedener Beschäftigtengruppen relevant. Arbeitsqualität ist ein multidimensionales Konstrukt, wobei den jeweiligen Arbeits- und Beschäftigungsbedingungen eine unterschiedliche Relevanz für die Arbeitsqualität der Beschäftigten zukommt (Hauff/Kirchner 2013). Eine Annäherung an die Frage der Ausgestaltung verschiedener HRM-Strategien könnte hier detaillierte Hinweise liefern, da eben Kombinationen von HRM-Praktiken analysiert werden und nicht singuläre Aspekte im Vordergrund stehen.[3]

3 Dabei geht es nicht nur um die Frage, welche HRM-Praktiken in den jeweiligen Strategien zu Anwendungen kommen. Vielfach werden sich hier Überschneidungen ergeben, da alle Beschäftigtengruppen rekrutiert, ausgewählt, beurteilt, motiviert, weitergebildet werden müssen. Entscheidend ist zudem, wie sich die Ausgestaltung der HRM-Praktiken über verschiedene Beschäftigtengruppen hinweg unterscheidet (Huselid/Becker 2011).

Zweitens können wir nicht genau sagen, welche Wirkungen von einer HRM-Differenzierung ausgehen. Wie oben dargestellt, kann eine HRM-Differenzierung insbesondere unter ökonomischen Gesichtspunkten sinnvoll sein: Hohe Investitionen werden nur bei denjenigen Beschäftigten getätigt, die einen hohen strategischen Wert für das Unternehmen haben; Investitionen in Beschäftige mit einem geringen strategischen Wert scheinen dagegen wenig zielführend, da das Humankapital dieser Beschäftigten keinen großen Einfluss auf den Unternehmenserfolg hat (Huselid/Becker 2011; Lepak/Snell 1999, 2002; Schmidt et al. 2018). Dem lässt sich allerdings entgegenhalten, dass eine HRM-Differenzierung potenziell negative Effekte hat, wenn Beschäftigte dies im Rahmen von sozialen Vergleichsprozessen als unfair wahrnehmen und mit negativen Einstellungen (z. B. Arbeitsunzufriedenheit) und Verhaltensweisen (z. B. verringerte Zusammenarbeit, Fluktuation) reagieren (Lepak et al. 2007; Marescaux et al. 2013, O'Connor/Crowley-Henry 2017). Die möglichen positiven Wirkungen einer HRM-Differenzierung könnten somit verringert oder gar neutralisiert werden.

Die konkreten Wirkungen der HRM-Differenzierung lassen sich mithilfe der Social Exchange Theorie (Blau 1964) sowie der Equity Theorie (Adams 1963) näher spezifizieren (O'Connor/Crowley-Henry 2017). Die Social Exchange Theorie betont das Prinzip der Reziprozität zur Analyse sozialen Handelns. Demnach werden Handlungen von Individuen durch erwartete Gegenleistungen (extrinsischer und intrinsischer Art) motiviert, wobei die Balance zwischen Beitrag und Belohnung entscheidend für die Bewertung einer sozialen Beziehung ist. Eine HRM-Differenzierung kann somit als fair wahrgenommen werden, solange die Balance zwischen Beitrag und Belohnung gewährleistet wird. Haben Beschäftigte dagegen das Gefühl, dass ihr Unternehmen keine angemessene Gegenleistung erbringt, werden sie mit negativen Einstellungen und Verhaltensweisen reagieren.

Im Rahmen der Equity Theorie (Adams 1963) wird die wahrgenommene Fairness ebenfalls durch das Verhältnis aus Beiträgen und Belohnungen bestimmt. Das entsprechende eigene Input-Output-Verhältnis wird aber immer auch zum Input-Output-Verhältnis von Referenzpersonen in Relation gesetzt, wobei eine Situation nur dann als fair wahrgenommen wird, wenn das eigene Input-Output Verhältnis gleich dem Input-Output-Verhältnis der Referenzperson ist. Die Wahrnehmung einer HRM-Strategie wird somit nicht nur durch die reine Balance zwischen Input und Output bestimmt, vielmehr spielen soziale Vergleichsprozesse eine entscheidende Rolle. Interessant hierbei ist die Frage, wer als Referenzperson fungiert. Da sich Menschen normalerweise mit Menschen vergleichen, die eine gewisse Ähnlichkeit zu ihnen selbst aufweisen, sind Vergleichsprozesse innerhalb einer Beschäftigtengruppe wahrscheinlich.[4] Derartige Vergleichsprozesse innerhalb von Beschäftigtengruppen beziehen sich allerdings nicht auf die HRM-Differenzierung im oben dargestellten Sinne, bei der es um eine unterschiedliche HRM-Strategie für verschiedene Beschäftigtengruppen geht. Vielmehr ist hiermit die Konsistenz innerhalb eines HRM-Systems bzw. die Stärke eines HRM-Systems (Bowen/Ostroff 2004) angesprochen. In dem hier vertretenen Verständnis von HRM-Differenzierung stehen dagegen Vergleichsprozesse zwischen unterschiedlichen Beschäftigtengruppen im Fokus, also etwa zwischen strategisch wertvollen Mitarbeitern vs. Mitarbeitern, denen kein hoher strategischer Wert zugeschrieben wird.

Für die Wirkung der HRM-Differenzierung spielt die wahrgenommene organisationale Gerechtigkeit eine entscheidende Rolle, wobei angenommen werden kann, dass der Effekt der HRM-Differenzierung auf die Einstellungen und Verhaltensweisen der Beschäftigten durch die wahrgenommene Gerechtigkeit mediiert wird (Gelens et al. 2013, 2014; O'Connor/Crowley-Henry 2017). Die wahrgenommene organisationale Gerechtigkeit beschreibt das Ausmaß, in dem die Beschäftigten das organisationale Handeln als fair empfinden (Greenberg 1990). Hierbei lassen sich drei Aspekte unterscheiden: die distributive Gerechtigkeit, die prozedurale Gerechtigkeit sowie die interaktionale Gerechtigkeit. Die distributive Gerechtigkeit betrachtet die Verteilung von Outcomes und spielt somit für die Frage, wie eine HRM-Differenzierung wahrgenommen wird und welche Reaktionen sich jeweils ergeben, eine zentrale Rolle. Unklar ist allerdings, wie die Bewertungen im Einzelnen vorgenommen werden. Nach dem Leistungs-prinzip könnte eine ungleiche Behandlung durchaus als fair wahrgenommen werden, falls Beschäftigte die unterschiedlichen Beiträge und Leistungen der jeweiligen Beschäftigtengruppen ebenfalls wahrnehmen. Im Gegenteil spricht das Gleichheitsprinzip eher für eine Uniformität im HRM. Darüber hinaus sind aber auch die prozedurale und interaktionale Gerechtigkeit von Relevanz, da z. B. Einflussmöglichkeiten der Beschäftigten oder das Verhalten von Führungskräften bei der Imple-

---

4 Daher analysieren z. B. Marescaux et al. (2013) nur die wahrgenommene Günstigkeit von HRM-Praktiken innerhalb einer Beschäftigtengruppe.

mentierung von HRM-Praktiken einen Einfluss auf die Wahrnehmung der HRM-Strategien haben können.

Eine unterschiedliche Behandlung von Beschäftigtengruppen im Rahmen der HRM-Differenzierung kann sich unter Beachtung der wahrgenommenen Fairness bzw. organisationalen Gerechtigkeit positiv, neutral oder negativ auswirken (Marescaux et al. 2013). *Positive* Wirkungen sind bei denjenigen Beschäftigten zu erwarten, die von der HRM-Differenzierung profitieren bzw. diese als richtig emfpinden. Dies wird z. B. in Studien zu I-Deals bestätigt, wonach I-Deals bei den Begünstigten zu einem höheren Commitment, gesteigerten Organizational Citizenship Behaviour und höheren Engagement führen (Anand et al. 2010, Hornung et al. 2010).[5] Eine HRM-Differenzierung kann auch eine eher *neutrale* Wirkung haben, da zwischen Beschäftigten unterschiedliche Normen und Annahmen dahingehend bestehen, welche HRM-Praktiken für eine bestimmte Beschäftigtengruppe angemessen sind (Krausert 2017; Nishii et al. 2008). Ganz im Sinne der Equity Theorie ließe sich hier argumentierten, das High-Potentials und Talente ganz einfach mehr bekommen, da sie eben mehr leisten. Die anderen Mitarbeitergruppen erhalten weniger, weil sie eine geringere Leistung erbringen. Die Welt ist in Ordnung, sofern die Relationen stimmen. Demgegenüber können sich aber auch *negative* Reaktionen zeigen, wenn Beschäftigte die vorgenommene HRM-Differenzierung als unfair bzw. ungerecht wahrnehmen. Exklusive High-Potential-Programme oder Talentmanagement können in diesem Sinne problematisch werden, da sie andere Beschäftigtengruppen ausgrenzen.[6] Letztere können sich dadurch möglicherweise benachteiligt fühlen und mit negativen Einstellungen und Verhaltensweisen reagieren (O'Connor/Crowley-Henry 2017).

Um diese potenziellen negativen Effekte einer HRM-Differenzierung zu minimieren oder zu umgehen, sehen Keeps und Delery (2007) zwei Alternativen: 1) den Austausch zwischen unterschiedlichen Beschäftigten zu

5 Kritisch an diesen Studien anzumerken ist, dass sie sich ausschließlich auf Beschäftigte konzentrieren, die I-Deals erhalten und damit die potenziellen negativen Effekte bei anderen Beschäftigtengruppen ausblenden (Marescaux et al. 2013).

6 Eine extreme Form der Ausgrenzung findet bei denjenigen Beschäftigten statt, die nicht über einen regulären Arbeitsvertrag an ein Unternehmen gebunden sind. Dies betrifft beispielsweise Leiharbeiter und Crowdworker. Vgl. hierzu auch Kirchner/Beyer (2016) sowie Hanau/Matiaske (2019) in diesem Band.

minimieren oder 2) die HRM-Systeme über die verschiedenen Beschäftigtengruppen abzustimmen. Die erste Alternative versucht die potenziellen Probleme einer HRM-Differenzierung durch eine Abschottung der jeweiligen Beschäftigtengruppen in den Griff zu bekommen. Dabei heben die Autoren allerdings auch hervor, dass dies in der modernen Arbeitswelt, in der Beschäftige in hohem Maße auf Kooperation und Austausch angewiesen sind, kaum realistisch ist. Daher empfehlen die Autoren auch eher die zweite Alternative, nach der Unternehmen versuchen sollten, die verschiedenen HRM-Systeme über eine gemeinsame HRM-Philosophie aufeinander abzustimmen. Durch diesen »between-HRM system fit« soll – ganz im Sinne Bowen und Ostroffs (2004) – ein »shared mindset« zwischen den Beschäftigten kreiert werden, welches negative Einstellungen und Verhaltensweisen verhindern soll (Banks/Kepes 2015: 362). Statt einer HRM-Differenzierung wird somit wieder die Uniformität im HRM gepriesen.

4. Fazit und Ausblick

In diesem Beitrag wurden die möglichen Vor- und Nachteile der Uniformität und Differenzierung im HRM diskutiert. Deutlich wurde, dass auf Basis der bisherigen Literatur keine eindeutigen Aussagen zu den Wirkungen der jeweiligen Strategien getroffen werden können. Für die universalistischen Ansätze bzw. Best-Practice-Strategien sprechen ihre starke Mitarbeiterorientierung, da diese Ansätze mit positiven Arbeits- und Beschäftigungsbedingungen (z. B. hoher Autonomie und Beteiligung, Weiterbildung und Beschäftigungssicherheit) einhergehen, die mutmaßlich nicht nur zu einer höheren Zufriedenheit und Motivation der Beschäftigten führen, sondern auch die Unternehmensleistung steigern können. Gegen die umfassende Anwendung dieser Strategien sprechen aus personalwirtschaftlicher Sicht vor allem Kosten- und Flexibilitätsgesichtspunkte. Vor diesem Hintergrund ist es nicht verwunderlich, dass Unternehmen in der Regel plurale HRM-Strategien in Bezug auf unterschiedliche Beschäftigtengruppen einsetzen. Dabei profitieren insbesondere die High Potentials und Talente, da ihnen umfassende Investitionen zuteilwerden. Beschäftigte, denen ein geringerer strategischer Wert zugschrieben wird, werden dagegen weniger großzügig behandelt.

Die HRM-Differenzierung wird in der bisherigen Literatur meist nur über die damit verbundenen ökonomischen Vorteile erklärt. Diese Makro-

Perspektive ignoriert allerdings die möglichen Folgen der HRM-Differenzierung für die Einstellungen und für das Verhalten der Beschäftigten. Eine HRM-Differenzierung kann sich unter diesem Gesichtspunkt schnell als ein zweischneidiges Schwert erweisen, da den potenziellen ökonomischen Gewinnen negative Einstellungen (z. B. Arbeitszufriedenheit, Commitment) und Verhaltensweisen (z. B. verringerte Zusammenarbeit, Unterstützung, Leistung, Fluktuation) derjenigen Beschäftigten gegenüberstehen, die nicht von der Differenzierung profitieren. Dies spricht mitunter für eine stärkere Uniformität im HRM, wobei die Best-Practice-Strategien im HRM als Standards guter Arbeit fungieren könnten.

Die strategische HRM Forschung betont seit einiger Zeit, dass die Wirkungen des HRM nur dann richtig verstanden werden können, wenn nicht nur auf die von Personalverantwortlichen intendierten und implementierten HRM-Praktiken geschaut wird, sondern wenn insbesondere die Wahrnehmung der HRM-Praktiken durch die Beschäftigten berücksichtigt wird (Wright/Nishii 2013). Entsprechend erfreut sich die Mikro-Perspektive einer zunehmenden Beliebtheit in der strategischen HRM-Literatur. Kaum Beachtung finden dabei allerdings die in diesem Beitrag fokussierten Aspekte der Fairness und organisationalen Gerechtigkeit. Demgegenüber setzt sich die Literatur zum Talent Management zunehmend mit den potenziell negativen Folgewirkungen eines exklusiven Talent Managements auseinander (z. B. Boeck et al. 2018; Gelens et al. 2013, 2014; O'Connor/Crowley-Henry 2017; Swailes 2013). Die (meist konzeptionellen) Beiträge liefern dabei wichtige Ansatzpunkte für die mit einer HRM-Differenzierung verbundenen Wirkungen. Aufbauend auf diesen Überlegungen bedarf es in der zukünftigen Forschung allerdings einer stärkeren Integration von Makro- und Mikro-Perspektiven (zu entsprechenden Forderungen vgl. z. B. auch Wright et al. 2014), da die Wirkungen einer HRM-Differenzierung nur so umfassend analysiert und verstanden werden können.

Literaturverzeichnis

Adams, J.S. (1963): Towards an understanding of inequity. In: *Journal of Abnormal and Social Psychology*, 67, 422–436.

Anand, S./Vidyarthi, P.R./Liden, R.C./Rousseau, D.M. (2010): Good Citizens in Poor-Quality Relationships: Idiosyncratic Deals as a Substitute for Relationship Quality. In: *Academy of Management Journal*, 53: 5, 970–988.

Appelbaum, E./Bailey, T./Berg, P./Kalleberg, A.L. (2000): Manufacturing advantage: Why high performance work systems pay off, Ithaca, NY.

Bainbridge, H.T.J./Sanders, K./Cogin, J.A./Lin, C.-H. (2017): The Pervasiveness And Trajectory Of Methodological Choices: A 20-Year Review Of Human Resource Management Research. In: *Human Resource Management*, 56: 6, 887–913.

Banks, G.C./Kepes, S. (2015): The influence of internal HRM activity fit on the dynamics within the »black box.« In: *Human Resource Management Review*, 25: 4, 352–367.

Blau, P.M. (1964): *Exchange and power in social life*, New York: Wiley.

Boeck, G. de/Meyers, M.C./Dries, N. (2018): Employee reactions to talent management: Assumptions versus evidence. In: *Journal of Organizational Behavior*, 39: 2, 199–213.

Bowen, D.E./Ostroff, C. (2004): Understanding HRM-Firm Performance Linkages: The Role of the »Strength« of the HRM System. In: *Academy of Management Review*, 29: 2, 203–221.

Busch, C./Vahle-Hinz, T. (2019): Gesundheit und Wohlbefinden in einer Arbeitswelt im Wandel: Aufrechterhaltung von Standards guter Arbeit bei multikulturellen Belegschaften und flexibler Arbeit. In: Alewell, D./Matiaske, W. (Hrsg.), *Standards Guter Arbeit – disziplinäre Positionen und interdisziplinäre Perspektiven*, Baden-Baden: Nomos, 39–61.

Collings, D.G./Mellahi, K. (2009): Strategic Talent Management: A review and research agenda. In: *Human Resource Management Review*, 19: 4, 304–313.

Gallardo-Gallardo, E./Dries, N./González-Cruz, T.F. (2013): What is the meaning of 'talent' in the world of work? In: *Human Resource Management Review*, 23: 4, 290–300.

Gelens, J./Dries, N./Hofmans, J./Pepermans, R. (2013): The role of perceived organizational justice in shaping the outcomes of talent management: A research agenda. In: *Human Resource Management Review*, 23: 4, 341–353.

Gelens, J./Hofmans, J./Dries, N./Pepermans, R. (2014): Talent management and organisational justice: Employee reactions to high potential identification. In: *Human Resource Management Journal*, 24: 2, 159–175.

Godard, J. (2004): A Critical Assessment of the High-Performance Paradigm. In: *British Journal of Industrial Relations*, 42: 2, 349–378.

Greenberg, J. (1990): Organizational justice: Yesterday, today, and tomorrow. In: *Journal of Management*, 16: 2, 399–432.

Hanau, H./Matiaske, W. (2019): Mitbestimmung im entgrenzten Betrieb – Arbeitsrechtliche und personalwirtschaftliche Perspektiven. In: Alewell, D./Matiaske, W. (Hrsg.), *Standards Guter Arbeit – disziplinäre Positionen und interdisziplinäre Perspektiven*, Baden-Baden: Nomos, 213–242.

Hauff, S./Alewell, D./Hansen, N.K. (2014): HRM systems between control and commitment: Occurrence, characteristics and effects on HRM outcomes and firm performance. In: *Human Resource Management Journal*, 24: 4, 424–441.

Hauff, S./Alewell, D./Hansen, N.K. (2017): HRM systems strength and HRM target achievement – Towards a broader understanding of HRM processes. In: *Human Resource Management*, 56: 5, 715–729.

Hauff, S./Kirchner, S. (2013): Wandel der Arbeitsqualität – Arbeits- und Beschäftigungsbedingungen zwischen 1989 und 2005 in einer evaluativ-relationalen Perspektive. In: *Zeitschrift für Soziologie*, 42: 4, 337–355.

Hornung, S./Rousseau, D.M./Glaser, J./Angerer, P./Weigl, M. (2010): Beyond top-down and bottom-up work redesign: Customizing job content through idiosyncratic deals. In: *Journal of Organizational Behavior*, 31: 2–3, 187–215.

Huselid, M.A. (1995): The Impact of Human Resource Management Practices on Turnover, Productivity, and Corporate Financial Performance. In: *The Academy of Management Journal*, 38: 3, 635–672.

Huselid, M.A./Becker, B.E. (2011): Bridging Micro and Macro Domains: Workforce Differentiation and Strategic Human Resource Management. In: *Journal of Management*, 37: 2, 421–428.

Jackson, S.E./Schuler, R.S./Jiang, K. (2014): An Aspirational Framework for Strategic Human Resource Management. In: *The Academy of Management Annals*, 8: 1, 1–56.

Jiang, K./Lepak, D.P./Hu, J./Baer, J.C. (2012): How Does Human Resource Management Influence Organizational Outcomes? A Meta-analytic Investigation of Mediating Mechanisms. In: *Academy of Management Journal*, 55: 6, 1264–1294.

Kaufman, B.E. (2015): Market competition, HRM, and firm performance: The conventional paradigm critiqued and reformulated. In: *Human Resource Management Review*, 25: 1, 107–125.

Kepes, S./Delery, J.E. (2007): HRM systems and the problem of internal fit. In: Boxall, P./Purcell, J./Wright, P. M. (Hrsg.): *The Oxford Handbook of Human Resource Management*, Oxford: Oxford University Press, 385–404.

Kirchner, S./Beyer, J. (2016): Die Plattformlogik als digitale Marktordnung. In: *Zeitschrift für Soziologie*, 45: 5, 324–339.

Krausert, A. (2017): HR differentiation between professional and managerial employees: Broadening and integrating theoretical perspectives. In: *Human Resource Management Review*, 27: 3, 442–457.

Lawler, E.E. (1986): *High-involvement management: Participative strategies for improving organizational performance*, San Francisco: Jossey-Bass.

Lepak, D.P./Liao, H./Chung, Y./Harden, E.E. (2006): A Conceptual Review Of Human Resource Management Systems In Strategic Human Resource Management Research. In: *Research in Personnel and Human Resource Management*, 25, 217–271.

Lepak, D.P./Snell, S.A. (1999): The human resource architecture: toward a theory of human capital allocation and development. In: *Academy of Management Review*, 24, 31–48.

Lepak, D.P./Snell, S.A. (2002): Examining the Human Resource Architecture: The Relationships Among Human Capital, Employment, and Human Resource Configurations. In: *Journal of Management*, 28: 4, 517–543.

Lepak, D.P./Taylor, M.S./Tekleab, A.G./Marrone, J.A./Cohen, D.J. (2007): An examination of the use of high-investment human resource systems for core and support employees. In: *Human Resource Management*, 46: 2, 223–246.

Marescaux, E./De Winne, S./Sels, L. (2013): HR practices and affective organisational commitment: (when) does HR differentiation pay off? In: *Human Resource Management Journal*, 23: 4, 329–345.

Nishii, L.H./Lepak, D.P./Schneider, B. (2008): Employee attributions of the »why« of HR practices: Their effects on employee attitudes and behaviors, and customer satisfaction. In: *Personnel Psychology*, 61: 3, 203–545.

O'Connor, E.P./Crowley-Henry, M. (2017): Exploring the Relationship Between Exclusive Talent Management, Perceived Organizational Justice and Employee Engagement: Bridging the Literature. In: *Journal of Business Ethics*: Online First.

Posthuma, R.A./Campion, M.C./Masimova, M./Campion, M.A. (2013): A High Performance Work Practices Taxonomy: Integrating the Literature and Directing Future Research. In: *Journal of Management*, 39: 5, 1184–1220.

Rousseau, D.M. (2005): *I-deals: Idiosyncratic deals workers bargain for themselves*, New York: Routledge.

Schmidt, J.A./Pohler, D./Willness, C.R. (2018): Strategic HR System Differentiation between Jobs: The Effects on Firm Performance and Employee Outcomes. In: *Human Resource Management*, 57: 1, 204. Available at 65–81.

Swailes, S. (2013): The ethics of talent management. In: *Business Ethics: A European Review*, 22: 1, 32–46.

Walton, R.E. (1985): From control to commitment in the workplace. In: *Harvard Business Review*, 63: 2, 77–84.

Wright, P.M./Coff, R./Moliterno, T.P. (2014): Strategic Human Capital: Crossing the Great Divide. In: *Journal of Management*, 40: 2, 353–370.

Wright, P.M./Nishii, L.H. (2013): Strategic HRM and organizational behaviour integrating multiple levels of analysis. In: J. Paauwe/D.E. Guest/P.M. Wright (Hrsg.): *HRM and performance: Achievements and challenges*, Chichester, West Sussex: Wiley, 97–110.

Vielfalt gleichstellen? Gleichstellung, Antidiskriminierung und Diversity Management im Kontext von digitalisierter Arbeit

Daniela Rastetter

1. Einleitung: das Feld der Gleichstellung

Chancengleichheit und Nichtdiskriminierung sind Merkmale »guter Arbeit.«[1] Im »DGB-Index Gute Arbeit« enthält der Bereich »Ressourcen« die Merkmale Aufstiegs- und Entwicklungsmöglichkeiten, Einfluss- und Gestaltungsmöglichkeiten, Betriebskultur sowie Kollegialität. Diese Merkmale können nur »gut« sein, wenn sie als fair und nichtdiskriminierend erlebt werden. Ebenso sind die Bereiche »Belastungen« sowie »Einkommen und Sicherheit« an Gerechtigkeitsvorstellungen gebunden. Gerechtigkeitsansprüche an gute Arbeit sind z. B. im Rahmen der Subjektivierung der Arbeit untersucht worden (vgl. Kleemann/Voß 2010; Kratzer et al. 2015); insbesondere im Aspekt der Verteilungs- und Beteiligungsgerechtigkeit weisen sie deutliche Bezüge zu Nichtdiskriminierung auf. Die Herstellung gerechter, nichtdiskriminierender Arbeit ist ein klassisches Thema der kritischen Arbeitsforschung, der Geschlechter- und der Ungleichheitsforschung sowie der Gewerkschaften und weiterer Institutionen, die sich um Arbeitnehmerrechte und Arbeitnehmerschutz kümmern. Bei steigender Heterogenität der Beschäftigungsformen und Arbeitsbedingungen im Zuge der Digitalisierung von Arbeit werden die Herausforderungen bezüglich Nichtdiskriminierung komplexer, sowohl was Steuerungsformen gesetzlicher und betrieblicher Art als auch was Ansprüche

1 Die Begriffe haben leicht unterschiedliche Bedeutungen, werden hier aber synonym verwendet. Chancengleichheit bedeutet, dass alle Menschen gleiche Bildungschancen und gleiche Startchancen auf dem Arbeitsmarkt haben. Nichtdiskriminierung heißt, dass Personen nicht aufgrund von Merkmalen, die nichts mit den Arbeitsaufgaben zu tun haben, abgelehnt oder schlecht bewertet werden. Gleichstellung wiederum legt den Akzent auf aktive Maßnahmen, mit deren Hilfe soziale Gleichheit unter den Beschäftigten hergestellt werden kann.

und Erwartungen der Beschäftigten selbst betrifft. Auf organisationaler Ebene treffen Arbeitsgesetze, betriebliche Gleichbehandlungsstrategien sowie Interessen verschiedener Beschäftigtengruppen und deren Vertretungen zusammen und gestalten das mikropolitische Feld, in dem Gleichbehandlung und Nichtdiskriminierung ausgehandelt werden. Unter den betrieblichen Strategien ist der Ansatz des Diversity Managements besonders interessant, da dessen Anspruch gerade im Managen der Heterogenität besteht. Es stellt sich deshalb die Frage, wie Gleichstellung im Rahmen fortschreitender Digitalisierung verhandelt wird und welche Rolle dabei Antidiskriminierungsgesetze auf der einen Seite und Diversity Management auf der anderen Seite spielen. Welche Interessen treffen in der Organisation aufeinander und welche Einflussmöglichkeiten haben verschiedene Akteursgruppen? Welche Gleichstellungsstandards resultieren daraus und welche Empfehlungen lassen sich für die Gestaltung diskriminierungsfreierer digitalisierter Arbeit ableiten?

Die in Deutschland aktuell geltenden Antidiskriminierungsgesetze sind zum einen eingebettet in übergreifende Gleichheitsgesetze (Grundgesetz), in Gesetze, die überwiegend, aber nicht nur auf den Arbeitsmarkt bezogen sind (Allgemeines Gleichbehandlungsgesetz/AGG[2]) sowie Gesetze, die direkt und ausschließlich Arbeitnehmende in Organisationen betreffen (Betriebsverfassungsgesetz,[3] Geschlechterquote bei Aufsichtsräten,[4] Entgelttransparenzgesetz[5]). All diese Gesetze müssen jedoch den Weg vom Papier in die Praxis finden (sog. »Rechtsdurchsetzung« oder »Rechtsmo-

---

2 Das Allgemeine Gleichbehandlungsgesetz (AGG), das seit 14.8.2006 in Kraft ist, hat zum Ziel, Diskriminierungen aus Gründen der zugeschriebenen Rasse, der ethnischen Herkunft, des Geschlechts, der Religion oder Weltanschauung, einer Behinderung, des Alters oder der sexuellen Identität zu verhindern oder zu beseitigen, verbietet Benachteiligungen aus einem dieser Gründe, sowohl unmittelbare als auch mittelbare sowie Belästigungen inklusive sexueller.

3 2001 wurde das Betriebsverfassungsgesetz um Antidiskriminierungs- und Gleichstellungsnormen erweitert (§ 75, § 80).

4 Am 1. Januar 2016 wurde eine fixe Geschlechterquote von 30 Prozent für neu zu besetzende Aufsichtsratsposten eingeführt, die für etwa 100 große Unternehmen gilt. Etwa 3500 weitere Unternehmen sind verpflichtet, sich eigene Zielgrößen zur Erhöhung des Frauenanteils in Aufsichtsräten, Vorständen und obersten Management-Ebenen zu setzen.

5 Ab Januar 2018 in Kraft, erlaubt es Beschäftigten in Betrieben ab 200 Mitgliedern, schriftlich Auskunft über das Einkommen der Kolleg_innen des jeweils anderen Geschlechts zu erhalten, die in vergleichbaren Positionen arbeiten.

bilisierung«, vgl. Kocher 2013), und dafür braucht es geeignete organisatorische Strukturen und engagierte Akteur_innen.

Parallel oder besser gesagt quer dazu entwickelte sich in Organisationen die betriebliche Strategie des Diversity Managements (DiM), das neben ethischen und juristischen Zielen auch Performance-Ziele formuliert. Anders als Gesetze, steht Diversity Management unter der Regie der Unternehmen und ist als freiwillige Strategie politisch wenig zu beeinflussen. Für die wachsende Diversität in Organisationen könnte Diversity Management die passende Strategie sein, die jedoch ebenso wie rechtliche Regelungen in der Praxis von machtvollen Akteur_innen und Institutionen umgesetzt werden muss, um nicht zur bloßen Legitimationsfassade zu werden.

Nichtdiskriminierung in Organisationen wird hier als ein Feld betrachtet, das konfliktreich und widersprüchlich gestaltet ist: Konfliktreich deshalb, weil verschiedene Akteur_innen unterschiedliche Ziele bezüglich Nichtdiskriminierung verfolgen oder unterschiedliche Wege für sinnvoll erachten, selbst wenn sie gleiche Ziele haben. Widersprüchlich deshalb, weil sich Werte und Ziele überlagern, die sich widersprechen können (z. B.: Antidiskriminierung und Profit), und weil der Gegenstand an sich ein »schlecht definierbares« Problem darstellt: Wer soll mit wem gleichgestellt werden, wo ist die Referenzgröße, wann genau ist Nichtdiskriminierung erreicht? In der jeweiligen Organisation sind mithin sowohl die Rechtsdurchsetzung als auch die Ausgestaltung von Diversity Management ein umkämpftes Terrain. Mit anderen Worten: Das Feld der Gleichstellung und Antidiskriminierung ist ein organisationales Kräftefeld mit verschiedenen kollektiven und individuellen Akteur_innen, die im Zusammenspiel bestimmte Formen und Prozesse von Nichtdiskriminierung oder auch Diskriminierung herstellen.

Dieses Feld wird durch die wachsende Heterogenität der Arbeitnehmerschaft (neu) konturiert; neben der steigenden demografischen Heterogenität (bezüglich Geschlecht, Alter, kultureller Herkunft etc.) ist vor allem die *beschäftigungsbezogene Heterogenität* bezüglich verschiedener arbeitsvertraglicher Beziehungen und verschiedener Beschäftigungsformen (Leiharbeit, geringfügige Arbeit, Werkvertrag, Mitarbeiter-Sharing, Crowdwork etc.) zu nennen, die alle unter den Begriff der »flexibilisierten Arbeit« fallen. Innerhalb dieser Beschäftigungsformen interessiert uns die digitalisierte Arbeit. Zum einen schreitet sie unaufhaltsam voran: 83 % der Beschäftigten in Deutschland in Betrieben ab 50 Mitarbeiter_innen nutzen digitale Technologien im Beruf, wobei die Nutzungsintensität mit der

Qualifikation der Beschäftigten steigt (BMAS 2016). Dreiviertel derjenigen, die mobile Geräte benutzen, arbeiten zumindest gelegentlich auch von unterwegs, ein Drittel arbeitet regelmäßig zu Hause (Bitcom 2013, S. 7). Damit sind flexible Arbeitszeiten und Arbeitsorte für einen großen Teil der Beschäftigten (vor allem im qualifizierten Bereich) zur Normalität geworden (siehe DGB-Index Gute Arbeit 2017). Zum anderen verändert die Entgrenzung von Arbeitszeit, Arbeitsort und Arbeitsverhältnissen die Kräfteverhältnisse in Organisationen und damit auch das Feld der Gleichstellung (vgl. auch Hanau/Matiaske 2019 in diesem Band). Nicht nur arbeiten die Beschäftigten selbst unter sehr unterschiedlichen Bedingungen und Vertragsverhältnissen zusammen, was neue Differenzlinien und Ungleichheiten nach sich zieht, sondern haben es die für Gleichstellung zuständigen Akteur_innen wie Betriebsrat und Gleichstellungsbeauftragte auch mit vielfältigen Ansprüchen und Anforderungen zu tun, für die sie zum Teil offiziell gar nicht zuständig sind. Für Unternehmensleitungen und Personalverantwortliche stellen sich neue Fragen der gerechten Gestaltung der Arbeitsorganisation und -aufgaben und der nichtdiskriminierenden Personalauswahl und -entwicklung.

Während vermehrt Studien zur Substitution von menschlicher durch digitale Arbeit sowie zu Arbeitsqualität bzw. Arbeitsbelastungen bei Digitalisierung vorliegen (vgl. DGB-Index Gute Arbeit 2017; HBS 2016; ver.di 2017), wurden bislang im deutschsprachigen Raum kaum Untersuchungen zum Diskriminierungspotential und zu Gleichstellungsstrategien bei digitalisierter Arbeit durchgeführt. In dieser Thematik überlagern sich demografische und beschäftigungsbezogene Heterogenität: So verteilen sich beispielsweise Männer und Frauen nicht gleichmäßig über verschiedene Formen digitalisierter Arbeit, mit je unterschiedlichen Folgen für Einkommen, Autonomie und Employability. Zu Geschlecht und Digitalisierung liegen mittlerweile einige Studienergebnisse vor, zu anderen Diversity-Dimensionen wie Alter, Migrationshintergrund oder Behinderung gibt es jedoch kaum Befunde. Diversity (Management) wurde in der Diversity-Forschung, soweit bekannt, bisher nicht auf dieses Themenfeld bezogen.

In zukünftigen Untersuchungen sollte das (umkämpfte) Feld der (Nicht)Diskriminierung und Gleichstellung vor dem Hintergrund steigender Digitalisierung untersucht werden: Erfüllt die betriebliche Strategie des Diversity Managements ihre eigenen Ziele, nämlich Vielfalt vorteilhaft zu gestalten, im Hinblick auf die Heterogenität digitalisierter Arbeit? Welche Wahrnehmungen und Erwartungen haben die Beschäftigten selbst bezüglich Fairness und Nichtdiskriminierung? Inwieweit sind Antidiskriminierungsgesetze wirksam, wenn es einerseits immer weniger eindeutige (Minderheiten-)Interessen gibt und damit die Interessenvertretungen zum Teil ihre Legitimation verlieren, andererseits jedoch mangels Standards des »Idealarbeitnehmers« auf verschiedene Gruppierungen mehr Rücksicht genommen werden muss? Welche alten und neuen Akteur_innen handeln mit wie viel Durchsetzungsmacht in diesem Feld? Welche Rolle spielen Interessenvertretungen, Gleichstellungsakteur_innen, die Politik, Gewerkschaften?

Zunächst wird gezeigt, inwiefern das betriebliche Instrument des Diversity Managements eine passende Strategie für die Förderung von Fairness und Nichtdiskriminierung bei flexiblen Beschäftigungsformen sein könnte. In der politischen Arena der Organisation ist es kein bloßes Steuerungsinstrument, sondern *Diversity Politik*, die auf plurale Interessenslagen und Machtprozesse trifft. Der Stand der Forschung zu Diskriminierung und Digitalisierung von Arbeit zeigt, dass das Feld noch offen und unbestimmt im Hinblick auf Ungleichheiten und Einflussmöglichkeiten von Akteur_innen ist. Aufgrund seiner Komplexität bietet sich empirisch ein qualitatives Vorgehen an, das die verschiedenen Facetten des Zusammenspiels betrieblicher Akteur_innen und Institutionen am besten erfassen kann. Entsprechende empirische Zugänge werden vorgestellt.

2. Diversity Management ist Diversity Politik

Zur Wirkung von Gleichbehandlungsgesetzen liegen inzwischen mehrere Studien vor (z. B. ADS 2016; Raasch/Rastetter 2013; Maschke 2010). Generell lässt sich feststellen, dass Gesetze allein kaum spürbare Veränderungen in Organisationen bewirken und dass es starker Institutionen und Kräfte bedarf, um die Gleichstellung voranzutreiben (Kocher 2013; Schönwälder 2006).[6] Ist Diversity Management eine solche starke Institution?

---

6 Vorgegebene Quoten wirken jedoch, wie das neueste Managerinnen-Barometer bezüglich der Zahlen von Frauen in Aufsichtsräten beweist (Holst/Wrohlich 2018).

2.1. Die Idee hinter Diversity (Management)

Diversity bedeutet Vielfalt, in Bezug auf Organisationen ist meist die Vielfalt ihrer Mitglieder gemeint, mitunter auch die Vielfalt der Kund_innen, Geldgeber_innen oder Geschäftspartner_innen der Organisation. Vielfalt als Konstrukt wird bezogen auf so verschiedene Dimensionen wie Geschlecht, Alter, Nationalität, Ethnizität, Religion[7], Behinderung, sexuelle Identität und Orientierung, familiäre bzw. Lebenssituation, Klasse, Ausbildung, Werte, Beruf, Verhaltensmuster, Persönlichkeit usw. Konzeptionell ist diese Liste unendlich lang und geht weit über die AGG-Kriterien hinaus. In der betrieblichen Praxis werden verschiedene Dimensionen je nach Organisation in unterschiedlichem Ausmaß berücksichtigt. In deutschen DAX-Unternehmen dominiert die Dimension »Geschlecht«, gefolgt von »Alter«, »Behinderung« und »Kulturzugehörigkeit« (Stand 2011, Jochmann et al. 2012).

Anders als Antidiskriminierungsgesetze, die teils auf deutsches, teils auf europäisches Recht zurückgehen, ist Diversity ein aus den USA importiertes Konzept. Dort wird als ein zentraler Ausgangspunkt häufig die Studie »Workforce 2000« genannt, die in den 1980er Jahren vorhersagte, dass der US-Arbeitsmarkt im 21. Jahrhundert wesentlich größere Anteile von Frauen, ethnischen Minderheiten und Einwanderern haben würde als damals. Eine andere Wurzel der zunehmenden Berücksichtigung von Diversity findet sich in Bürgerrechtsbewegungen der USA, insbesondere antirassistische, feministische und Arbeiterbewegungen, woraus die bis heute zentralen Dimensionen »class, race, sex« entstanden.

Diversity Management (oder Diversitätsmanagement, Managing Diversity) steht für eine betriebliche Steuerung von Vielfalt, bei der Bedingungen geschaffen werden, durch die alle Organisationsmitglieder, ungeachtet ihrer Gruppenzugehörigkeiten, ihre Potentiale entfalten können und durch die Konflikte vermieden werden. Differenz wird nicht mehr als Problem, sondern als Ressource betrachtet. Richtig durchgeführt binde Diversity Management qualifizierte Arbeitskräfte, biete besseren Service für diverse Märkte und fördere Kreativität, so der übliche Diskurs (vgl. Krell/Sieben 2011). Ziel sei ein Pluralismus an Werten, Einstellungen und Verhaltensweisen, die gleichermaßen wertgeschätzt werden. Denn das »homogene

7 Zu Religion siehe Alewell/Moll 2019 in diesem Band.

Ideal« – verkörpert durch heterosexuelle, weiße, der Mittelschicht zugehörige, nichtbehinderte Männer, die entscheidende Positionen, Werte und Normen bestimmen und denen eine Frau Hausarbeit und Kinderbetreuung abnimmt – führe zu Demotivation und mangelnder Entfaltung der Leistungswilligkeit und -fähigkeit (ebd.). Seit den 1990er Jahren wird Diversity Management als Teil der Personalpolitik in deutschen Großunternehmen implementiert, häufig in solchen mit US-amerikanischen Mutterkonzernen, aber auch Lufthansa war ein Vorreiter von DiM. Während Diversity Management in deutschen DAX-Unternehmen mittlerweile einen festen Stellenwert hat,[8] spielt es bei klein- und mittelständischen Unternehmen noch eine geringe Rolle.

2.2. Business Case und/oder Antidiskriminierung?

Der eher betriebswirtschaftlichen Herangehensweise an Vielfalt – dem »business case« – wurde eine Ökonomisierung und Instrumentalisierung von Differenzen vorgeworfen, eine Verwandlung von Gleichstellungspolitik zu einem Managementkonzept, das neue Ausschlüsse produziere und Ungleichheit dethematisiere (vgl. Eggers 2011). Dem marktförmigen Paradigma wurde deshalb ein gesellschafts- und herrschaftskritisches Paradigma gegenübergestellt, das an Chancengleichheit und Nichtdiskriminierung orientiert ist (ebd.).[9] Andere Herangehensweisen versuchen, Chancengleichheit und Ökonomie miteinander zu verbinden, z. B. der »ressourcenorientierte Lern- und Effektivitätsansatz«, nach dem Wissens- und Kompetenzbestände einer vielfältigen Belegschaft gefördert und gleichzeitig Diskriminierungen im Unternehmen verhindert werden sollen (Thomas/Ely 1996, S. 79; Segert et al. 2012, S. 6).

Eine simple Schwarz-Weiß-Sicht zwischen Fairness und Markt wird Diversity Management jedoch nicht gerecht. Vielmehr muss dessen gleichstellungspolitisches Potenzial erst geprüft werden, bevor es von

---

8 25 von 30 DAX-Unternehmen haben Diversity-Manager_innen und 23 haben die Charta der Vielfalt unterzeichnet (Stand 2013; Synergy Consult 2013).

9 Aus dieser Kritik entstanden Mitte der 1990er Jahre die sog. critical diversity studies, bei denen Macht- und Ungleichheitsaspekte in Gesellschaft und Arbeitswelt untersucht werden (vgl. Gotsis/Kortezi 2015; Ahonen et al 2014).

vornherein angezweifelt wird. Wichtiger als die Frage nach der Profitorientierung ist deshalb die Frage nach der organisationalen Umsetzung: Wer fördert Diversity Management, wer blockiert es, wer ist indifferent? Wo ist es angesiedelt, welchen Stellenwert hat es in der Unternehmensstrategie? Wie wird der interne Diskurs geführt, wer sind Subjekte und Objekte der Strategie (vgl. Bendl et al. 2008)? Welche Interessen sind damit verbunden und welche konkreten Wirkungen hat es? Auch bei einer vordergründigen Marktperspektive können Menschen Beschäftigungschancen erhalten, die vormals eher ausgegrenzt oder marginalisiert wurden, wie Migrant_innen oder Behinderte, vorausgesetzt, in ihnen werden Potenziale gesehen. Gewinnen sie dadurch Marktmacht, können sie für sich oder ihre Gruppe verbesserte Arbeitsbedingungen erlangen, und der »Normalarbeitnehmer« verliert an Durchsetzungs- und Normkraft. Vormals exkludierte und benachteiligte Gruppen in den Verwertungsprozess zu integrieren, schafft jedoch noch keine Wertschätzung der Vielfalt. Ein Gleichstellungseffekt könnte trotzdem genau dadurch entstehen, dass der Zugang zu Diversity am kapitalistischen Marktparadigma orientiert ist, nach dem die Unternehmen handeln (müssen). Während Gleichstellung eher in die betriebliche Sozialpolitik fällt, setzt Diversity Management am Kerngeschäft von Unternehmen an, nämlich wettbewerbsfähig zu bleiben (vgl. Riedmüller/Vinz 2007). Dies könnte ein Treiber für die stärkere Berücksichtigung von Beschäftigtengruppen jenseits des traditionellen Normalarbeitsverhältnisses sein. Gleichbehandlung könnte, wenn schon nicht im *Hauptfokus*, ein starkes *Nebenprodukt* sein.

2.3. Mikropolitische Diversity-Akteur_innen

Betrachtet man Diversity Management als Diversity *Politik*, sind daran verschiedene Akteur_innen beteiligt (hier nur eine Auswahl):

Die Beschäftigten: Manche sehen Vorteile darin und unterstützen es, manche betrachten es als gegen ihre Interessen gerichtet, manche finden es überflüssig und vielen ist es egal. Die Interessen sind zudem keineswegs innerhalb einer »typischen« Diversity-Gruppe identisch. Ähnlich verhält es sich mit ihrer Einstellung gegenüber Gleichbehandlungsgesetzen. Die Heterogenität der Beschäftigungsformen und der Belegschaftszusammensetzung erhöht vermutlich auch die Heterogenität der Interessen.

Betriebliche Interessenvertretung: Seit der Novellierung des Betriebsverfassungsgesetzes haben Betriebsräte die Aufgabe, die Gleichstellung von Frauen und Männern, die Vereinbarung von Familie und Erwerbstätigkeit, die Eingliederung Schwerbehinderter, die Beschäftigung Älterer sowie die Integration ausländischer Arbeitnehmer_innen zu fördern sowie Maßnahmen zur Bekämpfung von Rassismus und Fremdenfeindlichkeit im Betrieb zu beantragen. Zwar kann eine Diversity Management-Strategie als solche ohne formale Beteiligung des Betriebsrats eingeführt werden, einzelne Diversity-Maßnahmen sind jedoch der Mitbestimmung unterworfen, z. B. allgemeine Verhaltensregeln (Code of Conduct), Regelungen gegen Mobbing oder die Ausgestaltung betrieblicher Kinderbetreuung. Werden zu Antidiskriminierung Betriebsvereinbarungen abgeschlossen, ist deren formaler Rahmen im Betriebsverfassungsgesetz niedergelegt. Zudem bringen engagierte Betriebsrät_innen Diversity-Themen auf die Agenda (Losert 2011). Arbeitskräfte, die nicht beim Unternehmen angestellt sind, sondern auf Werkvertragsbasis oder als Soloselbstständige tätig sind, werden jedoch vom Betriebsverfassungsgesetz nicht erfasst.[10]

Gleichstellungs- und Diversitybeauftragte: Sie sind häufig im Spannungsfeld zwischen business case und Gleichstellung gefordert, eine Balance zu finden, die verschiedene Interessen gleichermaßen berücksichtigt. Ihre Durchsetzungskraft hängt davon ab, wo sie im Unternehmen angesiedelt sind, mit welchen Kompetenzen und Ressourcen sie ausgestattet sind und wie professionell sie agieren (Süß 2007). Häufig wurden aus den ehemaligen Gleichstellungsbeauftragten Diversityverantwortliche, ohne dass eine Erhöhung ihrer Ressourcenausstattung vorgenommen wurde. Darüber hinaus brauchen sie viel mikropolitische Kompetenz, um Verbündete zu finden und Rückhalt von der Geschäftsleitung zu erhalten (Edding 2000, Jüngling/Rastetter 2011). Bei steigender Heterogenität der Belegschaft stellt sich die Frage, inwieweit sie diese angemessen vertreten können bzw. dürfen.

Unternehmensleitung: Sie ist umso schneller von einer Diversity Management-Strategie zu überzeugen, je mehr Wert sie darin entdeckt, beispielsweise eine Profitsteigerung durch verbesserte Mitarbeiterbindung.[11] Zwischen offiziellem Leitbild und konkreten Maßnahmen besteht jedoch häufig ein Bruch, und nicht wenige Diversity-Strategien existieren

---

10 Von Gewerkschaftsseite wird gefordert, dass arbeitnehmerähnliche Personen in das Betriebsverfassungsgesetz einbezogen werden und dass die Betriebsverfassung auf Soloselbstständige ausgedehnt wird (Maschke 2016; siehe Hanau 2016).

11 Siehe den Beitrag von Sven Hauff 2019 in diesem Band.

nur auf dem Papier. Wenn aber Unternehmensleitungen hinter dem Konzept stehen und klare Vorgaben bzw. Sanktionen aussprechen, kann eine Diversity-Strategie Wirkung entfalten.

Von den externen Akteur_innen sei an dieser Stelle nur die Politik genannt: Die Einführung von Diversity-Kriterien in den Deutschen Corporate Governance Kodex 2009 und 2010 machte Diversity Management nochmals wichtiger für Unternehmen, fordert jedoch nur ein Reporting zu Gender und Internationalisierung. Die meisten DAX30-Unternehmen haben sich den Berichtsstandards der Global Reporting Initiative verpflichtet und integrieren (freiwillig) Diversity in ihre Nachhaltigkeits- und CSR-Berichte.[12] Dies tun sie jedoch in höchst unterschiedlichen Formen, nur wenige Unternehmen veröffentlichen beispielsweise Geschlechterverteilungen auf Einkommensgruppen, und es ist davon auszugehen, dass sie ungünstige Kennzahlen beschönigen oder verstecken (Werkmeister 2016). Nichtsdestotrotz wird durch die Reporte der Druck auf Unternehmen erhöht, aktiv zu werden und sich Ziele zu setzen.[13] Diese Ziele werden jedoch nicht automatisch von allen betrieblichen Akteur_innen geteilt.

3. Die Organisation als politische Arena

Der hier favorisierte akteurs- und handlungsbezogene Ansatz betrachtet die Organisation als (mikro-)politische Arena und die Arbeitsumgebung als mikropolitisches Geschehen (Küpper/Felsch 2000, S. 152). Aus strukturellen Bedingungen werden aus strategischer Sicht Ressourcen, Barrieren und Handlungsspielräume (Mucha et al. 2011). Dabei sind drei verschiedene politische Ebenen zu unterscheiden, die hier auf Diversity bezogen werden: Die Spielregeln (Polity) konstituieren das Spiel, die Spielstrategien (Policies) bündeln die Vorgehensweisen, die ein bestimmtes Ziel erreichen sollen, und die Spielzüge (Politics) setzen Strategien um,

---

12 Besonders prominent ist der Indikator »Diversity and Equal Opportunity« mit den Unterindikatoren »Diversity« und »salary ratio« (Werkmeister 2016).

13 Zudem gibt es auf europäischer und nationaler Ebene immer mehr konkrete Forderungen nach Berücksichtigung von Diversity: In einer 2014 eingeführten EU-Richtlinie wird eine nachhaltige Unternehmensführung unter Einbezug eines Diversitätskonzeptes gefordert, das eindeutige Zielsetzung, Implementierung und Ergebnisse enthalten soll. Ab 2017 soll dies in nationales Recht überführt werden.

nutzen aber auch die darin vorhandenen Spielräume aus (Neuberger 2006).

Die *Polity* markiert die Verfassung, in der basale Prinzipien kodifiziert sind, die eine Ordnung charakterisieren (Neuberger 2006, S. 27). Sie ist stets so allgemein gehalten, dass sie interpretiert und mit Leben gefüllt werden muss. Die »Diversity Polity« bezieht sich in erster Linie auf die geltenden Antidiskriminierungsgesetze. Unter welchen Umständen, in welchen Fällen und in welcher Form diese Polity anwendbar ist, darum wird immer wieder gerungen, niedergelegt u. a. in Gerichtsurteilen (vgl. Jochmann-Döll 2013). Dort geht es beispielsweise darum, inwieweit im konkreten Fall Qualifikationsgleichheit vorliegt und welche anderen Kriterien herangezogen werden dürfen. Riedmüller und Vinz (2007) fassen den Begriff der Diversity Polity weiter: Auf welchen normativen Grundlagen basiert eine »Politik der Verschiedenheit«: auf der Herstellung von Gerechtigkeit im Sinne von Anerkennung und/oder Umverteilung, auf dem Paradigma »Diversity and Inclusion« oder auf »Diversity anstelle von Equality«, bspw. durch die Legitimierung von Verschiedenheit als Ausdruck steigender Freiheitsgrade?

Die *Policies* werden konkreter: Sie legen die Konkretisierung der Polity in Form von Maßnahmen und Strategien fest. Die betriebliche Strategie des Diversity Managements oder eine Betriebsvereinbarung gegen sexuelle Belästigung sind Beispiele von Policies. Aber auch diese müssen durch Handlungen, die Politics, umgesetzt werden, um zu wirken, sonst steht die Policy nur auf dem Papier. Riedmüller und Vinz (2007) fragen in Bezug auf die Diversity Policy: Welche Unterscheidungen werden als Bezugspunkt für Policy-Maßnahmen steuerungsrelevant, welches Verständnis von Verschiedenheit bzw. Diversity liegt dem zugrunde und welche Anforderungen an Steuerung ergeben sich daraus?

Mit den *Politics* kommt Bewegung ins Spiel: Diese wenden die Polities und die Policies nicht einfach in der Praxis an, sondern wirken auch gestaltend zurück. So kann durch Erfahrungen im Alltag eine Policy verändert werden, wenn sie sich in der Praxis nicht bewährt hat, oder eine Polity wird veränderten Gegebenheiten – und Interessen – angepasst (etwa das Gesetz um einige Klauseln ergänzt). Auf allen Ebenen gibt es Freiheitsgrade und Spielräume. So können die Politics auch dafür genutzt werden, dass Policies oder Polities *nicht* wirken.[14] Riedmüller und Vinz (2007) stellen bezüglich Diversity Policies folgende Fragen: Welche Unterscheidungen benennen individuelle und kollektive Akteure? Wie bringen sie als Ergebnis von »Differenzhandeln« Verschiedenheit hervor und wie konstituieren sich Macht- und Herrschaftsverhältnisse im Kontext dieser »Klassifizierungskämpfe«?

Polity, Policies und Politics in Organisationen auf der einen Seite und zunehmend heterogene Beschäftigte auf der anderen Seite gestalten also das Feld der (Nicht-)Diskriminierung als Teil »guter Arbeit.«

4. Diskriminierung und Gleichstellung bei digitalisierter Arbeit

Als ein Hauptargument für Diversity Management wird immer wieder die sich wandelnde Beschäftigtenstruktur genannt (Krell/Sieben 2011), angefangen von der erwähnten Studie »Workforce 2000« bis zu aktuellen Erhebungen in Deutschland zum demografischen Wandel und zur Zusammensetzung der Bevölkerung bzw. der Arbeitnehmenden. In Deutschland steigen bis 2030 die Anteile der Älteren, der Frauen und der Teilzeitbeschäftigten an der Erwerbsbevölkerung, bei einem insgesamten Rückgang der Zahl der Erwerbstätigen, aber auch des Arbeitsangebots (BMAS 2013). Damit zusammenhängende Trends der Globalisierung und Migration sowie der gesellschaftliche Wertewandel ziehen eine Diversität an Identitäten, Lebensformen und Lebenslagen nach sich (Krell et al. 2007).[15] Es ist nicht zu erwarten, dass diese Trends zu weniger Diskriminierung führen, eher im Gegenteil.[16]

---

14 Sie sind dann reine Legitimationsfassade, hinter der das »wahre Leben« (ohne Gleichstellungsaktivitäten) stattfindet, was u. a. im Rahmen des Ansatzes des Neoinstitutionalismus untersucht wird (vgl. Rastetter 2017).

15 Siehe den Beitrag von Müller/Seibert/Vornfeld in diesem Band.

16 Die Hoffnung, dass kulturelle Ungleichheiten durch Globalisierung eingeebnet werden, hat sich bis jetzt nicht erfüllt (Moosmüller 2016). Häufig herrscht in multinationalen Unternehmen eine ethnozentrische Politik, die nur die Meinung des Headquarters gelten lässt. Nur wenn die entscheidenden Personen eine »globale« Weltsicht haben, Diversity wertschätzen und bereit sind, interkulturell zu lernen, wird kulturelle Diversity fair gemanagt (ebd.).

4.1. Digitalisierte Arbeitsformen: empirische Evidenz zu sozialer Ungleichheit

Insgesamt zeichnen neue Beschäftigungsformen zunehmend kleinteiligere Formen von Arbeit aus: Mehr Projektarbeit, Job Rotation und Weiterbildung, weniger Hierarchie und mehr kollaborative Elemente (Kalev/Roscigno 2016). Solche Arbeitsformen werden durch Digitalisierung weiterentwickelt: Teams arbeiten mithilfe digitaler Kommunikations- und Informationstechnologien häufig dezentral, sowohl was die Entfernung zu Leitungsebenen als auch untereinander (virtuelle Teams) betrifft. Beschäftigte erledigen Arbeitsaufgaben vermehrt von unterwegs oder vom Homeoffice aus, mit entsprechend weniger persönlichem Kontakt zu Vorgesetzten oder Kolleg_innen. Einige sind nur kurzfristig für das Unternehmen tätig oder arbeiten für mehrere Unternehmen gleichzeitig als Online-Arbeitskräfte. Onlinearbeit wird häufig über Internetplattformen vermittelt, die die Aufträge koordinieren (crowdworker, vgl. Leimeister et al. 2016; Maier et al. 2017).[17] Die Vertragsformen digitalisierter Arbeit reichen von unbefristeten Vollzeitanstellungen (etwa bei Führungskräften, die auch zunehmend digitale Arbeitsanteile aufweisen) bis zur Soloselbstständigkeit (häufig bei crowdworkern), wobei Vertragsformen jenseits des Normalarbeitsverhältnisses zunehmen (Absenger 2016). Damit einher geht eine Verringerung der Wirkmächtigkeit der arbeitsrechtlichen Schutzinstrumente (Hanau 2016).[18]

Studien zu Diskriminierung im Rahmen von digitalisierter Arbeit liegen bislang in geringem Umfang bezüglich Geschlecht vor (vgl. Kutzner/Schnier 2017). Eine Studie von ver.di (2017) ergab, dass die Beurteilung von digitalisierten Arbeitsbedingungen im Dienstleistungsbereich durch Frauen häufig schlechter ausfällt als durch Männer. Frauen haben in geringerem Maße Einflussmöglichkeiten auf die Gestaltung des Technikeinsatzes an ihrem Arbeitsplatz und der Anteil derer ist größer, die sich der digitalen Technik ausgeliefert fühlen. Was drohende Arbeitsplatzverluste angeht, liegen verschiedene Prognosen vor, die jedoch uneinheitlich und umstritten sind (Herzog-Stein 2016). Berufe mit einem hohen Frauenanteil

17 Siehe den Beitrag vonKirchner/Beyer 2016.

18 Siehe Hanau/Matiaske in diesem Band sowie Schuler-Harms/Goldberg in diesem Band zu den sozialversicherungstechnischen Implikationen.

sind nach ver.di sowohl stark (Büro- und Sekretariatsberufe, Berufe im Verkauf sowie im Gastronomiesektor) als auch schwach (Kinderbetreuung, Gesundheits- und Krankenpflege) von Automatisierung betroffen, wobei die schlechter bezahlten eher erhalten bleiben, was die Lohnlücke zwischen Frauen und Männern vergrößern könnte (vgl. ver.di 2017). Jedoch entstehen gemäß anderer Szenarien auch neue Arbeitsplätze und Tätigkeiten bzw. verschwinden zwar manche Tätigkeiten, aber nicht gleich die Arbeitsplätze (Herzog-Stein 2016). Diese sind vermutlich stärker als heute polarisiert in einerseits qualifizierte Tätigkeiten mit gutem Einkommen und andererseits einfache Arbeiten mit schlechtem Einkommen (Kutzner/Schnier 2017).

Technik, auch digitale Technik, ist auf der symbolischen Ebene männlich konnotiert, Digitalisierung und Geschlecht sind mithin miteinander verwobene soziale und politische Prozesse (vgl. Kutzner/Schnier 2017; Freudenschuss 2014; Mucha 2014).[19] Zudem ist die Software von Menschen gemacht und deshalb nicht frei von Stereotypen: In Algorithmen werden Ungleichheitsstrukturen und Stereotype nicht nur unsichtbar, sondern durch scheinbare Objektivität sogar legitimiert (Freudenschuss 2014).

Breitere Betrachtung findet das Thema der Vereinbarkeit von Beruf und Privatleben, da durch Digitalisierung die Grenzen zwischen den Sphären weiter verschwimmen. Als Chance für Frauen betrachtet ver.di die potenzielle Angleichung der Arbeitszeiten bei Erwerbs- und Sorgearbeit zwischen Frauen und Männern durch bessere Nutzungsmöglichkeiten von Homeoffice. Bezüglich Work-Life-Balance gibt es unter den Befragten eine leicht positive Bilanz, besonders positiv ist sie in Branchen mit hohem Anteil an digitaler Arbeit und bei hochkomplexen Tätigkeiten (zu ähnlichen Ergebnissen kommt der DGB-Index Gute Arbeit 2017).[20] Nach einer Studie des IfD Allensbach (2015) verwenden sowohl Väter als auch Mütter ihre Zeitersparnis durch digitalisierte Homeoffice-Arbeit für Kinderbetreuung, Haushalt und Entlastung des Partners/der Partnerin. Ergebnisse zur Flexibilisierung der Arbeitszeit zeigen jedoch umgekehrt, dass

---

19 In der Geschlechterforschung wird schon seit den 1990er Jahren die Ko-Konstruktion von Technik und Geschlecht beleuchtet, dies wurde später auf digitale Technologien übertragen (z. B. Youngs 2002).

20 Dies spielt auch eine wichtige Rolle bei der Gefährdungsbeurteilung psychischer Belastungen, vgl. Busch/Vahle-Hinz 2019 in diesem Band.

diese bei Männern zur Erhöhung ihrer Arbeitszeit und ihres Einkommens führt, bei Frauen jedoch nicht, sodass sich durch Digitalisierung traditionelle Geschlechterrollen weiter verfestigen könnten (Lott 2015).[21] Selbstbestimmte Arbeitszeiten und Homeoffice stehen zurzeit vorwiegend hochqualifizierten Beschäftigten zur Verfügung, könnten aber in Zukunft durch Verbesserung der Technik und der Arbeitsorganisation benachteiligten Beschäftigtengruppen zugutekommen (Lott 2016). Außerdem, so Lott, dränge in Zukunft die Normalität flexiblen Arbeitens die Dominanz der Präsenzkultur zurück, die vor allem Frauen mit Familienpflichten Nachteile bringt. Das Sichtbarsein im Betrieb entscheidet dann nicht mehr über Einflussmöglichkeiten (Kutzner/Schnier 2017). Wird jedoch erwartet, dass die Arbeit trotz dieser Pflichten von Zuhause oder unterwegs erledigt wird, werden Frauen bei einer traditionellen Arbeitsteilung wiederum benachteiligt. Das Interesse der Beschäftigten an Selbstbestimmung und Selbstorganisation kollidiert dabei nicht selten mit dem Schutz vor gesundheitsgefährdenden Arbeitsbelastungen (Ahlers 2016). Flexible Arbeitszeitmodelle sind seit langem Gegenstand von Betriebsvereinbarungen; durch zunehmende Entgrenzung der Arbeit kommen neue Handlungsfelder wie Regelungen des Homeoffice oder der Arbeit von unterwegs hinzu. Auf privater Ebene entstehen Spielräume für neue Rollenarrangements zwischen den Geschlechtern, die Aushandlungsprozesse in Gang setzen.

4.2. Szenarien zu (Nicht)Diskriminierung

Jenseits solcher begrenzten Befunde zu Geschlechtereffekten gibt es kaum Studien zu (Nicht-)Diskriminierung bei digitalisierter Arbeit. Verschiedene Szenarien sind denkbar, die im Folgenden nur kurz angedacht werden, da sie je nach Kontextbedingungen unterschiedlich gestaltet sind:

---

21 Die Beschäftigungsexpansion unter Frauen in den letzten zehn bis 15 Jahren erfolgte primär über flexible Formen der Beschäftigung. Vor allem verschiedene Formen der Teilzeitarbeit expandierten seit 2003, sodass diese Form mit 71 % (Stand 2010) zum Standardarbeitsverhältnis von Frauen avancierte (Dingeldey 2015). Eine Dominanz des Normalarbeitsverhältnisses zeigt sich vor allem in männlich dominierten Branchen des verarbeitenden Gewerbes, im Baugewerbe und den traditionellen und unternehmensbezogenen Dienstleistungen.

Auf der einen Seite kann mehr Zusammenarbeit auf der Basis von Wissen und Erfahrung statt auf der Basis formaler Positionen Vorurteile verringern (Kalev/Roscigno 2016). Gleichberechtigte und selbstorganisierte Arbeit in Arbeitskollektiven bietet Chancen für die Beseitigung sozialer Ungleichheit (Kutzner/Schnier 2017). Virtuelle Teams sind vermutlich weniger als face-to-face Teams durch ingroup-outgroup-Phänomene belastet, sodass die Aufmerksamkeit weniger auf Merkmale wie Geschlecht, Kultur oder Alter und mehr auf die Arbeitsinhalte gerichtet ist. Da Stereotype vor allem im persönlichen Kontakt wirken, kann Arbeiten mit digitalen Medien diese Wirkung vermindern und den Fokus mehr auf die Arbeitsergebnisse lenken. Bei ausschließlicher oder überwiegender Onlinearbeit mag die persönliche Sympathie oder »Chemie« zwischen den Akteur_innen, die häufig auf Ähnlichkeit in demografischen Merkmalen basiert, unwichtig werden, da sie sich ohnehin kaum begegnen.

Auf der anderen Seite ist weniger Hierarchie in Projektteams ambivalent zu bewerten: Wenn Führungskräfte diversity-sensibel sind, können sie auf Diskriminierungen und Ungleichheiten in Redebeiträgen und Konzepterarbeitungen entsprechend reagieren. Führungslose Teams haben es schwerer, ihre Vorurteile gegenüber Minderheiten abzubauen, da sie diese häufig unbewusst verwenden. Wenn jedoch die Führungskraft selbst stereotyp denkt und handelt, trägt sie nichts zur Gleichbehandlung bei. Auf sie kommen neue Aufgaben zu (Stichwort »digital leadership«), die nicht zuletzt darin bestehen, das Potenzial der Teamdiversity zu nutzen und Vertrauen aufzubauen (vgl. Hertel/Lauer 2012).

Auch bei virtueller Kommunikation gibt es Mikropolitik, z. B. Informationszurückhaltung, Einsatz von Taktiken in der email-Kommunikation (Jarren et al. 2015) oder Verbündungen unter Subgruppen. Studien aus der Gruppenforschung zeigen zudem, dass Druck und Zeitknappheit, wie sie häufig bei Projektteams vorliegen, dazu beitragen, dass Minderheiten sich Mehrheitsmeinungen anschließen, dass nicht verschiedene Ideen gehört und geprüft werden, sondern die Vorschläge von Meinungsführern angenommen werden, kurz, dass die Entfaltung der Potenziale des heterogenen Teams, wie bei Diversity Management angestrebt, nicht stattfindet (vgl. Rastetter 2006).

Ein traditionell großes Einfallstor für Diskriminierung ist die Einstellung neuen Personals, da Stereotype bei unbekannten Menschen besonders stark wirken und menschliche Urteilsprozesse in dieser Phase üblich sind. Bei virtuellen Einstellungen für Onlinearbeiten (ohne persönliche Vorstellung) könnten diese Formen von Diskriminierung reduziert werden. Zum immer größer werdenden Feld des E-Recruiting liegen soweit bekannt noch keine Studien bezüglich Diskriminierung vor. Dasselbe trifft für andere Bereiche der digitalisierten Personalarbeit zu wie Online-Tools bei Weiterbildungen oder den Einsatz von Algorithmen bei Matching-Prozessen und in der Personalplanung.[22] Die Körperferne im virtuellen Raum täuscht über trotzdem wirkende Körperpolitiken hinweg, siehe neuere Phänomene wie die Selbstoptimierung in Bewerbervideos oder in Skype-Einstellungsinterviews,[23] und auch sexuelle Belästigung ist im Netz möglich und durch niedrigere Hemmschwellen sogar erleichtert.

Die große Bedeutung schriftlicher und sprachlicher Kompetenzen bei digitalisierter Arbeit könnte Ungleichheit entlang sozialer Herkunft vergrößern. Der Austausch von implizitem Wissen (z. B. persönliche Erfahrungen und Fertigkeiten) ist über digitale Medien schwer realisierbar. Menschen mit körperlichen oder psychischen Beeinträchtigungen erlangen jedoch mehr Beschäftigungschancen, wenn digitale Techniken Barrieren am Arbeitsplatz abbauen. Der Einsatz digitaler Mittel zum Abbau von Ungleichheiten ist deshalb eine wichtige Zukunftsaufgabe betrieblicher Gleichstellungspolitik.

Einflussmöglichkeiten und Solidarität sind erschwert, wenn Beschäftigte vereinzelt zu Hause oder in virtuellen Teams an verschiedenen Orten arbeiten. Jedoch entstehen auch neue politische Handlungsräume und neue Kollektivitäten (vgl. Freudenschuss 2014).

Neue Technologien sind auch soziale Prozesse. Je nach organisationalen Bedingungen und subjektiven Interpretationen führen sie zu verschiedenen Aneignungsformen (z. B. Walker 2017). In ihrer Studie untersucht Walker, wie Beschäftigte ihre durch Digitalisierung eingeschränkten Handlungsspielräume durch verschiedene Strategien vergrößern bzw. aufrechterhalten (ebd.). Dass die Beschäftigten selbst ein wichtiger Treiber für Gleichstellung sind, gilt umso mehr, je weniger straff und top-down ein Unternehmen geführt wird bzw. je mehr es sich in Einzelbereiche und -segmente zergliedert. Ein betrieblicher Diversity-Diskurs bietet bestimm-

---

22 HR-Plattformen werden in Zukunft vermehrt personalbezogene Daten, auch unternehmensübergreifend, erheben, verarbeiten und miteinander vernetzen, um damit das Projekt-, Wissens- und Change Management zu unterstützen.

23 Siehe hierfür beispielsweise die onlinebasierte Plattform für Video Recruting *Cammio,* welche mittels sogenannter *video pitchs* »die ideale Ablöse des überkommenen Motivationsschreibens« verspricht (vgl. cammio.com).

te Sichtweisen auf Differenz an und macht Identitätsangebote, die Selbstführung und Selbstmanagement als »diverses« Subjekt nahelegen. Wer aber möchte sich überhaupt Gleichstellungsstandards unterwerfen, wer fühlt sich durch Gesetze und Diversity Management beschützt, wer bevormundet? Beschäftigte in flexiblen, digitalisierten Arbeitsformen wünschen wie oben angedeutet möglicherweise mehr Selbstbestimmung und Souveränität über ihre Arbeitszeiten und Arbeitsweisen und werden durch Arbeitszeitregelungen zu sehr eingeschränkt. Dies könnte aber auch nur auf bestimmte Bereiche zutreffen, während andere vor Selbstausbeutung geschützt werden müssen.

Arbeitsgesetze sind bei flexiblen Beschäftigungsverhältnissen schlechter anwendbar, da sie auf das Normalarbeitsverhältnis ausgerichtet sind. Die Chancen der Gleichbehandlung durch digitalisierte Arbeit hängen auch davon ab, wie sie betrieblich unterstützt werden. Dabei gelten die bisherigen Erkenntnisse zur betrieblichen Gleichstellungsarbeit weiter, nämlich, dass es Regeln und Verantwortlichkeiten für Fairness braucht, dass klare Kriterien, formale Entscheidungsprozesse und Sensibilität gegenüber Ungleichheit vorhanden sein müssen, um Gleichstellung voranzutreiben (Projektgruppe GiB 2010; Kalev/Roscigno 2016). Dass dies bei steigender Heterogenität der Beschäftigten und wachsender Entgrenzung der Arbeit schwieriger wird, ist einerseits naheliegend, da top-down-Prozesse weniger leicht durchzusetzen sind und kleinteiligere bzw. dezentrale Arbeitsformen die Transparenz und Kontrolle der Prozesse verringern. Andererseits können Beschäftigtengruppen, die bislang eher am Rand der Organisation mit wenig Macht agierten, mehr Durchsetzungsmacht gewinnen, wenn ihre Arbeitsformen zur Normalität werden. Mehr dezentrale Handlungsspielräume und partizipative Problemlösungsprozesse sind denkbar (Kutzner/ Schnier 2017). Bei Umstrukturierungsprozessen entstehen Machtverschiebungen und neue Aushandlungsmöglichkeiten, bei denen Akteur_innen versuchen, ihren Einfluss zu erhalten oder zu vergrößern. Welche Differenzlinien dabei bestehen bleiben oder sich ändern, ist eine zu untersuchende Frage.

Diversity Management mag aufgrund seiner Offenheit und seiner Organisationsbezogenheit hier flexible Gestaltungsmöglichkeiten bieten. Es könnte der Vereinzelung der Arbeitenden entgegenwirken und eine Klammer bieten, innerhalb der sich alle wertgeschätzt fühlen und einbringen können. Als Maßnahmen sind denkbar:

- professionelle Netzwerke in Organisationen zum sozialen Austausch;
- Betriebsvereinbarungen, die auch Arbeitskräfte auf Werkvertragsbasis etc. einschließen;
- Diversitybeauftragte, die sich für alle Beschäftigten zuständig fühlen;
- ein Leitbild, das explizit auch flexibel Beschäftigte mit einschließt;
- Transparenz bezüglich der Einkommensgruppen, Beschäftigungsverhältnisse etc.;
- Förderung von selbstorganisierten Veranstaltungen der Beschäftigten zu Themen der Gleichstellung;
- Schulungen der Führungskräfte und des Betriebsrats zu Gleichstellungsthemen usw.

5. Empirischer Zugang

Die Untersuchung der aufgeworfenen Fragen sollte idealerweise in großen Unternehmen der Privatwirtschaft durchgeführt werden, die verschiedene Beschäftigungsformen mit hohen Digitalisierungsgraden aufweisen, also neben klassischen Normalarbeitsverhältnissen flexible Formen der Beschäftigung, die von Homeoffice über virtuelle Teams bis zu crowdworkern reichen können. Zudem soll eine Diversity Management-Strategie vorhanden sein, die zumindest von einer zuständigen Stelle unterstützt wird sowie eine betriebliche Interessenvertretung. Die Branche kann sowohl im Dienstleistungsbereich als auch im industriellen Sektor angesiedelt sein. Denkbar ist sowohl eine Einzelfallstudie als auch ein Vergleich mehrerer Organisationen. Methodisch besonders ergiebig dürfte eine ethnografische Herangehensweise sein, bei der teilnehmende Beobachtungen, Interviews, Gruppendiskussionen und Dokumentenanalysen kombiniert werden, denn dadurch lassen sich schwer zu erfassende Phänomene wie Interessen, Strategien, Wahrnehmungen oder Einstellungen am besten untersuchen. Die Methode sollte offen gegenüber potenziellen Diversity-Dimensionen sein, denn die »offiziellen« Dimensionen könnten sich empirisch als weniger bedeutsam erweisen als subjektiv wahrgenommene, inoffizielle oder in einem Team situativ wirkende Dimensionen. Dies lässt sich nur mit einem qualitativen Vorgehen untersuchen. Gleichstellungsstandards sollen dabei zum einen nach herkömmlichen Kriterien geprüft werden, etwa die Anteile verschiedener demografischer Gruppen an hierarchischen Ebenen oder Einkommensklassen. Sie sollen aber auch zum anderen als sozial konstruierte Phänomene analysiert werden, die gemeinsam ausgehandelt und subjektiv interpretiert werden und erheblich von politisch gesetzten oder wissenschaftlich aufgestellten Standards abweichen können. Das Ziel eines solchen Vorgehens ist deshalb die Identifikation der subjektiven Theorien und mentalen Modelle zu Gleichstellung einschließlich der damit einhergehenden Interessen sein sowie die Analyse der Strategien, mit denen verschiedene Akteursgruppen versuchen, ihre Ansprüche an Nichtdiskriminierung zu verwirklichen. Damit verbunden ist auf der symbolischen Ebene die Berücksichtigung der Zusammenhänge zwischen digitaler Technik und Diversity-Dimensionen wie Geschlecht, Alter oder Kultur. Weiteres Ziel ist die Analyse der Gleichstellungspotenziale von Diversity Management und der Frage, ob die dargestellte Kritik daran gerechtfertigt ist. Die Betrachtung der betrieblichen Ebene ist notwendig, um Kontextbedingungen zu berücksichtigen, die das politische Feld der Gleichstellung strukturieren. Trotzdem können die Ergebnisse auf andere Organisationen verallgemeinert werden, wenn die Kriterien dafür geprüft und offengelegt werden. Praktische Implikationen bestehen in Weiterentwicklungen der Diversity Management-Strategien zur Förderung von Gleichstellung, Vorschlägen zum Empowerment von weniger machtvollen Gruppen (Förderung mikropolitischer Kompetenzen), Empfehlungen für Betriebsräte und Diversitybeauftragte zur Verbesserung ihrer Gleichstellungsarbeit im Hinblick auf die Rechtsdurchsetzung und die Entwicklung von Diversity-Maßnahmen, Schulungen für Führungskräfte bezüglich der Leitung heterogener Teams u. a.

6. Fazit: Gesetze, Diversity Management und Standards guter digitalisierter Arbeit

Gesetzliche Grundlagen zu Gleichbehandlung und Antidiskriminierung wurden seit der Jahrtausendwende stark erweitert, hinken jedoch gleichsam den Entwicklungen auf dem Arbeitsmarkt hinterher, da sie sich an vergangenen Standards und weniger an zukünftigen Gegebenheiten wie digitalisierten Beschäftigungsformen orientieren. So stellen sich etwa Fragen, inwiefern Arbeitskräfte durch das AGG geschützt sind, wenn sie Aufträge als Selbstständige annehmen, oder inwiefern Projektarbeitnehmer_innen das neue Entgelttransparenzgesetz nützt, bei dem Vergleichsfälle gefordert sind. Diversity Management hat hier mehr Flexibilität, auf neue Entwicklungen zu reagieren, da es als betriebliche Strategie leicht angepasst werden kann, z. B. um geeignete Maßnahmen für Arbeit im

Homeoffice zu schaffen. Außerdem kann Diversity Management an die spezifischen Gegebenheiten der jeweiligen Organisation angepasst werden. Ein multinationaler Industriekonzern hat bezüglich Gleichstellung andere Bedarfe als ein kleineres Dienstleistungsunternehmen. Jedoch steht der Arbeitnehmerschutz bei Diversity Management nicht (immer) im Vordergrund, sondern (häufig) die Motivations- und Leistungssteigerung. Außerdem ist auch hier die Frage, wer überhaupt in den Genuss der angebotenen Maßnahmen kommt, ob nur die Kernbelegschaft oder auch Werkvertragsnehmer_innen, Leiharbeitskräfte und Crowdworker. Umso wichtiger sind die Aushandlungen vor Ort unter den verschiedenen Akteur_innen darum, welche Standards für wen gelten sollen und wer von diesen profitiert. Dafür spielen Macht- und Einflussprozesse eine wichtige Rolle, denn wer seine Ansprüche und Erwartungen nicht durchsetzen kann, wird trotz Gleichbehandlungsgesetzen und trotz betrieblichen Gleichstellungsstrategien wenig tatsächliche Chancengleichheit genießen.

Literaturverzeichnis

Absenger, N. (2016): Welche Änderungen sind im Arbeits- und Sozialrecht in digitalisierten Arbeitswelten nötig? In: *Mitbestimmungs-Report*, 24, S.12–15.

Ahlers, E. (2016): Sind gesundheitsgefährdende Arbeitsbelastungen durch zeitgemäße Regulierung vermeidbar? In: *Mitbestimmungs-Report*, 24, S. 8–10.

ADS (Antidiskriminierungsstelle des Bundes) (2016): *Evaluation des Allgemeinen Gleichbehandlungsgesetzes*. Berlin.

Ahonen, P./ Tienari, J./ Meriläinen, S./ Pullen, A. (2014): Hidden contexts and invisible power relations: A Foucauldian reading of diversity research, in: *Human relations*, 67(3), S. 263–286.

Alewell, D./Moll, T. (2019): Religion, Religiosität und Spiritualität am Arbeitsplatz in deutschen Unternehmen, in: D. Alewell/ W. Matiaske (Hrsg.): *Standards Guter Arbeit – disziplinäre Positionen und interdisziplinäre Perspektiven*. Baden-Baden: Nomos, S. 107–137.

Bendl, R./ Fleischmann, A./ Walenta, C. (2008): Diversity management discourse meets queer theory, in: *Gender in Management: An International Journal*, 23(6), S. 382–394.

BMAS (Bundesministerium für Arbeit und Soziales) (2013): *Arbeitsmarktprognose 2030. Eine strategische Vorausschau auf die Entwicklung von Angebot und Nachfrage in Deutschland.* Bielefeld: W. Bertelsmann Verlag.

BMAS (Bundesministerium für Arbeit und Soziales) (2016): *Digitalisierung am Arbeitsplatz. Aktuelle Ergebnisse einer Betriebs- und Beschäftigtenbefragung*. Berlin.

Busch, C./ Vahle-Hinz, T. (2019): Gesundheit und Wohlbefinden in einer Arbeitswelt im Wandel: Aufrechterhaltung von Standards guter Arbeit bei multikulturellen Belegschaften und flexibler Arbeit, in: D. Alewell/ W. Matiaske (Hrsg.): *Standards Guter Arbeit – disziplinäre Positionen und interdisziplinäre Perspektiven.* Baden-Baden: Nomos, S. 39–61.

Cammio Video recruitment experts: Our Platform. Unter: https://cammio.com/our-platform/

Institut DGB-Index Gute Arbeit (2017): *Verbreitung, Folgen und Gestaltungsaspekte der Digitalisierung der Arbeitswelt.* Berlin.

Dingeldey, I. (2015): Institutionelle Dualisierung und Geschlecht, in: I. Dingeldey/ A. Holtrup/ G. Warsewa (Hrsg.): *Wandel der Governance der Erwerbsarbeit.* Wiesbaden: Springer, S. 101–129.

Edding, C. (2000): *Agentin des Wandels. Der Kampf um Veränderung im Unternehmen.* München: Murmann Verlag.

Herzog-Stein, A. (2016): Welche gesamtwirtschaftlichen Beschäftigungseffekte bringt die Digitalisierung mit sich? in: *Mitbestimmungs-Report*; 24, S. 5–7.

IfD (Institut für Demoskopie) Allensbach (2015): *Zu Hause arbeiten – Chancen der Digitalisierung für die Vereinbarkeit von Familie und Beruf. Bericht über eine Befragung im Herbst 2015 im Auftrag des Bundesministeriums für Familie, Senioren, Frauen und Jugend.* Allensbach.

Eggers, M. M. (2011): Anerkennung und Illegitimierung. Diversität als marktförmige Regulierung von Differenzmarkierungen, in: BrodenA. Broden/ P. Mercheril (Hrsg.): *Rassismus bildet. Bildungswissenschaftliche Beiträge zu Normalisierung und Subjektivierung in der Migrationsgesellschaft.* Bielefeld: transcript, S. 59–85.

Gotsis, G./ Kortezi, Z. (2015): *Critical studies in diversity management literature: a review and synthesis.* Dordrecht [u. a.], Wiesbaden: Springer.

Hanau, H. (2016): Schöne digitale Arbeitswelt? in: *Neue juristische Wochenschrift*, 36, S. 2613–2617.

Hanau, H./ Matiaske, W. (2019): Mitbestimmung im entgrenzten Betrieb – Arbeitsrechtliche und personalwirtschaftliche Perspektiven, in: D. Alewell/ W. Matiaske (Hrsg.): *Standards Guter Arbeit – disziplinäre Positionen und interdisziplinäre Perspektiven.* Baden-Baden: Nomos, S. 213–242.

Hauff, S. (2019): Human Resource Management zwischen Uniformität und Differenzierung, in: D. Alewell/W. Matiaske (Hrsg.): *Standards Guter Arbeit – disziplinäre Positionen und interdisziplinäre Perspektiven.* Baden-Baden: Nomos, S. 65–80.

Hertel, G./ Lauer, L. (2012): Führung auf Distanz und E-Leadership – die Zukunft der Führung? in: S. Grote (Hrsg.): *Die Zukunft der Führung.* Heidelberg: Springer, S. 103–118.

Holst, E./ Wrohlich, K. (2018): Spitzengremien großer Unternehmen: Geschlechterquote für Aufsichtsräte greift, in Vorständen herrscht beinahe Stillstand, in: *DIW Wochenbericht*, 85, 1/2, S. 3–17.

Jochmann, W./ Schawilye, R./ Schmidt, S. (2012): Nice to have oder unabdingbares Element nachhaltiger Personalarbeit? Stand der Umsetzung von diversity-

Programmen und deren personalwirtschaftliche Bedeutung, in: *Personalführung* 1, S. 27–34.

Jochmann-Döll, A./ Tonndorf, K. (2013): *Nach Leistung, Eignung und Befähigung? Beurteilung von Frauen und Männern im Polizeivollzugsdienst*, Arbeitspapier 276 der Hans Böckler Stiftung, Düsseldorf.

Jüngling, C./ Rastetter, D. (2011): Die Implementierung von Gleichstellungsmaßnahmen: Optionen, Widerstände und Erfolgsstrategien, in: G. Krell/ R. Ortlieb/ B. Sieben (Hrsg.): *Chancengleichheit durch Personalpolitik: Gleichstellung von Frauen und Männern in Unternehmen und Verwaltungen; Rechtliche Regelungen – Problemanalysen – Lösungen*. Wiesbaden: Gabler, S. 25–40.

Kalev, A./ Roscigno, V. J. (2016): Interview: Bureaucracy, Bias, and Diversity – Structural Constraints and Opportunities in Organization, in: C. Bradel-Kühner/ A. P. Müller (Hrsg.): *Re-thinking Diversity. Multiple Approaches in Theory, Media, Communities, and Managerial Practice*. Wiesbaden: VS Springer, S. 111–120.

Kirchner, S./Beyer, J. (2016): Die Plattformlogik als digitale Marktordnung, in: *Zeitschrift für Soziologie*, 45(5), S. 324–339.

Kleemann, F./ Voß, G.G. (2010): Arbeit und Subjekt, in: F. Böhle/ G. G. Voß/ G. Wachtler (Hrsg.): *Handbuch Arbeitssoziologie*. Wiesbaden: VS, S. 415–450.

Kocher, E. (2013): Unternehmen als Adressaten des Arbeitsrechts: die Bedeutung externer Akteurinnen und Akteure für die effektive Rechtsdurchsetzung, in: D. Alewell (Hrsg.): *Rechtstatsachen und Rechtswirkungen im Arbeits- und Sozialrecht*. München [u. a.]: Hampp, S. 41–57.

Kratzer, N./ Menz, W./ Tullius, K./ Wolf, H. (2015): *Legitimationsprobleme in der Erwerbsarbeit. Gerechtigkeitsansprüche und Handlungsorientierungen in Arbeit und Betrieb*. Baden-Baden: Nomos Verlag.

Krell, G./ Sieben, B. (2011): Diversity Management. Chancengleichheit für alle und auch als Wettbewerbsvorteil, in: G. Krell/ R. Ortlieb/ B. Sieben (Hrsg.): *Chancengleichheit durch Personalpolitik: Gleichstellung von Frauen und Männern in Unternehmen und Verwaltungen; Rechtliche Regelungen – Problemanalysen – Lösungen*. Wiesbaden: Gabler, S. 155–174.

Krell, G./ Riedmüller, B./ Sieben, B./ Vinz, D. (2007): *Diversity Studies. Grundlagen und disziplinäre Ansätze*. Frankfurt/New York: Campus Verlag.

Küpper, W/ Felsch, A.(2000): *Organisation, Macht und Ökonomie: Mikropolitik und die Konstitution organisationaler Handlungssysteme*. Wiesbaden: Westdeutscher Verlag.

Kutzner, E./ Schnier, V. (2017): Geschlechterverhältnisse in Digitalisierungsprozessen von Arbeit, in: *Zeitschrift Arbeit*, 26 (1), S. 137–157.

Leimeister, J. M./ Zogaj, S./ Durward, D./ Blohm, I. (2016): Systematisierung und Analyse von Crowdsourcing-Anbietern und Crowd-Work-Projekten, In: *Study der Hans-Böckler-Stiftung*, 324, https://www.boeckler.de/pdf/p_study_hbs_324.pdf.

Losert, A. (2011): Forschungsskizze: der Betriebsrat als Akteur im Diversity Management, in: G. Krell/ R. Ortlieb/ B. Sieben (Hrsg.): *Chancengleichheit durch Personalpolitik: Gleichstellung von Frauen und Männern in Unternehmen und Verwal-*

tungen; Rechtliche Regelungen – Problemanalysen – Lösungen. Wiesbaden: Gabler, S. 225–230.

Lott, Y. (2015): Costs and Benefits of Flexibility and Autonomy in Working Time: The Same für women and Men? in: *WSI-Diskussionspapier*, 196.

Lott, Y. (2016): Fördert die Digitalisierung Geschlechtergleichheit? in: *Mitbestimmungs-Report*, 24, S. 7–8.

Maschke, M. (2010): Instrumente und Akteure betrieblicher Gleichstellungspolitik, in: J. Achatz (Hrsg.): *Projektgruppe GiB: Geschlechterungleichheiten im Betrieb.* Berlin: edition sigma, S. 485–550.

Maschke, M. (2016): Vor welchen Herausforderungen steht die Mitbestimmung im Betrieb 4.0? in: *Mitbestimmungs-Report*, 24, S. 10–12.

Maier, M. F./ Viete, S./ Ody, M. (2017): *Plattformbasierte Erwerbsarbeit: Stand der empirischen Forschung.* Berlin: Bundesministerium für Arbeit und Soziales.

Moosmüller, A. (2016): Cultural Diversity in Multinational Corporations, in: C. Bradel-Kühner/ A. P. Müller (Hrsg.): *Re-thinking Diversity. Multiple Approaches in Theory, Media, Communities, and Managerial Practice.* Wiesbaden: VS Springer, S. 121–132.

Mucha, A. (2014): *Die mikropolitische Situation von Frauen in technischen Berufen: strategische Positionierung im nicht-habitualisierten Feld.* Baden-Baden: Nomos Verlag.

Mucha, A./ Nielbock, S./ Triebs, S. (2011): Mikropolitik-Coaching für den Aufstieg – drei Fallbeispiele, in: *Freie Assoziation. Zeitschrift für das Unbewusste in Organisation und Kultur*, 14(3+4), S. 155–168.

Neuberger, O. (2006): *Mikropolitik und Moral in Organisationen.* Stuttgart: Lucius & Lucius.

Raasch, S./ Rastetter, D. (2013): Das AGG auf dem Prüfstand, in: D. Alewell (Hrsg.): *Rechtstatsachen und Rechtswirkungen im Arbeits- und Sozialrecht.* München/ Mehring: Hampp Verlag, S. 88–104.

Rastetter, D. (2017): Geschlechterverhältnisse in Organisationen: Zur Relevanz von Akteur_innen, strategischem Handeln und Spielene – Inspirationsquelle Mikropolitik, in: M. Funder (Hrsg.): *Neo-Institutionalismus – Revisited.* Baden-Baden: Nomos Verlag, S. 339–366.

Rastetter, D. (2006): Managing Diversity in Teams. Erkenntnisse aus der Gruppenforschung, in: G. Krell/ H. Wächter (Hrsg.): *Diversity Management. Impulse aus der Personalforschung.* München/Mering: Hampp Verlag, S. 81–108.

Riedmüller, B./ Vinz, D. (2007): Diversity Politics, in: G. Krell/ B. Riedmüller/ B. Sieben/ D. Vinz (Hrsg.): *Diversity Studies. Grundlagen und disziplinäre Ansätze.* Frankfurt/New York: Campus Verlag, S.143–162.

Schuler-Harms, M./ Goldberg, K. (2019): Soziale Absicherung von alter und neuer Selbständigkeit als Herausforderung für das Sozialrecht, in: D. Alewell/ W. Matiaske (Hrsg.): *Standards Guter Arbeit – disziplinäre Positionen und interdisziplinäre Perspektiven.* Baden-Baden: Nomos, S. 189–212.

Segert, A./ Weghuber, E./ Wondrak, M. (2012): *Zukunftsfähige Managementstrategien. Diversity Management (DiM) & Corporate Social Responsibility (CSR) im Spannungsfeld zwischen Ethik und Betriebswirtschaft. Diversity Search & Factor-D.* http://factor-d.at/wp-content/uploads/2016/08/Diversity-Management-DiM-Corporate-Social-Responsibility-CSR.pdf.

Schönwälder, K. (2007): Diversity und Antidiskriminierungspolitik, in: G. Krell/ B. Riedmüller/ B. Sieben/ D. Vinz (Hrsg.): *Diversity Studies. Grundlagen und disziplinäre Ansätze.* Frankfurt/New York: Campus Verlag, S. 163–178.

Süß, S. (2007): Diversity-Management in Deutschland. Ergebnisse einer Intensivbefragung von in Deutschland agierenden Unternehmen, in: *Arbeitsbericht* Nr. 17, Hagen: Fernuniversität Hagen.

Thomas, D.A./ Ely, R.J. (1996): Making Differences Matter. A New Paradigm for Managing Diversity, in: *Harvard Business Review*, 74(5), S. 79–90.

ver.di Vereinte Dienstleistungsgewerkschaft (2017): *Digitalisierung und Arbeitsqualität. Eine Sonderauswertung auf Basis des DGB-Index Gute Arbeit 2016 für den Dienstleistungssektor.* https://innovation-gute-arbeit.verdi.de/++file++592fd69d086c2653a7bb5b05/download/digitalverdi_web.cleaned.pdf

Walker, E.-M. (2017): Subjektive Aneignungspraktiken digitaler Technologien und die zugrundeliegenden Gerechtigkeitsansprüche der Beschäftigten, in: *Zeitschrift Arbeit*, 26(3–4), S. 315–342.

Werkmeister, C. (2016): Diversity Reporting in Germany – an Empirical Investigation of DAX30 Companies, in: C. Bradel-Kühner/ A. P. Müller (Hrsg.): *Re-thinking Diversity. Multiple Approaches in Theory, Media, Communities, and Managerial Practice.* Wiesbaden: VS Springer, S. 169–192.

Youngs, G. (2002): Globalisierung und neue Kommunikationstechnologien: Geschlechterspezifische Perspektiven, in: Heinrich-Böll-Stiftung/ Feministisches Institut (Hrsg.): *Feminist_spaces. Frauen im Netz.* Königstein/Taunus, S. 11–25.

Religion, Religiosität und Spiritualität am Arbeitsplatz in deutschen Unternehmen

Dorothea Alewell und Tobias Moll

1. Spiritualität, Religion und Religiosität am Arbeitsplatz als neues Feld der Management-Forschung

Spiritualität, Religion(szugehörigkeit) und Religiosität der Arbeitnehmer werden in den meisten deutschen Unternehmen bzw. an den meisten Arbeitsplätzen bisher standardmäßig als »Privatsache« definiert und im Unternehmensalltag nicht weiter berücksichtigt. Auch in Bezug auf amerikanische Unternehmen wurde noch vor wenigen Jahren von Religion als dem letzten Tabu am Arbeitsplatz gesprochen (Fortune 2001). Dieser bisherige Standard beginnt sich jedoch möglicherweise zu verändern – so wird es zumindest für die angloamerikanischen Länder postuliert (Ashmos und Duchon 2000; Benefiel et al. 2014; Case und Gosling 2010, S. 264; Tourish und Tourish 2010).

Nach jahrzehntelangen Diskussionen um Work-Life-Balance, ganzheitliche Arbeit, Diversität sowie Corporate Social Responsibility kristallisiert sich derzeit ein neuer Diskussionsstrang zur Spiritualität, Religion und Religiosität am Arbeitsplatz heraus, der verschiedene Teilaspekte der vorherigen Diskurse aufgreift und verbindet. Dabei spielen sowohl die Interessen der Mitarbeiter als auch die Interessen der Unternehmen in diesem Diskurs eine Rolle: Wenn Menschen nicht nur als Arbeitskräfte, sondern als Personen mit ihren humantypischen spirituellen Bedürfnissen nach Identität und Sinn an den Arbeitsplatz kommen, ist Spiritualität und Religiosität am Arbeitsplatz potentiell ein wichtiger Bestandteil Guter Arbeit aus Sicht der Arbeitnehmer. Spiritualität, Religion(szugehörigkeit) und Religiosität der Menschen kann auch aus Sicht der Unternehmen im personalwirtschaftlichen Handeln eine relevante Ebene darstellen, wenn die Unternehmen Arbeitsplätze »ganzheitlich« gestalten wollen, um Kreativität, Innovationsfähigkeit und Sinnempfindung der Arbeitnehmer für sich nutzbar zu machen,[1] oder wenn international agierende Unternehmen nicht nur nach Alter, Geschlecht und Nationalität, sondern auch spirituell und religiös diverse Belegschaften und Kundengruppen aufweisen (Miller und Ewest 2013).

Dieser Beitrag untersucht aufbauend auf – überwiegend angloamerikanischen – Befunden der theoretisch-konzeptionellen sowie der empirischen Forschung im Themenfeld der Spiritualität, Religion und Religiosität am Arbeitsplatz, warum es lohnen könnte, dieses Themenfeld auch in Deutschland bzw. für deutsche Unternehmen näher zu untersuchen, und welche Fragen sich dabei stellen.

2. *Die personalwirtschaftliche Relevanz von Spiritualität, Religiosität und Religion am Arbeitsplatz*

2.1. Definition und Konzeptualisierung der zentralen Begriffe

Religion, Spiritualität und Religiosität sind keine Standardbegriffe der personalwirtschaftlichen Forschung. Sie werden in der Diskussion um Faith at Work bzw. im Spirituality Movement kontrovers diskutiert und sehr unterschiedlich konzeptualisiert (vgl. zu einem Überblick über diese Diskussionen z. B. Phipps und Benefiel 2013). Diese Diskussionen wiederholen wir aus Platzgründen nicht, sondern stellen direkt die von uns verwendete Begriffsfassung vor.

Wir begreifen Spiritualität als einen Oberbegriff zu Religiosität, und Religion als eine kollektiv geteilte mögliche Basis von Spiritualität.

Im Einzelnen lassen sich die Begriffe wie folgt bestimmen: Spiritualität bezeichnet einerseits den Bereich geistigen menschlichen Lebens, der mit dem Heiligen und Transzendenten sowie der Suche nach Sinn und Verbindung mit dem Großen und Ganzen in Verbindung steht, andererseits auch eine Haltung, Einstellung und Fähigkeit des Individuums, die spirituelles Erleben des Individuums überhaupt erst ermöglicht. Spirituelles Erleben beinhaltet den Ausdruck von und die Suche (und das mit dieser Suche verbundene Verhalten) nach Sinn und Bedeutung im Leben sowie

1 Vgl. Hauff (2019) in diesem Band zu HRM-Strategien, welche die Einzigartigkeit des Humankapitals in den Vordergrund stellen.

Verbundenheit mit Anderen, mit der Natur und mit dem über die eigene Person hinausgehenden »Großen und Ganzen«, auch dem Transzendenten.[2] Spiritualität ist damit auf der Ebene des Individuums definiert, als Teil des inneren, geistigen Lebens und als Haltung, Einstellung und Fähigkeit, sowie als Verhalten in diesem Suchprozess.

Unter Religion verstehen wir (in Anlehnung an Koenig 2012) ein multidimensionales und kollektiv geteiltes Konstrukt, das aus Glaubenssätzen, Glaubenspraktiken und Ritualen sowie Symbolen besteht, die sich auf eine übersinnliche, transzendente, »höhere« Macht beziehen. Die Glaubenssätze, -praktiken, Rituale und Symbole sind kollektiv geteilt, also anders als Spiritualität nicht in erster Linie individuell verortet. Religionen sind häufig über lange Zeiträume tradiert und institutionell verankert, z. B. über Organisationen wie Kirchen. Religion ist damit auch an Kollektive und Institutionen wie Kirchen, Glaubensgemeinschaften und Gemeinden gebunden und wird häufig auch innerhalb dieser Institutionen und ihrer Angebote ausgeübt. Die zentrale transzendente Macht wird in verschiedenen Religionen unterschiedlich mit Inhalt gefüllt und benannt, zum Beispiel als Gott, Allah, HaShem, Brahman, Buddha oder Dao (Koenig 2012). Religionen beinhalten mehrheitlich Vorstellungen über das Leben nach dem Tode sowie über die Beziehungen und Verantwortlichkeiten zwischen Menschen in sozialen Gemeinschaften, z. B. Postulate der Nächstenliebe oder Fürsorge für Schwächere sowie Achtung vor den Eltern oder Älteren.

Wie diese Begriffsbestimmung verdeutlicht, kann Religion eine spezifische, auf kollektiv geteilten und institutionalisierten Elementen beruhende mögliche Basis von individueller Spiritualität sein. Bezieht sich die individuelle Spiritualität auf eine Religion, so dass sich der Suchprozess nach Sinn und Bedeutung, nach Gemeinschaft und Transzendenz im Rahmen oder auf der Grundlage spezifischer religiöser Vorstellungen bewegt, so bezeichnen wir diesen Ausschnitt der Spiritualität als Religiosität.

Religiosität ist damit immer auch Spiritualität, aber umgekehrt ist Spiritualität nicht automatisch auch Religiosität – nämlich dann nicht, wenn der spirituelle Suchprozess ohne Bezug auf eine Religion auskommt. Nichtreligiöse Spiritualität baut nicht zwingend auf einem institutionellen Rahmen auf und benötigt keine inhaltliche Übereinstimmung zwischen

---

2 Vgl. zum Zusammenhang von Arbeit und Sinn Müller et al. (2019) in diesem Band.

mehreren Menschen. Spiritualität ohne Bezug auf Religion kann mit einer sehr individuellen, nicht kollektiv geteilten Suche nach Erfüllung und Lebenssinn einhergehen und ist daher eher subjektiv und persönlich, während Religiosität bzw. religiöse Spiritualität über den Bezug auf Religion auch kollektive und überindividuell geteilte Züge aufweisen kann.

Inwiefern können nun Spiritualität, Religion und Religiosität Relevanz an den Arbeitsplätzen und für die personalwirtschaftliche Arbeit in den Unternehmen entfalten?

2.2. Konzeptionelle und theoretische Überlegungen zur Relevanz von Spiritualität, Religion und Religiosität am Arbeitsplatz

Neal (2013) beschreibt die Geschichte der Managementtheorie als eine Entwicklung hin zu einem ganzheitlicheren Blick auf die Beziehung zwischen dem Individuum und dem Arbeitsplatz bzw. der Arbeitgeberorganisation. Vom Scientific Management über die Hawthorne-Experimente und die Human-Relations-Bewegung, die Qualitätszirkel-Entwicklungen mit ihrem Fokus auf den noch unerschlossenen intellektuellen Ressourcen von Arbeitskräften sowie Teamarbeit und Arbeitnehmerbeteiligung, bis hin zum Servant-Leadership-Ansatz (Greenleaf 1991) habe eine Entwicklung stattgefunden, bei der neben der physischen Energie von Arbeitnehmern zunächst auch die emotionale Eneregie und dann die intellektuelle Energie in das personalwirtschaftliche Denken und Handeln einbezogen worden sei. Der letzte Schritt sei, dass auch die vierte große energetische Kraft, die spirituelle Energie, gesehen und berücksichtigt werde. In der Tradition des Scientific Management wurden und werden Organisationen als rationale Gebilde konzeptualisiert, die nach effizienzorientierten Regeln gesteuert werden (sollten). Dieses rationale Leitbild präge nach wie vor große Teile der Wirtschaft. Nun jedoch mehrten sich in den letzten Jahren und Jahrzehnten die Stimmen der Wissenschaftler und der Praktiker, die neben Effizienz auch das innere Erleben der Arbeitnehmer, den wahrgenommenen Sinn am Arbeitsplatz bzw. in der Erwerbstätigkeit und den eigentlichen, den tieferen Zweck der wirtschaftlichen Tätigkeit sowie das Erleben von Gemeinschaft, Zugehörigkeit und Verbundenheit als wichtige Dimensionen von Organisationen ansehen. Zugleich werde ein wachsendes Interesse der Unternehmen und der Wissenschaftler an diesen Themen unterstellt (Ashmos und Duchon 2000; Benefiel et al. 2014; Neal 2013).

Für diese wahrgenommene oder postulierte (ggf. auch steigende?) Relevanz von Spiritualität am Arbeitsplatz lassen sich eine ganze Reihe von generellen und spezifisch personalwirtschaftlichen Gründen anführen (vgl. auch Ashmos und Duchon 2000; Benefiel et al. 2014; Neal 2013; Benefiel et al. 2014).

Erstens verdeutlicht die Definition von Spiritualität auch als *Suche nach Lebenssinn und Erfüllung*, dass Erwerbsarbeit, die mit dem Anspruch auf Selbstverwirklichung verbunden ist, Teil dieser spirituellen Suche sein kann (vgl. Müller et al. 2019 in diesem Band). Individuelle Spiritualität kann dann die Erwerbsarbeit als Teil der Suche nach Sinn und Erfüllung beeinflussen – und umgekehrt. In der arbeits- und organisationspsychologischen Forschung gibt es schon eine längere Diskussion um die positiven Wirkungen von Meaning at Work auf individuelle und organisationale Outcome-Variablen (vgl. z. B. Clausen und Borg 2011), etwa auf individuelles Wohlbefinden, Commitment, Arbeitsunfähigkeit und Fluktuationsneigung. In der Diskussion um veränderte Ansprüche und Bedürfnisse der sogenannten Generation Y im Arbeitsumfeld wird aktuell z. B. immer wieder deren Orientierungslosigkeit und, in gewissem Maße als Konsequenz, die daraus erwachsene Suche nach Sinn in bzw. hinter ihren Tätigkeiten genannt (Welk 2015; DGFP 2011, S. 12–15; Alewell und Brinck 2018). Zudem wird ein höheres Bewusstsein für Werte und Normen konstatiert, was sich z. B. in einem erhöhten Bedürfnis nach Übereinstimmung zwischen persönlichen und Unternehmenswerten widerspiegele (Deutsche Gesellschaft für Personalführung e. V. 2011, S. 24). Auch hier stellt sich die Frage, welche Rolle Spiritualität und Religion für den empfundenen Sinn am Arbeitsplatz und für die Entwicklung von solchen Normen und Werte spielen.

Nicht nur über Generationen, auch über das Lebensalter und den Lebensstandard als Einflussfaktoren auf Spiritualität und auf Werte wird diskutiert. Mit dem Wohlstand und der Erfahrung von Risiko, Komplexität und Unsicherheit in der Welt wachse das gesellschaftliche Interesse für spirituelle Bewegungen und für asiatische Religionen (Neal 2013), welche Meditation, die Suche nach der eigenen spirituellen Mitte und nach Sinn im Leben ins Zentrum stellen. Dieses Interesse wachse umso stärker, je mehr die große Gruppe der Babyboomer altere und sich daher mehr mit der eigenen Endlichkeit auseinandersetzen müsse. Wird dieses gesellschaftliche und individuelle Interesse an Spiritualität auch in die Unternehmen hineingetragen, so lässt sich die Hypothese ableiten, dass in Abhängigkeit von der Alters- und Generationsstruktur der Unternehmen unterschiedlich starke Bedürfnisse nach Spiritualität auftauchen. Garg (2017) zeigt in einer empirischen Untersuchung in Indien, dass Alter und Erfahrung positiv mit Spiritualität am Arbeitsplatz zusammenhängen. Außerdem fanden Marschke et al. (2011) bei Sales-Managern in den USA einen positiv moderierenden Effekt des Alters auf die Beziehung von Spiritualität und intrinsischer Arbeitsmotivation. Damit konnte auch in einer Untersuchung in der westlichen Welt ein positiver Zusamenhang zwischen Alter und Spiritualität am Arbeitsplatz gefunden werden.

Zweitens argumentiert Neal (2013), dass der in vielen Unternehmen stattfindende Personalabbau und die häufigen Umorganisationen und Re-Engineering-Prozesse vielfach *demoralisierte Belegschaften und eine wachsende Ungleichheit* bei den Löhnen und Gehältern hinterlassen haben. Damit entstehe eine wachsende Sehnsucht nach Gerechtigkeit und Zusammengehörigkeit, auf die Spiritualität am Arbeitsplatz eine Antwort darstellen könne. Spiritualität *vermindere also mögliche emotionale Ursachen für Entfremdung und Unzufriedenheit der Arbeitnehmer.* Trifft diese These zu, so kann man ggf. umgekehrt erwarten, dass mit stärkerer Ausprägung der Spiritualität am Arbeitsplatz auch die Arbeitszufriedenheit von Arbeitnehmern als personalwirtschaftlicher Outcome-Variable steigt. Hiermit ist ein bereits gut erforschtes Feld im Bereich der Spiritualität am Arbeitsplatz angesprochen (Houghton et al. 2016; Fry 2003; Karakas 2010) und es existieren neben konzeptionellen Studien auch eine Reihe empirischer Studien sowohl für Asien als auch für die USA als Vertreter der westlichen Welt. Häufig wird ein positiver Zusammenhang z. B. zwischen einem höheren Sinn in der Arbeit, der Verbundenheit mit der Firma und der Arbeitszufriedenheit gefunden (u. a. Gupta et al. 2014; Milliman et al. 2003; Marschke et al. 2011; Garg 2017). Altaf und Awan (2011) bestätigen in diesem Zusammenhang aber auch einen positiv moderierenden Effekt von Spiritualität am Arbeitsplatz auf den Zusammenhang zwischen Arbeitsüberlastung von Mitarbeitern und ihrer Arbeitszufriedenheit, was im Kontext von Personalabbau und laufenden Umstrukturierungen ebenfalls einen wichtigen Hinweis darstellt.

Im engen Zusammenhang mit diesem Argument zum Zusammenhalt in Unternehmen wird *drittens* auch darauf verwiesen, dass der nachlassende Zusammenhalt bzw. die *sinkende Bindungskraft von Familien, Kirchengemeinden, Nachbarschaften oder anderen zivilgesellschaftlichen Kollektiven* zur Konsequenz habe, dass die *Erwerbsorganisationen zur primären Quelle von Erlebnissen der Verbundenheit* mit anderen und der Zugehörigkeit zu einer Gemeinschaft werden. Organisationen, in denen

Individuen ihrer Erwerbstätigkeit nachgehen, würden somit stärker als früher zu einem Ort, an dem wesentliche Teile der spirituellen Suche nach Verbundenheit gelebt werden (Neal 2013). Aus Sicht der Organisationen betrachtet ergeben sich damit Zusammenhänge zwischen der Spiritualität der Arbeitnehmer und der Bindung an die Organisation bzw. mit dem organisationalen Commitment als personalwirtschaftlicher Outcome-Variable (vgl. dazu Hauff 2019 in diesem Band). Ein positiver Zusammenhang von Spiritualität am Arbeitsplatz und Commitment konnte in mehreren empirischen Untersuchungen in Asien und den USA bereits nachgewiesen werden (u. a. Garg 2017; Crawford et al. 2009; Pawar 2009; Milliman et al. 2003). Milliman et al. (2003) stellen zwar ein höheres Commitment durch das Erleben eines höheren Sinns der Arbeit, eines besonderen Gemeinschaftsgefühls und einer Kongruenz zwischen den persönlichen Werten und den Unternehmenswerten fest. Jedoch verringert das Erleben eines höheren Sinns nicht die Wahrscheinlichkeit einer Kündigung durch den Mitarbeiter. Auch einige Meta-Studien und Literature Reviews attestieren einen positiven Zusammenhang zwischen Spiritualität am Arbeitsplatz und Commitment (u. a. Reave 2005; Houghton und Neck 2016; Krishnakumar und Neck 2002). Krishnakumar und Neck stellen zusammenfassend fest, dass für den Bereich von Spiritualität, der durch die drei großen Weltreligionen Christentum, Islam und Judentum geprägt wird, positive Verbindungen zwischen Spiritualität am Arbeitsplatz und Mitarbeiter-Commitment am Arbeitsplatz abgeleitet werden können.

Viertens beziehen sich die Debatten um *Work-Life-Balance* auf die Frage, wie »Work« und »Life« ins Gleichgewicht gebracht werden können, Konflikt- und Spannungsfelder zwischen ihnen vermieden oder abgemildert werden können oder sich die beiden unterschiedlichen Bereiche menschlichen Lebens im besten Fall positiv befruchten könnten. Zentrale Nicht-Erwerbs-Anteile des Menschseins werden damit in den Blick genommen – und in der Personalarbeit nicht länger als blinder Fleck behandelt. Bislang wurde dabei in Deutschland insbesondere die Frage nach der Balance zwischen Familien- und Freizeitbedürfnissen auf der einen Seite und Arbeitsplatzanforderungen auf der anderen Seite thematisiert. Teilweise wird die »Balance« auch im Kontext von Stressentstehung und Stressvermeidung thematisiert und in den Bereich des betrieblichen Gesundheitsmanagements eingeordnet (und spielt daher auch bei der Gefährdungsbeurteilung psychischer Belastung eine Rolle, vgl. Busch/Vahle-Hinz 2019 in diesem Band). Religiöse und spirituelle Bedürfnisse in Balance mit den Bedingungen an den Arbeitsplätzen zu bringen, wurde dagegen bisher eher wenig thematisiert. In deutschen Unternehmen scheint Religion meistens jedenfalls überhaupt kein Thema zu sein.[3] Einige Autoren sprechen gar von Religion als dem letzten großen Tabu am Arbeitsplatz (Fortune 2001). Und Neubert und Dougherty (2013) stellen noch im Jahr 2013 fest, dass das Thema auch von der Management-Wissenschaft ganz überwiegend ausgelassen, ignoriert oder seine Adressierung explizit verweigert worden sei. Einige sporadische Verweise lassen sich trotzdem finden: Z. B. spricht Voggenreiter (2013) Spiritualität als Element der Life-Domain und damit als relevant für die Work-Life-Balance an. Allerdings wird daraus kein Handlungsfeld für Unternehmen abgeleitet. Im Bereich der internationalen Forschung beobachtet Laabs (1995) schon sehr früh bei Arbeitnehmern die Frage bzw. Verwunderung darüber, dass Spiritualität im Rahmen der Diskussionen um »Life« in der Work-Life-Balance nicht berücksichtigt wird. Trotz dieser nur sporadischen Thematisierung gibt es aber auch schon erste empirische Erkenntnisse. So konnten Allen und Paddock (2017) eine positive Verbindung zwischen Mindfulness (als Teilaspekt von Spiritualität) und Work-Family-Balance aufzeigen. Garg (2017) fand in Indien positive Auswirkungen von Spiritualität am Arbeitsplatz auf die Work-Life-Balance. Dabei wurden die positiven Effekte von Spiritualität auf die Work-Life-Balance positiv durch das Geschlecht (männlich) und den Sektor (öffentlich Beschäftigte) moderiert.

Debatten um *Diversität in Unternehmen,* um potenzielle Diskriminierung und Antidiskriminierungs- und Gleichstellungstrategien fokussieren *fünftens* häufig auf die Merkmale Geschlecht, ethnische Herkunft und Alter als Unterscheidungsmerkmale von Personen. Die Religion(szugehörigkeit) und die spirituelle Ausrichtung von Beschäftigten als Diversitätsmerkmal, obwohl zum Beispiel in der populären Charta der Vielfalt, im Grundgesetz und im Allgemeinen Gleichstellungsgesetz explizit als relevante Kriterien genannt, werden nach unserem Kenntnisstand dagegen kaum diskutiert (vgl. auch Alewell und Rastetter 2018 und Rastetter in diesem Band). Jedoch sind in international agierenden Unternehmen möglicherweise auch die Belegschaften, Lieferanten und Kunden religiös und spirituell divers zusammengesetzt, so dass zu prüfen ist, ob und wie ein Unternehmen auf diese Vielfalt reagieren muss und ggf. kann. Dabei wer-

3 Zu einigen empirischen Belegen hinsichtlich der expliziten Behandlung von Religionsfragen in Unternehmen vgl. weiter unten in diesem Beitrag.

den bestimmte Typen von Produkten oder von Arbeitsplätzen eher religionssensibel sein als andere. Beispielsweise sind vermutlich Arbeitsplätze von Intensiv-Kranken- und Altenpflegern, die regelmäßig mit Tod und Sterben von Patienten in Berührung kommen, durchaus religionssensibel. Das Gleiche könnte für Trainingsdienstleistungen im Bereich der Arbeits- und Wirtschaftsethik oder Verantwortlicher Personalführung gelten. Es gibt zudem ganz *konkrete und praktische Zusammenhänge, die zu beachten sind.* Hierzu zählt die Frage nach der Zusammenarbeit in Teams mit hoher religiöser Diversität. Auch der Marktauftritt von Unternehmen in anderen Kulturkreisen kann von Religion und Spiritualität innerhalb und außerhalb des Unternehmens abhängen – welche Werbung ist zum Beispiel in islamischen Ländern wirksam, welche Gestaltung von Finanzprodukten für internationale Märkte ist angesichts des islamischen Zinsverbotes möglich? Religionen können über die jeweiligen Speisevorschriften – wie zum Beispiel zu koscherem Essen im Judentum, dem Verbot von Schweinefleisch und Alkohol im Islam oder dem üblichen fleischlosen Freitag in christlich geprägten Regionen – Einfluss auf die Ernährung in den Betriebskantinen nehmen. Auch Religion und Arbeitszeitgestaltung können sich über die religiös begründeten Gebetszeiten, Fastenzeiten und Feiertage tangieren. Nicht zuletzt kann es Zusammenhänge zwischen der Religion und betrieblichen Kleidungsvorschriften geben, wie an der sogenannten Kopftuchfrage oder dem Tragen von religiösen Symbolen wie dem Kreuz am Arbeitsplatz deutlich wird.

Da wir angesichts der Entwicklung bei den weltweiten Flüchtlingsströmen vermutlich auch weiterhin mit Migrationsprozessen und einer potenziell ansteigenden religiösen Pluralität rechnen können, dürften diese Themen in Deutschland in Zukunft eher noch an Bedeutung gewinnen. Es ist zudem zu erwarten, dass das Themenfeld Religion in Unternehmen, die entweder religiös diverse Belegschaften, Bewerbergruppen oder Kundengruppen haben, oder die religionssensible Produkte oder Arbeitsplätze aufweisen, eine größere Rolle spielt als in Unternehmen, für die das nicht der Fall ist.

Hierzu haben wir erste empirische Hinweise gefunden in qualitativen Experteninterviews, die Mitglieder unserer Forschungsgruppe im Sommer 2017 mit Personalleitern und Geschäftsführern Hamburger Unternehmen geführt haben (zu einer ausführlicheren Darstellung siehe unten, Abschnitt 2.3.). In der Mehrheit der privatwirtschaflichen Unternehmen wird eine mehr oder weniger strikte Neutralität in Bezug auf alle Fragen rund um Religion, Religiosität und Spiritualität, die als Privatsache der Mitarbeiter angesehen werden, vertreten. Dagegen werden in den von uns interviewten Organisationen, deren Produkte und Dienstleistungen mit diesen Feldern inhaltlich zu tun haben, Religion und Spiritualität explizit als wichtige Ressourcen angesehen, die aktiv gepflegt und genutzt werden. Hierzu bekamen wir entsprechende Angaben von einer diakonischen Einrichtung und von einem Verlag, dessen Produkte ganz überwiegend aus den Themenfeldern Religion und Spiritualität stammen.

Die Vernachlässigung von Religion als Diversitätskriterium überrascht *sechstens* auch deswegen, weil der Business-Case zur Förderung von Diversität in den Unternehmen nicht selten über die durch Diversität potenziell steigende Kreativität und Innovationsfähigkeit von Unternehmen begründet wird (Alewell und Rastetter 2018). Mit Kreativität ist aber bereits eine geistige oder auch kognitive Ressource angesprochen, die enge Verbindungen zur Spiritualität als Suche nach Sinn und Erfüllung haben dürfte. Das wird unmittelbar am Beispiel der Meditation als einer zugleich kreativitätsfördernden und spirituellen Praxis deutlich. Die Einbeziehung von Spiritualität und Religion erscheint daher als logische Fortsetzung der bisherigen Diskussionen um Diversität. Man könnte also erwarten, dass in kreativen Industrien, Unternehmen oder Arbeitsplatzbereichen Religion und Spiritualität eher als Diversitätskriterien verwendet werden als in anderen Unternehmen.

Eine Verbindung zwischen Spiritualität bzw. Religion und Kreativität wird entsprechend auch von mehreren Autoren theoretisch, aus Interviews oder aus Literaturanalysen abgeleitet (u. a. Krishnakumar und Neck 2002; Luis Daniel 2010; Mitroff und Denton 1999; Gupta et al. 2014; Kudesia 2017; Neal 2013). Argumentiert wird, dass Unternehmen die volle Kreativität ihrer Mitarbeiter benötigten, um im härter werdenden Wettbewerb zu überleben, aber diese Kreativität sei ohne das Empfinden von Sinn am Arbeitsplatz in der Regel nicht zu haben (vgl. zu dieser Argumentation Neal 2013; Ashmos und Duchon 2000). Trifft diese These zu, so würde man mit steigendem Empfinden von Sinn am Arbeitplatz als Teilbereich der Arbeitsplatzspiritualität auch höhere Leistungen der Beschäftigten in kreativen Beschäftigungsfeldern beobachten, so dass eine weitere zentrale personalwirtschaftliche Outcome-Variable angesprochen ist. Z. B. fand Freshman (1999) im Rahmen einer Analyse mittels der Grounded Theory Zusammenhänge zwischen Spiritualität am Arbeitsplatz, Achtsamkeit/Bewusstsein, Intuition und Kreativität. Zysberg und Schenk (2013) konnten im Rahmen einer explorativen Faktorenanalyse Religion als einen erklärenden Faktor von Kreativität ausmachen. Duchon und Plowman

(2005) fanden in Unternehmen in den USA entsprechend eine höhere Produktivität in Abteilungen, die Spiritualität ermöglichen. Dabei kommt auch der Führung ein entscheidender Anteil zu, indem sie Aspekte von Sinn und Gemeinschaft vermittelt (Duchon und Plowman 2005).[4] Faro Albuquerque et al. (2014) konnten ähnliche Zusammenhänge im europäischen Kulturkreis bei einer Untersuchung im Gesundheitswesen in Portugal 2008 feststellen. In Literaturanalysen und Zusammenstellungen (u. a. Karakas 2010; Garcia-Zamor 2003; Luis Daniel 2010; Giacalone und Jurkiewicz 2003; Houghton et al. 2016) werden eine Vielzahl weiterer Untersuchungen zum Zusammenhang von Spiritualität und Performance vorgestellt, wobei die große Mehrheit der Studien ähnliche Zusammenhänge wie bei Douchon, Plowman und Albuquerque konstatiert. Insgesamt ist die empirische Basis dieses Zusammenhangs jedoch sehr schmal (Houghton et al. 2016).

Angesichts des *War-for-Talents* und eines in vielen Bereichen verschärften Fachkräftemangels reicht es heute *siebtens* für viele Unternehmen nicht mehr, sich auf die bloße Aktivierung der stillen Reserve der Frauen mit Familienpflichten und die längere Gesunderhaltung von Mitarbeitern in der zweiten Lebenshälfte zu konzentrieren, um ihren Personalbedarf zu decken. Diese Maßnahmen werden zwar weiterhin erforderlich sein, greifen aber möglicherweise zu kurz: Der Fachkräftemangel, Flüchtlingswellen und überall in der Welt lodernde Konflikte (die häufig zumindest auch als Religionskonflikte interpretiert oder geframt werden) führen zu der Frage, ob personalstrukturelle Strategieüberlegungen Bewerber- und Arbeitnehmergruppen mit unterschiedlichen Religionen und spirituellen Ausrichtungen adressieren müssen. Unterschiedliche ethnische Zugehörigkeiten und eine spezifische religiös-spirituelle Prägung von Menschen werden häufig genauso Hand in Hand gehen wie die Landeskultur in vielen Ländern auch durch die vorherrschende Religion geprägt ist. Der Versuch einer systematischen Fokussierung aller möglicherweise relevanten Gruppen von potenziellen und vorhandenen Mitarbeitern müsste also wohl zumindest eine explizite Entscheidung hinsichtlich dieser Fragen beinhalten. Man könnte daher erwarten, dass in Organisationen mit beson-

---

4 Zudem ist Spiritualität ggf. auch ein Element gesundheitsförderlicher Führung, vgl. Felfe/Klug (2019) in diesem Band.

ders starkem Fachkräftemangel Spiritualität und Religion eher als Themenfelder berücksichtigt werden.

Im Kontext einer Untersuchung zu religiöser Vielfalt am Arbeitsplatz in Deutschland wurden tatsächlich in einigen befragten Unternehmen Maßnahmen zur Förderung von religiöser Vielfalt mit der besonderen Ansprache von Migranten als Arbeitnehmern in Verbindung gebracht (Antidiskriminierungsstelle des Bundes 2016). Gyo (2016) sieht in der Migration eine Chance zur Bewältigung des Fachkräftemangels in Deutschland einerseits, sieht aber auch potentielle Spannungsfelder zwischen Arbeitsanforderungen und religiösen Vorschriften: Er berichtet über Konflikte um Arbeitsverweigerungen wegen des Umgangs mit Schweinefleisch oder bei der Pflege von Patienten des anderen Geschlechts (Gyo 2016). Diese Befunde zu betriebsrelevanten Chancen und Spannungsfeldern unterstützen die Empfehlungen zur expliziten Adressierung von Fragen der Religion und Spiritualität in der Personalarbeit.

Achtens wurden im Gefolge der Finanz- und Wirtschaftskrise zu Beginn dieses Jahrtausends zahlreiche Debatten um unverantwortliches Handeln in den Management- und Führungsebenen, um die Rolle von Gier und unmäßigen Renditeansprüchen als Auslöser der Krise, um das Eingehen überhöhter Risiken sowie die Privatisierung von Gewinnen bei Sozialisierung von Risiken geführt. Hiermit sind durchweg ethische Fragen sowie Fragen rund um Anreizsysteme und die Sozialisation von Personal angesprochen. Wenig überraschend boomen denn auch Ansätze einer *wertorientierten Unternehmensführung*. Dass jedoch die Herkunft und der Inhalt von Werten auf individueller Ebene sehr häufig eng mit Spiritualität und Religion verbunden sind, lässt sich gar nicht übersehen. Mit welchen Werten eine wertorientierte Unternehmensführung agiert bzw. inhaltlich gefüllt wird, wird vermutlich von der im Umfeld vorherrschenden Religion und/oder der religiös-spirituellen Ausrichtung der Unternehmensgründer, Eigentümer oder leitenden Führungskräfte mit beeinflusst.

In Unternehmen spielt auch Moral (als eng verwandter Begriff zu Werten und Ethik) durch interne und externe Stakeholder (z. B. Management und Kunden) und deren moralische Prägung potentiell eine Rolle (Aguilera et al. 2007). Ursprünge solcher (moralischen) Vorstellungen können wertebasierte Glaubenssysteme sein, welche unter anderem Religion einschließen (Cropanzano et al. 2003). Gümüsay (2017) zeigt in diesem Kontext die möglichen Einflüsse institutioneller Logik von Religionen (z. B. Glaubens- und Wertesysteme) auf Unternehmen sowie den Prozess, durch den die Beeinflussung der unternehmensinstitutionellen Logik zustande kommt, auf. Breite empirische Untersuchungen zur Herkunft von Unternehmenswerten liegen nach unserem Kenntnisstand nicht vor.

Im engen Zusammenhang mit unternehmensethischen Fragen ergeben sich *neuntens* analog auch *arbeitsethische Verbindungslinien*. Denn es geht ja bei den Diskussionen um die Wirtschaftskrisen und ihre Auslöser und Folgen nicht nur um das Verhalten der oberen Führungskräfte oder des Managements, sondern auch um die Frage, wie andere Mitarbeitergruppen mit Risiken oder Entscheidungskonflikten umgehen und welche zentralen Motive und Werte hinter ihrem Verhalten liegen. Nicht zufällig boomen Compliance-Themen gerade auch im praxisorientierten Schrifttum. Die Frage also, ob und mit welcher Motivation Mitarbeiter sich an Regeln halten, welche Regeln sie akzeptieren und aus vollem Herzen mittragen und welche Regeln sie zu umgehen versuchen, hängt nicht zuletzt wohl auch von ihrer *Arbeitsethik* ab. Und spätestens seit Max Webers Arbeiten zur protestantischen – genauer: calvinistischen – Arbeitsethik wird immer wieder diskutiert, ob arbeitsethische Einstellungen großer Bevölkerungsteile möglicherweise von der im Lande vorherrschenden oder bei der Erziehung eingeprägten Religion mit abhängen können (vgl. zu einem Überblick auch Miller und Ewest 2013) – und ggf. auch ein Beitrag zu einer hohen, vielleicht unter gesundheitlichen Gesichtspunkten auch übersteigerten Produktivität sind. Während uns aber das Stichwort »protestantische Arbeitsethik« noch vergleichsweise geläufig ist und sich mithilfe einer kurzen Internetrecherche schnell und leicht mit wenigstens kursorischem Inhalt füllen lässt, gilt dies nicht für verwandte Schlagworte zum Beispiel zu islamischer oder jüdischer Arbeitsethik – und erst recht nicht für entsprechende Suchworte zu kleineren und nicht-monotheistischen Religionen (vgl. aber die Beiträge zur Arbeitsethik unterschiedlicher Religionen in Neal 2013, Teil 2: Miller und Ewest 2013 zum Christentum, Lurie 2013 zum Judentum, Al Arkoubi 2013 zum Islam, Lips-Wiersma 2013 zum Baha'i, Spiller und Stockdale 2013 zur Maori-Perspektive, Miley und Read 2013 zur indigenen Spiritualität Australiens). Auch hier zeigt sich die potenzielle Relevanz religiöser Fragen in Bezug auf personalwirtschaftliche Aspekte, bei gleichzeitig vermutlich nur rudimentär ausgeprägtem systematischem Hintergrundwissen von Personalern und Führungskräften zu diesen Fragen.

Empirisch ergibt die Frage, ob Religion Einfluss auf arbeitsethisches Verhalten bzw. auf die Arbeitswerte (als Manifestation von Arbeitsethik) hat, ein uneinheitliches Bild (Parboteeah et al. 2008; Weaver und Agle 2002). Neuere Forschungen festigen jedoch den Eindruck eines Zusammenhangs zwischen Religion und Arbeitswerten. Parboteeah et al. (2009a) leiten theoretisch Auswirkungen auf Arbeitswerte aus Arbeitsethiken bzw. Werteaussagen der großen Religionen Christentum, Islam, Hinduismus und Buddhismus ab und testen diese anschließend empirisch in einer internationalen Studie. Sie finden unterschiedliche Einflüsse der großen Religionen auf intrinsische Arbeitswerte (u. a. sinnvoller Arbeit nachgehen und einen Beitrag zur Gesellschaft leisten) und extrinsische Arbeitswerte (Sicherheit des Arbeitsplatzes und Erfolg). In einer weiteren internationalen Studie stellen Parboteeah et al. (2009b) einen grundsätzlich positiven Effekt von Religion auf das Pflichtbewusstsein von Arbeitnehmern in Bezug auf ihre Arbeit fest. Darüber hinaus gibt es Evidenz zum Zusammenhang von spezifischen Arbeitsethiken und arbeitsrelevanten Werten und Normen mit religiöser Prägung: Unter anderem stellen Murtaza et al. (2016) einen positiven Effekt islamischer Arbeitsethik auf Organizational Citizenship Behavior fest oder Furnham (1984) und Jones (1997) fassen Evidenzen zu Auswirkungen der protestantischen Arbeitsethik auf eine Vielzahl von arbeitsrelevanten Charakteristika zusammen.

Zehntens tragen die viel diskutierten *charismatischen Führungsansätze* schon von ihrer Benennung her den Zusammenhang zwischen Führung und Religion in sich. Der Begriff Charisma kommt aus dem Griechischen und bedeutet so viel wie Gnadengabe, eine aus Wohlwollen dem Menschen von Gott geschenkte geistige oder geistliche Fähigkeit. Verwandte Ansätze fordern, dass Leadership visionäre Führung beinhalten und die Begeisterung der Mitarbeiter sicherstellen soll. Auch hier verweisen die Fragen, wo der Geist in der BeGEISTerung herkommt und woher die Visionen in der visionären Führung stammen, ursprünglich und vom Wortsinn her auf transzendente, über den einzelnen Menschen hinausweisende Zusammenhänge. Auch wenn diese Begriffe heute vermutlich überwiegend »entkernt« von ihrem ursprünglich religiösen Inhalt verwendet werden und dieser möglicherweise vielen Anwendern kaum noch bekannt ist, so lässt sich doch der ursprünglich spirituell geprägte Charakter der Begriffe nicht übersehen.

Diese Überlegungen zeigen, dass es zahlreiche thematische und theoretische Verbindungslinien zwischen der Personalarbeit in Unternehmen und der Religion, Religiosität und Spiritualität der Führungskräfte und der Mitarbeiter sowie eine ganze Reihe von unterstützenden empirischen Befunden überwiegend aus den angloamerikanischen und asiatischen Ländern gibt. Diese legen eine systematische Beschäftigung mit und explizite Berücksichtigung von Spiritualität, Religion und Religiosität des Personals in der Personalarbeit nahe. Allerdings lassen sich bezüglich des öffentlichen Umgangs mit Religion, Religiosität und Spiritualität große kulturelle Unterschiede zwischen verschiedenen Weltregionen vermuten, so dass damit die Relevanz für Deutschland noch nicht ausreichend belegt werden kann.

Und tatsächlich ist unser Eindruck, dass die theoretisch abgeleitete thematische Relevanz nicht umstandslos auch zu einer hohen empirischen Relevanz des Themas in Deutschland und in deutschen Unternehmen führt. Spiritualität, Religion und Religiosität am Arbeitsplatz ist ein eher unterbelichtetes Gebiet in der (deutschsprachigen) Forschung. Möglicherweise ist es auch eher ein Nicht-Thema oder sogar ein tabuisiertes Themenfeld in der großen Mehrheit der Unternehmen am Standort Deutschland. Um der Relevanz in den deutschen Unternehmen nachzuspüren, haben wir einige explorative Interviews geführt, deren Ergebnisse wir im nächsten Abschnitt vorstellen.

2.3. Erste qualitativ-empirische Befunde zu Religion, Religiosität und Spiritualität in deutschen Unternehmen

In der Forschungsgruppe, die die Erstautorin dieses Beitrags leitet, wurden im Sommer 2017 zehn qualitative Interviews mit insgesamt elf Personen (Geschäftsführern, Vorstandsmitgliedern, Personalleitern, Produktionsleitern) von Unternehmen oder Organisationen im Hamburger Raum geführt. Die Interviews waren Bestandteil der am Lehrstuhl betreuten Masterarbeit von Tobias Moll und wurden teilweise alleine von Tobias Moll, teilweise gemeinsam geführt (vgl. hierzu und auch zu allen folgenden Aussagen auch Moll 2017). Der Kontakt zu sieben Interviewten wurde über die gemeinsame Mitgliedschaft der Erstautorin und der späteren Interviewpartner im Dialog »Kirche und Wirtschaft«, der von Bischöfin Fehrs der evangelischen Nordkirche geleitet wird, angebahnt. Befragte, die über diesen Zugang gewonnen werden konnten, sind vermutlich entweder christlich-konfessionell gebunden oder doch einem Dialog zwischen Wirtschaft und Religion sowie dem Sprechen über Religion auch in der Öffentlichkeit gegenüber aufgeschlossen. Zudem wurde die Interviewanfrage über den Verteiler des kirchlichen Dienstes in der Arbeitswelt der Nordkirche versandt, darüber meldete sich ein weiterer Teilnehmer. Zu einem Interview wurde spontan der Produktionsleiter mitgebracht, ein weiteres Interview wurde über einen persönlichen Kontakt einer wissenschaftlichen Mitarbeiterin angebahnt. Von den elf interviewten Personen waren zwei weiblich. Alle gehörten entweder einer christlichen Konfession an oder waren nicht religiös-konfessionell gebunden, andere Religionen waren nicht im Sample vertreten. Insofern sind alle unsere Ergebnisse auf dem Hintergrund zu interpretieren, dass wir eine religionsnahe oder doch der christlichen Religion gegenüber offene Gruppe angesprochen und daraus unsere Teilnehmer rekrutiert haben. Die Unternehmen bzw. Organisationen gehören den Bereichen Wirtschaftsprüfung, Unternehmens- und Rechtsberatung, Versandhandel, Ver- und Entsorgung, Banken- und Verlagswesen sowie Diakonie an. Die Interviews dauerten zwischen 45 und 95 Minuten und wurden leitfadengestützt durchgeführt, später transkribiert und mit MaxQDA ausgewertet.

Die Interviews ergeben ein komplexes und teilweise auch ambivalentes Bild, was den Umgang deutscher Unternehmen und Organisationen mit Religion, Religiosität und Spiritualität angeht (vgl. ausführlicher Moll 2017).

In den Wirtschaftsunternehmen, in denen wir unsere Interviews geführt haben, wird für die Unternehmen insgesamt ganz überwiegend zunächst eine *strikte Neutralitätslinie* formuliert. Religion bleibt offiziell außerhalb des Unternehmens und wird als Privatsache der Mitarbeiter definiert, die nicht Inhalt der unternehmensbezogenen Tätigkeiten ist und sein kann bzw. sein soll. Anders sieht das in den von uns interviewten Einheiten nur in den beiden Organisationen mit religionsbezogenen Produkten oder Dienstleistungen aus, wo Religion, Religiosität und Spiritualität der Mitarbeiter explizit als wichtige Ressource angesehen und gepflegt und genutzt werden (Moll 2017). Religion und Wirtschaft werden als zwei strikt getrennte Sphären angesehen, die wenig oder gar nichts miteinander zu tun haben. Ob jemand religiös sei oder nicht, habe keine Auswirkungen auf seine fachlichen Aufgaben und deren Erledigung im Unternehmen, so eine häufig zu hörende Botschaft (Moll 2017). Die Wirtschaft sei ein komplett säkularisierter Bereich. Religion sei offiziell genauso ein Tabu-Thema im Unternehmen wie Politik, lautete die Aussage eines anderen Befragten dazu. In einem Unternehmen wurde auf die potentielle Konflikthaftigkeit von Gesprächen über Religion verwiesen, an anderer Stelle wurde angedeutet, dass man auf keinen Fall als »Apostel«, als missionarisch, oder als jemand, »an dem die Welt genesen solle«, wahrgenommen werden wolle (Moll 2017).

Diese Neutralitäts- und Trennungsperspektive auf den Zusammenhang zwischen Wirtschaftsunternehmen und Religion tritt allerdings in Kombination mit verschiedenen anderen Umgangsweisen mit Religion, Religiosität und Spiritualität auf, die die Neutralitätslinie teilweise durchbrechen und teilweise ergänzen, so dass sich insgesamt ein komplexes und teilweise auch ambivalentes Muster ergibt (Moll 2017):

- In acht von zehn Interviews fanden wir Hinweise auf *unternehmensexternes Engagement von Mitarbeitern mit Religionsbezug*, welches in vielen dieser Unternehmen entweder durchaus gern gesehen oder sogar auch *aktiv gefördert* wurde. Das Engagement reicht von direkten Projekten mit örtlichen Kirchengemeinden bis hin zum Engagement von Führungskräften in der Kirchensynode oder in Arbeitskreisen der Kirchenleitung. In einem Unternehmen aus dem Finanzsektor wurde ein unternehmensinterner Wettbewerb zum Mitarbeiter des Jahres veranstaltet, bei dem sich Mitarbeiter mit ihrem sozialen, auch religiösen Engagement außerhalb des Unternehmens bewerben können und dafür unternehmensintern ausgezeichnet werden. Die Begründung eines Vorstandsmitglieds für diesen Wettbewerb lautete, dass es aus Sicht des Unternehmens hoch erwünscht und gern gesehen sei, wenn sich Mitglieder des Unternehmens im lokalen Umfeld sozial und gesellschaftlich engagieren. Ganz ähnlich wurde in mehreren Unternehmen in Bezug auf das Engagement von Führungskräften in örtlichen Kirchengemeinden oder in Arbeitskreisen der Nordkirche argumentiert.
- Dieser positive Blick auf die Förderung des sozialen, aber auch Kirchengemeinde-bezogenen Engagements von Mitarbeitern geht bei unseren Interviewpartnern mit einer grundsätzlich positiven Haltung zu Religion und religiöser Vielfalt einher. Die positive Haltung gegenüber Religion, konkreter der christlichen Religion, wird allerdings zumindest teilweise der Methode der Rekrutierung der Gesprächspartner über den Dialog Kirche und Wirtschaft geschuldet sein. Religion wird von unseren Befragten grundsätzlich mit einem Set an positiven Werten für das Zusammenleben in einer Gesellschaft und mit der individuellen Orientierung in einer komplexer und turbulenter werdenden Welt, also auch mit individueller Resilienz, in Verbindung gebracht (Moll 2017). In einem Interview wurde berichtet, dass über Religion unter Kollegen häufig dann gesprochen werde, wenn Menschen z. B. durch Krankheit oder Tod in ihren Familien in Krisensituationen gerieten oder grundsätzliche Sinnkrisen in Bezug auf ihre Tätigkeiten durchlebten, und jeweils ihre Arbeitsfähigkeit darunter

leide. Diese Gespräche fänden aber durchweg entweder »in der Kanntine« statt – als mehr oder weniger privates Gespräch unter Kollegen nur am Rande des Arbeitskontextes. Mit dem jeweiligen Vorgesetzten dagegen spräche man darüber nicht. Oder die Gespräche fänden im Coaching-Kontext statt, wenn es darum gehe, in Krisen und an Wendepunkten neue Orientierung zu finden.

- Fast durchgängig fanden wir in den interviewten Unternehmen Hinweise auf eine *wertorientierte Unternehmensführung*. Auf die Frage nach den *Inhalten der Werte*, die zur Orientierung in der Führung des Unternehmens und der Personalführung dienen, wurden Werte (wie z. B. Nächstenliebe und Erhalt der Schöpfung und der natürlichen Lebensgrundlagen) genannt, die auch religiös sind. Teilweise wurden diese auch explizit als religiöse, genauer christliche Werte, verortet. In manchen Unternehmen wurde berichtet, dass die Werte stark durch den Gründer oder eine zentrale Führungskraft geprägt seien und es bei dieser Person individuell durchaus einen religiösen Hintergrund gegeben habe.
- Dagegen spielt die *Herkunft der Werte* aus einer religiösen Tradition in den meisten der interviewten Unternehmen keine Rolle und wird nicht thematisiert. Der Inhalt der Werte und die konsequente Orientierung an diesen Werten, damit auch die Vorbildwirkung der jeweiligen Führungskraft, seien entscheidend. In einem Unternehmen wurde weitergehend eine bezüglich der Herkunft der Werte aus dem religiösen Bereich eher negativ konnotierte Auffassung vertreten, nach der es eine große Aversion im Unternehmen dagegen gäbe, überhaupt anzuerkennen, dass wir in einem christlich geprägten Land lebten, das Christentum die Kultur (mit)geprägt habe und die Werte des Unternehmens möglicherweise christliche Werte seien (vgl. auch Moll 2017). Insgesamt ergab sich damit die Botschaft, dass zwar christliche Werte teilweise gelebt werden, aber eher ihr Inhalt als ihre religiöse Einbettung relevant seien und letztere auch nicht so benannt werde (und wohl auch nicht so benannt werden dürfe, wolle man nicht Widerstand im Unternehmen dagegen aktivieren).

In Bezug auf den nicht-religiösen Bereich der Spiritualität finden wir sehr viel eindeutigere Aussagen.

- Angebote zu spirituellen Praktiken und Techniken, wie z. B. Yoga und Meditation oder Achtsamkeitstrainings, werden in einigen der

Unternehmen gemacht. Sie werden aber häufig nicht mit dem Themenfeld Spiritualität in Verbindung gebracht, sondern eher als Teil des allgemeinen Gesundheits- und Sportprogramms der Unternehmen interpretiert (vgl. auch Moll 2017).

- Spiritualität wird in einen positiven Argumentationszusammenhang mit Stress- und Burnoutprophylaxe gebracht.Teilweise geschieht dies in unspezifizierter Form, teilweise wird der Zusammenhang darüber begründet, dass Spiritualität dabei helfen könne, die Fragen nach Sinn und Wert der eigenen Arbeit sowie nach der Bedeutung auch in einem umfassenderen Kontext zu beantworten, und diese Faktoren zu einer höheren Resilienz gegenüber hoher Arbeitsbelastung oder widrigen Umständen beitragen (vgl. auch Moll 2017).

Auffällig ist der Unterschied in den grundsätzlichen Haltungen zu Religion bzw. Religiosität auf der einen Seite und Spiritualität auf der anderen Seite: Spiritualität wird durchgängig eher positiv konnotiert, wird auf der rein individuellen Ebene verortet und mit positiven individuellen Wirkungen in Bezug auf Gesundheit und Belastbarkeit verbunden. Probleme mit der Privatsphäre oder dem Schutz dieses sensiblen Persönlichkeitsbereiches werden hier kaum thematisiert, da Spiritualität ohnehin als individuell auszulebender Persönlichkeitsbereich angesehen wird. Es ist auch in unseren Interviews nicht erkennbar, dass die Unternehmen sich von Spiritualität am Arbeitsplatz offiziell abgrenzen möchten oder müssten, z. B. in Form einer Neutralitätsaussage. Dagegen wird Religion eher auch im kollektiven Bereich verortet und eine abgrenzende Neutralitätsaussage wird von den meisten der Befragten für ihre Organisation, ihr Unternehmen (mit Ausnahme der beiden kirchennahen Organisationen) getätigt. Religion bzw. Religiosität am Arbeitsplatz zu berücksichtigen, dagegen gibt es durchaus Bedenken. Diese haben mit potentieller Missionierung oder ideologischen Manipulation von Mitarbeitern, mit Diskriminierung oder Ungleichbehandlung verschiedener religiöser Gruppen und der Konflikthaftigkeit religiöser Fragen, wenn diese kollektiv diskutiert werden, zu tun. Man kann diese Befunde möglicherweise so interpretieren, dass bei Spiritualität (im Sinne nicht-religiöser Spiritualität) die Wahrnehmung und Hoffnung besteht, dass diese auf individueller Ebene eine nützliche Ressource für den einzelnen Mitarbeiter sein kann, während Religiosität über das an die Religion gebundene auch kollektive Element eher auch mit kollektiv negativen Auswirkungen verbunden wird.

Schließlich liegen uns auf der Ebene konkreter Maßnahmen und Einrichtungen einige Befunde zu Religion und Spiritualität am Arbeitsplatz vor (Moll 2017):

- In fast allen der von uns befragten Unternehmen und Organisationen gibt es Aussagen entweder zur Nutzung von Yoga oder von Tai Chi und von Achtsamkeitstrainings. Andere Unternehmen könnten sich das Angebot durchaus vorstellen oder planen es. In einem Fall wird jedem Mitarbeiter ein Betrag von 500 Euro pro Jahr zur Verfügung gestellt, der für Gesundheitsmaßnahmen ausgegeben werden kann, also auch für Yoga und Tai Chi und verwandte Angebote. Häufig gibt es dabei eine Kostenteilung zwischen dem Unternehmen und den Mitarbeitern – diese stellen ihre Freizeit zur Verfügung, das Unternehmen stellt Räumlichkeiten und Trainer.
- Andachts- und Gebetsräume oder Räume der Stille sind eher die Ausnahme. Diese gibt es in drei der von uns befragten Organisationen, darunter die beiden kirchennahen, die je einen christlichen Andachtsraum haben, und ein Wirtschaftsunternehmen, welches über einen muslimischen Gebetsraum verfügt. Jedoch gibt es in drei weiteren Unternehmen Co-Working-Spaces oder allgemeine räumliche Rückzugsmöglichkeiten, die für ein individuelles »In-sich-Gehen« genutzt werden können.
- Religiöse Ernährungsge- und -verbote sind nur in zwei der befragten Unternehmen ein explizites Thema (Moll 2017). Das muslimische Verbot, Schweinefleisch zu essen, wird in einem Unternehmen dadurch berücksichtigt, dass generell in der Kantine ein vegetarisches Gericht angeboten wird. Es gibt also keine spezielle religionsbezogene Regelung und auch keine umfassende Berücksichtigung aller religionsbezogener Speisevorschriften. Sondern die Ernährungsbedürfnisse von Vegetariern und Muslimen werden gemeinsam und rudimentär dadurch berücksichtigt, dass eine der Speisen zur Auswahl kein Fleisch enthält. Im Übrigen orientiert sich aber das Angebot an den Speisegewohnheiten der (vermuteten) Mehrheit von atheistischen und christlichen Mitarbeitern.
- Es wird nur von wenigen Konflikten um Ernährungsfragen berichtet. Eine Befragte erzählte von expliziten Konflikten um die Ernährungsregelungen im Ramadan bei einem früheren Arbeitgeber. Dort gab es Arbeitsplätze, an denen unter großer Hitzeeinwirkung gearbeitet werden musste. Während des Ramadans kam es zur Dehydrierung von

muslimischen Mitarbeitern, die trotz Aufforderung des Betriebsarztes, wie in anderen Zeiten auch ausreichend zu trinken, tagsüber keine Flüssigkeit zu sich nahmen. Aus einem weiteren Unternehmen wird berichtet, dass das Unternehmen zu einem sommerlichen Grillfest einlud, woraufhin muslimische Mitarbeiter darum baten, auf Kosten des Unternehmens halal-Fleisch mitbringen zu dürfen. Das Unternehmen lehnte die Kostenübernahme ab. Dies wurde im Interview damit begründet, dass man wegen des Gleichbehandlungsgebots gar nicht erst in die Genehmigung von essensbezogenen Sonder- und Einzelwünschen zu der Betriebsfeier habe einsteigen wollen.

- In Bezug auf religiöse Feste, Feiern und Feiertag(sgebräuch)e gilt, dass die deutliche Mehrheit der von uns befragten Unternehmen und Organisationen Weihnachtsfeiern veranstalten und häufig auch Weihnachtskarten mit Weihnachtswünschen verschicken. Die generell favorisierte strikte Neutralitätsperspektive wird also in diesem Aspekt nicht so ausgelegt, dass jeder Religionsbezug vermieden wird und demzufolge »Jahres-« oder »Saisonabschlussfeiern« veranstaltet oder nach angloamerikanischem Vorbild »seasonal greetings« verschickt werden. Auf Nachfrage wurde der Bezug auf das christlich-religiöse Element »Weihnachten« bisweilen auch vehement verteidigt und sinngemäß als Teil der deutschen Leitkultur interpretiert (Moll 2017).
- Andachten und andere kollektive religiöse Rituale wurden uns nur aus den beiden kirchennahen Organisationen berichtet. Lediglich ein Befragter aus Wirtschaftsunternehmen berichtete über einen inoffiziellen, aber in den Räumen des Unternehmens stattfindenden Gebetskreis, und zwei Befragte über die Möglichkeit, die die Unternehmen muslimischen Mitarbeitern gewähren, sich in einer Pause nach Absprache mit den jeweiligen Vorgesetzen »in irgendeine Ecke« oder einen freien Raum im Unternehmen zum Gebet zurückzuziehen. Was allerdings die Arbeitszeitflexibilität angeht, betonten sechs Unternehmen, dass in allen religiösen Fragen bei der Urlaubs- und Pausengewährung möglichst viel Flexibilität für die Mitarbeiter gewährt werde – im Rahmen der allgemeinen Arbeitszeitregelungen.
- Zum Thema Kleidung und Schmuck mit Religionsbezug äußerten sich die Befragten eher ambivalent. Betont wurde z. B., dass man »glücklicherweise« noch keine größeren Konflikte um diese Fragen habe regeln müssen. Einige Befragte wiesen darauf hin, dass die rechtlichen Regelungen dazu führten, dass das Tragen von Kopftüchern oder von Kreuzen als religiösen Symbolen in der Regel zu tolerieren sei – meh-

rere Befragte ließen aber als ihre persönliche Einzelmeinung erkennen, dass sie große Schwierigkeiten damit hätten, eine Person mit Kopftuch einzustellen oder mit ihr zusammenzuarbeiten. Insgesamt wurde deutlich, dass Bekleidungs- und Schmuckregelungen ein viel diskutiertes Thema mit derzeit aber offenbar noch geringer praktischer Alltagsrelevanz in deutschen Unternehmen sind.

Wir stellen also insgesamt fest, dass entgegen der Erwartung einer gewissen Relevanz von Religion und Spiritualität am Arbeitsplatz der Standard jedenfalls in den wenigen von uns interviewten Unternehmen eher noch dort zu liegen scheint, wo Religion ein Tabu ist und kaum angesprochen wird und werden kann. Die Gründe für diese Kluft zwischen den Erwartungen und den Befunden sind noch gründlich zu eruieren. Jedoch sind aus unserer Sicht verschiedene Ansatzpunkte denkbar:

- Es könnte sein, dass Teilaspekte von Spiritualität und Religion in den Unternehmen durchaus gelebt werden, aber unter anderen Begriffen behandelt werden – und nicht als Ausdruck von Spiritualität und Religion interpretiert werden. So werden vielleicht Yoga und Meditation unter Gesundheitssport verortet und im Gesundheitsmanagement eingeordnet. Oder das Ringen um die eigene Berufung und den Sinn am Arbeitsplatz wird im Rahmen eines individuellen Coachings behandelt und damit in den Bereich der Personalentwicklung eingeordnet.
- Fraglich ist für uns auch, welche Zuschreibungen bzw. Attributionen Religions- und Glaubensfragen im betrieblichen Kontext auslösen. Glaube mit seinen stark emotionalen Komponenten wird möglicherweise als Gegensatz zu oder als unvereinbar mit Rationalität und Wissen interpretiert. Und ein Mensch, der seinem Gott das letzte Wort im eigenen Leben überlässt, wird möglicherweise als jemand wahrgenommen, der nicht genauso glatt in einer Hierarchie funktioniert wie ein anderer Mensch, der sich keiner höheren Macht außerhalb des Betriebes unterstellt sieht. Gibt es solche Zuschreibungen, so beschädigt potentiell ein Individuum, welches sich als gläubig outet, seine oder ihre Reputation in Bezug auf Rationalität, Durchsetzungstärke, Verhandlungsfähigkeit, Loyalität in einer Hierarchie und Planungsfähigkeit. Mit anderen Worten könnte das Rollenstereotyp von Managern mit dem Stereotyp des gläubigen Menschen in Konflikt stehen.
- Möglicherweise überwiegt die Interpretation von Religion als einem sehr konflikthaften Themenfeld, welches die Zusammenarbeit und den

Betriebsfrieden stören kann und deswegen lieber tabuisiert wird. Oder die individuelle Spiritualität wird als privates, sensibles und zu schützendes Feld definiert, in welches das Unternehmen nicht eindringen sollte.

- Religion als zunächst unsichtbares Merkmal einer Person müsste zunächst offen gelegt werden am Arbeitsplatz, bevor es systematisch berücksichtigt werden kann. Hier unterscheidet sich Religion z. B. von anderen, häufiger verwendeten Diversitätskriterien wie Alter und Geschlecht, die sichtbar sind und damit offen zu Tage treten. Genau dieser Akt des individuellen Offenlegens von Religion kann aber möglicherweise schon als eine missionarische Handlung verstanden werden, mit der das Individuum andere in unzulässiger Weise bedrängt (vgl. auch Gebert et al. 2014).

3. Forschungsbedarf und Perspektiven

Dass auf den ersten Blick die Hypothese von der potentiellen Relevanz von Spiritualität, Religion und Religiosität am Arbeitsplatz und damit für das personalwirtschaftliche Handeln der Unternehmen für Deutschland nicht unterstützt werden kann, löst Fragen auf verschiedenen Ebenen aus:

- Generell stellt sich die Frage, ob die im angloamerikanischen Sprach- und Kulturraum formulierte Hypothese von der Relevanz von Religion und Spiritualität am Arbeitsplatz (auch) für Deutschland mit seiner anders gelagerten und in Bezug auf Religionsfragen zurückhaltenderen Kultur (Pickel 2013) gilt?
- Finden wir (Teil-)aspekte von Spiritualität und Religion im individuellen oder betrieblichen Handeln in deutschen Unternehmen?
- Sind Spiritualität und Religion zwar im personalwirtschaftlichen Handeln verortet, aber werden ggf. unter anderen Begriffen anderen Bereichen zugeordnet? Finden sich z. B. Meditation und Yoga als Betriebssport im Bereich des Gesundheitsmanagements oder charismatische Führung im Bereich des Führungstrainings und die Suche nach Sinn im Rahmen der Karriereplanung?
- Fragen wir nach der normativen Relevanz bzw. nach der Erwünschtheit und Akzeptanz von Spiritualität und Religion am Arbeitsplatz aus der Perspektive verschiedener Beteiligter, so lohnt ein Blick darauf, welche Bedeutung Religion, Religiosität und Spiritualität an den Ar-

beitsplätzen aus Sicht der in den Unternehmen relevanten Gruppen (z. B. des Arbeitgebers, der Arbeitnehmer, der Betriebsräte) genau haben (vgl. zum folgenden auch Benefiel et al. 2014): Sind Religion, Religiosität und Spiritualität aus Sicht der Unternehmensleitungen und/oder HR-Abteilungen in erster Linie private und möglicherweise auch konfliktträchtige Felder, die man zur Vermeidung von Konflikten am Arbeitsplatz soweit möglich aus dem Arbeitsleben ausblenden sollte oder werden sie als Ressource betrachtet, die das Wohlbefinden und/oder das Sozial- und Extrarollenverhalten und/oder die Leistungen der Arbeitnehmer beeinflussen?
Stellen Religiosität und Spiritualität in der Perspektive der Arbeitnehmer am Arbeitsplatz relevante und nach Möglichkeit dort auch zu befriedigende humane Bedürfnisse dar (vgl. auch Case und Gosling 2010)? Streben Arbeitnehmer die Integration von spirituellen Bedürfnissen in das Arbeitsleben an? Oder lehnen sie eine solche Integration ab und betrachten Religion und Spiritualität als gut zu schützende Privatangelegenheit?

Neben den grundsätzlichen Interessen der verschiedenen Gruppen stellen sich die Fragen nach Instrumenten und ihren Wirkungen:

- Welche Instrumente, Praktiken, Verhaltensweisen oder Konzeptionen sind mit Religion und Spiritualität am Arbeitsplatz ggf. verbunden? Wie werden diese Aspekte am Arbeitsplatz konkret sichtbar? Welche Instrumente, Praktiken, Verhaltensweisen oder Konzeptionen sind wie bzw. in welchen Unternehmen oder an welchen Typen von Arbeitsplätzen in welchem Ausmaß verbreitet?
- Welche Wirkungen des Einsatzes von religions- oder spiritualitätsbezogenen Instrumenten oder Praktiken oder der Implementierung von Konzeptionen auf personalwirtschaftliche Outcomes auf Arbeitgeber- und Arbeitnehmerseite sind zu beobachten? Wovon hängen diese Wirkungen möglicherweise ab, wodurch werden sie moderiert oder mediiert?
- Werden Spiritualität, Religiosität und Religion der Arbeitnehmer im personalwirtschaftlichen Handeln instrumentalisiert, um Unternehmensziele zu erreichen? Wenn ja, wie ist das zu bewerten (vgl. z. B. auch Saks 2011; Vandenberghe 2011; kritisch Case und Gosling 2010)?

- Welche Einflussfaktoren moderieren oder mediieren die entsprechenden Zusammenhänge?

Um diese Fragen zu beantworten, sind aktuelle empirische Daten für Deutschland vonnöten, die es bisher nur in sehr rudimentärer Form bzw. gar nicht gibt. Solche Daten zu erheben, setzt erstens die nähere Bestimmung der Begriffe Religion, Religiosität und Spiritualität am Arbeitsplatz für den deutschen Sprach- und Kulturraum voraus (vgl. auch Case und Gosling 2010) und zweitens die valide und reliable Operationalisierung und Messung von Variablen zu Religion, Spiritualität und Religiosität (vgl. auch Zwingmann et al. 2011). Darauf aufbauend ergeben sich als wesentliche weitere Teilschritte die Identifikation und ggf. Anpassung von für den deutschen Sprach- und Kulturraum geeigneten Skalen und Messinstrumenten zur Erfassung von Variablen zu Religion, Religiosität und Spiritualität in quantitativen empirischen Untersuchungen, die Durchführung und Auswertung einer größeren empirischen Befragung von deutschen Unternehmen und Arbeitnehmern zur Bedeutung, Relevanz und den (potentiellen, erwarteten, tatsächlichen) Wirkungen von Religion und Spiritualität am Arbeitsplatz.

4. Ausblick: Religion, Religiosität und Spiritualität und die »Standards Guter Arbeit«

»Gute Arbeit« wird arbeitnehmerseitig immer auch mit Bezug auf die menschlichen Bedürfnisse, die Menschen mit an den Arbeitsplatz bringen und deren Befriedigung am Arbeitsplatz sie sich wünschen, erhoffen oder erwarten, definiert. Gehören zu diesen Bedürfnissen auch spirituell-religiöse Bedürfnisse, so ist deren Ausprägung bei verschiedenen Arbeitnehmergruppen ebenso wie das Maß ihrer Befriedigung am Arbeitsplatz eine für die Thematik »Standards Guter Arbeit« relevante Fragestellung. Spirituelle Bedürfnisse richten sich auf den Sinn der eigenen Tätigkeit und die Einbindung in ein größeres Ganzes sowie in transzendente, das eigene Ich übersteigende Zusammenhänge. Erwerbsarbeit und Lebenssinn ebenso wie Erwerbsarbeit und gesellschaftliche Teilhabe und Integration werden immer schon im engen Zusammenhang miteinander diskutiert (vgl. Opaschowski 1983, Hardering et al. 2016). Insofern liegt der Gedanke nicht fern, dass spirituelle (und religiöse) Bedürfnisse von Menschen auch am Arbeitsplatz relevant sind und mitdefinieren können, wodurch Gute

Arbeit für Menschen bestimmt wird. Ob und wie auf Religion und Spiritualität bezogene Standards Guter Arbeit in Deutschland ausgeprägt sind, ist aber bisher kaum untersucht. Zu vermuten ist, dass eine breite Gruppe von Einflussfaktoren dazu führen kann, dass sich diese Standards verändern. Hierzu gehören Veränderungen in den Arbeitstätigkeiten, in der Gesellschaft, in der Zusammensetzung von Arbeitskräfte- und Bewerbergruppen, Fachkräftemangel, aber auch gesamtgesellschaftliche Entwicklungen. Weiterhin ist fraglich, wie in dem normativen (arbeits- und datenschutz-)rechtlichen Rahmen, in dem die Unternehmen in Deutschland handeln, Religion, Religiosität und Spiritualität am Arbeitsplatz im Spannungsfeld zwischen Religionsfreiheit, Persönlichkeitsrechten und Diskriminierungsgefahren gehandhabt werden und werden können (vgl. auch Alewell und Rastetter 2019 und Rastetter in diesem Band). Es besteht damit breiter und grundlegender Forschungsbedarf in diesem Feld.

Literaturverzeichnis

Aguilera, R. V., D. E. Rupp, C. A. Williams und J. Ganapathi. 2007. Putting The S Back in Corporate Social Responsebility: A multilevel Theory of Social Change in Oraginzations. In: *Academy of Management Review* 32 (3): 836–863. Doi: 10.5465/AMR. 2007.25275678.

Al Arkoubi, Khadija. 2013. The Islamic Faith: Implications for Business Management. In: *Handbook of Faith and Spirituality in the Workplace*, Hrsg. Judi Neal, 103–118. New York, NY: Springer New York.

Alewell, Dorothea und Karla Louise Brinck. 2018. Generationsunterschiede inden Vorstellungen über »gute Arbeit« – Fakt oder Fiktion? In: *Die Zukunft des Personalmanagements: Herausforderungen, Lösungsansätze und Gestaltungsoptionen*, Hrsg. Heike Surrey und Victor A. Tiberius, 79–91. Zürich: vdf.

Alewell, Dorothea und Daniela Rastetter. 2018. *Religious Diversity: A topical subject for German Firms' HR and diversity management?* Unveröffentlichtes Manuskript, Hamburg.

Allen, Timmy D. und E. Layne Paddock. 2017. How beeing mindful impacts individuals' work-family balance, conflict, and enrichment: a review of existing evidence, mechanisms and future directions. In: *Mindfulness in organizations: Foundations, research, and applications*, Hrsg. Jochen Reb und Paul W.B. Atkins, 213–238. Cambridge: Cambridge University Press.

Altaf, Amal und Mohammad Atif Awan. 2011. Moderating Affect of Workplace Spirituality on the Relationship of Job Overload and Job Satisfaction. In: *Journal of Business Ethics* 104 (1): 93–99. Doi: 10.1007/s10551-011-0891-0.

Ashmos, Donde P. und Dennis Duchon. 2000. Spirituality at Work: A Conceptualization and Measure. In: *Journal of Management Inquiry* 9 (2), 134–145.

Benefiel, Margaret, Louis W. Fry und David Geigle. 2014. Spirituality and religion in the workplace: History, theory, and research. In: *Psychology of Religion and Spirituality* 6 (3): 175–187. Doi: 10.1037/a0036597.

Busch, Christine und Tim Vahle-Hinz. 2019. Gesundheit und Wohlbefinden in einer Arbeitswelt im Wandel: Aufrechterhaltung von Standards guter Arbeit bei multikulturellen Belegschaften und flexibler Arbeit. In: Alewell, Dorothea und Wenzel Matiaske (Hrsg.) *Standards Guter Arbeit – disziplinäre Positionen und interdisziplinäre Perspektiven*. Baden-Baden: Nomos, 39–61.

Case, Peter und Jonathan Gosling. 2010. The spiritual organization: Critical reflections on the instrumentality of workplace spirituality. In: *Journal of Management, Spirituality & Religion* 7 (4): 257–282. Doi: 10.1080/14766086.2010.524727.

Clausen, Thomas und Vilhelm Borg. 2011. Job demands, job resources and meaning at work. In: *Journal of Managerial Psychology* 26 (8): 665–681. Doi: 10.1108/026839 41111181761.

Crawford, Alleah, Susan S. Hubbard, Steven R. Lonis-Shumate und Martin O'Neill. 2009. Workplace Spirituality and Employee Attitudes within the Lodging Environment. In: *Journal of Human Resources in Hospitality & Tourism* 8 (1): 64–81. Doi: 10.1080/15332840802274445.

Cropanzano, Russell, Barry Goldman und Robert Folger. 2003. Deontic justice: The role of moral principles in workplace fairness. In: *Journal of Organizational Behavior* 24 (8): 1019–1024. Doi: 10.1002/job.228.

Deutsche Gesellschaft für Personalführung e. V. (DGFP). 2011. Zwischen Anspruch und Wirklichkeit Generation Y finden, fördern und binden: Generation Y finden, fördern und binden. Düsseldorf. *PraxisPapier* 9.

Duchon, Dennis und Donde Ashmos Plowman. 2005. Nurturing the spirit at work: Impact on work unit performance. In: *The Leadership Quarterly* 16 (5): 807–833. Doi: 10.1016/j.leaqua.2005.07.008.

Faro Albuquerque, Isabel, Rita Campos Cunha, Luís Dias Martins und Armando Brito Sá. 2014. Primary health care services: Workplace spirituality and organizational performance. In: *Journal of Organizational Change Management* 27 (1): 59–82. Doi: 10.1108/JOCM-11-2012-0186.

Felfe, Jörg und Katharina Klug. 2019. Leadership – State of the Art and a Research Agenda. In: Alewell, Dorothea und Wenzel Matiaske (Hrsg.) *Standards Guter Arbeit – disziplinäre Positionen und interdisziplinäre Perspektiven*. Baden-Baden: Nomos, 19–37.

Freshman, B. 1999. An Exploratory Analysis of Definitions and Applications of Spirituality in the Workplace. In: *Journal of Organizational Change Management* 12 (4): 318–329.

Fry, Louis W. 2003. Toward a theory of spiritual leadership. In: *The Leadership Quarterly* 14 (6): 693–727. Doi: 10.1016/j.leaqua.2003.09.001.

Furnham, A. 1984. The protestant work ethic: A review of the psychological literature. In: *European Journal of Social Psychology* 14 (1): 87–104. Doi: 10.1002/ejsp.2420 140108.

Garcia-Zamor, Jean-Claude. 2003. Workplace Spirituality and Organizational Performance. In: *Public Administration Review* 63 (3): 355–363. Doi: 10.1111/1540-6210.00295.

Garg, Naval. 2017. Workplace Spirituality and Employee Well-being: An Empirical Exploration. In: *Journal of Human Values* 23 (2): 129–147. Doi: 10.1177/09716858 16689741.

Gebert, Diether, Sabine Boerner, Eric Kearney, James E. King, Kai Zhang und Lynda Jiwen Song. 2014. Expressing religious identities in the workplace: Analyzing a neglected diversity dimension. In: *Human Relations* 67 (5): 543–563. Doi: 10.1177/001 8726713496830.

Giacalone, R. A. und C. L. Jurkiewicz (Hrsg.). 2003. *The handbook of workplace spirituality and organizational performance.* New York: Armonk.

Greenleaf, Robert K. 1991. *Servant Leadership: A Journey into the Nature of Legitimate Power and Greatness.* New Jersey: Paulist Press.

Gümüsay, Ali A. 2017. The Potential for Plurality and Prevalence of the Religious Institutional Logic. In: *Business & Society* 14, 1–26. Doi: 10.1177/00076503177 45634.

Gunther, Marc. 2001. God and Business. In: *Fortune,* 9. Juli.

Gupta, Manu, Vinod Kumar und Mandeep Singh. 2014. Creating Satisfied Employees Through Workplace Spirituality: A Study of the Private Insurance Sector in Punjab (India). In: *Journal of Business Ethics* 122 (1), 79–88. Doi: 10.1007/s10551-013-17 56-5.

Gyo, Christoph. 2016. *Beschäftigung von Flüchtlingen.* Wiesbaden: Springer Fachmedien Wiesbaden.

Hardering, Friedericke, Mascha Will-Zocholl und Heather Hofmeister. 2016. Sinn der Arbeit und sinnvolle Arbeit: Zur Einführung. In: *Arbeit* 24 (1-2): 3–12. Doi: 10.1515/ arbeit-2016-0002.

Hauff, Sven. 2019. Human Resource Management zwischen Uniformität und Differenzierung. In: Alewell, Dorothea und Wenzel Matiaske (Hrsg.) *Standards Guter Arbeit – disziplinäre Positionen und interdisziplinäre Perspektiven.* Baden-Baden: Nomos, 65–80.

Houghton, Jeffery D., Christopher P. Neck und Sukumarakurup Krishnakumar. 2016. The what, why, and how of spirituality in the workplace revisited: A 14-year update and extension. In: *Journal of Management, Spirituality & Religion* 13 (3): 177–205. Doi: 10.1080/14766086.2016.1185292.

Jones, Harold B. 1997. The Protestant Ethic: Weber's Model and the Empirical Literature. In: *Human Relations* 50 (7), 757–778. Doi: 10.1177/001872679705000701.

Karakas, Fahri. 2010. Spirituality and Performance in Organizations: A Literature Review. In: *Journal of Business Ethics* 94 (1): 89–106. Doi: 10.1007/s10551-009-0251-5.

Koenig, Harold G. 2012. Religion, spirituality, and health: The research and clinical implications. In: *ISRN psychiatry* 2012: 278730. Doi: 10.5402/2012/278730.

Krishnakumar, Sukumarakurup und Christopher P. Neck. 2002. The »what«, »why« and »how« of spirituality in the workplace. In: *Journal of Managerial Psychology* 17 (3), 153–164. Doi: 10.1108/02683940210423060.

Kudesia, Ravi S. 2017. Mindfulness and creativity in the workplace. In: *Mindfulness in organizations: Foundations, research, and applications*, Hrsg. Jochen Reb und Paul W.B. Atkins, 190–212. Cambridge: Cambridge University Press.

Laabs, Jennifer. 1995. Balancing spirituality and work. In: *Personnel Journal* 74 (9), 60–72.

Lips-Wiersma, Marjolein. 2013. A Baha'i Perspective on the Nature and Purpose of Work. In: *Handbook of Faith and Spirituality in the Workplace*, Hrsg. Judi Neal, 119–126. New York, NY: Springer New York.

Luis Daniel, Jose. 2010. The effect of workplace spirituality on team effectiveness. In: *Journal of Management Development* 29 (5), 442–456. Doi: 10.1108/02621711011 039213.

Lurie, Alan. 2013. Faith and Spirituality in the Workplace: A Jewish Perspective. In: *Handbook of Faith and Spirituality in the Workplace*, Hrsg. Judi Neal, 85–102. New York, NY: Springer New York.

Marschke, E., R. Preziosi, W. J. Harrington. 2011. How Sales Personnel View the Relationship between Job Satisfaction and Spirituality in the Workplace. In: *Journal of Organizational Culture, Communications & Conflict* 15 (2), 71–110.

Miley, Frances und Andrew Read. 2013. Indigenous Spirituality at Work: Australia. In: *Handbook of Faith and Spirituality in the Workplace*, Hrsg. Judi Neal, 175–194. New York, NY: Springer New York.

Miller, David W. und Timothy Ewest. 2013. The Present State of Workplace Spirituality: A Literature Review Considering Context, Theory, and Measurement/Assessment. In: *Journal of Religious & Theological Information* 12 (1–2), 29–54. Doi: 10.1080/10477845.2013.800776.

Milliman, John, Andrew J. Czaplewski und Jeffery Ferguson. 2003. Workplace spirituality and employee work attitudes. In: *Journal of Organizational Change Management* 16 (4), 426–447. Doi: 10.1108/09534810310484172.

Mitroff, I. I. und E. A. Denton. 1999. A Study of Spirituality in the Workplace. In: *Sloan Management Review* 40 (4): 83–92. Doi: 10.1016/B978-1-85573-386-2.50003-3.

Moll, Tobias. 2017. Spiritualität, Religiosität und Religion am Arbeitsplatz: Eine explorative empirische Untersuchung in deutschen Unternehmen. Unveröffentlichte Masterarbeit, Universität Hamburg.

Müller, Barbara, Christoph Seibert und Oliver Vornfeld. 2019. Von Arbeit und Sinn. Analyse eines Problemfeldes. In: Alewell, Dorothea und Wenzel Matiaske (Hrsg.) *Standards Guter Arbeit – disziplinäre Positionen und interdisziplinäre Perspektiven*. Baden-Baden: Nomos, 139–173.

Murtaza, Ghulam, Muhammad Abbas, Usman Raja, Olivier Roques, Afsheen Khalid und Rizwan Mushtaq. 2016. Impact of Islamic Work Ethics on Organizational

Citizenship Behaviors and Knowledge-Sharing Behaviors. In: *Journal of Business Ethics* 133 (2): 325–333. Doi: 10.1007/s10551-014-2396-0.

Neal, Judi. 2013. Faith and Spirituality in the Workplace: Emerging Research and Practice. In: *Handbook of Faith and Spirituality in the Workplace*, Hrsg. Judi Neal, 3–18. New York, NY: Springer New York.

Neal, Judi (Hrsg.). 2013. *Handbook of Faith and Spirituality in the Workplace*. New York, NY: Springer New York.

Neubert, M. J. und K. D. Dougherty. 2013. Christian Perspectives on Faith an Work: An Empirical Exploration of Faith and Work Associations Across Christian Religious Traditions. In: *Handbook of Faith and Spirituality in the Workplace*, Hrsg. Judi Neal, 47–68. New York, NY: Springer New York.

Opaschowski, Horst W. 1983. *Arbeit. Freizeit. Lebenssinn?* Wiesbaden: VS Verlag für Sozialwissenschaften.

Parboteeah, K. P., M. Hoegl und J. Cullen. 2009a. Religious dimensions and work obligation: A country institutional profile model. In: *Human Relations* 62 (1), 119–148. Doi: 10.1177/0018726708099515.

Parboteeah, K. Praveen, Martin Hoegl und John B. Cullen. 2008. Ethics and Religion: An Empirical Test of a Multidimensional Model. In: *Journal of Business Ethics* 80 (2), 387–398. Doi: 10.1007/s10551-007-9439-8.

Parboteeah, K. Praveen, Yongsun Paik und John B. Cullen. 2009b. Religious Groups and Work Values. In: *International Journal of Cross Cultural Management* 9 (1), 51–67. Doi: 10.1177/1470595808096674.

Pawar, Badrinarayan Shankar. 2009. Individual spirituality, workplace spirituality and work attitudes. In: *Leadership & Organization Development Journal* 30 (8): 759–777. Doi: 10.1108/01437730911003911.

Phipps, Kelly und Margaret Benefiel. 2013. Spirituality and Religion: Seeking a Juxtaposition That Supports Research in the Field of Faith and Spirituality at Work. In: *Handbook of Faith and Spirituality in the Workplace*, Hrsg. Judi Neal, 33–43. New York, NY: Springer New York.

Rastetter, Daniela. 2019. Vielfalt gleichstellen? Gleichstellung, Antidiskriminierung und Diversity Management im Kontext von digitalisierter Arbeit. In: Alewell, Dorothea und Wenzel Matiaske (Hrsg.) *Standards Guter Arbeit – disziplinäre Positionen und interdisziplinäre Perspektiven*. Baden-Baden: Nomos, 81–105.

Reave, Laura. 2005. Spiritual values and practices related to leadership effectiveness. In: *The Leadership Quarterly* 16 (5): 655–687. Doi: 10.1016/j.leaqua.2005.07.003.

Saks, Alan M. 2011. Workplace spirituality and employee engagement. In: *Journal of Management, Spirituality & Religion* 8 (4): 317–340. Doi: 10.1080/14766086.2011.630170.

Spiller, Chellie und Monica Stockdale. 2013. Managing and Leading from a Maori Perspective: Bringing New Life and Energy to Organisations. In: *Handbook of Faith and Spirituality in the Workplace*, Hrsg. Judi Neal, 149–174. New York, NY: Springer New York.

Tourish, Dennis und Naheed Tourish. 2010. Spirituality at Work, and its Implications for Leadership and Followership: A Post-structuralist Perspective. In: *Leadership* 6 (2), 207–224. Doi: 10.1177/1742715010363210.

Vandenberghe, Christian. 2011. Workplace spirituality and organizational commitment: An integrative model. In: *Journal of Management, Spirituality & Religion* 8 (3), 211–232. Doi: 10.1080/14766086.2011.599146.

Voggenreiter, Gudrun. 2013. Work-Life-Balance. In: *Psychologie der Wirtschaft*, Hrsg. Miriam Landes und Eberhard Steiner, 197–216. Wiesbaden: Springer Fachmedien Wiesbaden; Springer.

Weaver, G. R. und B. R. Agle. 2002. Religiosity and Ethical Behavior in Organizations: A Symbolic Interactionist Perspective. In: *Academy of Management Review* 27 (1), 77–97. Doi: 10.5465/AMR.2002.5922390.

Welk, Svenja. 2015. *Die Bedeutung von Führung für die Bindung von Mitarbeitern: Ein Vergleich unterschiedlicher Führungsstile im Kontext der Generation Y.* Wiesbaden: Springer Gabler.

Zwingmann, Christian, Constantin Klein und Arndt Büssing. 2011. Measuring Religiosity/Spirituality: Theoretical Differentiations and Categorization of Instruments. In: *Religions* 2 (4), 345–357. Doi: 10.3390/rel2030345.

Zysberg, Leehu und Tal Schenk. 2013. Creativity, Religiosity, and Political Attitudes. In: *Creativity Research Journal* 25 (2), 228–231. Doi: 10.1080/10400419.2013.783761.

Von Arbeit und Sinn. Analyse eines Problemfeldes

Barbara Müller, Christoph Seibert und Oliver Vornfeld

Wer nach dem Zusammenhang von Arbeit und Sinn fragt, richtet sein Augenmerk auf einen elementaren Sachverhalt menschlicher Existenz, zumindest dann, wenn gilt, dass Menschen darauf aus sind, einen Sinn in dem, was sie tun, zu sehen. Dass damit ganz Verschiedenes in den Blick gerät,[1] zeigt sich bereits daran, dass jene Frage in zweifacher Weise gestellt werden kann: Zum einen kann nach der Bedeutung gefragt werden, welche die Tätigkeit der Arbeit für die menschliche Suche nach dem hat, was gemeinhin als Lebenssinn bezeichnet wird; zum anderen richtet sie sich auf die Gestaltung von Strukturen, die es ermöglichen sollen, konkrete Arbeitsabläufe als ein sinnhaftes Tun zu erfahren. Während im ersten Fall also übergeordnete, das Leben als solches strukturierende, Gesichtspunkte in den Blick geraten, wird im zweiten Fall nach den strukturellen Bedingungen gefragt, die es erlauben, einen ganz bestimmten Arbeitsvorgang in sich bereits als wertvolles Tun zu qualifizieren. Die beiden Perspektiven sind natürlich nicht unabhängig voneinander, sie scheinen sich vielmehr zu ergänzen, da die erste ihre Konkretion in der zweiten und die zweite ihren allgemeinen Bestimmtheitsrahmen in der ersten findet. Allerdings liegen sie nicht auf einer Ebene. Denn die erste Perspektive ist semantisch umfassender als die zweite und nimmt diese in sich auf. Käme dem, was Arbeit heißt, nämlich keine Bedeutung für das Leben zu, dürfte es nicht sonderlich weiterführend sein, überhaupt nach den Bedingungen zu fragen, die erfüllt sein müssen, damit konkrete Arbeitsvorgänge als sinnhaft erfahren werden können.[2]

---

1 Vgl. hierzu auch die Verbindungslinien, die Dorothea Alewell/Tobias Moll, *Religion, Religiosität und Spiritualität am Arbeitsplatz in deutschen Unternehmen* (in diesem Band) zwischen dem personalwirtschaftlichen Diskurs und Sinnsuche als Teil individueller Spiritualität ziehen.

2 Darauf zielt auch die für den Bereich der evangelischen Theologie immer noch unübertroffene Studie von Torsten Meireis ab; vgl. Ders., *Tätigkeit und Erfüllung.*

Gegen diese Unterstellung eines Konnexes zwischen Arbeit und Lebenssinn könnte man einwenden, dass einzelne Arbeitsvorgänge sich sehr wohl als sinnvolles Tun begreifen ließen, ohne sie in einen Zusammenhang mit Gesichtspunkten zu sehen, welche nicht nur für Arbeit, sondern auch für andere Formen menschlichen Tätigseins eine strukturierende Funktion erfüllen. Eine solche Position einzunehmen, ist zweifellos möglich, sie kann allerdings keine Erklärung für das Phänomen liefern, dass Arbeit für viele Menschen westlicher Gesellschaften zu denjenigen Ressourcen gehört, die es ermöglichen sollen, einen gelungenen Lebensentwurf auszubilden. Will man diese Erklärungslücke nicht hinnehmen, bietet es sich somit an, die zweite Perspektive auf die erste zu beziehen, zumindest dann, wenn sie bis in ihre letzten Konsequenzen hinein durchdacht wird. Denn letztlich, so ein Resümee Volker Gerhardts, »bleibt kein Erfahrungsbereich von der dem Menschen wesentlichen Fähigkeit zur Sinngebung ausgenommen«[3]. Das gilt auch für die Arbeit. Die nachfolgenden Überlegungen werden dieser Ausgangsvermutung näher nachgehen, wobei zunächst versucht wird, den angezeigten Zusammenhang zwischen Sinn- und Arbeitsthematik in einer sehr elementaren Schicht menschlichen Wirklichkeitsbezugs zu verankern, um im Anschluss daran ausgewählte historische Möglichkeiten zu erörtern, wie jener Zusammenhang ausgestaltet werden kann. In einem letzten Schritt erfolgt schließlich eine soziologische Ausweitung der Gedankenführung.

1. Anthropologische Lokalisierung

Eine Bearbeitung der gestellten Aufgabe mit anthropologischen Überlegungen beginnen zu lassen, impliziert die These, dass der Arbeitsbegriff in seinem weitesten Verständnis kein rein ökonomischer Begriff ist und seine ökonomische Fassung deshalb weder als ursprünglich noch als erschöpfend angesehen werden sollte. Zwar bildete er sich erst im Zuge der in-

---

Protestantische Ethik im Umbruch der Arbeitsgesellschaft, Tübingen 2008, bes. Teil 3.6.

3 Volker Gerhardt, *Art. Sinn des Lebens*, in: *HWPh* 9, Sp. 815–824, Sp. 819. Alle Abkürzungen in diesem Artikel sind vorgenommen nach Siegfried M. Schwertner, *IATG3. Internationales Abkürzungsverzeichnis für Theologie und Grenzgebiete*, Berlin/Boston 32014.

dustriellen Transformation westlicher Gesellschaften zu einem theoretischen Zentralbegriff heraus, von der Sache her lässt er sich auf diesen Entwicklungskontext jedoch nicht beschränken. Die für uns so selbstverständliche Identifikation von Arbeit und Gelderwerb ist also keineswegs notwendig, sondern kulturell durchaus kontingent; in gleicher Weise markiert die Rede von der sogenannten »Berufsarbeit« auch nur einen Eckpunkt im Spektrum möglicher Redewendungen, die ein prima vista weiteres Verständnis ausdrücken wollen, wie etwa die Formulierungen »Arbeit am Selbst« oder »Beziehungsarbeit« bezeugen. Eine ursprünglichere Bedeutungsschicht als die ökonomische gibt schließlich auch der bemerkenswerte sprachliche Befund zu erkennen, dass die Wörter, die in vielen Sprachen zur Bezeichnung für Arbeit verwendet werden, eine Tätigkeit meinen, die überall mit großer Mühe und Anstrengung verbunden ist.[4] Damit sind ökonomische Sachverhalte mit eingeschlossen, fungieren aber als Teilbestimmungen eines komplexeren, existentiell verankerten Bedeutungsspektrums. Die Tätigkeit der Arbeit in diesem Umfang zu sehen, ist natürlich nicht neu. Sie steht in einer langen Tradition, die im neunzehnten Jahrhundert insbesondere mit Hegel und Marx[5] und zu Beginn des zwanzigsten Jahrhunderts mit so unterschiedlichen philosophischen Denkern wie Scheler[6] oder Marcuse[7] verbunden ist. Im Folgenden werden Einsichten dieser Vorgeschichte mit aufgenommen, allerdings nicht mit dem Anspruch versehen, eine umfassende Theorieinterpretation liefern zu wollen. Es geht allein darum, eine systematische Ansatzstelle für die nachstehende materiale Entfaltung des Themas zu markieren. Eine handlungstheoretisch akzentuierte Annäherung an den Sinnbegriff soll als Ausgangspunkt dienen.

---

4 Vgl. Marie-Dominique Chenu, *Art. Arbeit*, in: *HWPh* 1, S. 480–482, bes. S. 480f.

5 Georg Wilhelm Friedrich Hegel, *Grundlinien der Philosophie des Rechts* (1820), Frankfurt a. M. 1995, §§ 189–208; Karl Marx/Friedrich Engels, *Die deutsche Ideologie. Kritik der neuesten deutschen Philosophie in ihren Repräsentanten Feuerbach, B. Bauer und Stirner und des deutschen Sozialismus in seinen verschiedenen Propheten* (1845f.), in: *MEW* 3, S. 9–530, bes. S. 21.

6 Vgl. Max Scheler, *Arbeit und Ethik* (1899), in: Ders., *Frühe Schriften*, hgg. v. Maria Scheler/Manfred S. Frings, Bern/München 1971, S. 161–195.

7 Herbert Marcuse, *Über die philosophischen Grundlagen des wirtschaftswissenschaftlichen Arbeitsbegriffs* (1933), in: Ders., *Schriften*, Bd. 1, Frankfurt a. M., S. 556–594.

1.1. Sinn

Das Problem, ob sich in den vielfältigen semantischen Dimensionen des Begriffs eine gemeinsame Grundbedeutung zu erkennen gibt, kann hier umgangen werden. Interessant ist indessen, dass »Sinn« zunächst die Operationen von Sinnesorganen bezeichnet, also die elementar organisch-rezeptive Dimension des Lebens meint, die auch in ihren reflexiv-abstrakten Leistungen nie ganz fehlt.[8] Dabei kommt bereits auf dieser Ebene zum Vorschein, dass »Sinn« sich ganz allgemein als Beziehungsbegriff bestimmen lässt, mithin als eine Funktion der komplexen Relationen zwischen Teil-Kontext-Ganzem. Sinn entsteht, wenn etwas in einem Kontext verortet ist, im Zusammenhang mit anderem erscheint, darin Handlungsanschlüsse eröffnet und in letzter Konsequenz auf ein wie auch immer gegebenes, begrifflich-imaginiertes Ganzes bezogen werden kann. Ein vermeintlich Einzelnes als solches, also etwas, das unabhängig von Bezugs- und Verwendungskontexten besteht, kann im Umkehrschluss deshalb auch nicht als sinnvoll angesehen werden, es kann vielmehr überhaupt nicht stimmig zum Ausdruck gebracht oder gedacht werden. Sinn stellt sich somit immer als eine Funktion von Zusammenhängen ein. Diese Grundbestimmung des Sinnbegriffs lässt sich weiter spezifizieren, wenn man etwa im Anschluss an die wissensphänomenologischen Arbeiten von Alfred Schütz den Sachverhalt hervorhebt, dass die Genese von Sinn einen durchgängig selektiven Charakter annimmt.[9] Geht man dabei von der Prämisse aus, dass sich der menschliche Organismus als »*selecting agency*«[10] verhält, ist es insbesondere deshalb unverzichtbar, von Selektivität zu reden, weil bereits die Identifizierung von etwas *als* eines Teils im

---

8 Vgl. Volker Gerhardt, *Der Sinn des Sinns. Versuch über das Göttliche*, München 2014, S. 114–134.

9 Vgl. Alfred Schütz, *Theorie der Lebensformen. Frühe Manuskripte aus der Bergson-Periode*, hg. v. Ilja Srubar, Frankfurt a. M. 1981, S. 108; 114; 134f. An dieser differenztheoretischen Einsicht hat Schütz auch nach seinem Kontakt mit Husserl festgehalten, wenngleich in anderer Terminologie. Vgl. Ders., *Der sinnhafte Aufbau der sozialen Welt. Eine Einleitung in die verstehende Soziologie* (1932), Frankfurt a. M. 1993, S. 54; 94f. Vgl. dazu Jan Straßheim, *Sinn und Relevanz. Individuum, Interaktion und gemeinsame Welt als Dimensionen eines sozialen Zusammenhangs*, Wiesbaden 2015, S. 132–137.

10 Vgl. William James, *The Principles of Psychology I* (1890), New York 1950, S. 139. Hervorhebung im Original.

Verhältnis zu Elementen seines Kontextes einer Auswahl aus dem Spektrum an Möglichkeiten entspringt, die eine Situation bietet. Diese Auswahl muss natürlich weder reflektiert noch kognitiv-bewusst sein, ereignet sich in vielen Fällen vielmehr unwillkürlich und kann dann symbolisch-reflexive Formen annehmen. Letztere können wiederum als Selektionen begriffen werden, allerdings kommt ihnen die Eigenart zu, sich gegenüber den eher unwillkürlich vollzogenen Akten in relative Distanz zu bringen, um nun explizit nach ihrer Bedeutung für weitere Verhaltenssteuerung zu fragen. Ohne auswählendes Verhalten, so lässt sich festhalten, lassen sich keine Sinneinheiten ausmachen, wenngleich nicht jeder Auswahlakt reflektierenden Charakter hat. Zwei Aspekte seien an diesem Gesamtbefund gesondert hervorgehoben: Realisiert sich die jeweils im Vordergrund stehende Beziehung zwischen Teil-Kontext-Ganzem im Modus von Selektionen, heißt das erstens, dass »Sinn« als Relations- zugleich ein Differenzbegriff ist, für den die *Spannung* zwischen allen in einer Situation *möglichen* Beziehungen und der *faktisch realisierten* Beziehung strukturell konstitutiv bleibt. Anders gewendet vereinigt er in sich die Differenzen zwischen Wirklichem und der Fülle des Möglichen, zwischen Form und Dynamik, Immanenz und Transzendenz oder zwischen Besonderem und Allgemeinem. Etwas als »sinnvoll« auszuzeichnen, schließt somit stets diese Differenzen mit ein. Daraus ergibt sich zweitens, dass praktisch wirksame Sinnunterstellungen immer nur »bis auf wieteres«[11] gelten, also in sich selbst bereits Potentiale ihrer Transformation tragen. Das muss nicht wundern, wenn gilt, dass jede Auswahl sich perspektivisch vollzieht, d. i. standortverhaftet immer nur einen Ausschnitt aus einem gegebenen Möglichkeitsspektrum realisiert und damit auf einen anderen möglichen Sinn verweist, welcher wiederum in neuen Verweisungskontexten steht usw. Diese Überlegungen lassen sich mit Blick auf einen für die ethische Orientierung grundlegenden Umstand weiter entfalten.

1.2. Weltorientierung

Menschen sind nicht nur darauf aus, das, was sie tun, an einer partikularkontextuellen Sinnunterstellung auszurichten, sie wollen darüber hinaus,

11 Straßheim, *Sinn und Relevanz*, S. 103.

dass ihr Leben als solches Sinn macht, welche Worte auch immer gewählt werden,[12] um diesen Umstand auszudrücken: »We want our lives to have meaning, or weight, or substance, or grow towards some fulness [...]. But this means our *whole* lives«[13]. Folgt man diesem Gedanken, lassen sich drei eng miteinander verwobene Aspekte nennen, die jene selektive Grundcharakteristik des Lebens näher konturieren können: Zunächst ist der voluntative Aspekt offenkundig. Er lässt sich so deuten, dass Menschen ein vitales Interesse daran haben, ihr Leben als etwas zu verstehen, das einen Wert hat und von Bedeutung ist. Wir wollen, dass die Dinge, die wir tun, einen Sinn ergeben. Wäre dem nicht so, liefe das auf das zutiefst kontraintuitive Vorhaben hinaus, in unseren praktischen Weltbezügen prinzipiell kein Woraufhin[14] sehen zu wollen, also auf eine Position, die sich nur aufrechterhalten lässt, wenn die sich in ihr aussprechende Negation wiederum Ausdruck einer Absicht ist. Eine indifferente Haltung ist damit nicht ausgeschlossen, allerdings ist sie ihrerseits ein Ausdruck des Weltverhältnisses, d. i. eine ethische Perspektive. Angesichts dessen lässt sich der Sinnbezug somit als konstitutives Merkmal menschlicher Weltorientierung ausweisen. Dieser Gedanke zielt schließlich auf eine zentrale Einsicht hermeneutischer Anthropologie ab, die es erlaubt, die zuletzt erwähnten Selektionsleistungen auf einer höheren Stufe als *Artikulations-* und *Selbstauslegungsakte* zu identifizieren. Menschliche Weltorientierung erfolgt also ganz wesentlich im Modus von Selbstauslegungsakten.[15] Damit ist freilich nicht gesagt, dass das Weltverhältnis durch derartige Akte konstituiert wird, es wird allerdings behauptet, dass es erst vermöge ihrer zu seiner eigentümlichen, eine Handlungssteuerung ermöglichenden, Konkretion und Regelstruktur findet:

> [O]ur interpretation of ourselves and our experience is constitutive of what we are, and therefore cannot be considered as merely a view on reality, separable from

---

12 Die Begriffe »Lebensqualität« oder »Lebenszufriedenheit« bringen ebenfalls eine Einstellung zum Leben in seiner Ganzheit zum Ausdruck. Sie sollte allerdings nicht exklusiv verstanden werden, sondern inklusiv, d. i. in Bezug auf alle relevanten Teilaspekte. Nur deshalb kann es empirische Forschungen zur Lebensqualität etc. geben.

13 Charles Taylor, *Sources of the Self. The Making of Modern Identity* (1989), Cambridge Mass., 81996, S. 50. Hervorhebung im Original.

14 Vgl. Winfried Löffler, *Art. Sinn*, in: *NHPhG* 3, S. 1984–2000, bes. S. 1992f.

15 Vgl. dazu Matthias Jung, *Der bewusste Ausdruck*, Berlin 2009.

reality, nor as an epiphenomenon, which can be by-passed in our understanding of reality.[16]

Dies eingestanden, zeichnet sich bereits ab, dass das Arbeitsthema zum einen mit einer Tätigkeitsweise konfrontiert, vermittels derer Menschen sich *selbst* in ihrer *Welt* zu verstehen trachten, mithin in ihr heimisch zu werden suchen. Zum anderen ist deutlich, dass der Sinn ihres Tuns und infolge auch ihres Arbeitens nur »bis auf weiteres« gilt. Denn er realisiert sich bekanntlich stets in Differenz zu noch ausstehenden Selektionen, ist also entwicklungsoffen. Diese anthropologische Einbettung des Themas kann natürlich dazu verleiten, eine Sicht der Dinge zu favorisieren, die bereits die spezifisch menschliche Art, in der Welt zu sein, ganz wesentlich als Arbeit versteht. Wenn nämlich gilt, dass der Mensch sein »Dasein selbst *tun* muß – derart, daß er es als Aufgabe zu ergreifen und zu erfüllen hat«[17], dann fehlt nicht viel, um seine Lebenspraxis in toto schon als Arbeit zu bezeichnen, und zwar unabhängig von den einzelnen institutionellen Vorgängen des Arbeitens. Eine derartige Ausweitung des Begriffsumfangs nach dem Motto »Leben ist Arbeit« mag vielleicht konsequent erscheinen, ist ihrerseits aber eine nicht ganz unproblematische Totalbestimmung des Menschen, die zudem mit der Schwierigkeit konfrontiert, konkrete Prozesse des Arbeitens u. U. nicht mehr genau identifizieren und von anderen Tätigkeitsweisen abgrenzen zu können. Dieses Problem sei nur angedeutet, ohne an dieser Stelle geklärt werden zu müssen. Dringend klärungsbedürftig ist allerdings eine zweite Problemkonstellation. Im Ganzen gesehen können die bisherigen Ausführungen nämlich den Anschein erwecken, einer radikal individualethischen Position das Wort reden zu wollen. An diesem Eindruck ist zwar richtig, dass die sich in ihrer Lebenspraxis auslegenden Handlungssubjekte bei der Bestimmung dessen, was für sie Arbeit heißt, nicht umgangen werden können. So gesehen ist Arbeit immer auch das, was einzelne Akteure unter Arbeit verstehen. Allerdings sollte dabei nicht übersehen werden, dass unsere Selbstauslegungsakte in keinem geschichtlichen Vakuum vonstattengehen, sondern kulturelle Sinnressourcen in Anspruch nehmen, die über die Perspektive Einzelner sowohl in diachroner als auch in synchroner Hinsicht weit hin-

16 Charles Taylor, *Self-Interpreting Animals*, in: Ders., *Human Agency and Language. Philosophical Papers I*, Cambridge 1985, S. 45–76, S. 47.

17 Marcuse, *Über die philosophischen Grundlagen*, S. 568. Hervorhebung im Original.

ausgehen. Um dieses sozial-kulturelle Eingebundensein individueller Verstehensakte näher zu bestimmen, bietet sich der Begriff der Lebensform an.

1.3. Lebensform

Der Begriff verweist auf eine komplexe Geschichte, die von der keineswegs eindeutigen antiken Unterscheidung zwischen *bios* und *zoe* ausgeht und sich in der Moderne schließlich mit Denkern wie Schleiermacher, Schütz, Spranger oder Wittgenstein theoretisch verzweigt. Mit Blick auf gegenwärtige Debattenlagen ist außerdem festzustellen, dass das Interesse an dem Lebensformkonzept wieder verstärkt Konjunktur erlebt, wobei eine pluralistisch-gesellschaftliche Gesamtlage durchweg affirmativ vorausgesetzt ist.[18] Achtet man in diesem Zusammenhang auf den gängigen Sprachgebrauch, so fällt auf, dass sich eine Verwendungsweise, die Lebensform unter evolutionsbiologischen Gesichtspunkten versteht, mit einer solchen überschneidet, die darunter ausschließlich Formen menschlich-kultureller Praxis begreift.[19] Es geht im Folgenden allerdings weder um das Verhältnis dieser Verwendungsweisen noch darum, den Begriff der Lebensform gegenüber inhaltlich verwandten Ausdrücken wie Lebensführung, Lebensstil oder Lebensweise abzugrenzen.[20] Worauf es allein ankommt ist, die soeben aufgeworfene Problembestimmung etwas näher zu klären, woraus sich ergibt, dass »Lebensform« hier ausschließlich in der zweiten Bedeutung verstanden wird. Wie bereits angezeigt, soll die vorgenommene Einführung des Begriffs dazu dienen, einem individualistischen Missverständnis menschlicher Weltorientierung vorzubeugen. Denn obgleich sich diese im Modus von Selbstauslegungsakten vollzieht, partizipieren jene Akte unweigerlich an vorgängigen kollektiven Sinnressourcen, die sich in gemeinsamen Praktiken, Gewohnheiten oder Traditionen mit ihren *impliziten* Normierungen niederschlagen, mithin als Ermöglichungsfaktoren sinnhafter Weltorientierung der Einzelnen fungieren.

---

18 Vgl. Burkhard Liebsch, *Zerbrechliche Lebensformen. Widerstreit – Differenz – Gewalt*, Berlin 2001; Rahel Jaeggi, *Kritik von Lebensformen*, Berlin 2014.

19 Vgl. Burkhard Liebsch, *Art. Lebensform/Lebenskunst*, in: *NHPhG* 2, S. 1404–1418, bes. S. 1404f.

20 Vgl. Jaeggi, *Kritik von Lebensformen*, S. 70–76.

Dabei ist es wichtig zu sehen, dass die Ablaufstrukturen jener Praktiken durchaus als verpflichtend erlebt werden, ohne jedoch institutionell ausdrücklich als Normen, Regeln etc. fixiert worden zu sein. Ihr normativer Status unterscheidet sich deshalb auch von explizit kodifizierten Regelsätzen, wirken sie doch vielfach implizit im Modus des Selbstverständlichen. Auf diese Weise strukturieren sie gewissermaßen das gemeinschaftliche Spektrum der überhaupt zur Verfügung stehenden Optionen, um sich in einer bestimmten situativen Lage entsprechend verhalten zu können. Wir verstehen uns selbst also immer im Horizont der geschichtlich geronnenen Sinnverdichtungen vielfältiger Lebensformen, die mit Rahel Jaeggi wie folgt charakterisiert werden können:

> Lebensformen stellen sich dar als Bündel von sozialen Praktiken [...]. Sie umfassen Einstellungen und habitualisierte Verhaltensweisen mit *normativem Charakter*, die die *kollektive Lebensführung* betreffen, obwohl sie weder *streng kodifiziert* noch *institutionell verbindlich* verfasst sind.[21]

Dies eingestanden, gestaltet sich der Konnex zwischen Arbeit und Sinnstiftung freilich komplexer als bisher angezeigt. Es stellt sich nicht nur die Frage, ob es überhaupt möglich ist, sogenannte berufsspezifische Lebensformen voneinander abzuheben, um dann beispielsweise von einer vermeintlich professoralen, pastoralen, handwerklichen oder industriellen Lebensform zu reden. Es gerät zudem der Zusammenhang zwischen Lebensformen und darin eingelassenen Verständnissen des Verhältnisses von Arbeit und Sinn in den Blick. Fasst man den Begriff nämlich weit genug, ist zu erwarten, die genaue Fassung der Beziehung zwischen Arbeit und Sinnstiftung ihrerseits als Implikat ausgewählter Optionen zu erachten, wie Lebensmodelle kulturell strukturiert sein können. Das ist natürlich alles andere als einfach zu erörtern. Der nächste Abschnitt zielt daher auf eine erste Erkundung der zuletzt genannten Fragestellung in historischer Perspektive.

2. Historische Entfaltung

Im Folgenden soll anhand von ausgewählten historischen Beispielen dargelegt werden, wie sich Arbeit in einen umfassenden weltorientierenden

---

21 A. a. O., S. 77. Hervorhebungen im Original.

Sinn- und Handlungskontext bestimmter Lebensformen einfügt. Dabei interessieren in einem weiten Horizont die Verknüpfungen von Arbeit mit einem übergreifenden Ganzen.[22] In einem engeren Horizont interessieren strukturelle Bedingungen der Arbeit, insbesondere deren Begründungen. Es geht somit weniger darum, Einblicke in die Geschichte der Arbeit zu geben, als Modelle aufzuzeigen, wie die Arbeit zu bestimmten Zeiten und von bestimmten Autoren in einem umfassenden Lebens- und Sinnkontext wahrgenommen wurde.

Der Rückgriff auf die Geschichte hat mehrere Gründe. Historische Modelle und Beispiele stellen alternative Entwürfe dar. Dies impliziert ganz und gar nicht, dass sie, wird heute nach neuen Formen guter Arbeit und sinnvollen Lebens gesucht, reproduziert werden sollten. Dies wäre angesichts der heutigen, fundamental anders organisierten Gesellschaften weder wünschenswert noch überhaupt möglich. Dennoch kann der Rekurs auf historische Lebensformen und die sie begründenden Reflexionen im vorliegenden Kontext nützlich sein, um Typen der Koppelung von Sinn und Arbeit als Impulsgeber für aktuelle Reflexionen ausfindig zu machen. Im Folgenden wurden Beispiele ausgewählt, die einen prägnanten Fokus auf eine stimmige Sinnzuschreibung aufweisen. Beim zweiten und dritten Beispiel (2.2. und 2.3.) handelt es sich überdies um Umbruchs- und Transformationsphänomene, die auch mit historisch-innovativen Sinnzuschreibungen von Arbeit verbunden sind.[23] Bereits die vorliegende kleine Auswahl, die durch weitere und umfassendere Analysen zu ergänzen wä-

---

22 Vgl. Giorgio Agamben, *Höchste Armut. Ordensregeln und Lebensform*, Frankfurt a. M. 2012, der mit historischem Rückbezug die »Lebens-Form« in seiner Termino-logie »Leben« und »Regel« der Franziskaner analysiert (S. 9), d. i. was hier Sinnhorizont und Praxis (Arbeit) genannt wird.

23 Daraus lassen sich eventuell auch Lehren für den aktuell zu beobachtenden Wandel von Standards Guter Arbeit ziehen. So lässt sich die Digitalisierung als ein Treiber für aktuelle Veränderungen mit Auswirkungen auf die Kopplung von Sinn und Arbeit sehen. Vgl. dazu Stefan Kirchner und Jürgen Beyer, *Die Plattformlogik als digitale Marktordnung*, in: Zeitschrift für Soziologie, 45 (5), 324–339, 2016 sowie aus diesem Band: Hans Hanau und Wenzel Matiaske, *Mitbestimmung im entgrenzten Betrieb – Arbeitsrechtliche und personalwirtschaftliche Perspektiven*; Sven Hauff, *Human Resource Management zwischen Uniformität und Differenzierung*; Daniela Rastetter, *Vielfalt gleichstellen?*; Christine Busch und Tim Vahle-Hinz, *Gesundheit und Wohlbefinden in einer Arbeitswelt im Wandel*; Margarete Schuler-Harms und Katharina Goldberg, *Soziale Absicherung von alter und neuer Selbständigkeit als Herausforderung für das Sozialrecht.*

re, weist auf verschiedenartigste Weisen der Verbindung von Sinn und Arbeit hin: Arbeit kann vom Lebenssinn weitgehend losgelöst werden (2.1. Aristoteles), ein menschlich-notwendiges Übel mit mehr oder weniger sinnhaftem Potential darstellen (2.2. Mönchtum), aber auch organisch in den Sinnkosmos integriert werden (2.3. Luther).

2.1. Aristoteles: Unverbundenheit von Sinn und Arbeit

Aristoteles entwirft keine Theorie der Arbeit im engeren Sinne, und er äußert sich auch nirgendwo systematisch und konzentriert zum Thema Arbeit.[24] Gleichwohl sind seine Gedanken relevant, wenn es gilt, mit dem auf Sinnfragen geweiteten Blick ein antikes und im konkreten Falle weit darüber hinaus einflussreiches Modell für gutes Tun und Leben zu suchen. Es bedarf dazu insbesondere der Auseinandersetzung mit den aristotelischen Ethiken, konkret mit den Reflexionen über Handlungen, Tugenden und Glück. Handlungsbezogen interessiert sich Aristoteles vor allem für die Absicht des Handelnden.[25] Gut zu handeln (*eu prattein*) verbindet sich für Aristoteles letztlich mit dem übergeordneten und besten Ziel des Glücks (*eudaimonia*). Unter Glück versteht Aristoteles das gelingende Leben, das sich durch eine gute Lebensweise sowie gutes, nämlich tugendhaftes Handeln auszeichnet.[26] Die Frage nach dem Glück verbindet sich bei Aristoteles somit unmittelbar mit Handeln und insofern für uns Heutige potentiell auch mit Arbeit. Für den gegenwärtigen Arbeitsdiskurs interessiert dabei insbesondere die von Aristoteles herausgestrichene Verbindung von Glück und Tugend. Demnach sollte der handelnde Mensch, um sein Mensch-Sein adäquat zu realisieren, seine Vernunft in tugendhafter Weise benutzen. Wer dazu nicht fähig ist, wie z. B. Tiere, Kinder und Sklaven, partizipiert in diesem Sinne nicht am glücklichen Leben.[27] Aris-

---

24 Johannes Engels, *Merces auctoramentum servitutis. Die Wertschätzung bestimmter Arbeiten und Tätigkeiten durch antike heidnische Philosophen*, in: Verena Postel (Hg.), *Arbeit im Mittelalter. Vorstellungen und Wirklichkeiten*, Berlin 2006, S. 57–77, S. 67f.

25 Vgl. z. B. *Rhetorik* I,13 (1374a14).

26 Vgl. Philipp Brüllmann, *Art. Glück*, in: Christof Rapp/Klaus Corcilius (Hgg.), *Aristoteles-Handbuch. Leben – Werk – Wirkung*, Stuttgart/Weimar 2011, S. 232–238, S. 232.

27 Vgl. z. B. *Nikomachische Ethik* I,10 (1099b32–1100a4); X,6 (1177a8–9).

toteles denkt durchaus nicht weltfremd, schließt er doch konkrete, für ein glückliches Leben relevante, »freundliche« Lebensumstände mit ein; dazu gehört etwa, über ausreichende finanzielle Mittel zu verfügen, Freunde und Kinder zu haben oder schlicht durch glückliche Zufälle begünstigt zu sein.[28] Mit Blick auf die Erwerbsarbeit fällt hier auf, dass die Erlangung bzw. das Vorhandensein materieller Mittel zu den Voraussetzungen für ein glückliches Leben gezählt wird. Übertragen auf die Thematik der Erwerbsarbeit meint dies: Wessen Unterhalt gedeckt ist, hat ein geeignetes Fundament, um ein gutes Leben zu führen. In der Unterhaltsarbeit, in Produkten ohnehin, liegt das Glück nach Aristoteles nicht. Reichtum ist etwa nur insofern glücksrelevant, als man ihn verteilen und damit tugendhaft handeln kann; umgekehrt ist Reichtum als Selbstzweck nicht relevant für ein gelungenes Leben.

Aristoteles reflektiert ausgiebig über die besten Lebensweisen. Das bestmögliche Leben besteht für ihn darin, sich der theoretischen Betrachtung zu widmen: »Was also hindert, jenen glücklich zu nennen, der gemäß der vollkommenen Tugend tätig und mit äußeren Gütern hinlänglich versehen ist, nicht eine beliebige Zeit hindurch, sondern durch ein ganzes Leben?«[29] Die Betrachtung (*theoretike*) besteht darin, sich dem reinen Geist zuzuwenden, mindestens so ausgiebig und so weit es die äußeren Umstände erlauben. Dies meint konkret Philosophieren und Meditieren, nicht aber Arbeiten im heutigen Sinne der Erwerbsarbeit. Die zweitbeste Lebensweise sieht Aristoteles im politischen Dienst für das Gemeinwesen, der mit der Ausübung von Tugenden wie Gerechtigkeit, Tapferkeit und Klugheit einhergeht. Mit Recht problematisiert die Aristoteles-Forschung die mit dieser Theorie einhergehende reduktionistische Überzeugung, wonach es gleichsam die *eine* ideale menschliche Lebensform gibt, und weist überdies auf Unschärfen und Widersprüche der aristotelischen Argumentation hin.[30] Angewandt auf die Arbeit macht die Lektüre des Aristoteles nichtsdesto trotz darauf aufmerksam, dass für Aristoteles Erwerbsarbeit eine idealerweise zu vermeidende Beschäftigung darstellt, jedenfalls keinen Sinn in sich hat. Sinn und Arbeit sind in seinem Denken voneinander losgelöste Kategorien. Aktualisiert formuliert ist Arbeit für Aristoteles nur

28 A. a. O., I,9 (1099a32–b2).

29 A. a. O., I, 11 (1101a14–16); dt. nach Brüllmann, *Art. Glück*, S. 235.

30 Brüllmann, *Art. Glück*, S. 236,

dann sinnvoll, wenn sie beispielsweise Phasen der Muße ermöglicht, um sich mit Geistigem zu beschäftigen, oder wenn sie mit tugendhaftem Handeln einhergeht.[31]

Aristoteles und auch sein Lehrer Platon vertreten ein Lebensideal, das durch eine prinzipiell ablehnende Haltung gegenüber der Erwerbs- und vor allem der Handarbeit charakterisiert ist.[32] Der wahre Sinn des Lebens liegt für Platon und Aristoteles vielmehr in der Betrachtung und in ethisch wertvollem Handeln. Die Erwerbsarbeit liefert, so man nicht zu den wenigen gänzlich davon Entbundenen gehört, als notwendiges Übel das materielle Fundament dafür; ein Eigenwert oder eine positive konstitutiv-orientierende Rolle für das Weltverhältnis kommt ihr jedoch nicht zu. Vielmehr ist Erwerbsarbeit negativ konnotiert, insofern als sie sich mit Armut, untergeordneten Tätigkeiten, wie sie insbesondere Frauen verrichten, bis hin zu Sklaverei assoziiert. Bei dieser Sicht handelt es sich um ein elitäres, antik-aristokratisches Ideal, das nicht nur inkompatibel mit heutigen Verhältnissen ist, sondern auch an der Lebenssituation von mindestens 90 Prozent der damaligen Zeitgenossen vorbeigeht, die größtenteils in der Landwirtschaft tätig und somit Arbeiter und nicht Philosophen waren. Gleichwohl sind die Reflexionen des Aristoteles bedeutsam, weisen sie doch darauf hin, dass der Mensch ein Bedürfnis nach der Kontemplation und dem Tun des Guten zu haben scheint, basaler noch: Dass die Frage nach dem guten Leben überhaupt von grundlegender Relevanz ist.

2.2. Die christlich-monastische Lebensform: Arbeit als menschlich-notwendiges Übel

Der Blick auf die christlich-monastische Lebensform ist insofern besonders lohnend, als in monastischen Lebensformen eine christliche Interpretation und zugleich radikale Variante des philosophischen Lebens begegnet. Eine sorgfältige Relecture monastischer Texte auf die Verbindung von Lebensform und Arbeit legt sich gerade auch deshalb nahe, weil vorliegende Arbeiten nicht selten durch die theoretische Brille von Max Weber und Michel Foucault mit ihrer prinzipiell negativen Sicht auf das

31 Zur Muße, vgl. Engels, *Merces*, S. 60; Karin Schlapbach, *Art. Muße*, in: *RAC* 25, Sp. 357–369.

32 Zu Platons Arbeitsverständnis vgl. Engels, *Merces*, S. 66f.

Mönchtum vorgenommen sind.[33] Dies führt gezwungenermaßen zu vornehmlich negativen Resultaten; die Sinnhaftigkeit und damit auch der positive monastische Beitrag zur vorliegenden Fragestellung bleiben dabei unausgelotet. Im Verlauf der Geschichte des christlichen Mönchtums war Arbeit stets ein entscheidendes Thema, um die eigene Lebensform zu konturieren. Im Folgenden werden daher (stellvertretend für viele) zwei prägnante monastische Momentaufnahmen präsentiert: Zum einen das monastische Anfangsphänomen der Wüstenväter, zum anderen die mittelalterliche Aufspaltung des benediktinischen Mönchtums im 12. Jahrhundert.

2.2.1. Die ägyptischen Wüstenväter

Monastisches Leben, verstanden als christlich-philosophische Lebensweise, ist dadurch gekennzeichnet, die in der späteren antiken Philosophie, insbesondere der Stoa, beobachtbare kontinuierliche Aufwertung der Arbeit übernommen zu haben.[34] Diese grundsätzlich positive Haltung der Arbeit gegenüber hängt nicht zuletzt damit zusammen, dass das Christentum von Anfang an keine elitäre Bewegung war und daher den Bereich der Arbeit als wesentlichen Lebensbereich seiner AnhängerInnen gleichsam positiv in seinen Deutungshorizont integrieren musste. Gerade über die positive Bewertung der Arbeit ließen sich wichtige christliche Ideale verwirklichen: Die Pflege der Seele sowie die Herausbildung egalitärer sozialer Strukturen.

Eine frühe Spielart christlich-monastischen Lebens repräsentieren die ägyptischen Wüstenväter. Ihre Anfänge reichen mit dem Kopten Antonios (251–356) ins 3. Jahrhundert; ihre Hochblüte ist im 4. Jahrhundert anzu-

33 So z. B. Hubert Treiber/Heinz Steinert, *Die Fabrikation des zuverlässigen Menschen. Über die »Wahlverwandtschaft« von Kloster- und Fabrikdisziplin*, Münster 2005 mit Bezug auf Michel Foucault, *Überwachen und Strafen. Die Geburt des Gefängnisses* (1975), Frankfurt a. M. 1976. Klostervergleiche dort v. a. in Teil III: Disziplin, S. 173–292. Bei aller Differenziertheit, mit der Weber Klöster analysiert, liegt bei ihm doch die von Harnack übernommene These der »Weltflucht« zugrunde, vgl. Max Weber, *Wirtschaft und Gesellschaft. Grundriss der verstehenden Soziologie* (1921f.), Frankfurt a. M. 2005, S. 882; Weber zitiert und rezipiert damit Adolf Harnack, *Das Mönchtum, seine Ideale und seine Geschichte*, Berlin 1907, S. 5.

34 Zur Arbeitsauffassung der antiken Stoa, vgl. Engels, *Merces*, S. 68–75.

setzen. In einer zentralen Quelle über die Wüstenväter, den Apophthegmata Patrum, wird deren Lebensweise programmatisch als »*askesis*«, d. i. Übung, »wunderbare[r] Lebenswandel (*thaumaste biou diagoge*)« sowie als »geglückte himmlische Lebensführung (*ouranion politeian*)« bezeichnet.[35] Die Arbeit nahm bei den Wüstenvätern einen hohen Stellenwert ein.[36] Dies ist im monastischen Kontext nicht selbstverständlich; nur verwiesen sei an dieser Stelle etwa auf die sogenannten Euchiten (die Beter), welche ihren Tag gänzlich mit Gebet verbrachten, derweilen andere ihren materiellen Unterhalt sicherten. Arbeit ist gerade in einem radikalen Kontext wie der monastischen Lebensweise, in dem die Protagonisten all ihr Tun in ihr göttliches Streben und damit einen umfassenden Sinn einzuordnen versuchen, ein auch spirituell relevantes Thema. Der Blick auf die Wüstenväter und deren Arbeit führt zum einen zu einem Ideal der Autarkie und Caritas: Man will niemandem äußerlich zur Last fallen, vielmehr sogar andere mit einem kleinen Arbeitsüberschuss unterstützen. Darüber hinaus bildet die meist körperliche Arbeit eine Begleithandlung zu parallel ablaufenden geistigen Übungen. Der prototypische Wüstenvater sitzt in seiner monastischen Behausung, flicht Palmwedel zu Seilen und rezitiert parallel dazu die Heilige Schrift oder andere sinnstiftende Worte.[37] Solchermaßen ist die Erwerbsproduktion nicht genau abgrenzbar von der geistlichen Übung und damit von der Arbeit am Sinn.[38] Dies zeigt sich auch an der Terminologie, beispielsweise am zentralen monastischen terminus technicus »*ponos*« (Mühe):[39] Dieser bezeichnet sowohl die Mühsal der Arbeit als auch die monastische Lebensweise. Insgesamt nimmt die Arbeit gegenüber der geistlichen Fokussierung jedoch einen untergeordne-

35 *Gerontikon-Prolog*, in: *PG* 65, Sp. 72; dt. in: *Apophthegmata Patrum (Teil 1). Das Alphabetikon – Die alphabetisch-anonyme Reihe*, hg. v. Erich Schweitzer, *Weisung der Väter* 14, Beuron 2012, S. 19.

36 Vgl. Antoine Guillaumont, *Die Handarbeit im Alten Mönchtum: Bestreitung und Wertung*, in: Ders., *An den Wurzeln des christlichen Mönchtums. Aufsätze, Weisung der Väter* 4, Beuron 2007, S. 142–153.

37 Vgl. z. B. *Gerontikon, Apophthegma 1, Antonios 1*, in: *PG* 65, Sp. 76AB; dt. in: *Apophthegmata Patrum*, S. 21.

38 Agamben (*Höchste Armut*, S. 43) spricht hier in sinnvoller Weise von »Hybridisierung«, darunter versteht er die »Vermischung« von »Handarbeit und Gebet, von Leben und Zeit«; dies meine die monastische *meditatio*.

39 Zu »*ponos*« vgl. Pierre Miquel, *Lexique du désert. Etude de quelque mots-clés du vocabulaire monastique grec ancien*, *SpOr* 44, S. 233–240; Engels, *Merces*, S. 59.

ten Stellenwert ein. Dies reflektieren etwa Texte, die von der mutwilligen Zerstörung eigener Arbeiten handeln: Da das materielle Resultat dieser Arbeiten ohne Sinn und Nutzen erscheint – wertvoll ist allein der geistliche Prozess, der mit der Herstellung einhergeht – sind die Produkte entbehrlich. Der Mönch wird somit als tätiges Wesen beschrieben, das aus jedem Tun, nicht jedoch aus jedem Produkt, Nutzen für die seine Lebensweise schöpfen kann. An dieser Stelle zeigt sich die Wichtigkeit des Begriffs »Askese«; darunter ist in der monastischen Frühzeit der kontinuierliche Prozess des Einübens in die Lebensform zu verstehen, dem auch die Produktionsarbeit untergeordnet ist.[40] Umgekehrt kann die Arbeit als Mittel oder Übungsfeld genutzt werden, um gezielt spirituellen Fortschritt zu erzielen. So praktiziert, stärkt Arbeit die persönliche Beharrlichkeit und Stabilität. Arbeit vereinfacht und fördert damit nachgerade das monastische Leben, indem sie den Mönch bindet und erdet. Typischerweise wird die Arbeit in monastischen Texten den Anfängern als Übungsfeld und den Angefochtenen als Therapeuticum anempfohlen.

Nur sekundär im Denkhorizont der Wüstenväter steht Arbeit im heutigen modernen Sinn als relevanter Faktor etwa für den persönlichen Selbstwert oder für soziale Integration. Ein vorbildlicher Arbeiter ist in frühmonastischen Lebensformen vielmehr einer, der sich stetig um sein monastisches Werk bemüht, arbeitsbezogen formuliert: Einer, der parallel zur Arbeit seine geistlichen Übungen konzentriert verfolgt, die letztlich relevant sind für seinen Selbstwert, seine Sinnstiftung und seine Orientierung in der Welt. Vorbildlich erscheint keinesfalls derjenige, der die Arbeit gegenüber anderen Tätigkeiten in den Vordergrund rückt. Arbeit ist bei den Wüstenvätern eine wichtige und auch spirituell nützliche Aufgabe, insgesamt jedoch von untergeordneter Relevanz. Wer nicht arbeiten kann, wird von den Mitmönchen klaglos unterhalten. Wer nicht arbeiten will, riskiert derweilen den Vorwurf des Hochmuts, da er meint, sich über menschliche Grundbedingungen erheben zu können. Überdies nutzt er im Falle einer Arbeitsverweigerung die Mitmönche aus. Um soziale Integration geht es hier aber nur am Rande, vielmehr um tugend- oder lasterhaftes Verhalten. Ein über nötige Erholungspausen hinausgehendes Ausruhen

40 Zur antiken Vorstellung von Askese vgl. Mark Sheridan, *Monastic Culture: A Comparison of the Concepts of Askesis and Asceticism*, in: Philippe Nouzille/Michaela Pfeifer (Hgg.), *Monasticism between Culture and Cultures*, *AnMo* 14, S. 17–34.

von der Arbeit ist sowohl im produktionsbezogenen als auch spirituellen Sinne erst im Jenseits vorgesehen. Im Hier und Jetzt gehört das Mühen konstitutiv zum Leben.[41] Wie das Bemühen um die Perfektionierung der monastischen Lebensform, gehört für die Wüstenväter auch die Arbeit zeitlebens zu den Aufgaben des Mönchs.

2.2.2. Der benediktinische Reformorden der Zisterzienser

Von jeher im besonderen Fokus wirtschafts- und arbeitsbezogener Fragestellungen stand der Zisterzienserorden.[42] Die Zisterzienser sind ein im Jahr 1098 von Robert von Molesmes gegründeter Reformorden, der aus dem benediktinischen Mönchtum hervorging.[43] Es handelt sich somit um eine für jene Zeit neue Lebensform. Gemeinsam mit den Benediktinern befolgen die Zisterzienser die Benediktsregel als Grundnorm. Ein zentraler Grund, der zur Gründung der Zisterzienser führte, waren Roberts besondere Vorstellungen von Inhalt und Stellenwert der Arbeit, die von der in zeitgenössischen benediktinischen Klöstern gängigen Praxis abwichen.[44] Roberts Arbeitsideal ähnelt in manchem mehr demjenigen der Kartäuser und der außermonastisch Armutsbewegten als dem mittelalterlichen benediktinischen Feudalsystem. Insgesamt lag ihm daran, zu einer möglichst wörtlichen Befolgung der Benediktsregel zurückzukehren.

---

41 »Wir sind fleischlich [i. e. menschlich] und wollen essen. Deshalb arbeiten wir auch. ... auch Maria braucht ganz und gar die Martha [Lk 10,38–42].« *Gerontikon, Apophthegma 860, Silvanos 5*, in: *PG* 65, 409BD; dt. in: *Apophthegmata Patrum*, S. 300.

42 Vgl. Bernhard Nagel, *Die Eigenarbeit der Zisterzienser. Von der religiösen Askese zur wirtschaftlichen Effizienz*, Marburg 2006.

43 Vgl. Jörg Oberste, *Die Zisterzienser*, Stuttgart 2014, S. 12–212; zur Arbeit S. 183–212; Klaus Schreiner, *»Brot der Mühsal.« Körperliche Arbeit im Mönchtum des Mittelalters*, in: Postel (Hg.), *Arbeit im Mittelalter*, S. 133–170, bes. S. 147–154.

44 »Die Mönche unseres Ordens müssen ihren Lebensunterhalt durch Handarbeit (*de labore manuum*), Ackerbau und Viehzucht verdienen.« *Summa Cartae Caritatis*, Cap. 15, in: *Einmütig in der Liebe. Die frühesten Quellentexte von Cîteaux / Antiquissimi textus cistercienses, lat.–dt., Quellen und Studien zur Zisterzienserliteratur 1*, hgg. v. Hildegard Brem/Martin Altermatt, Langwaden 21998, S. 50f. Dieser Text stammt wahrscheinlich aus dem Jahr 1124, *Einleitung*, in: A. a. O., S. 23. Ebenso: *Exordium parvum*, 15, 10–14, a. a. O., S. 88f. Wichtig ist hier, für die Zisterzienser insgesamt, auch das Institut der Konversen.

Kontroversen der Zisterzienser mit Vertretern divergierender monastischer Lebensformen, namentlich den Benediktinern, beziehen sich häufig auf die Arbeit und damit zugleich auf die Auslegung der Benediktsregel.[45]

Die gegenüber den Benediktinern beobachtbare divergierende Arbeitspraxis der Zisterzienser rührt maßgeblich von Unbestimmtheiten in der Benediktsregel her. Dort werden der Mönch zwar als »Arbeiter« (*operarius*) und wahre Mönche als solche, die »wie unsere Väter und Apostel von ihrer Hände Arbeit (*labore manuum*) leben«, bezeichnet.[46] Insgesamt ist die arbeitsbezogene Terminologie in der Benediktsregel aber inkonsequent: Bisweilen ist von *labor*, oder gar *labor manuum* die Rede, bisweilen auch von *opus* und *operari*. Mit den diversen Begriffen verbinden sich verschiedene Arbeitsvorstellungen und Wertungen. *Labor* und sprachliche Derivate assoziieren sich mit Mühe und Anstrengung und damit potentiell mit einer negativen Bedeutung der Arbeit. Ganz im antiken Sinne schimmert so bei Benedikt die mit Arbeit verbundene Anstrengung durch. Gleichzeitig attestiert er, was typisch für den Mönch ist, gerade dieser Mühe, namentlich in Form von Handarbeit, einen hohen Nutzen. Mit dem zweiten häufigen Wortfeld, *opus,* ist ursprünglich ein Werk, ein Resultat oder eine Tagesarbeit gemeint, auf die man durchaus stolz sein kann.[47] Nicht selten verbindet sich ein *opus* mit beachtlichem fachlichen Können und Kunstfertigkeit. Derselbe Begriff wird in der Benediktsregel auch verwendet für den Gottesdienst (*opus Dei*) und für Gebete. Bei genauem Hinsehen ist für Benedikt recht eigentlich alles Arbeit. Der Versuch, Arbeit und Nicht-Arbeit konsequent voneinander abzugrenzen, scheitert. Das heutige Konzept der Work-Life-Balance ist etwa völlig inkompatibel mit

45 Die Zisterzienser gehen nach Bernhard von Clairvaux in den Augen der Cluniazenser, d. i. Benediktiner, »in Lumpen und schäbigen Arbeitskleidern« (*Apol.* I,1, S. 146f.), umgekehrt verrichten die Cluniazenser in den Augen der Zisterzienser die in der Benediktsregel gebotene »Handarbeit (*opus manuum*)« nicht (*Apol.* VI,12, S. 166f.). Bernhard von Clairvaux, *Apologia ad Guillelmum Abbatem / Apologie an den Abt Wilhem* (1125), in: Ders., *Sämtliche Werke lat.–dt.*, Bd. 2, hg. v. Gerhard B. Winkler, Innsbruck 1992, S. 145–201; zu den frühen Kontroversen zwischen Cluniazensern und Zisterziensern vgl. Joachim Wollasch, *Cluny. Licht der Welt. Aufstieg und Niedergang der klösterlichen Gemeinschaft*, Düsseldorf/Zürich 1996, S. 265–282.

46 Prol. 14; 48,8, in: *Die Benediktsregel lat.-dt., mit der Übersetzung der Salzburger Äbtekonferenz*, hg. v. Ulrich Faust, Stuttgart 2009, S. 8f.; 119.

47 Engels, *Merces*, S. 59f.

der benediktinischen Vorstellung vom Tätigsein, ebenso die Pole Arbeit und Freizeit. Sieht Benedikt doch verschiedene Tätigkeiten vor, die der Mönch abwechselnd, in einem festgelegten Rhythmus verrichtet, die aber letztlich alle demselben, nämlich spirituellen Zweck dienen. Im umfangreichsten Kapitel der Benediktsregel über die Arbeit wird diese zuerst als Mittel gegen den Müßiggang (*otiositas*) beschrieben, untergeordnet ist ihre Funktion zur Deckung des Lebensunterhaltes.[48] Insgesamt ist Arbeit für Benedikt primär eine Übung in Gehorsam und Demut: Der Mönch übt sich als Arbeitender darin ein, ohne Murren zu tun, was ihm aufgetragen ist, und gerade in der anstrengenden körperlichen Arbeit erfährt er, was es heißt zu dienen. Wie diverse monastische Vorgänger, u. a. die ägyptischen Wüstenväter, vertritt Benedikt somit ein arbeitstherapeutisches Ideal. Als typischer Vertreter einer gemeinschaftlich monastischen Lebensform setzt er Arbeit insbesondere auch ein, um die klösterliche Gemeinschaft zu festigen. Auch hier zeigt sich gegenüber Arbeit ein Vorrang von auf Religiöses bzw. Geistliches bezogenen Artikulations- und Selbstauslegungsakten für Sinnstiftung und Weltorientierung.

Robert von Molesmes und die Zisterzienser stießen sich im ausgehenden 11. Jahrhundert an einer einseitigen Interpretation der Benediktsregel, die das monastische Werk fast gänzlich von der Handarbeit und dem Mühen löste und in die liturgische Praxis verschob, sowie einer monastischen Ökonomie, die zu Reichtum und Abhängigkeit von den weltlich Mächtigen führte. Demgegenüber sollte ihrer Überzeugung nach ein Kloster gänzlich frei sein, und der einzelne Mönch sollte sich seiner menschlichen Existenz, die darin besteht, im Gefolge Adams sich sein Brot im Schweiße seines Angesichts zu erarbeiten (Gen 3,19), täglich vergewissern.[49] Robert und die Zisterzienser kehrten daher zurück zu einem System der Eigenarbeit; die Motivation dazu war dabei nicht primär eine wirtschaftliche, sondern eine religiöse. Der Arbeit, insbesondere in Form von Hand- und Landarbeit, wurde sowohl für den Einzelnen als für die Gemeinschaft wieder eine spirituelle Funktion zugeschrieben. Dies bedeutet nicht, dass Robert von Molesmes und die Zisterzienser der Überzeugung waren, die Arbeit definiere die monastische Philosophie. Vielmehr erkannten sie Ar-

---

48 48,1, in: *Benediktsregel*, S. 116.

49 Franz J. Felten, *Arbeit, Armut und Askese und die Folgen bei den frühen Zisterziensern*, in: *CistC* 108 (2001), S. 59–87, S. 66.

beit als sinnstiftendes Tun, das mit ihrem übergeordneten monastische Ideal nicht nur kompatibel, sondern diesem förderlich erschien. Die Unwuchten, in denen sich die Mönche in den zeitgenössischen Benediktinerklöstern dem liturgischen Gottesdienst zuwandten, erschienen ihnen übermäßig, insbesondere einseitig auf Kosten des konkret-praktischen Tuns. Die weitere Geschichte der Zisterzienser zeigt, wie herausfordernd es war, über dem, sich mit diesem Arbeitsethos einstellenden, wirtschaftlichen Erfolg der eigenen Klosterunternehmungen, den monastischen Geist nicht in den Hintergrund zu drängen. Dies gelang nicht immer: Die Zisterzienser gelten deshalb auch als »Vorboten des Kapitalismus«[50].

2.3. Luther: Arbeit als integrativer Bestandteil des christlichen Lebens[51]

Mit Luthers neuer Theologie verbindet sich auch die Theorie und Praxis einer neuen Lebensform. Die dafür relevante Terminologie bildete Luther maßgeblich aus dem monastischen Vokabular. Gehörte Luther von 1505 dem Orden der Augustiner-Eremiten an, gab er das monastische Leben im Jahre 1525 auf.[52] Seinen endgültigen Bruch mit dem Mönchsleben markiert die Heirat mit Katharina von Bora im Jahre 1525. Bereits seit den 1520er-Jahren hatte er allerdings in diversen Schriften deutliche Kritik am monastischen Leben geäußert und auch Ordensleute dazu ermuntert, das Kloster zu verlassen. Luther selber hat seinen klösterlichen Wohnort nie aufgegeben. Nach seiner Eheschließung und der Auflösung des Klosters als solchem lebte er in dem nunmehr ehemaligen Klostergebäude mit seiner großen eigenen und erweiterten Familie. Nicht nur hinsichtlich seines Wohnortes, sondern auch denkerisch liegt bei Luther so manche Kontinuität zu seiner vorreformatorischen Lebensform vor. Dabei handelt es sich allerdings nicht um unbesehene Übernahmen, sondern um häufig sehr in-

50 Nagel, *Eigenarbeit der Zisterzienser*, S. 98.

51 Fritz-Rüdiger Volz, *Art. Arbeit und Beruf*, in: Volker Leppin/Gury Schneider-Ludorff (Hgg.), *Das Luther-Lexikon*, Regensburg 22014, S. 70–72.

52 Vgl. Ulrich Köpf, *Art. Mönchtum*, in: Albrecht Beutel (Hg.), *Luther Handbuch*, Tübingen 2005, S. 50–57; Luthers wichtigste anti-monastische Schrift: *De votis monasticis iudicium* (1521), in: *WA* 8, S. 573–669. Zu Luthers Haltung zu den Gelübden vgl. Martin Brecht, *Martin Luther, Bd 2: Ordnung und Abgrenzung der Reformation*, Stuttgart 1986, S. 30–34.

novative Transformationen und Neuinterpretationen überkommender Sinnkategorien – die er somit als solche nicht gänzlich aufgab, sich jedoch um eine neue Fassung bemühte. Dazu gehört auch seine Vorstellung von Arbeit und Beruf. Mit zu Luthers Fundamentalkritik am Ordensleben gehört das monastische Gelübde, das er als Angriff auf den einzig relevanten rituellen Bund, nämlich die Taufe, einschätzte: Gott spricht die Menschen nicht an, um sie in die Klöster zu holen, sondern um ihnen qua Mensch-Sein im Glauben Heil zu schenken. Diese Überzeugung führte Luther dazu, Ruf und Beruf, in den allgemein weltlichen Bereich zu transferieren: »Niemand [ist] on befehl und beruff.«[53] Luther führte den Begriff »Beruf« in die deutsche Sprache ein, und damit verbunden die Vorstellung, wonach jeder Mensch dazu aufgerufen sei, in der Welt die seinem Stand angemessene Tätigkeit zu versehen. Dem Beruf kommt also bei Luther durchaus eine weltorientierende Funktion zu. Dieses Neuverständnis bildet damit einerseits einen klaren Bruch mit seinem vormaligen und in anderen Konfessionen anhaltend gültigen Verständnis von Berufung als mit dem Klosterleben verbundenes Geschehen. Andererseits fallen dennoch Kontinuitäten auf: Luther kreierte mit seiner Verweltlichung des Berufskonzeptes nicht den Berufstätigen im heutigen Sinne oder eine Person, die gänzlich anders in der Welt heimisch war als die nicht von reformatorischem Gedankengut erfassten Zeitgenossen. Zwar ordnete er sämtliche Lebensbezüge der Menschen neu. Der umfassende Ordnungsrahmen blieb aber, nicht anders als beim Mönch, die Gottesbeziehung. In der für sein Arbeits- und Berufsverständnis aufschlussreichen Hauspostille (1534) spricht Luther folglich vom »Christenmensch, der an den Herrn Christum glaubt, und spricht: Ich will in meines Herrn Christi Namen jetztund beten, lesen, arbeiten und also ihm dienen.«[54] Zur Arbeit und damit letztlich dem weltlichem Gottesdienst gehört dabei die Schulpflicht der Kinder nicht weniger als das eigentlich »sehr gering Ding, daß ein Mägdlein im Hause kocht, spült, kehrt, Kinder umträgt, wischt, badet.«[55] Welchen Arbeitsdienst der Mensch ausübt, ist recht eigentlich irrelevant: »Bist du

---

53 *Kirchenpostille* (1522) zu Joh 21,19–24, in: *WA* 10,1,1, S. 305–324, S. 309; aufschlussreich für Luthers neues Verständnis von Beruf bes. S. 308–310; zum Begriff Beruf und dessen Vorgeschichte vgl. Volz, *Art. Arbeit und Beruf*, S. 70.

54 *Dr. Martin Luthers Haus-Postille nach Veit Dietrich, Am fünften Sonntage nach Trinitatis* (1534), § 7a, in: *W2* 13.1, S. 753–766, S. 766.

55 A. a. O., § 9, S. 754.

Knecht, Magd, Herr, Frau, Bürgermeister, Fürst: so thue, was deines Amts ist, denn es hindert dich an deinem Glauben nicht, und kannst Gott in solchem Stande recht und wohl dienen.«[56] Dies schließt auch den Beruf des Henkers ein.[57] Volz ist daher zuzustimmen, wenn er formuliert: »Die Zeitgenossen Luthers benötigten keinen neuen Arbeitsbegriff, sondern eine qualitativ neue – aber weiterhin christlich-theologische – Deutung ihrer Lebens- und Arbeitswirklichkeit insgesamt.«[58] Auf dem Fundament des lutherischen Arbeits- und Berufskonzepts wurden in der historischen Rezeption verschiedenartige Gesellschafts- und Sozialtheorien entworfen, die unterschiedliche Elemente des lutherischen Konzepts in den Vordergrund rücken, bisweilen Kernideen Luthers auch ignorieren. Will heißen: Luthers Vorstellung von Arbeit und Beruf ist nicht deckungsgleich mit der weiteren protestantisch-lutherischen Arbeitsauffassung. Gerade der Anknüpfungspunkt bei Luther selber lohnt jedoch auf der Suche nach Vorstellungen von Arbeit als in einen Gesamtentwurf des Lebens eingebettetes Konzept. Im engeren Sinne gilt es hier in gewisser Weise auch, dem monastischen Luther nachzuspüren. Mindestens für Luther selber trifft jedenfalls zu, dass nicht die Arbeit den Menschen ausmacht, sondern der Beruf, verstanden als an den Einzelnen ergehenden Ruf Gottes, selbstverantwortlich ein gottgefälliges Leben zu führen. Bezieht der Mönch die Verbindung zwischen Arbeit und Sinn aus der durch die Regel vorgegebenen Lebensform oder schlicht im Gehorsam, so leitet sie der lutherische Christ selber ab. Dabei bewegt er sich in seinem Akt der Selbstauslegung aber in demselben Sinnganzen wie der Mönch, wenngleich sein unmittelbares äußeres Lebensumfeld die Welt und nicht das Kloster ist.

2.4. Zwischenfazit

Aus den historischen Beispielen geht unter inhaltlichen Gesichtspunkten hervor, dass Arbeit als mehr oder weniger begrüßte Tätigkeit wahrgenommen wird, um ein – hier – radikales Sinnstreben konkret zu verwirklichen, wobei Arbeit zu unterschiedlichen Graden Bedeutung für die Welt-

---

56 A. a. O., § 18, S. 758.

57 Vgl. Martin Luther, *Von der weltlichen Obrigkeit, wie weit man ihr Gehorsam schuldig sei* (1523), in: *WA* 11, S. 245–281, S. 255.

58 Volz, *Arbeit und Beruf*, S. 70.

orientierung hat. Stört die Arbeit bei Aristoteles das höchste Sinnstreben, so wird ihr in der christlich-monastischen Tradition durchaus das Potential zugeschrieben, mit der gewählten Lebensform nicht nur zu konvergieren, sondern sie gar zu befördern. Die Geschichte des christlichen Mönchtums ist arbeitsbezogen die Geschichte von unterschiedlichen Bestrebungen, reine und arbeitsvermittelte Sinnsuche in ein stimmiges Verhältnis zu setzen. Wie das Beispiel der Zisterzienser zeigt, konnte dabei die von diesen bei den Benediktinern diagnostizierte Vernachlässigung der Arbeit durchaus auch als spirituell schädlich interpretiert werden. Mit welchen konkreten Arbeiten und damit strukturellen Bedingungen und Faktoren, wie z. B. dem geistig anspruchslosen Flechten, körperlich anstrengender landwirtschaftlicher Tätigkeit oder hochspezialisierter Technik, sich welche Bedeutungen verbinden, konnte hier nicht ausgebreitet werden. Nichtsdestotrotz ist das Sinnstreben, das mit der Arbeit verbunden wird, in allen Beispielen, selbst bei Luther, der konkreten Arbeit übergeordnet und vorgelagert. Arbeitskrisen, wie sie im christlichen Mönchtum fassbar sind, sind entsprechend Sinnkrisen, und der neue Beruf (Luther) ist Konsequenz einer Neuordnung der Weltbezüge.

Neben diesem inhaltlichen Gesichtspunkt liefert die Analyse aber auch einen übergeordnet-strukturellen. Sie führt nämlich vor Augen, dass die Kopplungsverhältnisse zwischen Lebensform, Arbeit und Sinn, von welchen die Überlegungen ausgingen, nicht nur *in sich* komplex sind, sondern darüber hinaus auch *unter einander* erheblich variieren. Daran hat sich bis heute nichts geändert, es spricht hingegen einiges dafür, im Kontext moderner Gesellschaftsformationen eher von einem Komplexitätszuwachs als von einem Komplexitätsabbau zu reden. Damit konfrontiert die historische Analyse exemplarisch mit einer Problemkonstellation, die traditionalen Gesellschaften zwar nicht unbekannt ist, aber erst in posttraditionalen Gesellschaften zu einem sozialen Konstitutionsmerkmal par excellence wird. Gemeint ist das sogenannte »Faktum des [u. U. vernünftigen] Pluralismus«[59] verschiedener Lebensformen, mitsamt den damit einher gehenden unterschiedlichen Ausgestaltungen des Verhältnisses von Arbeit und Sinn. Dieses Faktum wirft die Frage nach den für posttraditionale Gesellschaften wirksamen *Mechanismen sozialer Integration* auf – eine Frage, die sich mit den Mitteln der handlungstheoretischen Leitorien-

59 Vgl. John Rawls, *Politischer Liberalismus* (1993), Frankfurt a. M. 1998, S. 106.

tierung, die bisher im Vordergrund stand, freilich nur eingeschränkt bearbeiten lässt. Es bietet sich daher an, sie ohne ihre Negation in eine Theorieperspektive mit aufzunehmen, die zugleich in der Lage ist, die sozialen Bedingungen der Transformation von Lebensformen sowie die Mechanismen ihrer gesellschaftlichen Integration mit zu berücksichtigen. Ein kurzer Ausblick auf Einsichten aus der Gründungsphase der Soziologie soll diese Perspektive markieren, ohne freilich den Anspruch zu erheben, die schwierigen Vermittlungsprobleme schon gelöst zu haben.

3. Soziologische Weiterführung

Die Moderne ist geprägt von wachsender Abhängigkeit der Individuen untereinander einerseits und zunehmenden Individualisierungsprozessen andererseits. Diese scheinbar gegenläufigen Bewegungen drücken sich sowohl in wachsender gesellschaftlicher Arbeitsteilung, also einer Ausdifferenzierung von Lebensformen in Bezug auf Arbeit, als auch in damit verbundenen Differenzierungen von Sinngebungen aus. Dies bedeutet, dass hergebrachte Modi der Vergesellschaftung und somit der Weltorientierung generell fragwürdig werden und mit einem Pluralismus von Lebensformen in Bezug auf Arbeit umgegangen werden muss. Dies bot und bietet Gefahr für gesellschaftliche Krisen. Ende des 19. Jahrhunderts fasst Émile Durkheim dieses Problem wie folgt: »Wir arbeiten zusammen, weil wir es gewollt haben, aber unsere freiwillige Zusammenarbeit schafft uns Pflichten, die wir nicht gewollt haben.«[60] Im Folgenden soll anhand eines Beispiels aus der sich institutionalisierenden Soziologie an der Schwelle zum 20. Jahrhundert aufgezeigt werden, wie dieses Problem auch für aktuelle Debatten produktiv gemacht werden kann.

Hierfür wird die Soziologie als Wissenschaft eingeführt, die maßgeblich aus dem Bedürfnis des Umgangs mit sozialen Transformationsprozessen und mit diesen verbundenen Krisen entstanden ist. Es wird argumentiert, dass Durkheims Theorie der sozialen Arbeitsteilung in der Lage ist, Möglichkeiten der sozialen Integration in arbeitsteiligen Gesellschaften aufzuzeigen, die Arbeitsteilung als konstituierenden Faktor miteinbezie-

60 *Über soziale Arbeitsteilung. Studie über die Organisation höherer Gesellschaften* (1893), Berlin 62012, S. 271.

hen. Durkheim nimmt dabei eine Unterscheidung von sozialer Integration durch Ähnlichkeiten der Gesellschaftsmitglieder in nicht-arbeitsteiligen Gesellschaften und durch Abhängigkeiten in arbeitsteiligen Gesellschaften vor. Der scheinbare Gegensatz von Individualismus und gesellschaftlichem Zusammenhalt wird von ihm hierbei hin zu einem solidarischen Pluralismus von Lebensformen der Arbeit synthetisiert, anstatt einseitig aufgelöst. Damit dies gelingt, muss allerdings – so Durkheim – die gesellschaftliche Anomie, d. i. Orientierungs- und Regellosigkeit, welche die neue Wirtschaftsform mit sich bringt, überwunden werden. Nur dann sind Arbeit und Arbeitsteilung in der Lage, gesellschaftlichen Zusammenhalt zu sichern. Zur Überwindung der Anomie bedarf es, so Durkheims Pointe, einer gemeinsamen Vorstellung von Gerechtigkeit, die es den einzelnen Gesellschaftsmitgliedern erst ermöglicht, Arbeit und Arbeitsteilung als sinnhaft zu erleben.

3.1. Soziologie als Wissenschaft sozialer Integration

Als Geburtsstunde der Soziologie als wissenschaftlicher Disziplin lässt sich das »lange 19. Jahrhundert« ausmachen, in dem es in Europa zu tiefgreifenden Veränderungen fast aller Bereiche des öffentlichen und privaten Lebens kam: Der Aufstieg von Kapitalismus und Bürgertum, kulminierend in industriellen und bürgerlichen Revolutionen, brachte die *anciens régimes* zu Fall und mit ihnen ihre Werte- und Gesellschaftsordnungen, ihre Lebensformen und deren Formen der Sinnstiftung und Weltorientierung. Neben den bürgerlichen Freiheiten entstand durch die flächendeckende Durchsetzung der Fabrikarbeit mit dem Proletariat eine neue Klasse, deren Mitglieder sich häufig größter Prekarität ausgesetzt sahen. In dieser Konstellation gesellschaftlicher Umbrüche formierte sich die Soziologie als »Krisenwissenschaft«[61]. Als sie an der Schwelle zum 20.

61 Zu Entstehungsgeschichte und Selbstverständnis der Soziologie siehe auch: Werner Sewing, *Soziologie als Krisenwissenschaft?*, in: Friedrich Heckmann/Peter Winter (Hgg.), *21. Deutscher Soziologentag 1982. Beiträge der Sektions- und ad hoc-Gruppen*, Opladen 1983, S. 385–388; Jürgen Habermas, *Kritische und konservative Aufgaben der Soziologie* (1962), in: Ders., *Theorie und Praxis. Sozialphilosophische Studien*, Frankfurt a. M. 1971, S. 290–306. Dieser sieht die Soziologie

Jahrhundert schließlich institutionalisiert wurde, war bei ihren Protagonisten ein Ringen um die Fragen nach der Betrachtung sozialen Wandels, der Veränderung von Weltanschauungen und Arbeitsverhältnissen sowie der Möglichkeiten sozialer Integration zu spüren. So kommt Talcott Parsons in seinem ersten Hauptwerk nach vergleichender Lektüre soziologischer Klassiker zu der Definition von Soziologie als »the science which attempts to develop an analytical theory of social action systems in so far as these systems can be understood in terms of the property of common-value integration.«[62]

Mit der Beschäftigung mit dem Problem der sozialen Integration ist kaum ein Name so eng verbunden wie der des französischen Soziologen Émile Durkheim (1858–1917). Durch dessen gesamtes Werk zieht sich die Frage nach Moral und sozialer Kohäsion, also dem sozialen Band (*lien social*), das Gesellschaften zusammenhält.[63] So beendet er seine Studie über gesellschaftliche Arbeitsteilung mit einem programmatischen Arbeitsauftrag: »Unsere erste Pflicht besteht darin, uns eine neue Moral zu bilden.«[64] Im Vergleich zu vielen anderen – und darin besteht sein Vorteil – geht er bei der Suche nach dieser neuen Moral weder reduktionistisch-individualistisch noch kollektivistisch vor, sondern akzeptiert eine Pluralität von Lebensformen als Grundbedingung der Moderne.

Durkheim beobachtet, dass die Arbeitsteilung den Modus gesellschaftlicher Integration fundamental umstellt: Von einer Solidarität durch Ähnlichkeit der Individuen (mechanisch) zu einer Solidarität aus Arbeitsteilung (organisch). Er wehrt sich hierbei entschieden gegen die Auffassung, dass die Arbeitsteilung zu gesellschaftlicher Desintegration führt: Diesen

---

zusammen mit der Ökonomie bereits in der 2. Hälfte des 18. Jahrhunderts (mit den schottischen Moralphilosophen Smith, Ferguson und Miller) entstehen.

62 *The Structure of Social Action. A Study in Social Theory with Special Reference to a Group of Recent European Writers, Vol. 2* (1937), New York 1968, S. 768.

63 Vgl. Hans Joas, *Das Problem der Entstehung neuer Moral als Leitfaden durch Durkheims Werk*, in: Ders., *Die Kreativität des Handelns*, Frankfurt a. M. 1992, S. 76–99; Matthias Koenig, *Wie weiter mit Émile Durkheim?*, in: Hamburger Institut für Sozialforschung (Hg.): *Wie weiter mit....?*, Hamburg 2008; Niklas Luhmann, *Arbeitsteilung und Moral. Durkheims Theorie* (1977), in: Emile Durkheim, *Über soziale Arbeitsteilung*, S. 19–38; Hans-Peter Müller/Michael Schmid, *Arbeitsteilung, Solidarität und Moral. Eine werkgeschichtliche und systematische Einführung in die »Arbeitsteilung« von Emile Durkheim* (1987), in: Emile Durkheim, *Über soziale Arbeitsteilung*, S. 481–532.

64 Emile Durkheim, *Über soziale Arbeitsteilung*, S. 480.

Effekt sieht er in den »anormalen Formen«[65] der Arbeitsteilung begründet und gibt Kriterien, die erfüllt sein müssen, damit Arbeitsteilung gelingt. Durkheim betrachtet die Arbeitsteilung somit unter Aspekten der Stiftung von Solidarität (also gesellschaftlichem Sinn) und nicht, wie er es den Ökonomen vorwirft, verengt als Hilfsmittel zur »Erhöhung der Rendite«[66]. Dabei verweist er darauf, dass die soziale Akzeptanz eines Marktes »auch an die Erfüllung vormarktlicher Normen und Werte gebunden ist«[67], wie Axel Honneth schreibt. Dieser liest Durkheim, wie auch Hegel, als Vertreter eines »normative[n] Funktionalismus«[68], der die Sittlichkeit von kapitalistischen Märkten aus vormarktlicher Solidarität begründet. Um diese vormarktlichen Bedingungen des Marktes aufzuzeigen, muss zunächst Durkheims Theorie der Arbeitsteilung beleuchtet werden.

3.2. Mechanische und organische Solidarität

Durkheim arbeitet zwei unterschiedliche Formen gesellschaftlicher Solidarität heraus: die mechanische und die organische Solidarität. In dem Verständnis des Begriffs nach Jaeggi, können auch sie grosso modo als Lebensformen angesehen werden: Sie sind Bündel sozialer Praktiken, haben normativen Charakter und betreffen die kollektive Lebensführung ohne streng kodifiziert oder institutionell fixiert zu sein.

Das kollektive Leben, das Durkheim als ursprünglicher als und als Bedingung für das individuelle Leben ansieht,[69] ist die Voraussetzung für mechanische Solidarität. Diese beruht auf gemeinsamen Weltorientierungen und Sinnbezügen in Form von Ähnlichkeiten in Vorstellungen, Gefühlen und Bewusstseinen.[70] Die Ähnlichkeiten entstehen dadurch, dass die Gesellschaft segmentär und funktional nicht differenziert ist, ihre Mitglieder also weitgehend dieselbe Lebenswelt teilen. Die individuellen Persönlichkeiten sind dabei wenig ausgeprägt. Durkheim nennt diese Solidaritäts-

---

65 A. a. O., Drittes Buch.

66 A. a. O., S. 442.

67 Axel Honneth, *Das Recht der Freiheit. Grundriß einer demokratischen Sittlichkeit*, Berlin 2011, S. 347.

68 A. a. O., S. 346.

69 Vgl. Durkheim, *Über soziale Arbeitsteilung*, S. 339f.

70 Vgl. a. a. O., S. 181.

form »mechanisch,« da sie wie die Kohäsion der Elemente fester Körper starr ist.[71] Die Rechtsform von durch mechanische Solidarität zusammengehaltene Gesellschaften ist das repressive Strafrecht.[72] Bestraft, also als kriminell angesehen, wird eine Handlung »wenn sie starke und bestimmte Zustände des Kollektivbewusstseins verletzt.«[73] Mit repressiven Maßnahmen wird eine Einheit in Glauben, Praktiken und Gefühlen aufgezwungen. Je mehr dies geschieht, »umso eher verschmilzt das soziale Leben mit dem religiösen Leben«[74]. Durkheim greift zum Aufzeigen der Vorherrschaft von mechanischer Solidarität in Gesellschaften zwar immer wieder auf historische Beispiele vom antiken Rom bis zu frühneuzeitlichen Gesellschaften zurück, lässt aber keinen Zweifel daran, dass er die mechanische Solidarität idealtypisch in vorhistorischen Horden- und Klangesellschaften verortet.[75]

In der historischen Entwicklung bemerkt Durkheim einen Rückgang des Strafrechts und ein stetig wachsendes kooperatives Vertragsrecht.[76] Das kooperative Recht macht er als vorherrschende Rechtsform in einer durch organische Solidarität zusammengehaltenen Gesellschaft aus. Im Vergleich zur Solidarität durch Ähnlichkeiten entsteht diese Form durch wachsende Abhängigkeiten der Mitglieder der Gesellschaft untereinander, die sich auf Arbeitsteilung, also einer Ausdifferenzierung unterschiedlicher Lebensformen in Bezug auf Arbeit, zurückführen lassen. Während die mechanische Solidarität zwar »die Sache an die Person bindet«[77], aber die Gesellschaftsmitglieder nicht untereinander miteinander verbindet, stellt eine funktional differenzierte Gesellschaft, in der die verschiedenen Individuen durch Arbeitsteilung darauf angewiesen sind, miteinander zusammenzuarbeiten, einen Organismus mit spezialisierten Funktionen dar. Der Vertrag ist eines der wesentlichen Merkmale für diese Zusammenarbeit. Das kooperative Recht ist mit dem die Körperfunktionen regelnden

---

71 Vgl. a. a. O., S. 182.
72 Vgl. a. a. O., S. 118ff.
73 A. a. O., S. 129.
74 A. a. O., S. 283f.; vgl. auch a. a. O., S. 234f.
75 Vgl. a. a. O., S. 229–237.
76 Vgl. a. a. O., S. 200f.
77 A. a. O., S. 167.

Nervensystem des Organismus vergleichbar, dem die Aufgabe zukommt, »die verschiedenen Funktionen des Körpers zu regeln.«[78]

Durkheim erachtet bei seiner Untersuchung zwei Dinge für evident: Erstens, dass die mechanische Solidarität über eine geringere Bindungskraft verfügt als die organische und zweitens, dass die mechanische Bindung »in dem Maß, wie die soziale Entwicklung voranschreitet, immer lockerer«[79] wird. Er weist aber zugleich darauf hin, dass auch in funktional stark differenzierten Gesellschaften das kollektive Bewusstsein transformiert, nämlich universalisiert (allgemeiner und unbestimmter), weiterbesteht und somit der gesellschaftlichen Pluralität Rechnung trägt.[80] Ein »Kult des Individuums«[81] entsteht und eine Vorstellung von Gerechtigkeit.

3.3. Anomie als Dauerzustand der wirtschaftlichen Sphäre

Durkheim ist der Auffassung, dass wenn Arbeitsteilung keine organische Solidarität erzeugt, dies daran liegt, dass »die Beziehungen der Organe nicht geregelt sind, weil sie in einem Zustand der *Anomie* verharren.«[82] Diesem Problem widmet er sich in seiner zweiten groß angelegten empirischen Studie *Der Selbstmord* von 1897, in der er verschiedene Motivationen und Begründungszusammenhänge für Suizide herausarbeitet. Für relevant hält er in funktional differenzierten Gesellschaften den egoistischen und den anomischen Suizid,[83] wobei dieser einen »nahen Verwandten«[84] von jenem darstellt. Der egoistische Suizid entsteht dadurch, dass der innere Zusammenhalt der Gesellschaft nicht ausreicht, um ihre Mitglieder in Abhängigkeit zu halten.[85] Die Lösung des Problems ist darum darin zu suchen, dass »der einzelne sich wieder solidarischer mit einem Kollektivwe-

---

78 Vgl. a. a. O., S. 180f.
79 A. a. O., S. 205.
80 Vgl. a. a. O., S. 227.
81 Vgl. a. a. O., S. 478.
82 A. a. O., S. 437. Hervorhebung im Original.
83 Vgl. Emile Durkheim, *Der Selbstmord* (1897), Frankfurt a. M. 1983, S. 242ff.; 442.
84 A. a. O., S. 454.
85 Vgl. a. a. O., S. 442.

sen fühlt«[86], denn der »Selbstmord steht im umgekehrten Verhältnis zum Integrationsgrad der Kirche, der Familie und des Staates.«[87] Je mehr der Mensch auf sich selbst zurückgeworfen wird, desto größer wird die Gefahr des Suizids.

Die Auflösung traditioneller Bande trägt auch zu dem bei, was Durkheim als »Anomie« bezeichnet und dem anomischen Suizid zugrunde liegt. Anomie kann als nicht gelingende Form der Aktualisierung von Weltorientierung und sinnstiftenden Selbstauslegungsakten in sich transformierenden Rahmenbedingungen angesehen werden. Ausgehend davon, dass ein Mensch nicht zufrieden sein bzw. leben kann, wenn »seine Bedürfnisse nicht mit den ihm zur Verfügung stehenden Mitteln einigermaßen im Einklang stehen«[88], bezeichnet Durkheim Anomie als einen Zustand gestörter Ordnung – gleichgültig ob es sich um eine Krise oder einen Anstieg des Wohlstands handelt –, der dadurch entsteht, dass soziale Kräfte sich verändern und ein Gleichgewicht zwischen Bedürfnissen und Mitteln noch nicht hergestellt ist, da es noch keine entsprechenden gesellschaftlichen Institutionen gibt, die dieses herstellen könnten bzw. die bestehenden sich darauf noch nicht eingestellt haben. In der wirtschaftlichen Sphäre macht Durkheim die Anomie als Dauerzustand aus, da stetig Gewerbe von Reglementierung befreit werden und es wirtschaftlicher Logik folgt, immer mehr zu wollen, sodass einen nichts dauerhaft befriedigt und gleichzeitig bei Rückschlägen ein Fall ins Bodenlose stattfindet.[89]

Deshalb setzt Durkheim zur Lösung des Problems auch in der wirtschaftlichen Sphäre an: Er schlägt »Vereinigungen aller Arbeiter derselben Sparte«[90] vor, denn hier könnten soziale Bindungen über Gefühle und Werte am besten gelingen: Diese Verbindungen nach Berufen – die als Lebensformen nach Jaeggi charakterisiert werden können, wenngleich dafür die definitorische institutionelle Unverbindlichkeit aufgegeben werden müsste – können nahezu jederzeit und überall wirken, da ständiger Kontakt über einen Großteil des Lebens des Individuums hergestellt ist.[91] Dabei dürften sie aber nicht die Zünfte des *ancien régime* rekapitulieren,

86 A. a. O., S. 443.
87 A. a. O., S. 231. Hervorhebung gelöscht.
88 A. a. O., S. 279.
89 Vgl. a. a. O., S. 288ff.
90 A. a. O., S. 449.
91 Vgl. a. a. O., S. 450.

sondern müssten Formen der Kollektivorganisation mit Kollektivinstanzen unterhalb der Staatsebene schaffen, damit Anomie und Egoismus aufgehoben werden können, also damit sie Kollektivkräfte freisetzen, die den Zusammenhalt stärken, Beschränkungen und Verbundenheit erzeugen und somit eine neue Moral entstehen helfen.[92]

3.4. Gerechtigkeit oder Anomie: Durkheims aktuelle Relevanz

Anhand der beruflichen Korporationen, deren Konzeption bei Durkheim stark kritisiert worden ist,[93] stellt sich die tiefer gehende moralische Frage nach Gerechtigkeit im wirtschaftlichen Sinne. Bellah schreibt: »One might almost say that justice, the highest form of organic solidarity, *is* the new 'common faith' or common conscience.«[94] Durkheim macht Gerechtigkeit als Maßstab für die Gültigkeit von Verträgen aus.[95] Dass er die Kontrolle über die Gerechtigkeit im wirtschaftlichen Prozess den beruflichen Korporationen geben möchte, muss nicht geteilt werden, um diesen Maßstab produktiv zu machen.[96]

Durkheims Suche gilt der in-der-Welt-orientierenden und sinnstiftenden

> moralische[n] Kraft, die die individuellen Egoismen zügeln, im Herzen der Arbeiter ein lebhafteres Gefühl ihrer Solidarität erhalten und das Gesetz des Stärkeren daran hindern kann, sich derart brutal auf die gewerblichen und kommerziellen Beziehungen auszuwirken.[97]

Für ihn ergibt sich – im Gegensatz zu den Utilitaristen – das Allgemeinwohl, der gemeinsame Nutzen, nicht einfach aus der Summe der individuellen Nutzen.[98] Dafür, dass sich das Allgemeinwohl als Maßstab durch-

---

92 Vgl. a. a. O., S. 454ff.

93 Vgl. z. B. Jürgen Habermas, *Theorie des kommunikativen Handelns, Bd. 2: Zur Kritik der funktionalistischen Vernunft*, Frankfurt a. M. 1981, S. 129f.

94 Robert N. Bellah, *Introduction*, in: Émile Durkheim, *On Morality and Society. Selected Writings*, Chicago/London 1973, S. ix–lv, S. xxivf. Hervorhebung im Original.

95 Vgl. Emile Durkheim, *Über soziale Arbeitsteilung*, S. 453; Ders., *Vorwort zur zweiten Auflage. Einige Anmerkungen zu den Berufsgruppen*, in: Ders., *Über soziale Arbeitsteilung*, S. 41–75.

96 Vgl. Habermas, *Theorie des kommunikativen Handelns, Bd. 2*, S. 122ff.

97 Durkheim, *Vorwort*, S. 51.

98 Vgl. Durkheim, *Über soziale Arbeitsteilung*, S. 455.

setzt, müssen Verträge gerecht sein, was eine gerechte Entlohnung der Arbeit ebenso beinhaltet[99] wie eine radikale Chancengleichheit, die darin besteht, dass Reichtum nicht vererbt wird.[100] Zudem muss Arbeit für den Arbeiter auch mit Sinn gefüllt sein. Nur wenn der arbeitende Mensch »fühlt, daß er zu etwas dient«[101], kann soziale Integration gelingen, d. i. der Pluralismus an Lebensformen der Arbeit bedarf des gegenseitigen Verständnisses von der Sinnhaftigkeit der eigenen Tätigkeit ebenso wie von der Tätigkeit des/der anderen. Honneth beschreibt dies als »Fairness und Transparenz der gesellschaftlichen Arbeitsteilung.«[102] Er sieht hierin die Aktualität Durkheims begründet, dass er »Forderungen nach einer qualitativ sinnvollen Arbeit als immanente Ansprüche der neuen Wirtschaftsordnung«[103] begreift. Die Erfüllung dieser Forderungen, bzw. der Glaube an ihre Erfüllung, stellt also die vormarktlichen Bedingungen des Marktes dar, die soziale Integration gewährleisten. Qualitativ sinnvolle Arbeit bzw. Sinnstiftung durch Arbeit wird somit interpretierbar als Maßstab für das Gelingen oder Nichtgelingen von sozialer Integration und Gesellschaft überhaupt. Durkheim beleuchtet dabei sozialethische Probleme (bspw. Verteilungsgerechtigkeit), deren Aktualität sich unmittelbar erschließt.

Wenngleich Durkheim die Konstellation von Arbeit und Sinnstiftung in der organischen Solidarität als eine sieht, die insbesondere mit dem Entstehen von Industrialisierung und Kapitalismus aufkommt, so bietet er, wie er selbst andeutet (da er Arbeitsteilung nicht als reines Phänomen der Moderne versteht), auch für andere Epochen der Menschheitsgeschichte Erklärungsmöglichkeiten. Ein gewichtiges Alleinstellungsmerkmal der Moderne ist für ihn jedoch die räumliche Entgrenzung von Arbeitsteilung und somit auch von organischer Solidarität.[104]

Es ergeben sich unweigerlich Anknüpfungspunkte für die historische Betrachtung: Mit Durkheim wäre davon auszugehen, dass dort, wo es zu Transformationen von Arbeitsverständnissen und Sinnstiftungen in Bezug auf Arbeit kommt, diese mit Transformationen der gesellschaftlichen Or-

---

99 Vgl. a. a. O., S. 452

100 Vgl. a. a. O., S. 454; Durkheim, *Vorwort*, S. 73.

101 Durkheim, *Über soziale Arbeitsteilung*, S. 442.

102 Axel Honneth, *Arbeit und Anerkennung. Versuch einer Neubestimmung*, in: *DZPh*, Berlin 56 (2008) 3, S. 327–341, S. 339.

103 A. a. O., S. 338.

104 Vgl. Durkheim, *Vorwort*, S. 66.

ganisation von Arbeit und der Form der sozialen Integration korrespondieren.

Literaturverzeichnis

Agamben, Giorgio: *Höchste Armut. Ordensregeln und Lebensform*, Frankfurt a. M. 2012.

Alewell, Dorothea/Moll, Tobias: *Religion, Religiosität und Spiritualität am Arbeitsplatz in deutschen Unternehmen*, in: Alewell, Dorothea/Matiaske, Wenzel (Hgg.): *Standards Guter Arbeit – disziplinäre Positionen und interdisziplinäre Perspektiven*, Baden-Baden 2019, S. 107–139.

Apophthegmata Patrum (Teil 1). Das Alphabetikon – Die alphabetisch-anonyme Reihe, hg. v. Erich Schweitzer, *Weisung der Väter* 14, Beuron 2012.

Apophthegmata Patrum, Gerontikon, in: *PG* 65, Sp. 71–440.

Bellah, Robert N.: *Introduction*, in: Émile Durkheim: *On Morality and Society. Selected Writings*, Chicago/London 1973, S. ix–lv.

Die Benediktsregel lat.-dt., mit der Übersetzung der Salzburger Äbtekonferenz, hg. v. Ulrich Faust, Stuttgart 2009.

Bernhard von Clairvaux: *Apologia ad Guillelmum Abbatem / Apologie an den Abt Wilhelm*, in: Ders.: *Sämtliche Werke lat.–dt.*, Bd. 2, hg. v. Gerhard B. Winkler, Innsbruck 1992, S. 145–201.

Brecht, Martin: *Martin Luther, Bd 2: Ordnung und Abgrenzung der Reformation*, Stuttgart 1986.

Brüllmann, Philipp: *Art. Glück*, in: Rapp, Christof/Corcilius, Klaus (Hgg.): *Aristoteles-Handbuch. Leben – Werk – Wirkung*, Stuttgart/Weimar 2011, S. 232–238.

Busch, Christine/Vahle-Hinz, Tim: *Gesundheit und Wohlbefinden in einer Arbeitswelt im Wandel: Aufrechterhaltung von Standards guter Arbeit bei multikulturellen Belegschaften und flexibler Arbeit*, in: Alewell, Dorothea/Matiaske, Wenzel (Hgg.): *Standards Guter Arbeit – disziplinäre Positionen und interdisziplinäre Perspektiven*, Baden-Baden 2019, S. 39–61.

Chenu, Marie-Dominique: *Art. Arbeit*, in: *HWPh* 1, S. 480–482.

Dr. Martin Luthers Haus-Postille nach Veit Dietrich, Am fünften Sonntage nach Trinitatis (1534), in: W^2 13.1, S. 753–766.

Durkheim, Emile: *Über soziale Arbeitsteilung. Studie über die Organisation höherer Gesellschaften* (1893), Berlin ^{6}2012.

Ders.: *Der Selbstmord* (1897), Frankfurt a. M. 1983.

Ders.: *Vorwort zur zweiten Auflage. Einige Anmerkungen zu den Berufsgruppen*, in: Ders.: *Über soziale Arbeitsteilung. Studie über die Organisation höherer Gesellschaften* (1893), Berlin ^{6}2012, S. 41–75.

Einmütig in der Liebe. Die frühesten Quellentexte von Cîteaux / Antiquissimi textus cistercienses, lat.–dt., *Quellen und Studien zur Zisterzienserliteratur* 1, hgg. v. Hildegard Brem/Martin Altermatt, Langwaden ^{2}1998.

Engels, Johannes: *Merces auctoramentum servitutis. Die Wertschätzung bestimmter Arbeiten und Tätigkeiten durch antike heidnische Philosophen*, in: Postel, Verena (Hg.): *Arbeit im Mittelalter. Vorstellungen und Wirklichkeiten*, Berlin 2006, S. 57–77.

Felten, Franz J.: *Arbeit, Armut und Askese und die Folgen bei den frühen Zisterziensern*, in: *CistC* 108 (2001), S. 59–87.

Foucault, Michel: *Überwachen und Strafen. Die Geburt des Gefängnisses* (1975), Frankfurt a. M. 1976.

Gerhardt, Volker: *Art. Sinn des Lebens*, in: *HWPh* 9, Sp. 815–824.

Ders.: *Der Sinn des Sinns. Versuch über das Göttliche*, München 2014.

Guillaumont, Antoine: *Die Handarbeit im Alten Mönchtum: Bestreitung und Wertung*, in: Ders.: *An den Wurzeln des christlichen Mönchtums. Aufsätze*, *Weisung der Väter* 4, Beuron 2007, S. 142–153.

Habermas, Jürgen: *Kritische und konservative Aufgaben der Soziologie* (1962), in: Ders.: *Theorie und Praxis. Sozialphilosophische Studien*, Frankfurt a. M. 1971, S. 290–306.

Ders.: *Theorie des kommunikativen Handelns, Bd. 2: Zur Kritik der funktionalistischen Vernunft*, Frankfurt a. M. 1981.

Hanau, Hans/Matiaske, Wenzel: *Mitbestimmung im entgrenzten Betrieb – Arbeitsrechtliche und personalwirtschaftliche Perspektiven*, in: Alewell, Dorothea/Matiaske, Wenzel (Hgg.): *Standards Guter Arbeit – disziplinäre Positionen und interdisziplinäre Perspektiven*, Baden-Baden 2019, S. 213–242.

Harnack, Adolf: *Das Mönchtum, seine Ideale und seine Geschichte*, Berlin 1907.

Hauff, Sven: *Human Resource Management zwischen Uniformität und Differenzierung*, in: Alewell, Dorothea/Matiaske, Wenzel (Hgg.): *Standards Guter Arbeit – disziplinäre Positionen und interdisziplinäre Perspektiven*, Baden-Baden 2019, S. 65–80.

Hegel, Georg Wilhelm Friedrich: *Grundlinien der Philosophie des Rechts* (1820), Frankfurt a. M. 1995.

Honneth, Axel: *Arbeit und Anerkennung. Versuch einer Neubestimmung*, in: *DZPh*, Berlin 56 (2008) 3, S. 327–341.

Ders.: *Das Recht der Freiheit. Grundriß einer demokratischen Sittlichkeit*, Berlin 2011.

Jaeggi, Rahel: *Kritik von Lebensformen*, Berlin 2014.

James, William: *The Principles of Psychology I* (1890), New York 1950.

Joas, Hans: *Das Problem der Entstehung neuer Moral als Leitfaden durch Durkheims Werk*, in: Ders.: *Die Kreativität des Handelns*, Frankfurt a. M. 1992, S. 76–99.

Jung, Matthias: *Der bewusste Ausdruck*, Berlin 2009.

Kirchner, Stefan/Beyer, Jürgen: Die Plattformlogik als digitale Marktordnung, in: *Zeitschrift für Soziologie*, 45 (5), S. 324–339.

Koenig, Matthias: *Wie weiter mit Émile Durkheim?*, in: Hamburger Institut für Sozialforschung (Hg.): *Wie weiter mit…?*, Hamburg 2008.

Köpf, Ulrich: *Art. Mönchtum*, in: Beutel, Albrecht (Hg.): *Luther Handbuch*, Tübingen 2005, S. 50–57.

Liebsch, Burkhard: *Zerbrechliche Lebensformen. Widerstreit – Differenz – Gewalt*, Berlin 2001.

Ders.: *Art. Lebensform/Lebenskunst*, in: *NHPhG* 2, S. 1404–1418.

Löffler, Winfried: *Art. Sinn*, in: *NHPhG* 3, S. 1984–2000.

Luhmann, Niklas: *Arbeitsteilung und Moral. Durkheims Theorie* (1977), in: Emile Durkheim: *Über soziale Arbeitsteilung. Studie über die Organisation höherer Gesellschaften* (1893), Berlin [6]2012, S. 19–38.

Luther, Martin: *De votis monasticis iudicium* (1521), in: *WA* 8, S. 573–669.

Ders.: *Kirchenpostille* (1522) *zu Joh 21,19–24*, in: *WA* 10,1,1, S. 305–324.

Ders.: *Von der weltlichen Obrigkeit, wie weit man ihr Gehorsam schuldig sei* (1523), in: *WA* 11, S. 245–281, S. 255.

Marcuse, Herbert: *Über die philosophischen Grundlagen des wirtschaftswissenschaftlichen Arbeitsbegriffs* (1933), in: Ders.: *Schriften*, Bd. 1, Frankfurt a. M., S. 556–594.

Marx, Karl/Engels, Friedrich: *Die deutsche Ideologie. Kritik der neuesten deutschen Philosophie in ihren Repräsentanten Feuerbach, B. Bauer und Stirner und des deutschen Sozialismus in seinen verschiedenen Propheten* (1845f.), in: *MEW* 3, S. 9–530.

Meireis, Torsten: *Tätigkeit und Erfüllung. Protestantische Ethik im Umbruch der Arbeitsgesellschaft*, Tübingen 2008.

Miquel, Pierre: *Lexique du désert. Etude de quelque mots-clés du vocabulaire monastique grec ancien*, *SpOr* 44, S. 233–240.

Müller, Hans-Peter/Schmid, Michael: *Arbeitsteilung, Solidarität und Moral. Eine werkgeschichtliche und systematische Einführung in die »Arbeitsteilung« von Emile Durkheim* (1987), in: Emile Durkheim: *Über soziale Arbeitsteilung. Studie über die Organisation höherer Gesellschaften* (1893), Berlin [6]2012, S. 481–532.

Nagel, Bernhard: *Die Eigenarbeit der Zisterzienser. Von der religiösen Askese zur wirtschaftlichen Effizienz*, Marburg 2006.

Oberste, Jörg: *Die Zisterzienser*, Stuttgart 2014.

Parsons, Talcott: *The Structure of Social Action. A Study in Social Theory with Special Reference to a Group of Recent European Writers, Vol. 2* (1937), New York 1968.

Rastetter, Daniela: *Vielfalt gleichstellen? Gleichstellung, Antidiskriminierung und Diversity Management im Kontext von digitalisierter Arbeit*, in: Alewell, Dorothea/Matiaske, Wenzel (Hgg.): *Standards Guter Arbeit – disziplinäre Positionen und interdisziplinäre Perspektiven*, Baden-Baden 2019, S. 81–105.

Rawls, John: *Politischer Liberalismus* (1993), Frankfurt a. M. 1998.

Scheler, Max: *Arbeit und Ethik* (1899), in: Ders.: *Frühe Schriften*, hgg. v. Maria Scheler/Manfred S. Frings, Bern/München 1971, S. 161–195.

Schlapbach, Karin: *Art. Muße*, in: *RAC* 25, Sp. 357–369.

Schreiner, Klaus: *»Brot der Mühsal.« Körperliche Arbeit im Mönchtum des Mittelalters*, in: Postel, Verena (Hg.): *Arbeit im Mittelalter. Vorstellungen und Wirklichkeiten*, Berlin 2006, S. 133–170.

Schuler-Harms, Margarete/Goldberg, Katharina: Soziale Absicherung von alter und neuer Selbständigkeit als Herausforderung für das Sozialrecht, in: Alewell, Dorothea/Matiaske, Wenzel (Hgg.): *Standards Guter Arbeit – disziplinäre Positionen und interdisziplinäre Perspektiven*, Baden-Baden 2019, S. 189–212.

Schütz, Alfred: *Theorie der Lebensformen. Frühe Manuskripte aus der Bergson-Periode*, hg. v. Ilja Srubar, Frankfurt a. M. 1981.

Ders.: *Der sinnhafte Aufbau der sozialen Welt. Eine Einleitung in die verstehende Soziologie* (1932), Frankfurt a. M. 1993.

Schwertner, Siegfried M.: *IATG³. Internationales Abkürzungsverzeichnis für Theologie und Grenzgebiete*, Berlin/Boston ³2014.

Sewing, Werner: *Soziologie als Krisenwissenschaft?*, in: Heckmann, Friedrich/Winter, Peter (Hgg.): *21. Deutscher Soziologentag 1982. Beiträge der Sektions- und ad hoc-Gruppen*, Opladen 1983, S. 385–388.

Sheridan, Mark: *Monastic Culture: A Comparison of the Concepts of Askesis and Asceticism*, in: Nouzille, Philippe/Pfeifer, Michaela (Hgg.): *Monasticism between Culture and Cultures*, *AnMo* 14, S. 17–34.

Straßheim, Jan: *Sinn und Relevanz. Individuum, Interaktion und gemeinsame Welt als Dimensionen eines sozialen Zusammenhangs*, Wiesbaden 2015.

Taylor, Charles: *Self-Interpreting Animals*, in: Ders.: *Human Agency and Language. Philosophical Papers I*, Cambridge 1985, S. 45–76.

Ders.: *Sources of the Self. The Making of Modern Identity* (1989), Cambridge Mass., ⁸1996.

Treiber, Hubert/Steinert, Heinz: *Die Fabrikation des zuverlässigen Menschen. Über die »Wahlverwandtschaft« von Kloster- und Fabrikdisziplin*, Münster 2005.

Volz, Fritz-Rüdiger: *Art. Arbeit und Beruf*, in: Leppin, Volker/Schneider-Ludorff, Gury (Hgg.): *Das Luther-Lexikon*, Regensburg 22014, S. 70–72.

Weber, Max: *Wirtschaft und Gesellschaft. Grundriss der verstehenden Soziologie* (1921f.), Frankfurt a. M. 2005.

Wollasch, Joachim: *Cluny. Licht der Welt. Aufstieg und Niedergang der klösterlichen Gemeinschaft*, Düsseldorf/Zürich 1996.

Teil III

Standards Guter Arbeit und der Einfluss des rechtlichen Rahmens

Dispositives Arbeitsrecht – Das Beispiel der Arbeitszeitrichtlinie

Florian Schramm und Ines Kanngießer

1. Zusammenfassung

Das Arbeits(schutz-)recht ist für die Qualität von Arbeitsverhältnissen relevant, indem es neben inhaltlichen Maßstäben auch Instrumente der Gestaltung von Arbeitsverhältnissen bereitstellt. Für die Arbeitszeit ist neben dem Arbeitszeitgesetz auf der europäischen Ebene die Arbeitszeitrichtlinie 2003/88/EC für die betriebliche Arbeitszeitgestaltung maßgeblich. Die dort genannten Ziele und Inhalte sind für die Mitgliedsstaaten rechtlich bindend. Optional räumt die Richtlinie – wie auch das Arbeitszeitgesetz – den Mitgliedsstaaten auf Ebene der Sozialpartner (Tarifparteien) einen begrenzten Spielraum zur weiteren Ausgestaltung der Arbeitszeit ein, wodurch nationale, branchenspezifische und wirtschaftliche Bedürfnisse Berücksichtigung finden sollen. Dieser verhandelbare Ausgleichszeitraum, welcher zur Ermittlung der durchschnittlichen wöchentlichen Höchstarbeitszeit der Arbeitnehmer dient, stellt neben einigen anderen Regelungen im Arbeitsrecht eine Flexibilisierung dar, mit dem ggf. auch ein Unterschreiten des vorgesehenen Mindeststandards ermöglicht wird.

In diesem Beitrag wird in folgenden Schritten vorgegangen: Zuerst wird der in der Europäischen Arbeitszeitrichtlinie bzw. dem Arbeitszeitgesetz formulierte Ausgleichszeitraum für das Überschreiten der zulässigen Arbeitszeiten erläutert. In einem zweiten Schritt wird die sozioökonomische Perspektive auf das Arbeitsrecht als eine geeignete Grundlage für die empirische Forschung skizziert. In einem dritten Schritt werden Ergebnisse der bisherigen Analyse vorgestellt. Mit einem Fazit endet der Beitrag.

2. Law in books – Law in practice

Das Arbeitszeitrecht wird als Arbeitnehmerschutzrecht verstanden (Charter of Fundamental Rights of the European Union, Artikel 31). Zusammenfassend liegen die gesetzlichen Aufgaben in der Lösung des Interessenkonflikts zwischen der Arbeitgeber- und Arbeitnehmerseite. Arbeitnehmer sollen vor unangemessenen Regelungen durch den Arbeitgeber geschützt werden, während zugleich günstige Rahmenbedingungen im wirtschaftlichen und konjunkturellen Kontext für eine flexible Arbeitszeitgestaltung geschaffen werden sollen (Directive 2003/88/EC, Erwägungsgründe 1–17 sowie Artikel 1; § 1 ArbZG; Hahn et al. 2014: 33). Zur Wahrung der Schutzziele und Grundsätze wurde auf europäischer Ebene die Directive 2003/88/EC über Aspekte der Arbeitszeitgestaltung des europäischen Parlaments erlassen. Diese Richtlinie umfasst eine Ansammlung von zwingenden Mindestschutzbedingungen zugunsten der Arbeitnehmer, welche durch die Mitgliedsstaaten in nationales Recht umzusetzen sind. Eine nicht fristgerechte oder nur ungenügende Umsetzung setzt der unmittelbaren Wirkung der Richtlinien nichts entgegen (Treaty establishing the European Economic Community, Artikel 10 und 249).

Bezogen auf die wöchentliche Höchstarbeitszeit legt die Arbeitszeitrichtlinie fest, dass die Mitgliedsstaaten die erforderlichen Maßnahmen zu treffen haben, dass nach dem Verhältnis des Erfordernisses der Sicherheit und des Gesundheitsschutzes der Arbeitnehmer a) »the period of weekly working time is limited by means of laws, regulations or administrative provisions or by collective agreements or agreements between the two sides of industry;« and does b) »the average working time for each seven-day period, including overtime, does not exceed 48 hours.« (Directive 2003/88/EC, Artikel 6). Artikel 16 Ziffer b sieht zunächst einen Ausgleichszeitraum von bis zu vier Monaten vor. Die Arbeitszeitrichtlinie erlaubt von diesem Mindeststandard abzuweichen. Konkret ist es den Mitgliedsstaaten nach Artikel 19 Abs. 1 der Arbeitszeitrichtlinie gestattet, den Ausgleichszeitraum per Gesetz für eine bestimmte Auswahl von Berufstätigkeiten und Arbeitnehmergruppen auf sechs Monate zu verlängern. Darüber hinaus ist eine nationale Verlängerung des Ausgleichszeitraums auf bis zu maximal zwölf Monate nur möglich, sofern diese Verlängerung gemeinschaftlich durch die entsprechenden Tarifvertragsparteien beschlossen und in Tarifverträgen verankert wird (Directive 2003/88/EC, Artikel 19 Abs. 2). Innerhalb des Ausgleichszeitraums darf die durchschnittliche wöchentliche Höchstarbeitszeit der Arbeitnehmer 48 Stunden nicht überschreiten (Directive 2003/88/EC).

Die deutschen Regelungen des Arbeitszeitgesetzes sind weitestgehend konform mit den europäischen Vorgaben. Mit Blick auf den Ausgleichszeitraum ist jedoch dahingehend eine Abweichung festzustellen, dass Deutschland uneingeschränkt für sämtliche Tätigkeiten einen sechsmonatigen Ausgleichszeitraum zur Ermittlung der durchschnittlichen Wochenarbeitszeit von 48 Stunden vorsieht (§ 3 Satz 2 ArbZG), während die europäischen Vorgaben diesen nur eingeschränkt für ganz bestimmte Tätigkeiten und Arbeitnehmergruppen erlauben (EC 2010: 4). Hahn et al. (2014: 88) sowie Schubert und Jerchel (2011: 77) bezweifeln, dass diese Regelung mit den unionalen Vorgaben der Arbeitszeitrichtlinie vereinbar ist und stufen den sechsmonatigen Ausgleichszeitraum als europarechtswidrig ein. Hieran würden auch die Ausnahmeregelungen der Arbeitszeitrichtlinie nach den Artikeln 17 und 19 nichts ändern, welche Verlängerungen auf sechs oder zwölf Monate in benannten Ausnahmefällen vorsehen, denn »§ 3 Satz 2 ArbZG formuliert den Regel- und nicht einen abschließenden vorgesehenen Ausnahmefall,« argumentieren Hahn et al. (2014: 88). Die juristische Prüfung, ob die im deutschen Arbeitsrecht vorgesehene verlängerte Ausgleichsfrist von 6 Kalendermonaten den Vorgaben der Arbeitszeitrichtlinie entspricht hält an (EC 2016).

Neben dem obigen Arbeitszeitrecht ist für die Bewertung die vom Recht oftmals stark abweichende Rechtswirklichkeit von zentraler Bedeutung. So ist unbestimmt, wie das Recht in der betrieblichen Praxis wahrgenommen und eingeschätzt wird, was wiederum die Basis für das eine soziale Wirklichkeit konstruierendes Verhalten der beteiligten Akteure bildet. Die Wirkung von Recht und Gesetz hängt demgemäß unweigerlich mit dem Verhalten der Handelnden zusammen, welches wiederum durch Normkenntnisse, Legimitationsvorstellungen sowie Erwartungshaltung im Hinblick auf Sanktionen gesteuert wird (Röhl 1987: 252).

3. Die sozioökonomische Perspektive auf das Recht

Mit einer sozioökonomischen Perspektive ist eine Perspektive gemeint, welche dem methodologischen Individualismus verpflichtet ist, ohne dabei kollektive Phänomene zu vernachlässigen. So werden zur Erklärung kollektiver Phänomene auf der Makroebene sozialer Systeme, die im Mittelpunkt des Forschungsinteresses stehen, die Handlungen der Akteure auf der Mikroebene herangezogen, die in einen Kontext eingebunden sind (Coleman 1995). So ist etwa die Machtverteilung in einem sozialen System nicht allein auf strukturelle Gegebenheiten zurückzuführen. Das Makrophänomen der Machtverteilung ist vielmehr das Ergebnis von Wahlhandlungen der Akteure auf der Mikroebene (Logik der Selektion), die auf Grund eines spezifischen Aggregationsmechanismus Folgen auf der Makroebene zeitigen (Logik der Aggregation). Zum Verständnis der Wahlentscheidungen der (ggf. kollektiven) Akteure sind bei Bedarf deren innere Zustände zur Erklärung heranzuziehen. Diese Perspektive teilt mit der systemtheoretischen Rechtstheorie (Vesting 2007) die Einsicht, dass Recht (als System) durch das Handeln der Akteure reproduziert wird.

Für die Analyse der Rechtswirklichkeit ist die Bedeutung psychologischer Aspekte des Wahrnehmens, Bewertens, Entscheidens etc. wichtig. Akteure beurteilen Alternativen vor dem Hintergrund ihrer Ziele und suchen nach möglichst vorteilhaften Lösungen. Das gilt für individuelle Akteure ebenso wie für kollektive Akteure – in letzterem Falle jedoch vermittelt durch die Interaktionen der Individuen, die in einen organisatorischen Kontext eingebunden sind.

Das Arbeitsrecht wirkt in der Interaktion der betrieblichen Akteure auch dann, wenn es nicht expliziter Gegenstand der Kommunikation ist. Es ist jedoch nicht nur implizites Wissen der Akteure, sondern auch explizit eine Ressource, die die Akteure z. B. im Falle von Konflikten nutzen können. Dabei geht es nicht allein um geschriebenes oder in Gerichten verhandeltes Recht, sondern um das Arbeitsrecht, wie es sich die Akteure für ihre Zwecke »zurechtlegen«. Auch streben die betrieblichen Akteure, selbst wenn sie sich des Arbeitsrechts explizit bedienen, nicht unbedingt die juristische Auseinandersetzung mit Hilfe von Rechtsanwälten und Gerichten an. So bleiben Verhandlungen und Konflikte unter dem Niveau einer justiziablen Auseinandersetzung, was aber gerade nicht bedeutet, dass das Arbeitsrecht dabei keine explizite *oder* implizite Rolle spielt. Implizit ist die Rolle des Arbeitsrechts immer dann, wenn die Akteure wissen, dass sie bei Bedarf auf die Ressource Recht zugreifen können, es aber momentan nicht tun, solange es andere Möglichkeiten gibt. Gerade diese Hintergrundfunktion dürfte einen wesentlichen Teil der Wirkung des Arbeitsrechts ausmachen.

4. Der Forschungsstand zum Ausgleichszeitraum

Das Ziel dieses Abschnitts liegt darin, über die tatsächliche Bedeutung der verlängerten Ausgleichszeiträume zur Berechnung der durchschnittlichen wöchentlichen Arbeitszeit zu informieren. Hierzu wurden zwei qualitative Forschungsmethoden eingesetzt. Im Rahmen einer Dokumentenanalyse (Lamnek 2010; Wolff 2013) wurden zunächst 36 Tarifverträge im Geltungsbereich von Hamburg dahingehend untersucht, ob abweichende

Ausgleichszeiträume in Tarifverträgen Anwendung finden und welchen Umfang diese haben. Zudem wurden Erfahrungen und Einstellungen von Tarifvertragsparteien durch neun Experteninterviews (Meuser & Nagel 1991; Liebold & Trinczek 2009) erfasst. Angesichts des dürftigen Forschungsstands stand nicht die Hypothesenprüfung, sondern die Hypothesen- beziehungsweise Theoriegenerierung im Vordergrund (Lamnek 2010: 20).

Gefragt wurde vorrangig danach, inwieweit abweichende arbeitszeitliche Regelungen zur Ermittlung der durchschnittlichen wöchentlichen Arbeitszeit (so genannter Ausgleichszeitraum) nach § 7 Abs. 1 Nr. 1 b ArbZG in der tariflichen Praxis tatsächlich vereinbart werden. Wie werden zudem die abweichenden Regelungen nach § 7 Abs. 1 Nr. 1 b ArbZG ausgestaltet (Ausschöpfungsgrad nach § 7 Abs. 8 ArbZG)? Schließlich waren die Gründe für die getroffenen Regelungen und die Erfahrungen der Tarifvertragsparteien von Interesse.[1]

Durch die Dokumentenanalyse konnten vier tarifliche Varianten zur (abweichenden) Vereinbarung von Ausgleichsfristen ausgemacht werden:

- *Erhöhung der Flexibilisierung durch Tarifvertrag:* Das heißt, dass der Tarifvertrag unmittelbar und zwingend eine Verlängerung des Ausgleichszeitraums auf über sechs Kalendermonate vorsieht.
- *Einschränkung der Flexibilisierung durch Tarifvertrag:* Das heißt, dass der Tarifvertrag unmittelbar und zwingend eine Verkürzung des gesetzlichen Ausgleichszeitraums auf unter sechs Kalendermonate vorsieht.

---

1 Eine inhaltliche Abgrenzung wird wie folgt vorgenommen: Die vorliegende Arbeit thematisiert auf europäischer Ebene neben den Zielen der Arbeitszeitrichtlinie 2003/88/EC die allgemeinen Regelungen zur wöchentlichen Arbeitszeit nach Artikel 6, dazugehörige Bezugszeiträume nach Artikel 16 b sowie die Grenzen der Abweichung von Bezugszeiträumen kollektivrechtlicher Art gemäß Artikel 19 der Arbeitszeitrichtlinie. In Deutschland entspricht dies der zulässigen Höchstarbeitszeit für Arbeitnehmer nach § 3 des Arbeitszeitgesetzes sowie Abweichungsmöglichkeiten durch Tarifvertrag nach § 7 Abs. 1 Nr. 1 b in Verbindung mit § 7 Abs. 8 ArbZG. Weitere arbeitszeitspezifische Regelungen und Besonderheiten wie beispielsweise die Abweichungsoptionen von der zulässigen wöchentlichen Höchstarbeitszeit auf individueller Ebene ohne Zeitausgleich (sogenannte »Opt-Out« Regelung (Directive 2003/88/EC, Artikel 22, Abs. 1) sind nicht Gegenstand dieses Beitrags.

- *Optionale Erhöhung der Flexibilisierung durch Öffnungsklausel im Tarifvertrag:* Das heißt, dass der Tarifvertrag optional eine Klausel vorsieht, welche eine Verlängerung des Bezugszeitraums auf ein festgeschriebenes Maximum (Anzahl Kalendermonate Ausgleichszeitraum) durch – erstens – Betriebsvereinbarung oder wenn kein Betriebsrat besteht, durch einzelvertragliche Regelung, oder – zweitens – ausschließlich durch Betriebsvereinbarung, oder – drittens – ausschließlich durch einzelvertragliche Regelung ermöglicht.
- *Beibehaltung der gesetzlichen Ausgleichsfrist:* Das heißt, dass der Tarifvertrag entweder keine, oder keine abweichende Vereinbarung zum gesetzlich festgelegten sechsmonatigen Ausgleichszeitraum vorsieht.

Die Dokumentenanalyse zeigt, dass innerhalb der Tarifverträge mehrheitlich abweichende Regelungen gewählt werden, die eine Verlängerung der Ausgleichsfrist auf zwölf Monate – und in Einzelfällen darüber hinaus auf bis zu 18 Monate[2] – vorsehen. Daneben wird die Beibehaltung gesetzlicher Fristen nur in einzelnen Fällen angestrebt, Verkürzungen gesetzlicher Fristen sind die seltene Ausnahme. Methodisch werden überwiegend Öffnungsklauseln verwendet. Hinsichtlich der Branchen zeigt sich, dass verlängerte Ausgleichszeiträume nicht nur in witterungsabhängigen Gewerben wie dem Baugewerbe (vergleiche Syben 2015) von zentraler Bedeutung sind, sondern auch in weiteren Branchen, die anderen externen Einflüssen unterliegen, anzutreffen sind.

Zusammenfassend eröffnen die Tarifverträge damit mehrheitlich einen arbeitszeitlichen Rahmen, der mehrere Wochen/Monate im Jahr eine 60 Stundenwoche zulässt (6 Werktage × 10 Stunden/Tag), solange die durchschnittliche Arbeitszeit von acht Stunden werktäglich im Ausgleichszeitraum (von überwiegend zwölf Monaten) nicht überschritten wird.

Im Rahmen der Experteninterviews kamen vier weitere Aspekte zum Vorschein.

Rolle der Sozialpartner: Die Arbeitnehmervertreter (Gewerkschaften) sehen sich in einer wichtigen Rolle, wenn es um die Verhandlung von abweichenden Ausgleichszeiträumen geht. Auch wenn die interviewten Experten auf Gewerkschaftsseite einen verlängerten Ausgleichszeitraum

2 Unter Umständen lässt sich dies in Anlehnung an Jachtenfuchs und Kohler-Koch (2004: 87) als ein Beispiel einer Fehlinterpretation der Richtlinie deuten.

auf bis zu zwölf Kalendermonate für Ihre Branche für notwendig halten, möchten sie dies nicht pauschal für alle Beschäftigen und Branchen im Gesetz verankert wissen. Eine gestaltende Mitbestimmung der Sozialpartner wird für notwendig erachtet, um branchenspezifische Korridore zu schaffen.[3] Die Festlegung eines gesetzlichen Ausgleichszeitraums von zwölf Monaten – wie es diskutiert wird – würde den Sozialpartnern einen Verhandlungspunkt in den Tarifverhandlungen nehmen, was ggf. eine reduzierte Wahrung der Arbeitnehmerinteressen und ein Absenken des Arbeitnehmerschutzes bedeuten könnte. Erwartungsgemäß plädieren die Arbeitgebervertreter für die diskutierte gesetzliche Verankerung eines generellen und für alle Arbeitnehmer geltenden zwölfmonatigen Ausgleichszeitraums (und gerne darüber hinaus auf bis zu 24 Monate) im Gesetz.

Vorteile verlängerter Ausgleichszeiträume: Die Gründe, die für eine Verlängerung des Ausgleichszeitraums sprechen, liegen den Experten folgend in branchenspezifischen Besonderheiten, der Reichweite des Tarifvertrages, also ob es sich um einen Firmen- oder Flächentarifvertrag handelt sowie den Bedürfnissen auf Arbeitnehmer- und Arbeitgeberseite. Hierzu zählt zum Beispiel die Berücksichtigung saisonaler Einflüsse, die Erfordernisse nach Sicherheit im Hinblick auf die Planung von Urlaub und Freizeit sowie das Begehren nach einer effizienten Personalplanung. Folglich ist nicht verwunderlich, dass den Experten zufolge die tarifliche Option zur Verlängerung des Ausgleichszeitraums in den Betrieben Anwendung finden und eine ungleichmäßige Verteilung der regelmäßigen wöchentlichen Arbeitszeit gelebte Praxis ist. Der verlängerte Ausgleichszeitraum ermöglicht den Unternehmen eine hohe Grundflexibilität in Bezug auf die Gestaltung der Arbeitszeit, aber auch Kostenvorteile durch einen effizienten Personaleinsatz. Die Möglichkeiten arbeitszeitlicher Flexibilisierung sind jedoch nicht nur für den Arbeitgeber vorteilig, um die Arbeitnehmer beispielsweise entsprechend der Auftragslage effizient einzusetzen. Vielmehr werden auch daraus resultierende Arbeitszeitmodelle von der Belegschaft gern in Anspruch genommen. Zudem verspricht ein Ausgleichszeitraum, der dem Kalenderjahr gleichgesetzt ist, der Belegschaft mehr Sicherheit in Bezug auf die Urlaubs- und Freizeitplanung. Den Arbeitnehmern wird dadurch im Vergleich zu kürzeren Ausgleichszeiträu-

3 Vgl. Hanau/Matiaske (2019) in diesem Band zur Auswirkung des Trends der »Entbetrieblichung« auf die Mitbestimmung.

men eine »freiere Gestaltung und Freizeitplanung« ihrer täglichen Arbeitszeit ermöglicht. Zieht man die Vorteile auf Arbeitnehmer- und Arbeitgeberseite zusammen, so kann nicht mehr davon gesprochen werden, dass es sich bei den Flexibilisierungsoptionen um ein Instrument ausschließlich zugunsten der Erfüllung von Arbeitgeberinteressen handelt. Seitens der Experten wird ein Zusammenhang zwischen arbeitszeitlicher Flexibilität, Arbeitszufriedenheit und geringerem Krankenstand der Arbeitnehmer postuliert, von dem wiederum der Arbeitgeber profitiert.
Gesundheitliche Aspekte: Dennoch betonen die Experten im Kontext aktueller demografischer Entwicklungen, Burnout und anderen multiplen Belastungsstörungen die zunehmende Bedeutung des Arbeitsschutzes und einer sachgemäßen Anwendung des Ausgleichszeitraums sowie die Bedeutung von Erholungsphasen für Arbeitnehmer. So wird auf die Ernsthaftigkeit gesundheitlicher Problematiken hingewiesen und Arbeitgeber sowie Betriebs- und Personalräte aufgerufen, die Einhaltung arbeitszeitlicher Bestimmungen zu überwachen, um gesundheitlichen Schäden und einem vorzeitigen Ausscheiden aus dem Unternehmen (zum Beispiel durch verfrühten Renteneintritt) vorzubeugen.[4] Dabei sind nicht zwangsläufig die Arbeitgeber die treibenden Kräfte, sondern auch die Arbeitnehmer mit ihren Präferenzen.

Rolle der Betriebsparteien im arbeitszeitlichen Gestaltungsprozess: Auch wenn sich die Flexibilität und ausgedehnte Ausgleichszeiträume zur ungleichmäßigen Verteilung der Arbeitszeit vermeintlich positiv auf die Arbeitnehmer auswirken, darf dies nicht als Argument gegen die Schutzvorschriften des Arbeitszeitgesetzes verstanden werden. Der Schutz der Arbeitnehmer ist bei der Anwendung des Arbeitszeitgesetzes zumindest gleichberechtigt zu den Zielen einer Flexibilisierung zu berücksichtigen. Zwei Experten konstatieren, dass hier ein hohes Maß an Kompetenz gefordert ist und schreiben den Betriebsparteien eine Schlüsselfunktion zu. Diese müssen in Anlehnung an den tariflich vorgegebenen Rahmen – mittels Betriebsvereinbarungen – die mit den Erfordernissen des Unternehmens abgestimmten Arbeitszeitmodelle und Stundenkontingente festlegen, und dabei die gesetzlichen Schutzinteressen der Arbeitnehmer wahren.

---

4 Dies geschieht zum Beispiel in Form von gesundheitsförderlicher Führung (Felfe/Klug 2019 in diesem Band) und durch die Gefährdungsbeurteilung psychischer Belastung (Busch/Vahle-Hinz 2019 in diesem Band).

5. Diskussion und Fazit

Die Aufgabe des Arbeitszeitrechts ist es, die Schutzinteressen der Arbeitnehmer mit den Flexibilisierungsabsichten des Arbeitgebers zu vereinbaren. Ein Instrument zur Flexibilisierung der Arbeitszeit stellt der so genannte Ausgleichszeitraum dar. Die mögliche Ausweitung des Ausgleichszeitraums durch die Tarifpartner stellt eine Ausnahme im Arbeitsrecht dar, bei der faktisch bestehende Schutzstandards unterlaufen werden. Der hierzu im engeren Sinne bestehende Forschungsstand ist ausgesprochen dürftig. Hier bietet sich eine sozioökonomische Perspektive an, die die verschiedenen Akteure (Arbeitgeber, Arbeitgeberverbände, Gewerkschaften, Betriebsräte, Beschäftigte, Gesetzgebung und Rechtsprechung) mit ihrem Verhalten berücksichtigen kann.

Bezüglich der realen Verhältnisse zeigt sich, dass abweichende Regelungen beim Ausgleichszeitraum in Tarifverträgen von zentraler Bedeutung sind. Bei rund drei Viertel der ausgewerteten Tarifverträge wurden verlängerte Ausgleichsfristen auf zwölf Monate vereinbart, in Einzelfällen sogar darüber hinaus auf bis zu 18 Monate. Nur ein Viertel orientiert sich an den allgemeinen gesetzlichen Bestimmungen des Arbeitszeitgesetzes, während nur ein Tarifvertrag diese auf zwei Monate reduziert. Die konkrete Ausgestaltung der tariflichen Bestimmungen im Hinblick auf die Flexibilisierungsoptionen durch die Ausgleichszeiträume obliegt überwiegend der Betriebsebene. Hierfür sehen die Tarifverträge entsprechende Öffnungsklauseln vor. Den Experten zufolge werden diese auch ausnahmslos in den Betrieben umgesetzt, von einer ungleichmäßigen Verteilung der regelmäßigen wöchentlichen Arbeitszeit in der betrieblichen Praxis kann somit ausgegangen werden. Dies ermöglicht den Unternehmen eine hohe Arbeitszeitflexibilität, aber auch Kostenvorteile durch einen effizienten Personaleinsatz. Auch die Arbeitnehmer scheinen von den flexiblen Arbeitszeitmodellen zu profitieren. Diese ermöglichen eine »freiere« Gestaltung ihrer täglichen Arbeitszeit, beispielsweise durch Gleitzeitsysteme und folglich eine bessere Planung ihrer Freizeit. In diesem Kontext wird sodann die Rolle der Arbeitgeber sowie der Betriebs- und Personalräte deutlich. Dem Verständnis der Experten folgend müssen diese verstärkt als Hüter der rechtmäßigen Umsetzung der Arbeitszeit fungieren, da die Vorschriften arbeitsrechtliche Schutznormen sind, wobei etliche Arbeitnehmer verlängerte Ausgleichszeiträume zu befürworten scheinen.

Die Ergebnisse dieser Forschungsarbeit sind jedoch zu limitieren. Sowohl die Dokumentenanalyse als auch die Experteninterviews beziehen sich nur auf den Geltungsbereich Hamburg. Bei der Dokumentenanalyse wurden 24 Tarifverträge analysiert. Auch die fünf Experteninterviews ermöglichen nur einen ersten Feldzugang, der durch weitere Interviews validiert werden müsste.

Aus der Analyse ergeben sich verschiedene Implikationen für die Wissenschaft und Praxis, die in Kürze genannt seien. *Erstens* ist eine fundierte Forschung in dieser terra incognita angesichts des politischen Diskurses um die Europäische Arbeitszeitrichtlinie und das Arbeitszeitgesetz in Deutschland und Europa geboten. *Zweitens* verdient die seltene Konstruktion des möglichen Unterlaufens von Schutzstandards (des öffentlichen Rechts) durch tarifpolitische Akteure Interesse. Nur in seltenen Fällen bestehen im deutschen Arbeitsrecht ähnliche Konstruktionen (z. B. Kündigungsschutz beim BGB). Tarifvertragliche Vereinbarungen sehen grundsätzlich vor, dass die Beschäftigten durch sie nicht schlechter gestellt werden dürfen. Das Tarifvertragsgesetz regelt für Ausnahmen Öffnungsklauseln (von Tarifverträgen). *Drittens* scheinen auch juristische Unstimmigkeiten zwischen der nationalen und der europäischen Regelung zu bestehen, so dass fraglich ist, ob das geltende und praktizierte Arbeitszeitgesetz im Hinblick auf den Bezugszeitraum europarechtskonform ist. *Viertens* schließlich zeigt die Analyse, wie dispositives Recht durch die Umsetzung der beteiligten Akteure Flexibilität unter Einhalten des Rechtsrahmens ermöglicht. Das Einbeziehen der Sozialpartner scheint die Berücksichtigung branchenspezifischer Besonderheiten und der Interessen der Arbeitnehmer zu gewährleisten. Dies könnte auch im europäischen Kontext gelten, da offensichtlich durch dispositive Elemente in einem für recht verschiedene Länder gleichen Rechtsrahmen Flexibilität innerhalb dieses Rechtsrahmens ermöglicht wird. Zudem scheint die Einbindung der Sozialpartner das Machtgefüge von Arbeitnehmer- und Arbeitgeberinteressenvertretungen zu stabilisieren. Dies weist auf die Vorteile einer reflexiven Regulierung (vgl. Kremer/Bothfeld 2012) hin, die die rechtliche Selbstregulierung gegenüber einer alleinigen Gesetzgebung bevorzugt. Nach der bisherigen Forschung scheint es sich bei der reflexiven Regulierung weder um den Königsweg noch um eine Sackgasse (vgl. Kremer/Bothfeld 2012) der zukünftigen Gestaltung des Arbeitsrechts zu handeln. Ganz gewiss aber verdient sie im Kontext arbeitsrechtlich fundierter Standards der Arbeit vertiefte Forschungsbemühungen.

Literaturverzeichnis

Arbeitszeitgesetz (1994) vom 6. Juni 1994. Zuletzt geändert 20.04.2013.

Busch, C. & Vahle-Hinz T. (2019): Gesundheit und Wohlbefinden in einer Arbeitswelt im Wandel: Aufrechterhaltung von Standards guter Arbeit bei multikulturellen Belegschaften und flexibler Arbeit. In: Alewell, D. & Matiaske, W. (Hrsg.): *Standards Guter Arbeit – disziplinäre Positionen und interdisziplinäre Perspektiven*. Baden-Baden: Nomos, 39–61.

Charter of fundamental rights of European Union (2000). http://www.europarl.europa.eu/charter/pdf/text_en.pdf (10/12/2016).

Coleman, J. S. (1995): *Grundlagen der Sozialtheorie*. Band 1. München, Wien: Oldenbourg.

Directive 2003/88/EC of the European Parliament and of the Council of 4 November 2003 concerning certain aspects of the organization of working time. Brussels.

European Commission (2010) Report form the Commission to the European Parliament, the Council, the European Economic and Social Committee and the Committee of the Regions on implementation by Member States of Directive 2003/88/EC. COM(2010) 802. Brussels.

European Commisson (2016) February infringements package: main decisions. Employment: Commission requests Germany to respect the reference period to calculate average weekly working time for German civil service. http://europa.eu/rapid/ press-release_MEMO-15-4489_de.htm (10/12/2016).

Hahn, F., Pfeiffer, G. & Schubert, J. (2014): *Arbeitszeitrecht. Handkommentar*. Baden-Baden: Nomos Verlag.

Hanau, H. & Matiaske W. (2019). Mitbestimmung im entgrenzten Betrieb – Arbeitsrechtliche und personalwirtschaftliche Perspektiven. In: Alewell, D. & Matiaske, W. (Hrsg.): *Standards Guter Arbeit – disziplinäre Positionen und interdisziplinäre Perspektiven*. Baden-Baden: Nomos, 213–242.

Jachtenfuchs, M. & Kohler-Koch, B. (2004) Governance in der Europäischen Union. In: Benz, A. (Hrsg.) *Governance – Regieren in komplexen Regelsystemen*. Wiesbaden: Springer-Verlag, 77–101.

Kremer, S. & Bothfeld, S. (2012). In: Bothfeld, S. (Hrsg.): *Arbeitsmarktpolitik in der sozialen Marktwirtschaft*. Wiesbaden: Springer-Verlag.

Lamnek, S. (2010): *Qualitative Sozialforschung*. Weinheim, Basel: Beltz Verlag.

Lieboldt, R. & Trinczek, R. (2009): Experteninterview. In: Kühl, S., Strodtholz, P. & Taffertshofer, A. (Hrsg.): *Handbuch Methoden der Organisationsforschung. Quantitative und Qualitative Methoden*. Wiesbaden: VS Verlag, 32–56.

Meuser, M. & Nagel, U. (1991): ExpertInneninterviews – vielfach erprobt, wenig bedacht. Ein Beitrag zur qualitativen Methodendiskussion. In: Garz, D. & Kraimer, K. (Hrsg.): *Qualitativ-empirische Sozialforschung. Konzepte, Methoden, Analysen*. Opladen: Westdeutscher Verlag, 441–471.

Röhl, K. F. (1987): *Rechtssoziologie*. Köln, Berlin, Bonn, München: Heymanns Verlag.

Schubert, J. M. & Jerchel, K. (2011): *Handlungsspielräume für Tarifparteien und Interessenvertretungen bei der Arbeitszeitgestaltung. WSI Mitteilung 2/2011*. Düsseldorf: Wirtschafts- und Sozialwissenschaftliches Institut in der Hans-Böckler-Stiftung, 76–82.

Syben, G. (2015): *Arbeitszeiten zwischen tariflicher Regelung betrieblichem Alltag – Eine explorative Untersuchung tariflicher und tatsächlicher Arbeitszeiten im Branchenvergleich im Organisationsbereich der Industriegewerkschaft Bauen-Agrar-Umwelt*. http://www.boeckler.de/pdf_fof/S-2014-760-3-1.pdf (12/10/2016).

Treaty establishing the European Economic Community (2002). http://eur-lex.europa.eu/legal-content/EN/TXT/PDF/?uri=CELEX:12002E/TXT&from=EN (10/12/ 2016).

Vesting, Thomas (2007): *Rechtstheorie. Ein Studienbuch. Juristische Kurz-Lehrbücher*. München: Verlag C.H. Beck.

Wolff, S. (2013): Dokumenten- und Aktenanalyse. In: Flick, U., Kardorff, E. v. & Steinke, I. (Hrsg.): *Qualitative Forschung: Ein Handbuch*. 10. Auflage. Reinbek: Rowohlt Verlag, 502–513.

Soziale Absicherung von alter und neuer Selbstständigkeit als Herausforderung für das Sozialrecht

Margarete Schuler-Harms und Katharina Goldberg[1]

Soziale Sicherung ist ein Thema »guter Arbeit« in mehrfacher Hinsicht. So hat sie den Zweck, Risiken, die sich aus dem Ausfall der Erwerbstätigkeit und des Erwerbseinkommens ergeben, für die Erwerbstätigen und ihre Familien aufzufangen und durch Sach- und Geldleistungen abzufedern. Zugleich wirkt sie auf die Arbeitswelt zurück, indem sie Erwerbstätige von der Sorge um anderweitige Absicherung dieser Risiken entlastet. Pflichtmitgliedschaften und Pflichtbeiträge als wesentliches Element der Sozialversicherung gewährleisten von jeher funktionsfähige Systeme, die nicht nur das (Ver-)Sicherungsprinzip, sondern mit ihrer Orientierung am Arbeitsentgelt bzw. -einkommen und durch andere Solidarkomponenten wie z. B. die Berücksichtigung von Unterhaltsempfängern der Versicherten soziale Gerechtigkeit verwirklichen. Mit diesen Funktionen entlasten soziale Sicherungssysteme zugleich die Allgemeinheit von der Sicherung des Existenzminimums derer, die ohne diese Systeme im Risikofall nicht in der Lage wären, sich und ihre Angehörigen selbst zu unterhalten.[2] Die Frage nach sozialer Sicherung Selbstständiger ist auch insoweit von Belang, denn hinsichtlich der steuerfinanzierten Existenzsicherung (im Alter als sog. Grundsicherung, §§ 41 ff. SGB XII) stehen sich Beschäftigte und Selbstständige gleich.[3]

---

1 Die Autoren danken Wenzel Matiaske für die Ergänzung dieses Beitrages um die Fußnoten 9, 24, 41.

2 Vgl. statt vieler *R. Waltermann*, Sozialrecht, 11. Aufl. 2014, Rn.107.

3 Historisch lässt sich dies nachvollziehen am Beispiel der sog. Erwerbslosenfürsorge während der Weimarer Republik, die als Sonderfürsorgesystem auch Selbständige umfasste, und der seit 1927 bestehenden Arbeitslosenversicherung, die ausschließlich abhängig Beschäftige einbezog, vgl. *A. Hänlein/F. Tennstedt*, Geschichte des Sozialrechts, in: v. Maydell/Ruland/Becker (Hrsg.), Sozialrechtshandbuch (SRH), 5. Auflage 2012, § 2 Rn. 31.

Im Konzept der Verwirklichungschancen (*capability approach*) Amartya Sens[4] haben soziale Anwartschaften und Leistungen die Funktion materieller Ressourcen, die die individuelle Befähigung für ein gutes Leben positiv beeinflussen können. Gute Arbeit bildet zugleich eine Voraussetzung als auch einen Teil guten Lebens.[5] Pflichtmitgliedschaften und Pflichtbeiträge binden Versicherte in Solidarsysteme ein, die Risiken des Alters und Todes, der Krankheit und Pflegebedürftigkeit, teilweise auch der Arbeitslosigkeit, kollektivieren. Zugleich bewirken Pflichtmitgliedschaft und Beitragspflicht Bindungen in der autonomen Lebensführung, die die Chancen für die Verwirklichung eines guten Lebens auch mindern können. Innerhalb des *capability approaches* entsteht auf diese Weise ein Spannungsverhältnis zwischen den positiven und negativen Ressourcen, die die Einbindung in Sozialversicherungssysteme mit sich bringt.

Die Sozialversicherung des Bismarck'schen Typs kennzeichnen einige spezifische Merkmale.[6] Es handelt sich um einen *de jure* Standard mit einem gegliederten System von Pflichtversicherungen, die regelhaft (abhängig) Beschäftigte zu Mitgliedern haben. Beitragspflichtig sind – mit Ausnahme der gesetzlichen Unfallversicherung – regelmäßig Arbeitgeber und Arbeitnehmer zu etwa gleichen Teilen. Selbstständige sind in dieses System sozialer Sicherung weder prinzipiell noch systematisch standardisiert eingebunden. Einen Arbeitgeber haben sie nicht, sondern typischerweise Auftraggeber oder Kunden. Für sie gilt die Annahme, dass selbstständige Erwerbstätigkeit grundsätzlich mit eigenständiger Absicherung der mit einem Ausfall der Erwerbstätigkeit oder gar -fähigkeit verbundenen Risiken einhergeht, zu der die Erwerbstätigen (ggf. zusammen mit ihren Angehörigen) typischerweise imstande seien.

Ein solches Leitbild der Selbstständigkeit prägt das Sozialversicherungsrecht jedoch weder rein noch lückenlos. Dieses bindet

---

4 Vgl. *A. Sen*, Ökonomie für den Menschen, Wege zu Gerechtigkeit und Solidarität in der Marktwirtschaft, 2002. Zur Adaption auf die deutsche Situation siehe *R. Lehweß-Litzmann/O. Leßmann*, Kapitel 2. Wie Teilhabe produziert wird. in: Dritter Bericht zur sozioökonomischen Entwicklung in Deutschland: Exklusive Teilhabe – ungenutzte Chancen. Bielefeld 2016.

5 Zum Zusammenhand von Arbeit und einem sinnhaften Leben siehe *B. Müller/C. Seibert/O.Vornfeld,* Von Arbeit und Sinn – Analyse eines Problemfeldes, in: D. Alewell, W. Matiaske (Hrsg.), Standards Guter Arbeit – disziplinäre Positionen und interdisziplinäre Perspektiven, Baden-Baden 2019, S. 139–173.

6 Knapp zusammengefasst bei *R. Waltermann*, Sozialrecht, 11. Aufl. 2014, Rn. 108.

Selbstständige in unterschiedlichen Formen und aus unterschiedlichen Gründen in die sozialen Sicherungssysteme ein (1). Die Einbindung bleibt rechtstechnisch und -praktisch immer eine Ausnahme.[7] Auch »Pfade« zeichnen sich im Laufe der Rechtsentwicklung kaum ab. Die fehlende Systematik der Einbindung Selbstständiger in die Sozialversicherung dürfte auch in der Vielfalt und Wandelbarkeit der Selbstständigkeit und den mit ihr einhergehenden Sicherungsbedürfnissen ihren Grund finden. Dennoch sind Stimmen, die eine umfassendere oder systematischere Einbindung Selbstständiger in die sozialen Sicherungssysteme fordern, nie verstummt und gegenwärtig wieder deutlicher zu vernehmen. Konkreten Anlass zur Überprüfung der bestehenden Strukturen gibt der heute beobachtete Wandel der Arbeit nicht nur, aber auch als Begleiterscheinung der Digitalisierung (2). War und ist selbstständige Erwerbstätigkeit (noch) in dem beschriebenen Sinne »gute Arbeit«? Greift die deutsche Sozialversicherung in Bezug auf selbstständige Erwerbstätigkeit und neue Arbeitsformen hinreichend weit oder droht sie ihre Zwecke zu verfehlen und ihre Funktionen zu verlieren? Müssen hier neue Standards gesetzt werden? Diesen Fragen wird unter Nutzung des Konzepts der Verwirklichungschancen unter 3. nachgegangen. Bei entsprechendem Befund stellt sich außerdem die Frage nach einer Anpassung der Systeme und ihrer rechtlichen Grundlagen (4).

---

7 Vgl. nur *K. Windhövel*, Szenarien einer Eingliederung der Selbständigen ohne obligatorische Altersvorsorge in die gesetzliche Rentenversicherung, 2009; *K. Schulze Buschoff*, Sozialpolitische Perspektiven der neuen Selbständigkeit, in: A. D. Bührmann/H. J. Pongatz (Hrsg.), Prekäres Unternehmertum – Unsicherheiten von selbständiger Erwerbstätigkeit und Unternehmensgründung, 2010, S. 167 ff.; *D. Hedermann*, Krankenversicherungsschutz in der modernen Gesellschaft, 2014, S. 117 ff.; *O. Deinert*, Soloselbständige zwischen Arbeitsrecht und Wirtschaftsrecht, 2015, S. passim; *W. Brose*, Von Bismarck zu Crowdwork, NZS 2017, S. 7 ff. Die Neuschaffung des § 23 c Abs. 2 SGB IV 2017 hat die Regelungstechniken der Sozialversicherungspflicht von soloselbstständig tätigen Notärzten um eine neue Variante erweitert, indem ihre Einnahmen beitragsfrei gestellt werden, vgl. kritisch hierzu *S. Porten*, NZS 2017, S. 495, 500.

1. Bestandsaufnahme: Soziale Sicherung Selbstständiger

1.1. Grundlagen

Das Sozialversicherungsrecht definiert den Begriff der Selbstständigkeit nicht, sondern nennt ihn als Komplementärbegriff zum zentralen Systembegriff der Beschäftigung: Beschäftigung ist »nichtselbstständige Arbeit, insbesondere in einem Arbeitsverhältnis« (§ 7 Abs. 1 S. 1 SGB IV)[8]. Die Bedeutung der Abgrenzung zur Beschäftigung iSv §7 Abs. 1 S. 1 SGB IV sieht der Gesetzgeber durchaus: Über die Frage, ob Beschäftigung vorliegt, entscheidet auf Anfrage die Deutsche Rentenversicherung und trifft damit eine Regelung durch Verwaltungsakt, den die Betroffenen mit Widerspruch und Klage anfechten können (vgl. § 7a SGB IV). Der Gesetzgeber hat wenigstens die Abgrenzung für Hausgewerbetreibende, Heimarbeiter und sog. Zwischenmeister näher vorgezeichnet (§ 12 SGB IV) und

8 Rund 4,3 Mio. Personen waren 2017 selbständig, siehe *Destatis*, Erwerbsbeteiligung der Bevölkerung – Fachserie 1 Reihe 4.1, 2017. Mit einer Selbständigenquote von 9,8 % (9,5 % ohne Landwirtschaft) liegt Deutschland weit unterhalb des EU-Durchschnitts von 14,5 % (12,9 % ohne Landwirtschaft) bzw. der Länder in der Euro-Zone von 14,3 % (13,2 % ohne Landwirtschaft) (Quelle: EUROSTAT; eigene Berechnung). Jedoch ist die Selbständigenquote seit den 1980er Jahren nach zwei Jahrzehnten kontinuierlichen Rückgangs erheblich gestiegen. Insbesondere ab 2000 wuchs der Anteil der Selbständigen (*K. Kelleter*, Selbstständige in Deutschland, Wirtschaft und Statistik 2009, Nr. 12, S. 1204–1217). Im Zeitfenster von 2000–2012 stieg ihr Anteil um 14 %, wohingegen die Zahl der abhängig Beschäftigten im Zeitraum nur um 5 % aufwuchs. Dabei entwickelte sich insbesondere der Anteil der Solo-Selbständigen stark positiv, wohingegen der Anteil der Selbständigen mit Beschäftigten stagniert (*K. Brenke*, Allein tätige Selbständige: starkes Beschäftigungswachstum, oft nur geringe Einkommen, DIW Wochenbericht 2013, Nr. 7, S. 3–16). Wichtige Treiber der Entwicklung waren Förderinstrumente der Bundesagentur für Arbeit, die Liberalisierung im Handwerk, die ab 2004 die Gründung von Betrieben ohne Meisterbrief ermöglichte, sowie die EU-Erweiterung. Seit 2012 ist der Anteil der Solo-Selbständigen, der seinerzeit 6,3 %, betrug wieder leicht rückgängig (*K. Brenke*, Selbständige Beschäftigung geht zurück, DIW Wochenbericht 2015, Nr. 36, S. 790–796). Derzeit beträgt die Quote der Solo-Selbständigen in Deutschland 5,6 %. Die Vergleichszahl im EU Durchschnitt beträgt 10,6 % (*K. Schulze Buschoff*, Selbstständigkeit und hybride Erwerbsformen – Sozialpolitische Gestaltungsoptionen. Nr. 21, Policy Brief WSI 2018).

damit eine Schnittstelle von abhängiger und selbstständiger Tätigkeit für einen bestimmten Tätigkeitstyp selbst bearbeitet.

Selbstständigkeit als sozialrechtliche Kategorie bedarf der Differenzierung: Vor allem für kleine oder sog. Solo-Selbstständige ohne eigene oder mit nur wenigen sozialversicherungspflichtigen Arbeitnehmern wird Sozialversicherungspflicht erwogen oder bereits umgesetzt. Auch innerhalb dieser Gruppe sind unterschiedliche Formen und Typen der Selbstständigkeit für die Reichweite der Sozialversicherungspflicht zu unterscheiden. In einigen Zweigen der Sozialversicherung ist freiwillige Mitgliedschaft Selbstständiger möglich. Als Pflichtmitglieder werden Selbstständige den Beschäftigten teils gleichgestellt, teils wird ihr Versicherungsstatus abweichend gestaltet. Denkbar sind als weitere, wenn auch seltene Kategorien eine Versicherungspflicht auf Antrag oder die Möglichkeit der Befreiung von der Versicherungspflicht.

Dem für die Beitragsbemessung maßgeblichen Begriff des Arbeitsentgelts Beschäftigter (§ 14 SGB IV) entspricht bei selbstständiger Tätigkeit der Begriff des Arbeitseinkommens (§ 15 Abs. 1 SGB IV). Arbeitseinkommen ist der nach den allgemeinen Gewinnermittlungsvorschriften des Einkommensteuerrechts ermittelte Gewinn aus einer selbstständigen Tätigkeit. Die Einkünfte aus selbstständiger Arbeit regelt § 18 EStG. Besonderheiten gelten für die Bestimmung des Arbeitseinkommens bei Landwirten (§ 15 Abs. 2 SGB IV). Die rechtlichen Grundlagen für die einzelnen Sozialversicherungszweige können in der Beitragsbemessung abweichen und gehen in diesem Falle vor (vgl. § 1 Abs. 3 SGB IV).

Typischerweise haben Selbstständige keinen Arbeitgeber und müssen ihren Sozialversicherungsbeitrag vollständig selbst aufzubringen. Auch diese Regel gilt nicht ausnahmslos. § 28m SGB IV und besondere Regelungen (vgl. § 169 Nr. 3 SGB VI) sehen vor, dass für Hausgewerbetreibende ein halber Beitrag durch den »Arbeitgeber« zu entrichten ist. Für Künstler und Publizisten wird die zweite Hälfte des Aufkommens durch die »Verwerter« der künstlerischen oder publizistischen Leistung (Verlage, Galerien, Rundfunkanstalten)[9] in der Form der Künstlersozialabgabe aufgebracht. In der gesetzlichen Rentenversicherung wird ein halber Beitrag für Seelotsen durch die Lotsenbruderschaft übernommen (vgl. § 174 Abs. 3 Nr. 1 SGB VI).

9 Zum Kreis der »Verwerter« vgl. § 24 Abs. 1 KSVG.

Auch im zeitlichen Umfang einer Versicherungspflicht können sich die Gruppen der selbstständigen Versicherten unterscheiden. Für das Handwerk etwa wurde die Versicherungspflicht im Jahr 1960 auf 18 Jahre begrenzt.[10] Diese Begrenzung wurde später aufgehoben und die Möglichkeit einer Befreiung von der Versicherungspflicht vorgesehen.[11]

1.2. Soziale Sicherung Selbstständiger nach Versicherungszweigen

Für Selbstständige bestand und besteht grundsätzlich keine Pflicht zur Krankenversicherung. Dem Pflichtversicherungssystem der GKV gehören sie auch dann nicht an, wenn sie andernfalls keinen Versicherungsschutz hätten oder wenn sie unmittelbar vor Aufnahme der selbstständigen Tätigkeit pflichtversichert waren (vgl. § 5 Abs. 1 Nr. 13 i.V.m. Abs. 5 SGB V). Im Gegensatz zu dieser sehr restriktiven Regelung[12] steht die seit 1972 bestehende Pflichtversicherung für Landwirte[13] und die 1983 eingeführte Pflichtversicherung für Künstler und Publizisten.[14]

Selbstständige, die nicht diesen beiden Gruppen angehören, haben die Wahl, eine private Krankenversicherung abzuschließen oder sich freiwillig in einer gesetzlichen Krankenkasse zu versichern. Attraktiv war und ist die GKV für Selbstständige mit einem nicht oder geringfügig erwerbstätigen Ehe- oder Lebenspartner und minderjährigen sowie arbeitslosen oder sich in Ausbildung befindenden erwachsenen oder behinderten Kindern, die gem. § 10 SGB V in der GKV beitragsfrei mitversichert sind. Freiwillige Versicherung ist allerdings an enge Voraussetzungen gebunden, insbesondere ist sie nur möglich als Fortsetzung einer zuvor bestehenden Pflichtmitgliedschaft (im Zusammenhang eines Beschäftigungsverhältnis-

10 Vgl. Gesetz über eine Rentenversicherung der Handwerker (Handwerkerversicherungsgesetz – HwVG) vom 08.09.1960, BGBl. I, 737.

11 § 2 Nr. 8, § 6 Abs. 1 Nr. 4 SG VI.

12 Kritik bei *F. Hase*, Gesetzliche Krankenversicherung – Selbständige und Rückkehrer, in: K.J. Bieback (Hrsg.), Neue Mitgliedschaft in der Sozialversicherung – Auf dem Weg in die Volksversicherung?, 2010, S. 168 (174 f.), der »differenzierte Regelungskonzepte« vorschlägt.

13 Vgl. *C. Wirth*, Die agrarsoziale Sicherung, in: B. v. Maydell/F. Ruland/U. Becker (Hrsg.), Sozialrechtshandbuch (SRH), 5. Aufl. 2012, §19 Rn. 3, 84 ff., und im vorliegenden Beitrag am Ende des Abschnitts.

14 Zu diesem Sonderfall nochmals am Ende dieses Abschnitts.

ses) oder bei erstmaliger Beschäftigung im Inland (vgl. § 9 Abs. 1 SGB V). Die Option der freiwilligen Versicherung ist – mit Ausnahme der beschriebenen Gruppe – auch nicht allzu attraktiv, denn § 240 SGB V in Verbindung mit den Grundsätzen des Spitzenverbands der Krankenkassen[15] schreibt die Beitragsbemessung auf Grundlage des Gesamteinkommens vor und nicht etwa nur des Arbeitseinkommens.[16] Ein Korrektiv bildet die hierdurch unter Umständen schneller erreichte Beitragsbemessungsgrenze (§ 223 Abs. 3 SGB V).

In die Pflegeversicherung, eine Volksversicherung, sind auch Selbstständige verpflichtend eingebunden und gehören je nach gewähltem Typ der privaten oder sozialen Säule an. Für die Höhe des Beitrags in der sozialen Pflegeversicherung bleibt der Umstand der Pflicht- oder freiwilligen Mitgliedschaft in der Krankenversicherung relevant: Bei freiwilliger Mitgliedschaft in einer Krankenkasse wird auch bei der Beitragsbemessung in der Pflegepflichtversicherung das Gesamteinkommen im Sinne von § 240 SGB V zugrunde gelegt (§ 57 SGB XI). Die Beitragshöhe ist dabei wie in der gesetzlichen Krankenversicherung gedeckelt.

Das Unfallversicherungsrecht erstreckt die Pflichtmitgliedschaft auf einige Gruppen von Selbstständigen (§ 2 SGB VII). Neben Landwirten und ihren Angehörigen sind dies Hausgewerbetreibende und Zwischenmeister samt mitarbeitenden Ehegatten und Lebenspartnern, selbstständige Küstenschiffer und Küstenfischer unter denselben Voraussetzungen wie in der gesetzlichen Rentenversicherung sowie Personen, die im Gesundheitswesen oder in der Wohlfahrtspflege selbstständig tätig sind. Auch Notärzte im Rettungsdienst sind ohne weiteres unfallversichert, sofern sie nicht daneben als zugelassene Vertragsärzte oder Ärzte in privater Niederlassung tätig sind oder eine Beschäftigung im Umfang von mindestens 15 Stunden wöchentlich außerhalb des Rettungsdienstes ausüben. Unternehmer und ggf. ihre Angehörigen können außerdem durch Satzung einer Berufsgenossenschaft zur Versicherung verpflichtet werden (§ 3 Abs. 1 Nr. 1

15 Einheitliche Grundsätze zur Beitragsbemessung freiwilliger Mitglieder, Stand: 15.11.2017, und Katalog von Einnahmen und deren beitragsrechtliche Bewertung nach § 240 SGB V, Stand: 07.11.2017, beide abrufbar unter https://www.gkv-spitzenverband.de/krankenversicherung/kv_grundprinzipien/finanzierung/beitrags bemessung/beitragsbemessung.jsp.

16 Anders z. B. die Beitragsbemessung für Künstler und Publizisten, für die das Arbeitseinkommen maßgeblich bleibt, § 234 SGB V.

SGB VII) oder sich freiwillig versichern (§ 6 SGB VII). Für Ihre Beiträge haben Selbstständige allein aufzukommen; neben Zwischenmeistern und Hausgewerbetreibenden ist auch der »Auftraggeber« beitragspflichtig, soweit er zur Zahlung von Entgelt verpflichtet ist (§ 150 Abs. 2 S. 1 Nr. 1 SGB VII).
In der Arbeitslosenversicherung können Selbstständige ein Versicherungspflichtverhältnis auf Antrag begründen, wenn sie eine selbstständige Tätigkeit mit einem Umfang von mindestens 15 Stunden wöchentlich aufnehmen und ausüben (§ 28a Abs. 1 Nr. 2 SGB III) und entweder innerhalb der letzten zwei Jahre vor Aufnahme der Tätigkeit mindestens zwölf Monate in einem Versicherungsverhältnis gestanden oder unmittelbar vor Aufnahme der Tätigkeit Anspruch auf Arbeitslosengeld I hatten. Versicherungspflicht nach anderen Vorschriften oder Versicherungsfreiheit schließen die Möglichkeit der Versicherungspflicht auf Antrag aus. Die Einbindung Selbstständiger ist hier also besonders eng gehalten.

Am weitesten hat der Gesetzgeber die gesetzliche Rentenversicherung für Selbstständige geöffnet. Auch § 2 SGB VI, der die Pflichtversicherung bestimmter Gruppen von Selbstständigen vorsieht, ist aber als Ausnahmeregelung formuliert und lässt eine Systematisierung oder Typisierung der einbezogenen Tätigkeiten nur unvollkommen zu. Allerdings bezieht das Rentenversicherungsrecht die sog. Soloselbstständigen pauschal in die Rentenversicherungspflicht ein, ohne an einen bestimmten Beruf oder eine bestimmte Berufsgruppe anzuknüpfen (§ 2 S. 1 Nr. 9 SGB VI). Der Bezug zur Arbeitnehmerähnlichkeit im Arbeitsrecht ist hier nicht zu übersehen.[17] Versicherungspflichtig sind außer den in § 2 S. 1 SGB VI Aufgezählten die Künstler und Publizisten sowie die Landwirte und ihre Angehörigen. Eine Gemeinsamkeit bildet der Umstand, dass die hier erfassten Selbstständigen in der Regel keine bis (im Falle der Küstenschiffer und -fischer) maximal vier versicherungspflichtige Arbeitnehmer beschäftigen und somit typischerweise überwiegend von ihrer eigenen Hände Arbeit leben. Die Beiträge müssen regelmäßig selbst aufgebracht werden. Ausnahmen bestehen für Hausgewerbetreibende, deren Beitrag zur Hälfte der »Arbeit-

---

17 *O. Deinert*, Soloselbständige zwischen Arbeitsrecht und Wirtschaftsrecht, S. 80 ff.; *J. Heuschmidt/T. Klebe*, Erwerbsarbeit in der Plattformökonomie und Schutz des Arbeits- und Sozialrechts?, in: U. Faber/K. Feldhoff/K. Nebe/K. Schmidt/U. Waßer (Hrsg.), Gesellschaftliche Bewegungen – Recht unter Beobachtung und in Aktion, Festschrift für W. Kohte, 2016, S. 73 (83).

geber« übernimmt, und für Künstler und Publizisten, die ebenfalls nur den halben Beitrag selbst aufbringen müssen (vgl. § 169 SGB VI). Bemessungsgrundlage ist das Arbeitseinkommen (§ 165 SGB VI). Andere Selbstständige können sich seit 1972[18] freiwillig versichern. Das kann sinnvoll sein, um z. B. die durch Pflichtmitgliedschaft begründete Anwartschaft auf eine Erwerbsminderungsrente zu erhalten[19] oder um die für unterschiedliche Leistungen vorgesehenen Wartezeiten zu erwerben. Der Beitrag bemisst sich auch bei freiwilliger Versicherung nach dem Arbeitseinkommen (§ 165 Abs. 1 SGB VI).

Einige Gruppen von Selbstständigen sind in soziale Sondersysteme eingebunden. In diesen teilweise schon lange bestehenden Versicherungssystemen werden Berufsgruppen und Sicherungsbedürfnisse Selbstständiger stärker als in der allgemeinen Sozialversicherung typisiert.

Eine besondere Sozialversicherung besteht für die Landwirtschaft (vgl. § 2 Abs. 2 Nr. 3 SGB IV). Die älteren land-, forst- und gartenbauwirtschaftlichen Berufsgenossenschaften, Alters-, Kranken- und Pflegekassen wurden zum 1. Januar 2013 in die Sozialversicherung für Landwirtschaft Forsten und Gartenbau (SVLFG) überführt. Gesetzliche Grundlagen bilden die Gesetze über die Alterssicherung der Landwirte (ALG)[20] und über die Krankenversicherung der Landwirte (KVLG) sowie die Satzung der SVLFG.[21] Die landwirtschaftliche Sozialversicherung berücksichtigt besondere Merkmale dieser Form der Selbstständigkeit. So werden Angehörige nicht aufgrund ihrer Unterhaltsberechtigung abgeleitet, sondern als originäre, weil in die Erwerbsarbeit typischerweise eingebundene Mitglieder der Sozialversicherung geführt. Der Kreis der Angehörigen ist etwa in der Alterssicherung weit gefasst: Er umfasst neben dem Ehe- oder Lebenspartner Verwandte bis zum dritten, Verschwägerte bis zum zweiten Grad und Pflegekinder. Länger als die gesetzliche Rente wurde die Alterssicherung der Landwirte als Zuschuss konzipiert und trägt noch heute diese Zü-

---

18 Bezweckt war die Öffnung der Rentenversicherung für »große Gesellschaftsgruppen«, BT-Drs. VI/2916, S. 37.

19 Das ist wohl nur in geringem Maße zielführend, da innerhalb der letzten fünf Jahre vor Eintritt des Rentenfalls drei Jahre mit Pflichtbeitragszeiten liegen müssen, vgl. § 43 Abs. 1 Nr. 2 SGB VI.

20 Vom 29.7.1994, Stand: 17.7.2017.

21 Derzeit in der Fassung des 18. Nachtrags vom 15.11.2017, abrufbar unter http://www.svlfg.de/11-wir/wir03_satzung/svlfg_18nt_stand20171115.pdf.

ge mit Rücksicht auf den Umstand, dass Altbauer und Altbäuerin auf dem Hof im Altenteil verbleiben, mitarbeiten und von ihren Angehörigen versorgt werden. Ebenso wird die Möglichkeit schwankender Erträge berücksichtigt und für den Fall eines Einkommens unterhalb der Mindesteinkommensgrenze werden staatliche Beitragszuschüsse vorgesehen. Die konkrete Ausgestaltung dieses Systems verfolgt nicht zuletzt den Zweck einer Subventionierung der Agrarwirtschaft.[22]

Mit der Künstlersozialversicherung wurde zum 1. Januar 1983 ein weiteres Sondersystem zur sozialen Sicherung Selbstständiger eingeführt, aber anders als im Falle der Landwirtschaft in die allgemeine Sozialversicherung integriert. Die Künstlersozialkasse wurde organisatorisch der Unfallversicherung Bund und Bahn eingegliedert und bildet dort ein Sondervermögen. Die Kasse wird aus Beiträgen der Künstler und Publizisten sowie aus der Künstlersozialabgabe finanziert, die Verwerter der Leistung aufbringen.

Die berufsständische Versorgung ist als öffentlich-rechtliche Pflichtversicherung organisiert, ohne Sozialversicherung zu sein. Sie bildet das Sicherungssystem für die selbstständig arbeitenden Angehörigen der sog. Freien Berufe. Ihre Regelung und Organisation liegt in der Zuständigkeit der Länder. Berufsständische Versorgungssysteme bestehen ausschließlich als Alterssicherungssysteme. Sie knüpfen an die Zugehörigkeit zu einem spezifischen Standesberuf und für den Beitrag an das Arbeitseinkommen an.

Die soziale Sicherung Selbstständiger in den bestehenden Systemen erweist sich als disparat, in vielem schlüssig, in anderem inkonsistent und aus der Perspektive der Selbstständigen unübersichtlich. Konsistent verwirklichen am ehesten die Sondersysteme für die freien Berufe, die Landwirtschaft und – mit Einschränkungen – die Künstler und Publizisten den sozialen Schutz der jeweiligen Berufsgruppe.

22 Vgl. nur *C. Wirth*, Die agrarsoziale Sicherung, 5. Auflage 2012, § 19 Rn. 45 (46).

2. Wandel der Arbeit – Wandel der Selbstständigkeit am Beispiel der Plattformökonomie und ihrer dynamischen Entwicklung

Digitalisierung verändert die Arbeitswelt. Sie bietet die Chance, Arbeitsplätze den Wünschen der Arbeitenden entsprechend anzupassen, und damit auch die Chance für Erweiterung und Modifizierung selbstständiger Erwerbsarbeit. Aus Sicht des Unternehmens erhöht sie auch die Flexibilität in der Gestaltung der Produktivität. Die Chance, sich der eigenen sozialversicherungsrechtlichen Beitragspflicht zu entledigen, motiviert Unternehmen außerdem dazu, Produktivität seltener als bisher im klassischen Arbeitsverhältnis zu generieren und verstärkt auf »Outsourcing« zu setzen, mithin die Aufgabe sozialer Sicherung »Auftragnehmenden« zu übertragen[23]. Diese Tendenz wird nicht zuletzt durch technischen Fortschritt, Unternehmensverflechtungen und -netzwerkbildungen und Mobilisierung von Arbeitsplätzen begünstigt.[24] Vor allem das Internet und die fortschreitende Digitalisierung eröffnen den Erwerbstätigen neue Formen der Erwerbsarbeit und den Unternehmen neue Optionen der Gestaltung von Produktions- oder Leistungsprozessen. Es treten neue, digitale Akteure auf den Markt, die Arbeitsnachfrage und Arbeitsangebot in neuartiger Weise organisieren helfen.[25] Gerade hier gewinnt die Frage der Selbstständig-

23 Über die Zahl der Soloselbständigen im Kontext der Digitalisierung sind bislang keine verlässlichen Zahlen verfügbar (dies geht aus der Antwort auf eine große Anfrage der Abgeordneten Sabine Zimmermann (Zwickau), Herbert Behrens, Matthias W. Birkwald, weiterer Abgeordneter und der Fraktion DIE LINKE hervor, siehe BT Drucksache 18/8803). Auf Basis des Mikrozensus ermittelt *K. Brenke*, Die allermeisten Selbständigen betreiben Altersvorsorge oder haben Vermögen, DIW Wochenbericht 2016 Nr. 45, S. 1071–1076, rund 55.000 IT-Fachkräfte (nach ISCO). Das ist eine vergleichsweise kleine Gruppe gegenüber den am häufigsten vertretenen Kategorien von rund 112.000 Architekten, 134.500 Bauhandwerkern, 169.100 Verkäuferinnen und Verkäufern sowie 291.800 Technikern, Fertigungsberufen und Maschinenbedienern. Nach Qualifikationen findet sich eine große Spannbreite von wenig qualifizierten Berufsgruppen – im Bereich der Hauswirtschaft sowie Reinigungs- und andere Hilfskräfte – bis hin zu hochqualifizierten Berufen wie Lehrer, Wissenschaftler, IT-Kräfte, Autoren und kreative Berufe, siehe *K. Brenke*, Die allermeisten Selbständigen betreiben Altersvorsorge oder haben Vermögen, DIW Wochenbericht 2016 Nr. 45, S. 1071–1076.

24 Vgl. Hanau/Matiaske, S. 213–242 in diesem Band.

25 *S. Kirchner/J. Beyer,* ZfS 2016, S. 324 (328 ff.).

keit, ihrer Abgrenzung zur Beschäftigung in einem klassischen Arbeitsverhältnis und ihrer sozialen Sicherung eine neue Qualität[26].

Neue Modelle internetbasierter Tätigkeiten werden auf den sog. Plattformen vermittelt. Plattformen sind *websites*, die die notwendige Infrastruktur bieten, um einen Auftragnehmer mit einem Auftraggeber in einem bestimmten Bereich zu verbinden. Je nach Konzeption richten sie einen Arbeitsauftrag in unterschiedlicher Weise an die auf ihr angemeldeten Auftragnehmer (die sog. *crowd*). Unter dem Begriff der dort stattfindenden *Crowdwork* lassen sich zwei Typen identifizieren, denen sich das rechtswissenschaftliche Interesse zuwendet. Den ersten Typ bilden Plattformen für den Bereich der *Cloudwork* wie *Upwork, Amazon MTurk, Clickworker, twago* und *99designs*, bei denen digitale Tätigkeiten vom heimischen Computer ausgeführt werden.[27] Dem zweiten Typ sind Plattformen zuzuordnen, die für physische Dienstleistungen digitale Vermittlungsleistungen anbieten (*Gig-Work*). Bei *Gig-Work* gehört die erbrachte Leistung überwiegend der alten Arbeitswelt an, neu geordnetwird ihre Organisation und rechtliche Ausgestaltung. Der Begriff »*Gig*« entstammt der Musikerwelt und bezeichnet dort ein (kurzes) Engagement oder eine einmalige Verpflichtung. Mit *Gig-Work* entstehen nicht wie bei der *Cloudwork* neuartige Tätigkeiten (deren Charakter als Haupterwerbsquelle noch in Frage steht), sondern es verändert sich der klassische Arbeitsmarkt. Vor allem dieser Wandel erfordert unter dem Aspekt sozialer Sicherung Selbstständiger sorgfältige Beobachtung. Die weiteren Ausführungen dieses Beitrags werden sich deshalb hierauf konzentrieren.

Während die am Computer erbrachte *Click-, Crowd- und Cloudwork* stets ortsungebunden ist, findet *Gig-Work* ortsgebunden statt.[28] Wie auch bei der *Cloud-Work* können bei der *Gig-Work* sowohl Individuen als auch die ganze *Crowd* mit Aufgaben betraut werden. Ortsgebundene *Crowd*-Tätigkeiten sind oft solche im Bereich des lokalen *Micro-Taskings* (bspw. *App-Jobber* und *Streetspotr*) und dienen (bisher) dazu, kleinste Bewer-

---

26 Vgl zur Problematik aus arbeitsrechtlicher Perspektive *H. Hanau*, NJW 2016, S. 2614 ff.

27 Siehe zu den Formen und der arbeitsrechtlichen Einordnung des (hier *Crowdworking* genannten) *Cloudworking Wisskirchen/Schwindling*, ZESAR 2017, S. 318 ff.

28 Siehe hierzu die Graphik bei *F. Schmidt*, Publikation der Friedrich-Ebert-Stiftung, S. 6 (abrufbar unter http://library.fes.de/pdf-files/wiso/12826.pdf (letzter Abruf am 04.01.2018).

tungs- und Marktforschungstätigkeiten von unterwegs auszuführen. Individuelle *Gig-Work* wird dagegen über Plattformen wie *airbnb, wimdu* (Gastgewerbe) *uber, lyft, haxi* (Beförderung), *lieferando, instacart, deliveroo* (Logistik) und *Taskrabbit, Helpling, Kaufmich* (Haushalts- und persönliche Dienste) vermittelt.[29] Prägend für die individuelle *Gig-Work* ist, dass sich über die jeweilige Plattformen Individuen zu einem persönlichen Austausch verabreden und es bei einer abschließenden Bewertung des Auftraggebers stets auf die Leistung dieser konkreten Person ankommt. Das Geschäftsmodell der Plattformen sieht in der Regel vor, die gewünschten Arbeitskräfte als selbstständig tätige Unternehmer an Kunden zu vermitteln.[30] Arbeitsrechtlich werden die im Bereich der individuellen *Gig-Work* Arbeitenden daher mit dem Argument, ihnen fehle die persönliche Abhängigkeit, die sich im Weisungsrecht eines Arbeitgebers bezogen auf Inhalt, Ort und Zeit der Arbeitsleistung konkretisiert, der Kategorie der Selbstständigen zugeordnet.[31]

Mit der Anknüpfung an den Begriff der (abhängigen) Beschäftigung und mit ihrem historischen Ausgangspunkt als Arbeitnehmerversicherung bleibt die Sozialversicherung in ihrer aktuellen Form ebenfalls statisch an eine solche Einordnung gebunden.[32] Die Bestimmung der Beschäftigteneigenschaft als Typusbegriff gem. § 7 Abs. 1 SGB IV gilt zwar als flexibel, wird aber zugleich durch die Schaffung von Ausnahmen (bspw. in § 2 SGB VI) in ihren Möglichkeiten beschränkt.[33] Das Sozialversicherungsrecht bleibt auf diese Weise nahe an der arbeitsrechtlichen Klassifizierung und ordnet das Verhältnis nur bei belegbarer Divergenz zwischen Vertragsdurchführung und formaler Vereinbarung anders, nämlich als ab-

---

29 Siehe hierzu die Graphik bei *F. Schmidt*, Publikation der Friedrich-Ebert-Stiftung, S. 7 (abrufbar unter http://library.fes.de/pdf-files/wiso/12826.pdf, letzter Abruf am 04.01.2018).

30 Die privatautonome übliche Vereinbarung zwischen Unternehmer und Plattform, die für eine solche Bestimmung zunächst ausschlaggebend ist (vgl. *S. Greiner*, SGb 2016, S. 301 (303)), in der Regel also die AGB der Plattform, sieht also vor, dass kein Beschäftigungsverhältnis entsteht.

31 *H.-J. Bauschke*, öAT 2016, S. 225 (226); für das Sozialrecht siehe BSG v. 28.5.2008, B 12 KR 13/07 R, juris Rn. 15.

32 *O. Wintermann*, NZA 2017, S. 537 spricht von »korporatistischen Maßnahmen und Institutionen des letzten Jahrhunderts«, die für neue Arbeitsformen Anwendung finden sollen.

33 *W. Brose*, NZS 2017, S. 7, (13).

hängige Beschäftigung, ein.[34] Damit sind die meisten Formen von *Gig-Work* sozialversicherungsrechtlich der Selbstständigkeit zuzuordnen. Viele der dergestalt selbstständig Tätigen fallen zudem in den Bereich der kleinen Selbstständigkeit. Zugleich eröffnet die Scheidelinie zwischen Beschäftigung und Selbstständigkeit mit ihren weit reichenden Folgen für die soziale Sicherung der *Gig-Worker* erhebliche Spielräume für die Gestaltung durch Plattformen, Auftraggeber und *Gig-Worker*, wobei die Gestaltungsmacht der Plattform mit ihrer Attraktivität steigen dürfte.[35]

3. Wandel selbstständiger Erwerbsarbeit und Anpassungsbedarf im Sozialversicherungsrechts

Gewandelte Formen von Arbeit (auch) als Folge von Digitalisierung werfen die Fragen nach dem angemessenen sozialen Schutz der Erwerbstätigen auf. Sozialer Schutz, hier in Form sozialer Sicherung als Element »guter Arbeit« knüpft an den individuellen Schutzbedarf Erwerbstätiger an. Hinsichtlich des individuellen Schutzbedarfs erweist sich aber selbstständige Erwerbstätigkeit als bemerkenswert vielfältig. Gerade Selbstständige, vornehmlich die mit höherem Einkommensniveau, verbinden ihren Erwerbsstatus mit dem Potential zur Eigenvorsorge für den Fall der Krankheit, der Erwerbsunfähigkeit, des Alters und Todes, ja selbst für den Fall der Erwerbslosigkeit aus anderen Gründen. Einbindungen in Pflichtsysteme zum Zweck sozialer Sicherung werden von dieser Gruppe als paternalistisch empfunden.[36]

Auf der anderen Seite ist ein sozialer Schutzbedarf für spezifische Gruppen von Selbstständigen lange anerkannt, in der Rentenversicherung vor allem für solche, deren Erwerbstätigkeit eine große Nähe zur abhängigen Beschäftigung aufweist. Selbstständige *Gig-Worker* fallen zumeist aus dem locker geknüpften sozialen Netz, obwohl ein Sicherungsbedarf zumindest nicht fern liegt: Selbst die Einordnung als Soloselbstständige

34 *S. Greiner*, SGb 2016, S. 301, (303).

35 Zur Plattformsoziologie vgl. *S. Kirchner/J. Beyer*, ZfS 2016, S. 324 ff.

36 Zitat im Weißbuch 4.0, S. 167 über arbeitenviernull.de hierzu: »*Eine RV-Pflicht für Selbstständige kommt einer wirtschaftlichen Entmündigung verantwortungsbewusst handelnder Individuen gleich. Man kann es auch Entmündigung durch den Nanny-Staat nennen.*«

i.S.d. § 2 S. 1 Nr. 9 SGB VI dürfte typischerweise scheitern, da sie nicht auf Dauer und im Wesentlichen für einen Auftraggeber tätig sind.[37] Einige von Ihnen sehen sich zwar als Unternehmer, andere jedoch sind Geringverdiener, denen es unmöglich ist, eigenständig eine Altersvorsorge aufzubauen.[38] Am Beispiel der *Gig-Worker* zeigt sich das Spannungsverhältnis der Einordnung der Ressource Sozialversicherungsrecht in den *capability approach* und zugleich die Schwierigkeit, die Diversität der Selbstständigen in geeigneter Form abzubilden.

So steht die endgültige Einpassung neuer Arbeitsformen und -modalitäten wie von *Gig-Work* in die herkömmlichen Begriffe und Strukturen des Sozialversicherungsrechts noch aus. Das für die Frage ihrer Einbindung maßgebliche Schutzniveau der *Gig-Worker* bedarf – wie das anderer Selbstständiger – der Erhebung und ggf. Differenzierung je nach Art der Tätigkeit. Einige sind ebenso schutzbedürftig wie klassische Arbeitnehmer, da sie faktisch nur für eine Plattform arbeiten und von den Aufträgen dieser Plattform persönlich abhängig sind.[39] Andere erfüllen die Merkmale des selbstständigen Unternehmertums und bedürfen dieses Schutzes weniger, da ihre wirtschaftliche Abhängigkeit weniger ausgeprägt ist.[40]

---

37 Vgl. *S. Neumann*, SGb 2010, S. 463 (465). *A. Hartmann*, NWB 2016, S. 3808 ff. versucht anhand einer Rechtssprechungsanalyse den Begriff des »Auftragnehmers« auf die Plattform auszuweiten.

38 *U. Fachinger*, SZ 2017, S. 815 (820).

39 Siehe zudem zur Ertragsschwäche kleiner Selbstständiger *R. Waltermann*, SGb 2017, S. 425 (427).

40 Zur Schutzbedürftigkeit siehe *W. Brose*, NZS 2017, S. 7 (8). Bezüglich der Einkommen der Soloselbstständigen ist anzumerken, dass die Spreizung der Einkommen bei den Solo-Selbständigen im Vergleich zu den abhängig Beschäftigten deutlich größer ist. *K. Brenke*, Solo-Selbständige in Deutschland – Strukturen und Erwerbsverläufe, Forschungsbericht Nr. 423, 2011 ermittelt mit 1500.- Euro eine dem mittleren Haushaltseinkommen der abhängig Beschäftigten nahezu gleiche Größe. Das Haushaltseinkommen der einkommensstarken bzw. -schwachen Gruppen liegt dagegen bei den Solo-Selbstständigen erheblich über bzw. mit 533.- Euro unter demjenigen der 5 % einkommensschwächsten Haushalte abhängig Beschäftigter von 733.- Euro (vgl. auch *H. Hanau/W. Matiaske*, Mitbestimmung im entgrenzten Betrieb – arbeitsrechtliche und personalwirtschaftliche Perspektiven, in: D. Alewell, W. Matiaske (Hrsg.), Standards Guter Arbeit – disziplinäre Positionen und interdisziplinäre Perspektiven, Baden-Baden 2019, S. 213–242). Eine vergleichbare Spreizung wird bezüglich der Alterssicherung berichtet. *K. Brenke,* Selbständige Beschäftigung geht zurück, DIW Wochenbericht 2015, Nr. 36, S. 790–796, berechnet, dass 46 % der Solo-Selbstständigen bzw. 32 % der Selbst-

Eine ähnliche Schutzbedürftigkeit wie bei klassischen Arbeitnehmern zeigt sich vor allem in den Bereichen, in denen Dienstleistungen besonders persönlich sind (Beförderung, Logistik sowie Tätigkeiten im Privathaushalt und ähnliche Dienstleistungen). Eine solche Schutzbedürftigkeit ist z. B. im Bereich des Gastgewerbes weniger gegeben, da die Vermietung einer Wohnung eher den Charakter eines Kapitaleinsatzes hat.

Aufgrund des rasanten Voranschreitens der Digitalisierung, der wirtschaftlichen Attraktivität der Plattformökonomie für Plattformbetreiber und Unternehmen sowie dem Autonomiebedürfnis[41] vieler auf diesen Plattformen Tätiger ist es absehbar, dass in Zukunft weitere Arbeitsplätze in diesem Bereich entstehen werden. Für Unternehmen und ehemalige Arbeitgeber sind sie finanziell attraktiv. *Gig-Work* bietet in dem weitgehend unregulierten Bereich der Plattformökonomie Wettbewerbsvorteile gegenüber klassischen Dienstleistungsunternehmen, da nicht nur Sozialversicherungs-, sondern auch Steuerpflichten bisher nur in den alten Kategorien geregelt sind.[42] So ergeben sich auch für die *Gig-Worker* Vorteile, insbesondere auch durch die Möglichkeit, flexibler zu arbeiten.

Die in großem Stil entstehenden neuen Typen der Erwerbsarbeit, für die *Gig-Work* exemplarisch steht, generieren aber auch Gefahren, u. a. auf dem Feld der sozialen Sicherung. Soziale Standards, die regelhaft für Beschäftigte, punktuell aber auch für Selbstständige bestehen, treten außer Kraft. Die sozialen Risiken und Lasten verbleiben bei den Arbeitenden, aber auch bei der Gemeinschaft, die die soziale Sicherung über steuerfinanzierte Auffangnetze leisten muss.[43] Die Möglichkeit, sich als Arbeit-

---

ständigen mit Beschäftigten nicht über eine private Renten- oder eine Lebensversicherung verfügen. Von diesen Personen haben jedoch große Gruppen durch Geld- und Anlagevermögen oder Vermögen in Immobilien vorgesorgt. Nur 25 % der Solo-Selbständigen und 15 % der Selbständigen mit Angestellten verfügen weder über eine private Rentenversicherung oder Kapitallebensversicherung noch über ein Geld- oder Anlagevermögen von mindestens 100.000 Euro. Legt man die Messlatte mit 250.000 Euro deutlich höher, dann sind 34 % der Solo-Selbständigen und 21 % der Selbständigen mit Beschäftigten ohne hinreichende Altersvorsorge.

41 Auch persönliche Autonomie ist eine Basis für ein gutes Leben, vgl. *S. Bothfeld*, ZSR 2017, S. 355 (357).

42 *R. Waltermann*, SGb 2017, S. 425 (429).

43 Dieses zweite Schutzziel kommt aus dem Bereich der Pflegeversicherung, könnte zukünftig aber auch im Rentenversicherungsrecht fruchtbar gemacht werden, vgl. *W. Brose*, NZS 2017, S. 7 (8).

geber selbst zu entlasten, indem Beschäftigungsverhältnisse in selbstständige Tätigkeiten umgewandelt werden, setzt hohe Anreize.

4. Anforderungen an Systemanpassungen

Das Forschungsprogramm ist damit in Ansätzen vorgezeichnet: Es umfasst die Prüfung des Anpassungsbedarfs und der erforderlichen Anpassungen bestehender Standards in den Systemen und dem Recht der sozialen Sicherung unter Berücksichtigung der anhaltenden Dynamik des Wandels. Es gilt, ein System der sozialen Sicherung unter Einbeziehung neuer Arbeit zu entwickeln, das in erster Linie eine nachhaltige Sicherung derer bewirkt, die dieser Sicherung bedürfen,[44] und das in zweiter Linie auch seine Leistungsfähigkeit für diese Aufgabe nachhaltig erhält.

4.1. Systemdiskussion

Bei aller Unsicherheit über die künftige Entwicklung der Arbeitsmärkte als Folge der Digitalisierung lassen sich Unterschiede im Anpassungsbedarf der Sozialversicherungszweige feststellen. Besonderer Anpassungsbedarf lässt sich für die Alterssicherung konstatieren. Steigende Diskontinuität von Erwerbsbiografien bei steigender Lebenserwartung erfordern ihn nicht nur im Interesse der Betroffenen, sondern auch unter dem Aspekt der öffentlichen Ausgaben, da andernfalls steuerfinanzierte subsidiäre Sicherungssysteme wie die Grundsicherung in Anspruch genommen werden.

Neue Nahrung werden grundlegende Reformvorschläge wie die Bürgerversicherung in der Krankenversicherung[45] sowie die Erwerbstätigenversicherung[46], die Idee persönlicher Erwerbstätigenkonten[47] oder gar der

---

44 »Auch in schwierigen Situationen müssen sich Arbeiter auf ihr soziales Netz verlassen können« fordert das *BMAS*, Weißbuch 4.0, S. 93.

45 Grundlegend *A. Lenze*, Staatsbürgerversicherung und Verfassung, 2005; *K.-J. Bieback*, Sozial- und verfassungsrechtliche Aspekte der Bürgerversicherung, 2. Aufl. 2014.

46 *H. Rische*, Weiterentwicklung der gesetzlichen Rentenversicherung zu einer Erwerbstätigenversicherung: Einführung in die Problematik, Deutsche Rentenversicherung 2009, 285; aktuell *J. Ueckermann*, Für eine zukunftsfeste Rente: Genera-

Vorschlag einer Grundrente für alle[48] in der Rentenversicherung erfahren. Ihnen ist gemeinsam, dass sie die Verbindung von Beschäftigung und Arbeitnehmerstatus von der Mitgliedschaft in der Sozialversicherung und der Beitragstragung lösen. Diese Modelle mögen in Zukunft attraktiv sein, doch löst der grundlegende Systemwechsel einige drängende Fragen nicht – so etwa nicht die nach dem Schicksal des heutigen Arbeitgeberbeitrags. Daher werden sie hinsichtlich ihrer Qualität als Ressource für gute Arbeit zu untersuchen sein.

Auch Pfadabhängigkeit und Kontinuität der Sozialversicherungen sprechen nicht für einen raschen Prinzipien- und Systemwechsel.[49] Näher liegt es daher, Möglichkeiten der Systemanpassung auszuloten und hierbei nicht auszuschließen, dass diese ggf. Grundlage und Ausgangspunkt eines allmählichen Systemwechsels bilden könnten.

Eine grundlegende Anpassung des Systems durch systematische Einbeziehung Selbstständiger wird seit langem vor allem für die Rentenversicherung diskutiert.[50] Auch das Weißbuch Arbeiten 4.0 nimmt diesen Vorschlag für die gesetzliche Rentenversicherung auf, ohne allerdings pauschale Lösungen unter Einbeziehung anderer Sozialversicherungssysteme zu thematisieren.[51] Zu fragen ist zudem, wie das Rentenversicherungssys-

tionensolidarität und Erwerbstätigenversicherung, in: Köster (Hrsg.), Zukunftsfeste Rente: neue Impulse für die Alterssicherung, 2017, S. 198 ff., siehe hierzu auch das *BMAS*, Weißbuch 4.0, S. 179.

47 *BMAS*, Weißbuch 4.0, S. 181; G. Schmidt, Von der aktiven zur lebenslauforientierten Arbeitsmarktpolitik, in: Naegele (Hrsg.), Soziale Lebenslaufpolitik, 2010, S. 333.

48 *W. Leyendecker*, Grundrente – Rentenmodell für die Zukunft?, DRV 1986, 143 ff.; *F. Ruland*, Sozial- und rechtspolitische Bedenken gegen eine Grundrente, ZfR 1987, S. 354 ff.

49 Vgl. *P. Axer*, Strukturprobleme der Finanzierung sozialer Sicherheit aus rechtswissenschaftlicher Sicht, in: P. Masuch/W. Spellbrink/U. Becker/S. Leibfried (Hrsg.), Grundlagen und Herausforderungen des Sozialrechts – Bundessozialgericht und Sozialstaatsforschung, Band 2, 2015, S. 713 (733).

50 Vgl. aktuell *G. Wagner*, Rentenversicherungspflicht für Selbständige macht Sinn – auch wenn die Digitalisierung weniger stark sein sollte als viele glauben, ZfW Bd. 65 (2016), S. 123 ff.; *E. Welskop-Deffaa*, Die dynamische Rente 4.0 – Antworten der Alterssicherungspolitik auf die Digitalisierung der Arbeit, ZfW Bd. 65 (2016), S. 129 ff.; *R. Kreikebohm/U. Kolakowski/S. Kockert/J. Rodewald,* Die rentenpolitische Agenda 2030 – Die Zukunftsfähigkeit der gesetzlichen Alterssicherung vor dem Hintergrund der gesellschaftlichen Veränderungen, 2016.

51 *BMAS*, Weißbuch 4.0, S. 172 f.

tem auch zukünftig derart dynamische Entwicklungen wie die der Digitalisierung der Arbeit rechtlich abbilden kann.

Ein besonderes Augenmerk erfordert angesichts der Vielfalt von Selbstständigkeit die »kleine«, evtl. auch die Solo-Selbstständigkeit. Möglich wäre es, Arbeitende nach Art der *Gig-Worker* durch Erweiterung des Anwendungsbereichs in § 2 S. 1 Nr. 9 SGB VI oder durch Schaffung eines weiteren Tatbestands in die gesetzliche Rentenversicherung einzubeziehen.[52] An die arbeitsrechtlichen Kategorien lässt sich nicht gut anknüpfen, da auch sie, insbesondere die Kategorie der arbeitnehmerähnlichen Selbstständigkeit, wegen der gewandelten sozialen Arbeitswirklichkeit einer Neujustierung bedürfen.[53] Denkbar und zielführend erscheint aber eine Parallelführung der Überlegungen zum Reformbedarf wegen der Nähe von arbeits- und sozialrechtlicher Kategorienbildung.

4.2. Beschäftigung und Selbstständigkeit als bleibende Kategorien?

Ob eine Neujustierung der Konzeptbegriffe, insbesondere eine Erweiterung des Beschäftigten-Begriffs in § 7 Abs.1 SGB IV, die gewünschte dynamische Erfassung des Schutzbedarfs von *Gig-Work* in einer sich wandelnden Arbeitswelt zu leisten vermag,[54] ist ebenso zu prüfen wie die Alternative(n) neuer Begriffskategorien und mit ihnen einer Justierung im Wege der Gesetzgebung.

---

52 *S. Neumann*, SGb 2010, S. 463 (467); *R. Waltermann*, RdA 2010, S. 162 (167); *R. Waltermann*, SGb 2017, S. 425 (429).

53 Vgl. *A. Bücker*, Arbeitnehmer und arbeitnehmerähnliche Personen – Zur notwendigen Neujustierung der Begriffe in der vernetzten Arbeitswelt, in: U. Faber/K. Feldhoff/K. Nebe/K. Schmidt/U. Waßer (Hrsg.), Gesellschaftliche Bewegungen – Recht unter Beobachtung und in Aktion, Festschrift für W. Kohte, 2016, S. 21 (39 ff.); *U. Mückenberger*, Der Arbeitnehmerbegriff – aus arbeitspolitischer Perspektive, Diskussionspapier aus der Kommission »Arbeit der Zukunft« der Hans-Böckler-Stiftung, S. 6 ff., abrufbar unter https://www.boeckler.de/pdf/201701_adz_diskussionspapier_mueckenberger.pdf (letzter Abruf am 15.04.2018). Zur Arbeitnehmerähnlichkeit der Heimarbeit im Arbeitsrecht als »interessante Regelungsoption« *J. Heuschmidt/T. Klebe*, Erwerbsarbeit in der Plattformökonomie und Schutz des Arbeits- und Sozialrechts?, in: U. Faber/K. Feldhoff/K. Nebe/K. Schmidt/U. Waßer (Hrsg.), Gesellschaftliche Bewegungen – Recht unter Beobachtung und in Aktion, Festschrift für W. Kohte, 2016, S. 73 (78 f.).

54 Z. B. *W. Brose*, NZS 2017, S. 7 (8 f.).

4.3. Versicherungspflicht oder Versicherungsberechtigung?

Der Wandel der Arbeit wirft auch die Frage auf, ob Selbstständigen die Sozialversicherung lediglich stärker zu öffnen ist oder ob sich eine verpflichtende Einbindung empfiehlt. Die historischen Pfade legen ebenso wenig wie das geltende Recht eine bestimmte Konzeption nahe. Es wird zu prüfen sein, ob sich gerade für diese Frage das Theoriekonzept des *capability approach* nutzbar machen ließe. Dies verweist auf die grundsätzlicheren Fragen, unter anderem die, welcher Stellenwert dem Zweck, die Funktionsfähigkeit der Sozialversicherungen zu gewährleisten, in diesem Konzept zukommt.[55] Denn die Frage der Nachhaltigkeit sozialer Systeme ist nicht ohne Relevanz für die individuellen Verwirklichungschancen der in ihnen Versicherten, und zwar sowohl der Pflichtversicherten als auch der freiwillig Versicherten, die ihre Entscheidung auf diese Funktionsfähigkeit der Systeme gründen. Andererseits ist der Zusammenhang mit den Verwirklichungschancen der Betroffenen und folglich mit dem Thema »Gute Arbeit« locker.

4.4. Voller oder anteiliger Beitrag?

Reformüberlegungen sind auch unter dem Aspekt anzustellen, dass Selbstständige als Pflichtversicherte typischerweise die Beiträge ganz überwiegend allein aufbringen müssen. Für einen Teil der heutigen und künftigen *Gig-Worker* aus der kleinen Selbstständigkeit der alten Arbeitswelt ist das schwierig. Zudem kehrt in der Frage der vollen oder hälftigen Beitragslast die Frage nach der Abgrenzung von Beschäftigung nach § 7 Abs. 1 S. 1 SGB IV und Selbstständigkeit wieder und mit ihr das Problem eines Ausweichens der Arbeitgeber in Formen eines Personaleinsatzes abseits der abhängigen Beschäftigung. Deshalb wird erwogen, solchen Selbstständigen nur den halben Beitrag zur Renten- oder Krankenversicherung aufzuerlegen.[56] Anschauungsmaterial für mögliche Gestaltungen bieten

---

55 Vgl. *W. Brose*, NZS 2017, S. 7.

56 *S. Neumann*, SGb 2010, S. 463 (469) plädiert ebenso wie *R. Waltermann*, RdA 2010, S. 162 (169) dafür, sie wie andere Selbstständige selbst die Beiträge zahlen zu lassen. Anderer Ansatz möglicherweise bei *F. Nullmeier*, Digitale Ökonomie und ihre Folgen für die Entwicklungsrichtung der gesetzlichen Rentenversiche-

die Sozialversicherung der Hausgewerbetreibenden und Zwischenmeister[57] sowie die Künstlersozialversicherung[58]. Auch über eine Abgabe, mit der an die mittels der technischen Plattform erzielte Wertschöpfung anknüpfen lässt, ist nachzudenken.[59] *Gig-Worker* sind zumeist von der von ihnen gewählten Plattform abhängig, ohne auf dem nicht-plattformbasierten und sich monopolisierenden Markt ihre Dienste anbieten zu können. Andere Optionen gilt es auszuloten.

4.5. Weitere Fragen

Fragen weniger grundsätzlicher Art schließen sich an. An welches Einkommen der Selbstständigen wird für die Beitragsbemessung angeknüpft und wie wird es ermittelt? Wird der Fall der Erwerbsminderung rentenversicherungsrechtlich abgesichert, und ggf., wie?[60] Die Antwort auf solche Fragen hängt von der Systementscheidung und davon ab, welchen Schutz selbstständige Erwerbstätigkeit im System der Sozialversicherung künftig haben wird.

Literaturverzeichnis

Axer, Peter, Strukturprobleme der Finanzierung sozialer Sicherheit aus rechtswissenschaftlicher Sicht, in: P. Masuch/W. Spellbrink/U. Becker/S. Leibfried (Hrsg.),

---

rung, DRV 2017, S. 249–272; *ders.*, Einstürzende Neubauten. Statikprobleme im Säulenmodell der Alterssicherung, SF 2015, S. 196–202.

57 *J. Heuschmidt/T. Klebe*, Erwerbsarbeit in der Plattformökonomie und Schutz des Arbeits- und Sozialrechts?, in: U. Faber/K. Feldhoff/K. Nebe/K. Schmidt/U. Waßer (Hrsg.), Gesellschaftliche Bewegungen – Recht unter Beobachtung und in Aktion, Festschrift für W. Kohte, 2016S. 73 (84).

58 Über eine Einbeziehung anderer Selbstständiger in die Künstlersozialversicherung denkt auch das *BMAS*, Weißbuch 4.0, S. 167 nach.

59 Anknüpfen ließe sich an das Konzept der um 1980 diskutierten Maschinenabgabe, vgl. dazu den SPD-Politiker *Rudolf Dressler* im Interview, abrufbar unter http://www.zeit.de/1984/06/ohne-chance, mit Bezug auf eine Forderung seiner Partei aus dem Jahr 1978; Deutscher Bundestag, Plenarprotokoll der 63. Sitzung vom 11. November 1981, Anlage 17, abrufbar unter http://dipbt.Bundestag.de/doc/btp/ 09/09063.pdf.

60 Fragen dieser Art wirft auch *U. Fachinger*, SZ 2017, S. 815 (828 ff.) auf.

Grundlagen und Herausforderungen des Sozialrechts – Bundessozialgericht und Sozialstaatsforschung, Band 2, 2015, S. 713–735.

Bauschke, Hans-Joachim, Arbeitsrecht 4.0 – Eine kurze Bestandsaufnahme aus aktuellem Anlass, öAT 2016, S. 225–228.

Bieback, Karl-Jürgen, Sozial- und verfassungsrechtliche Aspekte der Bürgerversicherung, 2. Aufl. 2014.

Bothfeld, Silke, Autonomie – ein Kernbegriff moderner Sozialstaatlichkeit, ZSR 2017, S. 355–387.

Brenke, Karl, Allein tätige Selbständige: starkes Beschäftigungswachstum, oft nur geringe Einkommen, DIW Wochenbericht 2013, Nr. 7, S. 3–16.

Brenke, Karl, Selbständige Beschäftigung geht zurück, DIW Wochenbericht 2015, Nr. 36, S. 790–796.

Brenke, Karl, Die allermeisten Selbständigen betreiben Altersvorsorge oder haben Vermögen, DIW Wochenbericht 2016 Nr. 45, S. 1071–1076.

Brenke, Karl, Solo-Selbständige in Deutschland – Strukturen und Erwerbsverläufe, Forschungsbericht Nr. 423, 2011.

Brose, Wiebke, Von Bismarck zu Crowdwork, NZS 2017, S. 7–14.

Bücker, Andreas, Arbeitnehmer und arbeitnehmerähnliche Personen – Zur notwendigen Neujustierung der Begriffe in der vernetzten Arbeitswelt, in: U. Faber/K. Feldhoff/K. Nebe/K. Schmidt/U. Waßer (Hrsg.), Gesellschaftliche Bewegungen – Recht unter Beobachtung und in Aktion, Festschrift für Wolfhart Kohte, 2016, S. 21–46.

Deinert, Olaf, Soloselbständige zwischen Arbeitsrecht und Wirtschaftsrecht – Zur Notwendigkeit eines erweiterten Sonderrechts für Kleinunternehmer als arbeitnehmerähnliche Personen, 2015.

Fachinger, Uwe, Herausforderungen der sozialen Sicherung der Soloselbstständigen: Lehren aus der Krankenversicherung, Sozialer Fortschritt 2017, S. 815–842.

Greiner, Stefan, Die Vielfalt der modernen Arbeitsformen im Sozialrecht, SGb 2016, S. 301–309.

Hanau, Hans, Schöne Digitale Arbeitswelt, NJW 2016, S. 2614–2617.

Hanau, Hans; Matiaske, Wenzel, Mitbestimmung im entgrenzten Betrieb – arbeitsrechtliche und personalwirtschaftliche Perspektiven, in: D. Alewell, W. Matiaske (Hrsg.), Standards Guter Arbeit – disziplinäre Positionen und interdisziplinäre Perspektiven, Baden-Baden 2019, S. 213–242.

Hänlein, Andreas; Tennstedt, Florian, Geschichte des Sozialrechts, in: v. B. Maydell/F. Ruland/U. Becker (Hrsg.), Sozialrechtshandbuch, 5. Auflage 2012.

Hartmann, Andreas, Arbeit 4.0 und Rentenversicherungspflicht Soloselbstständiger – Neue Rechtsprechung erweitert den Auftraggeberbegriff des § 2 S. 1 Nr. 9 SGB VI,NWB 2016, S. 3808–3812.

Hase, Friedhelm, Gesetzliche Krankenversicherung – Selbständige und Rückkehrer, in: K.J. Bieback (Hrsg.), Neue Mitgliedschaft in der Sozialversicherung – Auf dem Weg in die Volksversicherung?, 2010, S. 168–175.

Hedermann, Dennis, Krankenversicherungsschutz in der modernen Gesellschaft, 2014.

Heuschmidt, Johannes; Klebe, Thomas, Erwerbsarbeit in der Plattformökonomie und Schutz des Arbeits- und Sozialrechts?, in: U. Faber/K. Feldhoff/K. Nebe/ K. Schmidt/U. Waßer (Hrsg.), Gesellschaftliche Bewegungen – Recht unter Beobachtung und in Aktion, Festschrift für Wolfhart Kohte, 2016, S. 73–84.

Kelleter, Kai, Selbstständige in Deutschland, Wirtschaft und Statistik 2009, Nr. 12, S. 1204–1217.

Kirchner, Stefan; Beyer, Jürgen, Die Plattformlogik als digitale Marktordnung – Platform Logic as a Digital Market Order, ZfS 2016, S. 324–339.

Kreikebohm, Ralf; Kolakowski, Uwe; Kockert, Svenja; Rodewald, Jürg, Die rentenpolitische Agenda 2030 – Die Zukunftsfähigkeit der gesetzlichen Alterssicherung vor dem Hintergrund der gesellschaftlichen Veränderungen, 2016.

Lehweß-Litzmann, René; Leßmann, Ortrud, Kapitel 2: Wie Teilhabe produziert wird, in: Forschungsverbund sozioökonomische Berichterstattung (Hrsg.), Dritter Bericht zur sozioökonomischen Entwicklung in Deutschland: Exklusive Teilhabe – ungenutzte Chancen, 2016.

Lenze, Anne, Staatsbürgerversicherung und Verfassung – Rentenreform zwischen Eigentumsschutz, Gleichheitssatz und Europäischer Integration, 2005.

Leyendecker, Wolfgang, Grundrente – Rentenmodell für die Zukunft?, DRV 1986, 143–160.

Müller, Barbara; Seibert, Christoph; Vornfeld, Oliver, Von Arbeit und Sinn. Analyse eines Problemfeldes, in: D. Alewell, W. Matiaske (Hrsg.), Standards Guter Arbeit – disziplinäre Positionen und interdisziplinäre Perspektiven, Baden-Baden 2019, S. 139–173.

Neumann, Sebastian, Alterssicherung und »Solo-Selbstständigkeit«, SGb 2010, S. 463–470.

Nullmeier, Frank, Digitale Ökonomie und ihre Folgen für die Entwicklungsrichtung der gesetzlichen Rentenversicherung, DRV 2017, S. 249–272.

Nullmeier, Frank, Einstürzende Neubauten. Statikprobleme im Säulenmodell der Alterssicherung, SF 2015, S. 196–202.

Porten, Stephan, Sozialversicherungsfreiheit für Notärzte – Bestandsaufnahme einer Neujustierung, NZS 2017, S. 495–500.

Rische, Herbert, Weiterentwicklung der gesetzlichen Rentenversicherung zu einer Erwerbstätigenversicherung: Einführung in die Problematik, DRV 2009, 285–293.

Ruland, Franz, Sozial- und rechtspolitische Bedenken gegen eine Grundrente, ZfR 1987, S. 354–359.

Schulze Buschoff, Karin, Selbstständigkeit und hybride Erwerbsformen - Sozialpolitische Gestaltungsoptionen. Nr. 21, Policy Brief WSI 2018.

Schulze-Buschoff, Karin, Sozialpolitische Perspektiven der neuen Selbständigkeit, in: A.D. Bührmann/H. J.Pongatz (Hrsg.), Prekäres Unternehmertum – Unsicherheiten von selbständiger Erwerbstätigkeit und Unternehmensgründung, 2010, S. 167–199.

Sen, Amartyra, Ökonomie für den Menschen – Wege zu Gerechtigkeit und Solidarität in der Marktwirtschaft, 2002.

Ueckermann, Johanna, Für eine zukunftsfeste Rente: Generationensolidarität und Erwerbstätigenversicherung, in: Köster (Hrsg.), Zukunftsfeste Rente: neue Impulse für die Alterssicherung, 2017, S. 198–209.

Wagner, Gert, Rentenversicherungspflicht für Selbständige macht Sinn – auch wenn die Digitalisierung weniger stark sein sollte als viele glauben, Zeitschrift für Wirtschaftspolitik Bd. 65, 2016, S. 123–128.

Waltermann, Raimund, Digitalisierung der Arbeitswelt und Schutz Kleiner Selbstständiger durch das Sozialversicherungsrecht, SGb 2017, S. 425–431.

Waltermann, Raimund, Welche arbeits- und sozialrechtlichen Regelungen empfehlen sich im Hinblick auf die Zunahme Kleiner Selbstständigkeit?, RdA 2010, S. 162–170.

Waltermann, Raimund, Sozialrecht, 11. Auflage 2014.

Welskop-Deffaa, Eva, Die dynamische Rente 4.0 – Antworten der Alterssicherungspolitik auf die Digitalisierung der Arbeit, Zeitschrift für Wirtschaftspolitik Bd. 65, 2016, S. 129–137.

Welskop-Deffaa, Eva, Die dynamische Rente 4.0 – Antworten der Alterssicherungspolitik auf die Digitalisierung der Arbeit, Zeitschrift für Wirtschaftspolitik Bd. 65 (2016), S. 129 ff.

Windhövel, Kerstin; Funke, Claudia; Möller, Jan-Christian; Thiede, Reinhold; Ehler, Jürgen, Szenarien einer Eingliederung der Selbständigen ohne obligatorische Altersvorsorge in die gesetzliche Rentenversicherung, Expertise im Auftrag des Fotschungsnetzwerks Alterssicherung (FNA) der Deutschen Rentenversicherung Bund, 2009.

Wintermann, Ole, Von der Arbeit 4.0 zur Zukunft der Arbeit, NZA 2017, S. 537–541.

Wirth, Christian, Die agrarsoziale Sicherung, in: v. B. Maydell/F. Ruland/U. Becker (Hrsg.), Sozialrechtshandbuch, 5. Auflage 2012.

Wisskirchen, Gerlind; Schwindling, Jan, Crowdworking im Lichte des Arbeitsrechts, ZESAR 2017, S. 318–327.

Mitbestimmung im entgrenzten Betrieb – Arbeitsrechtliche und personalwirtschaftliche Perspektiven

Hans Hanau und Wenzel Matiaske

1. Zusammenfassung

Dezentralisierung und Flexibilisierung im entgrenzten Betrieb sind sowohl für das Arbeitsrecht als auch für die personalwirtschaftliche Forschung Herausforderungen, die eine Kooperation der bislang einander meist ignorierenden Disziplinen nahelegen. Aus der Entgrenzung aufgrund technologischen und des, hier in den Vordergrund gerückten, organisationalen Wandels resultieren Veränderungen der Arbeitsbeziehungen, welche die grundlegenden Kategorien des Arbeitsrechts – Arbeitnehmer- und Betriebsbegriff – und die darauf basierenden Rechte in Frage stellen. Die betriebliche Mitbestimmung wurde durch Dezentralisierung und Flexibilisierung seit den 1990er Jahren faktisch erheblich gestärkt. In jüngerer Zeit ist jedoch eine Ausdünnung der Reichweite dieser – in der Terminologie der Wirtschaftswissenschaften – »immateriellen« Partizipation zu verzeichnen. Vor diesem Hintergrund eruiert der Beitrag den empirischen und institutionell gestaltenden Forschungsbedarf in Hinblick auf Empirie und institutionelle Gestaltung der Mitbestimmung im entgrenzten Betrieb.

2. Arbeitsrecht und Personalwirtschaft – ein in Bewegung geratenes Verhältnis

Als angewandte Disziplin macht die Betriebswirtschaftslehre nicht nur Gebrauch von ihren zahlreichen Nachbardisziplinen, sondern pflegt in aller Regel auch den wissenschaftlichen Austausch. In der Teildisziplin Personalwirtschaftslehre finden sich beispielsweise traditionell starke Kooperationen in den Schnittmengen mit der Arbeitsmarktforschung, der Arbeits- und Organisationspsychologie oder der Organisationsforschung. Erstaunlicherweise ist jedoch die wissenschaftliche Austauschbeziehung mit dem Arbeitsrecht weit unterdurchschnittlich ausgeprägt. Zwar kann das

Arbeitsrecht praktisch als »Geschäftsgrundlage« des Personalmanagements gelten (Matiaske 2018). Die Beziehungen von Arbeitgebern und Arbeitnehmern, Betrieb bzw. Unternehmen und Interessenvertretungen der Arbeitnehmer sowie Verbänden und Gewerkschaften werden maßgeblich durch das Arbeitsrecht geprägt und auf dieser Grundlage von Praktikern gestaltet.[1] Trotz dieser großen Bedeutung des Rechts fehlen betriebswirtschaftliche, aber auch rechtssoziologische Studien zu Rechtsfolgen oder -wirklichkeit (vgl. Schramm 2018; Rehder und Vogel 2015). Auch das Recht hatte sich bislang wenig für die Empirie des Arbeitsrechts interessiert.

Die Ignoranz »funktionierte« auch, weil beide Disziplinen die jeweils andere Seite als stabil wahrnehmen konnten oder wollten. Während in der betrieblichen Praxis seit einem Vierteljahrhundert – unter Stichworten wie (neuer) Dezentralisierung oder Flexibilisierung – an der »grenzenlosen Unternehmung« (Picot et al. 1996) gearbeitet wurde, konnten Personalwirte die Folgen der Entgrenzung für Arbeitnehmer und Betrieb ausblenden. Betriebliche Beschäftigungs- oder Personalstrategien und deren Bedeutung für die Entwicklung atypischer Beschäftigung sowie für die Arbeitsbeziehungen (Nienhüser 2007) ließen sich vernachlässigen, weil die eingesetzten Instrumente wie beispielsweise Leiharbeit als Form der sog. numerischen Flexibilisierung (Kalleberg 2001) aus Sicht des entleihenden Betriebes keine Veränderung des Direktionsrechts über den Arbeitnehmer impliziert. Das Personalmanagement lagert diese Arbeitsbeziehungen in die Beschaffung aus. Diese These behauptet keineswegs, dass nicht empirisch zu diesen Phänomenen gearbeitet worden ist. Innerhalb der Personalwirtschaftslehre stand die Forschung allerdings oft unter der Überschrift psychologischer Verträge, also subjektiver Wahrnehmungen, oder auch betrieblicher Personalstrategien, ohne die Folgen für die Arbeitsvertragsverhältnisse oder das Arbeitsrecht zu thematisieren.

Das Arbeitsrecht hat die Betriebswirtschaftslehre umgekehrt gleichsam als Schicksal wahrgenommen, dem man reaktiv durch Regulierung sowie

---

1 Das Cranet (Wehner et al. 2017), eine regelmäßige Befragung zur Institutionalisierung des Personalmanagements im internationalen Vergleich, weist mit der Frage nach dem Studienfach rund 58 % der leitenden Personalmanager als Betriebswirte, 13 % als Volkswirte und Sozialwissenschaftler und nur 11 % als Juristen aus (eigene Berechnungen Cranet 2015). Praktiker auf betrieblicher Ebene sind also i. d. R. keine Juristen, sondern Betriebswirte.

Nachführung des eigenen Systems doch immer irgendwie gewachsen sei. Man meinte, sich deshalb eine gewisse Ignoranz leisten zu können. Diese Passivität ist mittlerweile aufgrund der grundstürzenden technischen, aber auch organisationalen Umbrüche gewichen. Die Zumutungen haben ein solches Ausmaß angenommen, dass man sich nunmehr für die Empirie der Arbeitswelt, also die Voraussetzungen und Folgen des eigenen Tuns zunehmend interessiert: Vor dem Hintergrund der als Herausforderung breit diskutierten Digitalisierung der Arbeit hat die Rechtswissenschaft etwa auf dem 71. Juristentag 2016 mit der Frage, ob das Arbeitsrecht ein »Update 4.0« benötigt, jüngst eine erhebliche Nachfrage nach sozialwissenschaftlicher und insbesondere betriebswirtschaftlicher Forschung zur Arbeitsrechtswirklichkeit geltend gemacht.

Zu dieser Veränderung soll auch das nachfolgend skizzierte Forschungsprogramm beitragen, das nach der Zukunft der Mitbestimmung im entgrenzten Betrieb fragt. Dazu wollen wir jedoch zunächst die Entgrenzung von Arbeit und Betrieb, das Phänomen der Ausdünnung der betrieblichen Mitbestimmung sowie die Implikationen für Personalwirtschaft und Arbeitsrecht näher beleuchten.

3. Dezentralisierung und Flexibilisierung – Zwei Aspekte der Entgrenzung

Fragen nach Eigenproduktion oder Fremdbezug bzw. der Aufspaltung von Unternehmen oder der Ausgliederung von Unternehmensteilen gehören zu den konstitutiven betriebswirtschaftlichen Entscheidungen, nicht nur in der Praxis, sondern auch für die Disziplin. Dennoch sah sich die Betriebswirtschaftslehre in den 1990er Jahren mit dem Outsourcing als einem neuartigen Phänomen konfrontiert, das als »Paradigma der Neuen Dezentralisation« (Drumm 1996) charakterisiert worden ist. Neu war am Outsourcing nicht die grundlegende organisatorische Entscheidung, sondern zunächst die Kopplung mit informationstechnischen Fragen. Die prototypischen Fälle des Outsourcings waren die vollständige Ausgliederung der EDV-Betreuung von General Motors an den zuvor erworbenen EDV-Dienstleister EDS in den Jahren 1984/85 und vor allem die Übertragung der Datenverarbeitung und der Kommunikationsnetze an IBM und DEC durch Eastman Kodak im Jahr 1989 (Dirlewanger 1992). Die Informationstechnologie (IT) wurde von Kodak nicht intern an eine Konzerntochter, sondern extern an IT-Dienstleister vergeben. In Deutschland stieg IBM 1993 in das Outsourcing-Geschäft ein. FAG Kugelfischer gehörte zu den ersten Unternehmen, die ihre Datenverarbeitung an die IBM Tochter »Systeme und Netze« übertrugen. Mit dem Outsourcing wechselten auch 260 Arbeitnehmer das Unternehmen (Oehring 1994), d. h. mit der Entscheidung für den Fremdbezug löste das ausgliedernde Unternehmen die davon betroffenen Arbeitsverhältnisse. Die Engführung von Outsourcing auf die Ausgliederung von IT wurde allerdings in kürzester Zeit aufgegeben, und praktisch konnte jede Leistung, die nicht zur »Kernkompetenz« (vgl. Prahalad und Hamel 1990; Homp und Krüger 1997) der Unternehmung zählte, ausgegliedert werden. Vom Paradigma der Dezentralisation war auch die Rede, weil das Outsourcing wie eine Modewelle das Wirtschaftsleben erfasste (Kieser 1996).

Trotz der offenkundigen Prominenz des Outsourcing – 1996 wurde das schönfärberische »Imponierwort« für die »Vernichtung von Arbeitsplätzen« im Wettbewerb um das Unwort des Jahres nur von der »Rentnerschwemme« auf den zweiten Platz verdrängt[2] – blieben die empirischen Kenntnisse zum Phänomen rudimentär (Matiaske und Mellewigt 2002). Außerhalb besonders prominenter Fälle wie dem zitierten First-Mover-Beispiel der FAG wurden Zahlen über Unternehmen als Akteure oder Betriebsteile und Arbeitnehmer als »Betroffene« kaum bekannt, geschweige denn systematisch erhoben.[3] Es mangelt jedoch nicht nur an den deskriptiven Grundlagen. Die Personalforschung orientierte sich in den Erklärungsversuchen zum Outsourcing oft an grundlegenden organisationstheoretischen Konzeptionen – wie Institutionenökonomik, soziologischer Neoinstitutionalismus oder Strukturationstheorie und gelegentlich auch der sozioökonomischen Machttheorie – und selten an naheliegenden personalwirtschaftlichen und arbeitsrechtlichen Gesichtspunkten.

---

2 Vgl. www.unwortdesjahres.net.

3 Dies ist teilweise der mangelnden Forschungsinfrastruktur der Betriebswirtschaftslehre geschuldet, die nicht über Institutionen zur Dauerbeobachtung verfügt. Universitäre Erhebungen wie das Cranet fragen zwar nach dem Outsourcing, dies jedoch nur im Bereich des Personalmanagements. Darüber hinaus ist das Sampling der mehrfachen Querschnittserhebung eher für illustrative Zwecke geeignet. Für die Erhebung im Jahr 2000 ist zu berichten, dass zwischen 70 % (Ost) und mehr als 80 % (West) der befragten Unternehmen Outsourcing nutzten. Dieser Anteil korrelierte stark mit der Unternehmensgröße. Bei kleineren Unternehmen mit weniger als 100 MA machten rund 45 % gar keinen Gebrauch vom Outsourcing. Bei großen Unternehmen mit mehr als 2000 MA waren dies weniger als 10 % (eigene Berechnungen, Cranet 1999/2000).

Der Trend des Outsourcings verband sich mit dem Trend zur Konzernorganisation als Holding. Genauer gesagt, wandelte sich das Verständnis der Führung von Zentralbereichen im Konzern in den gegebenen Rahmenbedingungen des Aktiengesetzes zu Beginn der 1990er Jahre (Mellewigt und Matiaske 2000). Diese erhielten Kostenverantwortlichkeit und wurden häufiger als Cost-, Service- oder Profitcenter geführt, die auch am Markt reüssieren und externe Kunden finden konnten sowie von internen Kunden nicht zwingend gewählt werden mussten (vgl. Bühner 1992, 1996; Bach 2009). Damit war und ist jedoch keine Aussage darüber getroffen, entlang welcher Grenzen Zentralbereiche bzw. Center geschnitten werden sollten. In betriebswirtschaftlichen Studien sind wohl unschwer vermutbare Transaktionskosten häufiger als schwierig zu ermittelnde »harte« Personalkosten als Grundlage der Argumentation gewählt worden, obwohl in bekannten Fallbeispielen letztere wohl eine entscheidende Rolle gespielt haben. Das bis dahin einheitliche deutsche Unternehmen IBM wurde 1993 aufgespalten. Das nunmehr den Softwarebereich bündelnde Unternehmen wurde nicht Mitglied des Arbeitgeberverbandes, sondern schloss Haustarifverträge mit der Deutschen Angestellten Gewerkschaft (DAG) ab, die im Vergleich zu dem im Stammhaus geltenden Tarifvertrag mit der Industriegewerkschaft Metall eine unvergütete Verlängerung der Wochenarbeitszeit von 36 auf 38 Stunden vorsahen (Mayer 2000).

Das Beispiel macht auf einen weiteren Aspekt aufmerksam (Weitbrecht 2017). Die Kritik der Arbeitgeber an ihren Verbänden und dem Flächentarifvertrag, die damit verbundenen Austritte aus den Arbeitgeberverbänden und die Etablierung von Mitgliedschaften ohne Tarifbindung wurden aufgrund der Arbeitsteilung zwischen den Disziplinen vornehmlich im Forschungsfeld der industriellen Beziehungen beobachtet (vgl. Behrens 2011; Haipeter 2017). Die Beobachtungen in diesen Forschungsfeldern sind allerdings zusammenzuführen, um die Veränderungen im Zusammenhang zu verstehen. Der schwindende Organisationsgrad der Arbeitgeberbände, deren Mitglieder hinsichtlich der Tarifbindung eine große Hebelwirkung entfalten, ist dabei für die Erosion des Flächentarifvertrages sicherlich von ebenso großer Bedeutung wie der Mitgliederschwund auf Seiten der Gewerkschaften (vgl. Schnabel 2005; Ellguth und Kohaut 2010; Schnabel 2016).

Die Tendenz zur Verringerung der Fertigungstiefe und die Umstellung vom Betrieb als Ort der Wertschöpfung auf Wertschöpfungsarchitekturen (Dietl et al. 2009) hat sich seither fortgesetzt. Besonders deutlich wird dies am Beispiel von Unternehmensnetzwerken, die organisationstheoretisch gewissermaßen als Avantgarde der Entgrenzung des Betriebes gelten (Sydow und Wirth 1999; Helfen et al. 2016). Unternehmensübergreifende Netzwerkstrukturen treten vielgestaltig auf, in besonders verdichteter Form etwa als virtuelle Unternehmen, d. h. als Netzwerke mehrerer Unternehmen, die – über interorganisationale Informationssysteme verbunden – eine gemeinsame Leistung erstellen und nur dem Kunden gegenüber als Einheit erscheinen (Köhler 1999). Weitere Erscheinungsformen sind etwa Zulieferer- und Produktionsnetzwerke, die auch Produktionsformen wie Just-In-Time- oder In-House-Produktion umfassen (Krebber 2005, S. 67), ferner Cluster (Deinert 2014) und temporäre Projektnetzwerke, wie z. B. Arbeitsgemeinschaft/ARGE, Joint Venture oder Konsortium (Krebber 2005, S. 60 ff.). Arbeitsrechtlich problematisch sind Netzwerkstrukturen vor allem in Hinblick auf die fremdsteuernden Einflüsse. Ein fokales Unternehmen beispielsweise, das einen Netzwerkverbund führt und steuert, erlangt dadurch zwar noch keine rechtliche Verfügungsmacht über die Arbeitnehmer der anderen Netzwerkunternehmen. Gleichwohl hat es zumindest faktischen Einfluss auf die Arbeitsorganisation, da bei Beachtung der Steuerungs- und Führungsvorgaben regelmäßig kein substanzieller eigener Gestaltungsspielraum für die nachgeordneten Netzwerkunternehmen verbleibt (Hanau 2016).

Die vorgenannten Entwicklungen und der Trend zur Hierarchieverschiebung werden durch den Einsatz moderner Informations- und Kommunikationstechnologie ermöglicht, vereinfacht und beschleunigt (beispielsweise Alt et al. 2005; Stadlbauer 2007; Reinhart et al. 2008). Information und Kommunikation zwischen netzwerkförmig kooperierenden Akteuren werden ebenso erleichtert wie die gegenseitige Steuerung und Kontrolle. So werden Netzwerkbildungen auch über große räumliche Distanz und Unternehmensgrenzen hinweg begünstigt. Dies ermöglicht eine arbeitsteilige Wertschöpfung durch unternehmensübergreifende Planung und Steuerung von Geschäftsprozessen. Gleichzeitig werden damit aber auch die technischen und prozeduralen Grundlagen für eine fortschreitende Entbetrieblichung geschaffen: Wenn die Notwendigkeit der Konzentration von Betriebsmitteln und Mitarbeitern an einem physischen Ort entfällt, führt dies zur Erosion des Betriebes als einer räumlich-organisatorischen Einheit, in welche die Arbeitnehmer eingegliedert sind und in der sie ihrer Tätigkeit kontinuierlich nachgehen. Die zentrale Rolle des Betriebes als soziale Basis für institutionalisierte Einflussnahme der Arbeitnehmer auf arbeitgeberseitige Entscheidungsprozesse verliert an Bedeutung (Krause 2016, S. B 19; Bialeck und Hanau 2018).

Flexibilisierung kann als personalwirtschaftliches Pendant zur organisationalen Dezentralisierung verstanden werden. Der »flexible Mensch« (Sennett 1998) ersetzt den »organizational man« (Whyte 1956) und schließt die Lücken, welche der Abbau der Bürokratie in der Organisation hinterlässt. Der Arbeitgeber bietet statt stabilem Einkommen und Karrierechancen nunmehr Gelegenheiten zur Selbstverwirklichung, statt Leistungsbereitschaft des Arbeitnehmers zählt der Beitrag zur Wertschöpfung, der Input in Form von Wissen und Fähigkeiten statt bloßer Arbeitskraft verlangt lebenslanges Lernen und Adaption (Rousseau 1995). Der Arbeitnehmer wandelt sich zum Mitunternehmer in der Organisation und zum Unternehmer in eigener Sache (Pongratz und Voß 2003). Dieser Vorgang ist hoch ambivalent.

Einerseits seien die Stichworte »neuer« psychologischer Vertrag und Arbeitskraftunternehmer genannt, um grundlegende Aspekte flexibler Organisation, die allzu oft bloß die Flexibilität der Menschen in der Organisation meint, in Erinnerung zu rufen. Das Unbehagen in der zeitgenössischen Organisation hat jedenfalls auch damit zu tun, dass psychologische Verträge höchst einseitige Angelegenheiten sind, weshalb die Metapher des Vertrages häufig kritisiert worden ist (Mefebue 2013): Es sind lediglich die Gefühle der Arbeitenden, die in ein Arbeitsverhältnis einfließen und dort gebunden werden. Die Organisation antwortet gefühlskalt mit Personalstrategie und Arbeitsrecht. Auch die seit den 1990er Jahren vielfach erforschten Schattenseiten der neuen Flexibilität – Arbeitsplatz- und Einkommensunsicherheit, vor allem aber auch permanente Verfügbarkeit und Zeitstress (Busch und Vahle-Hinz 2019) – seien lediglich angedeutet. In den vergangenen Dekaden ist jedenfalls deutlich geworden, dass das Unbehagen im »stahlharten Gehäuse der Hörigkeit«, gegen das die Organisationstheorie (spätestens) seit der Human-Relations-Bewegung, über die humanistische Psychologie und das Organizational Behavior bis hin zur postmodernen Organisationskritik angeschrieben hat, mit Handlungsspielraum, Autonomie und positivem Feedback allein nicht aus der Welt zu schaffen ist (eine Übersicht geben Moldaschl und Voß 2003). Andererseits liegen in der Überwindung der tayloristischen Arbeitsweise durch dieses Wiederaufleben unternehmerischer Elemente im Arbeitsverhältnis auch nicht unbeträchtliche Chancen, gerade für Führungskräfte: die Lockerung der Hierarchie ermöglicht Souveränität hinsichtlich Arbeitserbringung, -ort und -zeit, Hierarchie kann sich zur Kooperation entwickeln (Hanau 2018). Den Chancen der Organisationsänderung und -entwicklung stehen allerdings Änderungskosten und organisationale Widerstände entgegen. Rückblickend lässt sich jedenfalls verstehen, warum eine Sehnsucht nach »alten Zeiten«, die so gut nicht waren, zu verspüren ist und warum es notwendig erscheint, dass die Personal- und Organisationsforschung eine Neupositionierung ihrer normativen Grundlagen in Angriff nimmt.

Flexibilisierung der Arbeitsverhältnisse wird in erster Linie als *numerische* Flexibilität (Kalleberg 2001) diskutiert. Darunter sind personalpolitische Maßnahmen zu verstehen, die intern oder extern (kurzfristige) Kapazitätsanpassungen ermöglichen wie beispielsweise Überstunden oder Kurzarbeit, Teilzeit oder Befristung, Leiharbeit bzw. Fremdbezug von Leistungen bzw. Arbeitsleistungen durch (Onsite-) Werkverträge (Dütsch und Struck 2010). Ein Teil dieser Instrumente – Befristungen, Teilzeit unter 20 Stunden, geringfügige Beschäftigung und Leiharbeit, nicht aber Solo-Selbständigkeit – fasst das Statistische Bundesamt in der Kategorie der atypischen Beschäftigung zusammen. Dabei hat sich der Anteil der atypischen Beschäftigung auf Basis des Mikrozensus von 1991 bis 2016 von 14,1 % aller abhängig Beschäftigten auf 22,3 % erhöht. Absolut betrug die Zahl der abhängig Beschäftigten im Jahr 2016 rund 33,3 Mio. Frauen und Männer. Die Teilzeitquote (über 20 Stunden) stieg von 5,6 % auf 10,8 %. Zugleich stieg der Anteil der Solo-Selbständigen im Zeitraum von 45,1 % auf 54,5 % bei insgesamt 3,65 Mio. Selbständigen im Jahr 2016 (Destatis Mikrozensus 1991 und 2016, eigene Berechnung).

Ein (wachsender) Teil dieser Arbeitsverhältnisse ist als prekär einzustufen, was in der sozioökonomischen Forschung intensiv diskutiert wird (vgl. Keller und Seifert 2013; Keller 2018; Schuler-Harms und Goldberg 2019). Die Bandbreite atypischer Arbeitsverhältnisse ist allerdings groß, weshalb die schlichte Gleichsetzung mit prekärer Beschäftigung nicht angemessen ist. Leiharbeit korreliert zwar beispielsweise sowohl in Deutschland als auch im europäischen Vergleich mit Merkmalen prekärer Beschäftigung (Nienhüser und Matiaske 2006), worunter die Autoren nicht nur eine geringere als die branchenübliche Entlohnung, sondern auch unterdurchschnittliche Teilnahme an Weiterbildung, überdurchschnittliche physische und psychische Belastungen sowie als gering wahrgenommene soziale Unterstützung und Handlungsspielräume verstehen. Jedoch finden sich selbst in diesem Beschäftigungssegment Formen wie das Interimsmanagement (Alewell 2006), die weder aus der Außenperspektive der Forschung noch der Binnensicht der Akteure Merkmale prekärer Beschäftigung tragen. Bei der deutlich gestiegenen Zahl der Solo-Selbständigen erzielt zwar eine ebenfalls gewachsene Zahl nur geringe Haushaltseinkommen (Brenke 2011). Jedoch ist diese Gruppe bezüglich des Einkommens sehr heterogen zusammengesetzt. Die im Vergleich zu abhängig Beschäftigten höhere Einkommensspreizung impliziert, dass ein Teil der Solo-Selbständigen auch deutlich höhere Einkommen als Arbeitnehmer erzielen.[4] Ein in jüngerer Zeit untersuchtes Beispiel untypischer atypischer Beschäftigung sind Honorarärzte (Keller und Wilkesmann 2014), wobei nicht nur die Lebenslage der Beschäftigten, sondern auch der Einfluss dieser Beschäftigungsform auf die Organisation thematisiert worden ist, da diese im Kern der Beschäftigung von Krankenhäusern angesiedelt ist (Wilkesmann et al. 2016).

Aufgrund der sozialen Folgen prekärer Beschäftigung ist die numerische Flexibilisierung jedoch auch außerhalb der Personal- und Organisationsforschung im Fokus. Anders die *funktionale* (Kalleberg 2001) oder *qualitative* Flexibilisierung (Dütsch und Struck 2010). Bezogen auf die Beschäftigung im Betrieb meint dies insbesondere Qualifizierung, also Aus- und Weiterbildung, Personalentwicklung oder Formen der Arbeitserweiterung (job enlargement, job enrichment). Die Flexibilisierung durch Investitionen in Humankapital ist mit Zahlen der amtlichen Statistik nicht ohne weiteres zu illustrieren, denn diese unterscheidet nicht nach dem Segment der Beschäftigung im Betrieb, worauf zurückzukommen ist. Die Weiterbildungsbeteiligung in Deutschland ist jedenfalls seit Anfang der 90er Jahre erheblich gestiegen. Die Beteiligungsquote lag 1991 bei 37 % und steigt bis zum Ende der Dekade auf rund 48 %. Um die Jahrtausendwende fällt die Beteiligung dann ab, um ab 2010 wieder anzusteigen. Derzeit liegt diese etwa bei 50 % (BMBF/Infratest 2011, www.datenportal.bmbf.de)[5]. Der Anteil weiterbildender Unternehmen liegt für 2016 bei rund 77 % mit einer durchschnittlichen Teilnahmequote

---

4 Brenke (2011) berechnet auf Basis des SOEP ein äquivalenzgewichtetes Haushaltseinkommen von 1500 Euro für Solo-Selbständige und von 1570 Euro für abhängig Beschäftige für das Jahr 2010. Während diese Beträge in etwa gleich sind, liegt das Haushaltseinkommen im unteren Bereich der Verteilung (5 %) bei den Solo-Selbständigen mit 533 Euro deutlich unter dem Haushaltseinkommen von Arbeitnehmern, die bei 733 Euro liegen. Umgekehrt verhält es sich bei den oberen 5 %. In dieser Teilgruppe schneiden die Solo-Selbständigen mit 4000 Euro deutlich besser ab als die Arbeitnehmer mit 3067 Euro.

5 Bei Zeitreihen zur Weiterbildung ist zu beachten, dass das nationale Berichtssystem Weiterbildung (BWB) ab 2007 vom europäischen Adult Education Survey (AES) abgelöst worden ist. Zur Methodik vgl. BMBF/Infratest 2011.

von 45 % (Destatis 2017). Die Zahlen variieren über die Branchen und steigen linear mit der Unternehmensgröße. Letzterer Befund wird besonders in Auswertungen von Betriebsvereinbarungen zur Weiterbildung deutlich (Heidemann 2015).

Aus Perspektive der Personalforschung sind diese Instrumente der Flexibilisierung unterschiedlichen Segmenten der Beschäftigten zuzuordnen. Das breit rezipierte Konzept der flexiblen Unternehmung von Atkinson und Meager (1984) unterscheidet dabei zwischen Kern- und Randbelegschaften, wobei erstere mit Instrumenten der funktionalen und letzteren mit solchen der numerischen Flexibilisierung verbunden wird (zur Diskussion vgl. Martin und Bartscher-Finzer 2015). Begründend wird dabei häufig auf eine transaktionskostentheoretische Argumentation zurückgegriffen. Williamson (1984) hat entlang der Dimensionen der Kontrollkosten, die mit dem Grad der Verflechtung in der Leistungserstellung oder Teamproduktion steigen, weil die Beiträge zum Ergebnis nicht einzelnen zuzurechnen sind, sowie der Kosten für die Wiedergewinnung von Personal, die mit der Spezifität des Humankapitals anwachsen, eine Segmentation des Personals vorgeschlagen. Danach ist es, im Sinne der Reduktion von Transaktionskosten, rational, wenn im Fall individuell zurechenbarer Produktivität und geringer Investitionen in spezifisches Humankapital ein Spot-Markt für Arbeitskraft implementiert wird. Steigen jedoch die Kontrollkosten durch den Einsatz von Teams bzw. die Wiedergewinnungskosten aufgrund von spezifischem Humankapital, wird Personalbindung zweckmäßig (Matiaske 1992; Kullak 1995). Diese These von der Dualität der Belegschaften, die im Übrigen früheren segmentationstheoretischen Überlegungen ähnelt, übersieht allerdings weitere, insbesondere machttheoretische Aspekte der Entstehung von Personalstrategien (Nienhüser 2007). Dies betrifft einerseits das Verhältnis von Angebot und Nachfrage am Arbeitsmarkt, den Stand der Arbeitsbeziehungen auf überbetrieblicher Ebene und selbstverständlich die Arbeitsgesetzgebung. Andererseits sind damit auch die betriebsinternen Arbeitsbeziehungen, also die betriebliche Mitbestimmung angesprochen.

4. Betriebliche Mitbestimmung – Eine »stille Revolution«

Dabei ist die Herstellung von Arbeitnehmer- und Entscheidungsnähe des Betriebsrats wesentlich: Das Mitbestimmungsgremium soll dort installiert werden, wo die arbeitnehmer- und mitbestimmungsrelevanten Entscheidungen getroffen werden (Koch 2017). Die zentralen Merkmale des Betriebsbegriffs setzen sich demnach zusammen aus einheitlichem Rechtsträger, einheitlicher Leitung, räumlicher Einheit, gewisser Dauer sowie organisierter Zweckverfolgung (Franzen 2016).

Die betriebliche Mitbestimmung galt, trotz ihrer historischen Wurzeln, die bis in das Revolutionsjahr 1848 und die Debatten in der Frankfurter Paulskirche reichen, dann aber erst in der Weimarer Republik gesetzlich verankert und in der bundesrepublikanischen Nachkriegsordnung mit dem Betriebsverfassungsgesetz von 1952 erneut kodifiziert wurden, als »Aschenputtel« der deutschen Arbeitsbeziehungen (Müller-Jentsch 2008). Auch die Neufassung des BetrVG von 1972, welche die Mitbestimmungsrechte erheblich erweiterte, änderte dies nicht. Kotthoff (1981), der die zentrale Studie zur Rechtswirklichkeit der Betriebsverfassung nach der Reform vorgelegt hat, typologisierte zwei Drittel der von ihm untersuchten Fälle als »ignoriertes«, »isoliertes« und von der Geschäftsleitung »instrumentalisiertes« Betriebsratshandeln. Die Situation wandelte sich in den 1990er Jahren grundlegend. In einer Nachfolgestudie stellte Kotthoff (1994) fest, dass nunmehr in zwei Drittel der Fälle wirksame Interessenvertretungen im Sinne des Gesetzes wie »respektierte« oder »standfeste« Betriebsräte bzw. Betriebsräte als »kooperative Gegenmacht« etabliert waren. Müller-Jentsch (1995) prägte den Begriff des »Co-Managements«.

Die Soziologie der industriellen Beziehungen macht u. a. institutionelles Lernen und Ko-Evolution für den Wandel der Grenzinstitution (Fürstenberg 1958) als Intermediär zur Verbindung von Interessen der Beschäftigten und wirtschaftlicher Belange verantwortlich (Müller-Jentsch 2018). Die ökonomische Theorie ist diesbezüglich zurückhaltend. Sie sucht vielmehr aus der Perspektive relevanter Akteure nach guten Gründen für die Vorteilhaftigkeit der Institution, um die Nutzung der Mitbestimmung zu erklären. Die Standardökonomie war (und blieb) diesbezüglich skeptisch, da Mitbestimmung in erster Linie als Verdünnung von Eigentums- und damit verbundenen Verfügungsrechten der Inhaber bzw. des Managements gesehen wurde. Erst die verstärkte Rezeption der Neuen Institutionenökonomik und deren Zugang zur Organisationstheorie schuf Akzeptanz für alternative Erklärungen (Dunn 1998).

Die sozioökonomische Theorie hatte schon früh argumentiert, dass Mitbestimmung den Beschäftigten die Artikulation ihrer Interessen ermöglicht. Für die Organisation ist dies vorteilhaft, insofern Widerspruch oder »voice« helfen kann, Abwanderung oder »exit« zu vermeiden (Hirschman 1974). Aus Perspektive des Transaktionskostenansatzes wird angeführt, dass die Mitbestimmung die Kosten der (internen) Kommunikation und Verhandlungen senkt, weil dem Management ein legitimierter Ansprechpartner gegenübersteht sowie Regeln und Routinen etabliert werden (Nienhüser 2014). Aus dieser Sicht hat der Gesetzgeber mit der Betriebsverfassung Instrumente wie »participation«, »feedback« und »codetermination« geschaffen, die im nordamerikanischen »Human Resource Management« in (akademischen) Modellen seit den 60er Jahren verschiedentlich als Elemente des Personalmanagements erst »erfunden« werden mussten, um Ziele wie »commitment«, »organizational citizenship« oder eine geringe Fluktuation zu erreichen (Pfeffer 1996). Dabei verfolgt der Staat mit der Kanalisierung von Konflikten im Betrieb durch die Mitbestimmung und ihre Institutionen durchaus auch eigene Ziele wie die Entlastung der Arbeitsgerichtsbarkeit und darüber hinaus die Einhegung des Konfliktes von Arbeit und Kapital (Keller 2008).

Die empirische Forschung zur Mitbestimmung konzentrierte sich in ökonometrischen Studien zunächst auf die Zielvariable des wirtschaftlichen Erfolges von Unternehmen in Abhängigkeit des Vorhandenseins und unter Berücksichtigung der Kosten der Mitbestimmung, ohne zu eindeutigen Ergebnissen zu kommen (vgl. Frick und Sadowski 1995; Dilger 2002; Stettes 2007; Jirjahn 2011). Die vor dem skizzierten theoretischen Hintergrund unterkomplexen Modellierungen sind ebenso wie die wenig aufschlussreichen Ergebnisse auch der mangelnden Datenbasis geschuldet. Diese hat sich zwischenzeitlich erheblich verbessert. Allerdings ist der wirtschaftliche Erfolg auch eine zu diffuse Variable, um den Wert der Mitbestimmung einzuschätzen. Dieser erweist sich möglicherweise nicht bei stabiler Geschäftslage und ökonomischem Erfolg, sondern gerade in wirtschaftlich schwieriger Situation oder bei organisatorischen Änderungen. In diesen Fällen sind Betriebe jedoch kaum ansprechbar für die Organisations- und Personalforschung, was das Wissen zur Wirksamkeit der Mitbestimmung systematisch einschränkt. Einigkeit besteht in der jüngeren empirischen Forschung jedoch, dass Mitbestimmung der Innovativität förderlich ist (Kraft und Stank 2004; Gerlach 2012). Neuere qualitative Studien belegen den Befund, »dass die für Deutschland typische Struktur und Kultur der Mitbestimmung positiv auf die Innovationsfähigkeit der Unternehmen wirkt« (Pfeiffer 2014, S. 402). Dies gilt insbesondere für

Innovationen der Arbeitsorganisation, weniger für Produktinnovationen.[6] Es ist jedenfalls keine allzu gewagte These, dass die Möglichkeit, Akzeptanz zu schaffen, und die konstatierte grundsätzliche Innovationsförderlichkeit nicht nur die zuvor erläuterten organisatorischen Änderungen erleichtert, sondern auch die Mitbestimmung selbst gestärkt haben.

Die organisatorischen und personalpolitischen Veränderungen wurden durch eine Entwicklung im dualen System der Arbeitsbeziehungen ergänzt, die unter den Begriffen der Dezentralisierung oder, präziser, Verbetrieblichung der Tarifpolitik diskutiert worden ist (Schmidt und Trincek 1999). Durch die Verlagerung von Kompetenzen von der tarifvertraglichen überbetrieblichen auf die betriebliche Ebene erhielten Betriebsräte und Management Spielräume, insbesondere in den Feldern der Arbeitszeit-, aber auch der Lohnpolitik, die bis dahin den Tarifparteien vorbehalten waren. Den Ausgangspunkt dieser Entwicklung bildeten Tarifverträge zur Arbeitszeitverkürzung Mitte der 1980er Jahre, welche die Umsetzung und Konkretisierung der Maßnahmen in einer zweiten Verhandlungsrunde an die Betriebe delegierten. Dies ermöglichte die rasche Ausbreitung flexibler Arbeitszeitmodelle, insbesondere in Form von Arbeitszeitkonten, und stärkte die Position der Betriebsräte. Einen zweiten Schub erhielt die Verbetrieblichung durch die Einführung tariflicher Härtefall- und Öffnungsklauseln Anfang der 1990er Jahre. Innerhalb tariflich vereinbarter Rahmenbedingungen und Korridore wurden Möglichkeiten geschaffen, um auf betrieblicher Ebene Konzessionen bei Einkommen und Arbeitszeit auszuhandeln, beispielsweise durch Verlängerungen der Arbeitszeit ohne Lohnausgleich oder temporäre Verkürzungen. Ferner war seitens der Betriebsräte häufig die Zustimmung zur Reorganisation Gegenstand der Vereinbarungen. Im Gegenzug verpflichteten sich die Arbeitgeber zu Beschäftigungsgarantien und zum Verzicht auf betriebsbedingte Kündigun-

6 Zwar ist diese These in der Literatur weitgehend Konsens, jedoch ist einschränkend anzumerken, dass insbesondere die zahlreichen qualitativen Studien einen systematischen Bias für innovative Unternehmen mit betrieblicher Mitbestimmung aufweisen. Es gälte, worauf auch Pfeiffer (2014) in ihrer zusammenfassenden Kommentierung hinweist, in gleicher Weise innovative Unternehmen ohne betriebliche Mitbestimmung zu untersuchen. Darüber hinaus wären insbesondere auch Unternehmen zu betrachten, in welchen Innovationen eine untergeordnete Rolle spielen.

gen für einen spezifizierten Zeitraum und sicherten standortbezogene Investitionen zu (Seifert 2002).

Die sukzessive Stärkung der betrieblichen Mitbestimmung lässt sich als Erfolgsgeschichte des deutschen Mehrebenenmodells der Arbeitsbeziehungen lesen (Müller-Jentsch 2018). Mit der Flexibilisierung von Arbeitszeiten und der kontinuierlichen Modernisierung der Berufsbilder seit den 1990er Jahren schienen »zukunftsfeste Strukturen« geschaffen worden zu sein, die der deutschen Wirtschaft die Anpassung an den erneuten Schub in der Digitalisierung erleichtern. Diese von Bosch (2018, S. 240) als »stille Revolution« bezeichnete Entwicklung wurde nicht zuletzt durch Co-Management und immaterielle Partizipation befördert.

5. Immaterielle Partizipation – Inklusion und Exklusion

Die Funktionalität der Mitbestimmung für Anpassungs- und Wandlungsfähigkeit von Betrieben einerseits und das i.d.R. angenommene partizipative Interesse der Arbeitnehmer (AN) sind in der Praxis indes keine hinreichenden Gründe, der appellativen Norm des § 1 Abs. 1 S. 1 BetrVG – »in Betrieben werden … Betriebsräte gewählt« – auch durchweg zu folgen. Für das Jahr 2000 beziffern Ellguth und Kohaut (2004) auf Basis des IAB-Betriebspanels den Anteil der mitbestimmungsfähigen Betriebe, die über einen Betriebsrat verfügen, auf 12 %. Aufgrund des starken Größeneffektes, der Anteil steigt mit zunehmender Betriebsgröße sprunghaft an, betrug der Deckungsgrad der Betriebsräte rund 50 % in West- und 41 % in Ostdeutschland.

Diese Anteile sind seither sogar gesunken. Schon früh hatte Hassel (1999), allerdings auf schwächerer Datenbasis, auf das Phänomen der Erosion der betrieblichen Mitbestimmung aufmerksam gemacht. In der jährlichen Fortschreibung der Schätzung auf Basis des IAB-Betriebspanels wird dieser Rückgang mittlerweile allerdings sehr deutlich. In 2017 verfügen nur noch 9 % der mitbestimmungsfähigen Betriebe in Deutschland über einen Betriebsrat. Unterdurchschnittlich ist dieser Anteil mit 5 % in Betrieben mit 50–100 Beschäftigten. In der Größenklasse von 101–199 Beschäftigen haben zwar bereits mehr als 53 % der Betriebe einen Betriebsrat und in den kleinen Großbetrieben zwischen 200 und 500 Arbeitnehmern sind dies schon 69 % (Ellguth und Kohaut 2018). Der Größeneffekt ist also weiterhin deutlich. Allerdings ist der Rückgang insbesondere im Bereich dieser mittleren Betriebsgrößen zu beobachten (Ellguth 2018).

Der Rückgang des Deckungsgrades ist für Gesamtdeutschland zu verzeichnen, fällt jedoch im Osten von einem ohnehin niedrigeren Niveau nochmals deutlich stärker aus. Rund 40 % der Beschäftigten in der westdeutschen Privatwirtschaft sind 2017 durch einen Betriebsrat vertreten. In Ostdeutschland sind dies nur noch 33 % (Ellguth und Kohaut 2018).

Das Bezugsjahr 2000 charakterisiert die Situation vor der Reform des Betriebsverfassungsgesetzes (BetrVG). Die Intention des Gesetzgebers war, mit der Novellierung des BetrVG den Erosionsprozess der Mitbestimmung umzukehren. Insbesondere durch Entbürokratisierung des Wahlrechts sollte die Bildung von Betriebsräten erleichtert werden (Deutscher Bundestag 2012). Diese Erwartungen haben sich nicht erfüllt. Vielmehr hat sich der Erosionsprozess fortgesetzt. Es ist weder gelungen, kleinere Betriebe in die Mitbestimmung einzubeziehen, noch die Ost-West-Differenz im Deckungsgrad der Mitbestimmung einzuebnen. In Verbindung mit der Erosion des Flächentarifvertrags (Kohaut 2018) – nur noch 27 % der Betriebe in West- und 16 % der Betriebe in Ostdeutschland sind an einen Flächentarifvertrag gebunden und in 2 % der Betriebe in West- und Ostdeutschland ist ein Haustarifvertrag gültig – resultiert eine Ausdehnung der »weißen Flecken« im dualen System der deutschen Arbeitsbeziehungen (Bellmann et al. 1999), in denen weder ein Tarifvertrag Anwendung findet, noch eine betriebliche Interessenvertretung vorhanden ist. Für 39 % der Beschäftigten in West- und 51 % der Beschäftigten in Ostdeutschland gilt kein Tarifvertrag und ist zugleich keine innerbetriebliche Interessenvertretung durch einen Betriebsrat vorhanden (Ellguth 2018; vgl. auch Schneider und Vogel 2018).

Die Erosion der betrieblichen Mitbestimmung ist ein empirisch bislang weitgehend unerforschtes Phänomen. Eine erste Dekompositionsanalyse der Determinanten des Rückgangs der betrieblichen Mitbestimmung auf Basis des IAB-Betriebspanels für den Zeitraum von 1996 bis 2014 haben Ellguth und Trinczek (2016) veröffentlicht. Danach lassen sich in Betrieben mittlerer Größe (51 bis 500 AN) rund 59 % des Zeiteffektes auf Veränderungen in strukturellen Variablen wie Branche, Personalstruktur oder Tarifbindung zurückführen. Einen Erklärungsbeitrag in der Größenordnung der Summe aller anderen berücksichtigten Variablen leistet die Variable Branchentarifvertrag. Die Ausdünnung der Mitbestimmung folgt gewissermaßen der Erosion des Flächentarifvertrages. Ferner liefern die Branche – konkret die Abnahme des Verarbeitenden Gewerbes und die Zunahme der Dienstleistungen – sowie die sinkenden Betriebsgrößen einen relevanten und signifikanten Erklärungsbeitrag. Geringen Einfluss haben auch der Anteil geringfügig Beschäftigter, der Teilzeitanteil und die Ausgründung des Betriebsteils. Tendenziell stärken dagegen der Anteil Qualifizierter, ein hoher Stand der technischen Ausrüstung, die organisatorische Einbindung als Zweigstelle bzw. Mittelinstanz sowie ein Haustarifvertrag die Mitbestimmung. Der Frauenanteil nimmt dagegen in multivariater Betrachtung nur verschwindend geringen Einfluss.

Diese ersten erklärenden Befunde sind noch zu wenig detailliert, um genauere Aussagen über strukturelle Änderungen und ihren Einfluss auf die betriebliche Mitbestimmung zu ermöglichen. Die Wirkungsrichtung der einbezogenen Variablen legt jedoch die Formulierung der Leitannahme nahe, dass die zuvor skizzierte Tendenz zur Entgrenzung von Betrieben der betrieblichen Mitbestimmung insgesamt nicht zuträglich ist. Es wird, theoretisch wie empirisch, zwischen Kern- und Randbelegschaften nunmehr über Betriebsgrenzen hinweg zu unterscheiden sein. Insgesamt folgern Ellgut und Trinczek (2016) aus dem Ergebnis der Dekompositionsanalyse, dass jenseits der einbezogenen strukturellen Variablen insbesondere auch veränderte Einstellungen zur immateriellen Partizipation – auf Seiten der Beschäftigen und des Managements – eine bedeutsame Rolle bei der Erklärung der Erosion der Mitbestimmung spielen. Dieser Einstellungsbegriff wird mit Blick auf weitergehende Forschung genauer zu klären sein. Darüber hinaus sind alternative institutionelle Arrangements zu entwickeln, die eine Partizipation der Arbeitnehmer ermöglichen. Den Forschungsbedarf zur Empirie und rechtlichen Ausgestaltung der betrieblichen Mitbestimmung wollen wir abschließend skizzieren.

6. Ansätze für ein Betriebsverfassungsrecht 4.0 – Empirische Fragen und institutionelle Überlegungen

Strukturelle Variablen können die Erosion der Mitbestimmung, die mit der Entgrenzung von Betrieben und Arbeit einhergeht, nicht erklären, wie auch Ellguth und Trinczek (2016) konzidieren. Sie bilden die Randbedingungen oder, anders ausgedrückt, formen die Situationen, in denen Akteure ihre Einstellungen bzw. – wie wir mit Coleman (1990) präzisieren möchten – ihre Interessen gegenüber der Mitbestimmung entwickeln. Der Begriff des Interesses signalisiert die Weichenstellung für eine handlungstheoretische, soziologische Konzeption, die sich allerdings tieferreichenden verhaltenstheoretischen Argumenten nicht grundsätzlich verschließt (Matiaske 2004). Vorrangig steht damit allerdings nicht die Einstellung zur Mitbestimmung im Fokus, sondern die Durchsetzung von Interessen in der Interaktion mit anderen Akteuren im Handlungsfeld der Mitbestimmung. Dies schärft den Blick für die Ressourcen, die Akteure mobilisieren können, um ihre Interessen in einer spezifischen Situation in höherem oder geringerem Maß zu verwirklichen (Nienhüser 1998).

Zur Bestimmung der Interessen an der Mitbestimmung liegen eine Reihe von Studien vor, u.a. auf Basis der Analyse von Betriebsratswahlen. Der Trendreport zur Betriebsratswahl 2014 von Greifenstein et al. (2017, S. 24) berichtet eine (weiterhin) sehr hohe betriebliche Wahlbeteiligung, die je nach Einzelgewerkschaft zwischen 73 und etwas über 80 % liegt (vgl. auch Stettes 2015). Dabei finden sich keine signifikanten Unterschiede zwischen west- und ostdeutschen Betrieben. Auf betrieblicher Ebene nimmt die Wahlbeteiligung mit der Betriebsgröße, was demokratietheoretisch gut erklärbar ist, und einem steigenden Frauenanteil ab. Die hohe Wahlbeteiligung insgesamt belegt ein hohes Interesse an der betrieblichen Mitbestimmung, sofern Betriebsräte zur Wahl stehen. Dies gilt auch im Fall neugegründeter Gremien. Insofern gelten initiierende Ereignisse und die Unterstützung durch und damit auch eine gewisse Bindung an Gewerkschaften als Schlüsselfaktoren (Artus et al. 2014). Die Ausdünnung der Mitbestimmung korrespondiert also möglicherweise mit dem langfristigen Rückgang des gewerkschaftlichen Organisationsgrades. Ferner werden einer Betriebsratsgründung entgegenstehende Interessen und Maßnahmen von Arbeitgebern berichtet (Behrens und Dribbusch 2014), die zwar keine zu vernachlässigende Randerscheinung darstellen, in ihrem Umfang aber nur schwer einzuschätzen sind (Müller 2018).

Unklar ist auch, inwieweit die seit der Reform des BetrVG 2001 mögliche Beteiligung von Leiharbeitnehmern an der Betriebsratswahl, wenn diese länger als drei Monate im entleihenden Betrieb eingesetzt sind (§ 7 S. 2 BetrVG), zu einer stärkeren Repräsentation der Interessen dieser Gruppe geführt haben. Die vorliegenden Arbeiten – beispielsweise von Artus (2014), Promberger (2012) oder Wassermann und Rudolph (2007) – weisen jedenfalls darauf hin, dass Betriebsräte ihren Einfluss auf die Bedingungen von Leiharbeit und für Leiharbeitnehmer im Betrieb nicht durchgängig nutzen. Es ist eine weitergehende empirische Frage, inwieweit die 2017 erfolgte gesetzliche Begründung eines Auskunftsrechts über den Einsatz von Leiharbeit im Betrieb (§ 80 Abs. 2 BetrVG) sowie die ebenfalls seit 2017 vorgesehene Berücksichtigung von Leiharbeitnehmern bei den betriebsverfassungsrechtlichen Schwellenwerten (§ 14 Abs. 2 S. 4 Arbeitnehmerüberlassungsgesetz) helfen, Leiharbeitnehmer faktisch besser in die Mitbestimmung zu integrieren. Ferner sind die Interessen von solchen »peripheren« Teilen der Belegschaft an der Mitbestimmung noch kaum erforscht. Wilkesmann et al. (2011) zeigen in einer typologischen Analyse von Befragungsdaten abhängig Beschäftigter, dass die Erwartungen an die Mitbestimmung mit dem sozialstrukturellen Milieu erheblich variieren. Darunter identifizieren sie u. a. mit einem »schutzsuchenden« und einem »mitbestimmungsbedürftigen« Milieu zwei größere Cluster (insgesamt rund 17 %), deren Mitglieder teilweise peripheren Beschäftigungsverhältnissen zugerechnet werden können. Jedoch handelt es sich bei den peripheren Gruppen im Betrieb keinesfalls durchgängig um Personen, die Mitbestimmung einfordern, wie exemplarisch Jansen (2018) für Solo-Selbstständige oder auch abhängig Beschäftigte im Feld der freien Berufe erläutert. Schließlich wäre zu klären, inwieweit die Kenntnis der Mitbestimmung (Nienhüser et al. 2016) und ihrer Potentiale überhaupt eine Rolle bei der Interessendurchsetzung durch diese Gruppen spielt.

Die Arbeitsrechtswissenschaft sieht sich durch die skizzierte Entbetrieblichung vor besondere Herausforderungen gestellt. Das »Normalarbeitsverhältnis« (Mückenberger 1985) als klassischer Bezugspunkt des Arbeitsrechts ist noch mit einer Vielzahl von Schutz- und Partizipationsrechten ausgestattet. Mit der Umstellung auf Wertschöpfungsketten und dem Gebrauch von den vielfältigen Möglichkeiten digitaler und vernetzter Technologien nähern sich Unternehmen immer mehr dem Ziel einer vollständigen digitalen Vernetzung der Wertschöpfungsprozesse. Damit einher gehen vielfältige Veränderungen der Arbeitsprozesse wie auch der Betriebs- und Unternehmensstrukturen. Durch die Fragmentierung der zugrundeliegenden Rechtsbeziehungen können sowohl Anknüpfungspunkte als auch Anwendungsvoraussetzungen der betrieblichen Mitbestimmung wegfallen, und das Partizipations- und Schutzinstrumentarium der Betriebsverfassung droht zunehmend, seine Passgenauigkeit zu verlieren. Denn ihre Anknüpfungspunkte und Anwendungsvoraussetzungen zielen auf klar definierte Akteure, abgrenzbare Organisationseinheiten und hierarchische Strukturen ab (Bialeck und Hanau 2018).

Von wesentlicher Bedeutung für die deutsche Betriebsverfassung ist der Begriff des Betriebes, er bildet ihre Grundlage. Als Betrieb im Sinne des BetrVG wird gemeinhin die organisatorische Einheit bezeichnet, innerhalb derer der Inhaber (Arbeitgeber) allein oder gemeinsam mit den von ihm beschäftigten Arbeitnehmern mit Hilfe von sachlichen oder immateriellen Betriebsmitteln fortgesetzt bestimmte arbeitstechnische Zwecke unmittelbar verfolgt. Diese betriebsverfassungsrechtliche Betriebsbegriffsbestimmung knüpft also räumlich-gegenständlich an und setzt eine in irgendeiner Weise materialisierte Arbeits- und Betriebsstätte voraus (Franzen 2016). Die in der Betriebsstätte vorhandenen Betriebsmittel müssen für die Verfolgung des oder der arbeitstechnischen Zwecke zusammengefasst, geordnet und gezielt eingesetzt und die menschliche Arbeitskraft von einem einheitlichen Leitungsapparat gesteuert werden, dessen Leitungsmacht sich auf alle wesentlichen Arbeitgeberfunktionen in personellen und sozialen Angelegenheiten erstreckt.[7] Dabei ist die Herstellung von Arbeitnehmer- und Entscheidungsnähe des Betriebsrats wesentlich: Das Mitbestimmungsgremium soll dort installiert werden, wo die arbeitnehmer- und mitbestimmungsrelevanten Entscheidungen getroffen werden (Koch 2017). Die zentralen Merkmale des Betriebsbegriffs setzen sich demnach zusammen aus einheitlichem Rechtsträger, einheitlicher Leitung, räumlicher Einheit, gewisser Dauer sowie organisierter Zweckverfolgung (Franzen 2016).

Das klassische Arbeitsverhältnis wird zunehmend durch alternative und neue selbständige Beschäftigungsformen verdrängt, so dass es schon an dieser zentralen Anwendungsvoraussetzung für die Betriebsverfassung fehlt. Doch selbst dort, wo noch reguläre Arbeitsverhältnisse begründet werden, kann der interne Bedeutungsverlust der Hierarchie im Unternehmen zum Problem des »machtlosen Vertragsarbeitgebers« (Däubler 2016) führen, der seine Rechte nicht ausübt oder nicht ausüben kann, weil er sie – etwa im Rahmen eines strategischen Netzwerks an ein fokales Unternehmen – delegiert hat. Der formelle Vertragsarbeitgeber ist in diesen Fällen also gar nicht mehr notwendigerweise auch der maßgebliche Unternehmer, der die zentralen Arbeitgeberfunktionen ausübt und/oder die wesentlichen Entscheidungen trifft. Damit läuft betriebliche Mitbestimmung, die diesen Arbeitgeber ohne Leitungsmacht adressiert, letztlich weitestgehend leer. Die betriebliche Mitbestimmung ist jeweils auf einen einheitlichen Entscheidungsträger im Betrieb, Unternehmen oder Konzern ausgerichtet und auch angewiesen; auf die neuen flüchtigen Beeinflussungs- und Entscheidungswege in einer in Verbünden außerhalb gesellschaftsrechtlicher Verflechtungen organisierten und vernetzten Wertschöpfungs-

7 Bundesarbeitsgericht, Beschluss vom 15.10.2014 – 7 ABR 53/12. *NZA* 2015 (16), 1014–1019.

kette ist sie kaum vorbereitet (Rieble 2014). Rechtswissenschaftliche Ansätze, das Netzwerk oder den Netzverbund als Entität greifbar und vor allem rechtlich handhabbar und zu einem Adressaten für das Arbeitsrecht zu machen (Rohe 1998; Lange 1998), konnten sich bislang nicht durchsetzen.

Erst recht ist der Betriebsverfassung die Institution eines »Netzwerkbetriebsrats« unbekannt, mit dessen Hilfe die Arbeitnehmerseite etwa analog einem Konzernbetriebsrat nach §§ 54 ff. BetrVG Einfluss auf die maßgeblichen Steuerungsinstanzen eines Netzwerkverbunds nehmen könnte (Hanau 2016).

Damit stellt sich die Frage, ob das geltende Betriebsverfassungsrecht Lösungsansätze bereithält, um mit den skizzierten Problemen, insb. der Erosion des Betriebes und dem Problem machtloser Arbeitgeber, umzugehen oder wie es sich gegebenenfalls entsprechend fortentwickeln ließe.

Wenn die faktische arbeitgeberische Entscheidungsmacht nicht mehr beim Vertragsarbeitgeber angesiedelt ist und sich der taugliche Ansprechpartner betrieblicher Mitbestimmung nicht mehr ohne weiteres lokalisieren lässt, erscheint es sinnfällig, die Einrichtung von Mitbestimmungsinstanzen auf den tatsächlich einschlägigen Entscheidungsebenen zuzulassen, etwa durch Ermöglichung des bereits angesprochenen Netzwerkbetriebsrats. Mit § 3 Abs. 1 Nr. 3 BetrVG hat der Gesetzgeber gerade Vorsorge für passgenaue Vertretungsstrukturen »aufgrund anderer Formen der Zusammenarbeit von Unternehmen« treffen wollen. Ausweislich der Gesetzesbegründung sollte dies auch außerhalb einer Konzernorganisation ermöglicht werden, etwa »entlang der Produktionskette« (BT-Drs. 14/5741, S. 34), so dass durch Tarifvertrag ein solches Vertretungsgremium etabliert werden könnte. Allerdings gelten die nach § 3 Abs. 1 Nr. 3 BetrVG gebildeten eigenen betriebsverfassungsrechtlichen Organisationseinheiten gem. § 3 Abs. 5 BetrVG als Betriebe i.S.d. BetrVG. § 3 Abs. 1 BetrVG ermöglicht damit nach zutreffender, aber nicht unumstrittener Auffassung (anderer Auffassung etwa Kania und Klemm 2006) nur die Festlegung der untersten Ebene der Betriebsverfassung, der jeweiligen Basisvertretungseinheit (vgl. Franzen 2016; Wisskirchen und Block 2017). Dadurch wird die gesetzliche Struktur abgelöst, und diese Vertretung tritt an die Stelle der vorhandenen Betriebsräte und nicht zusätzlich neben sie (Krebber 2005, S. 338). § 3 Abs. 5 BetrVG statuiert wegen vermuteter unauflösbarer Konflikte bei parallel bestehenden Vertretungseinheiten den von Rieble (2014) prägnant als betriebsverfassungsrechtliches »Highlander-Prinzip« bezeichneten Grundsatz, demzufolge es immer nur einen Betriebsrat geben kann, der »seine Belegschaft« im Rahmen seiner Zuständigkeit umfassend vertritt. In diesem Rahmen müssten alle in einem Netzwerk beschäftigten Arbeitnehmer einen gemeinsamen Betrieb bilden und einen gemeinsamen Betriebsrat wählen. An einer solchen Repräsentation werden sie in aller Regel jedoch wegen vorhandener widerstreitender Interessen kaum interessiert sein, da schließlich nicht alle sie berührenden Angelegenheiten auch immer einen Netzwerkbezug haben (Krause 2016). Hinzu kommen weitere Praktikabilitätsprobleme: Als informelle Zusammenschlüsse außerhalb gesellschaftsrechtlicher Verflechtungen sind Netzwerke häufig instabil und in ihrem Mitgliederbestand volatil. Auf Arbeitgeberseite müsste zudem erst einmal ein von allen beteiligten Unternehmen mit hinreichender Vertretungsmacht ausgestatteter Verhandlungspartner gefunden werden (Hanau 2016). Schließlich könnte sich das Erfordernis eines Tarifvertrages für die Begründung abweichender Strukturen entlang der Produktionskette angesichts der Instabilität von Netzwerken und Flüchtigkeit von Kunden- und Lieferantenbeziehungen als zu unflexibel und damit hinderlich erweisen (Günther und Böglmüller 2015).

Die zusätzliche Bildung von Arbeitnehmergremien auf Netzwerkebene bleibt damit § 3 Abs. 1 Nr. 4 und Nr. 5 BetrVG vorbehalten. Zusätzliche Arbeitnehmervertreter nach diesen Vorschriften können indes keine vollwertigen Mitbestimmungsrechte ausüben (Rieble 2014). Gänzlich verschlossen bleibt der Weg über eine Mitbestimmungsflexibilisierung durch Aufgabenübertragung auf Arbeitsgruppen nach § 28a BetrVG. Diese Option ist nämlich ausschließlich an den Betrieb gebunden und bezieht sich weder auf betriebsübergreifende Arbeitsgruppen innerhalb eines Unternehmens noch auf unternehmensübergreifende Arbeitsgruppen (Oetker 2016). Um einen Netzwerksbetriebsrat als zusätzliches Mitbestimmungsgremium zu ermöglichen, müsste der Gesetzgeber § 3 Abs. 5 BetrVG ändern (Hanau 2016).

Ist der Anwendungsbereich der betrieblichen Mitbestimmung im Zusammenhang mit vernetzten digitalen Techniken einmal eröffnet, stellt sich die Frage, inwieweit der Betriebsrat bei ihrer Einführung und Anwendung zu beteiligen ist. Als Kardinalnorm könnte sich insoweit § 87 Abs. 1 Nr. 6 BetrVG erweisen. Danach unterliegt die »Einführung und Anwendung von technischen Einrichtungen, die dazu bestimmt sind, das Verhalten oder die Leistung der Arbeitnehmer zu überwachen«, der stärksten Form der erzwingbaren Mitbestimmung. Nach aktueller Lesart und ständiger Rechtsprechung ist die Einführung technischer Einrichtungen bereits dann nach § 87 Abs. 1 Nr. 6 BetrVG mitbestimmungspflichtig, wenn sie objektiv geeignet ist, das Leistungsverhalten der Arbeitnehmer zu überwachen.[8] Die digitale Vernetzung von Maschinen und Beschäftigten mittels Informations- und Kommunikationstechnik führt zwangsläufig dazu, dass laufend Daten erhoben werden, die unmittelbar oder mittelbar Rückschlüsse auf Arbeits- und Leistungsverhalten der Arbeitnehmer zulassen (Günther und Böglmüller 2015). § 87 Abs. 1 Nr. 6 BetrVG würde damit dem Betriebsrat ein umfassendes Vetorecht gegenüber jeglicher Form digitaler Vernetzung im Arbeitsverhältnis eröffnen. Deshalb ist zu überlegen, ob hier eine Anpassung in umgekehrter Richtung erfolgen, die Mitbestimmung also restriktiver gehandhabt werden sollte, etwa in dem Sinne, dass erst die gezielte Auswertung von Leistungsdaten den Mitbestimmungstatbestand auslöst (so Hanau 2016; für gesetzgeberisches Tätigwerden hingegen tendenziell Zumkeller 2015 sowie Günther und Böglmüller 2015).

Zudem wird auch die Betriebspraxis bedarfsgerechtere und flexiblere Ausübungsformen betrieblicher Mitbestimmung entwickeln müssen. Etablierte Formen der Mitbestimmung hinken notwendig der technischen Entwicklung hinterher. Es wird für die Beteiligten immer schwerer, alle technisch relevanten Aspekte zu verstehen und rechtzeitig bzw. proaktiv regulativ zu gestalten. Selbst bereits eingeführte Technik wandelt sich bei *Software*-Updates, *Upgrades* oder *Crossgrades* zunehmend schneller und grundsätzlicher als bisher und erfordert immer wieder Neueinschätzungen und gegebenenfalls Anpassungen (Pfeiffer 2016). Beispielsweise gleichen allein die zugrundeliegenden technischen Prozessbeschreibungen bei IKT-Betriebsvereinbarungen nach § 87 Abs. 1 Nr. 6 BetrVG in der Praxis oft mehrbändigen Kompendien, sind aber häufig bereits kurz nach Fertigstellung inhaltlich schon wieder Makulatur. Die Hinzuziehung externer Sachverständiger zur Erfüllung der Betriebsratsaufgaben gem. § 80 Abs. 3 BetrVG sollte angesichts der steigenden spezifischen Know-How-Anforderungen durch vernetzte IKT eklatant an Bedeutung gewinnen.

Das immense Potential der digitalen Vernetzung von Wertschöpfungsketten ist also dazu geeignet, beträchtliche Teile der Arbeitswelt erheblich zu verändern, wenn nicht zu revolutionieren. Die bereits

---

8 Bundesarbeitsgericht, Beschluss vom 9.9.1975 – 1 ABR 20/74. *NJW* 1976 (6), 261–262.

vielerorts beklagte Erosion des klassischen »Normalarbeitsverhältnisses« und des »Normalbetriebs« wird unweigerlich fortschreiten. Betriebsgebundenheit und Verstetigung der Arbeitsbeziehungen mit klarer Rollenverteilung zwischen den Parteien werden in weiten Teilen weiter an Bedeutung verlieren. Die hergebrachten Rollenzuschreibungen und -funktionen der Parteien des Arbeitsverhältnisses werden zunehmend an Kontur verlieren. Damit einhergehend ist ein Bedeutungsverlust des Betriebsverfassungsrechts in seiner jetzigen Form absehbar. Es wird auf die Entwicklungen reagieren müssen, auf dem Wege legislatorischer Regulierung oder durch Änderung und Erweiterung im Wege richterlicher Rechtsfortbildung (zu einer Partizipation 4.0 Huchler 2017).

7. Partizipation als Norm »guter Arbeit« – Der Capability Approach

Empirische Forschung kann die Rahmenbedingungen erhellen, innerhalb derer sich die Mitbestimmung mehr oder weniger gut entfaltet: die Interessen verschiedener Gruppen von Arbeitnehmern bzw. Arbeitgebern an der Mitbestimmung explorieren sowie Funktionen und Folgen der Mitbestimmung aufzeigen. Allerdings lässt sich die Normativität der Mitbestimmung nicht auf die Empirie ihrer Umsetzungschancen reduzieren. Vielmehr ist die betriebliche Mitbestimmung eine integrale Institution der Wirtschaftsordnung und der Sozialordnung des Betriebes. Empirie kann allerdings helfen, Institutionen zu entwerfen oder zu modifizieren, die auch im entgrenzten Betrieb Mitbestimmung und damit Arbeitnehmern Teilhabe ermöglichen. Die normative Rückbindung an den sog. Befähigungsansatz oder Capability Approach (Sen und Nussbaum 1993; Nussbaum 1999; Sen 2005) interpretiert die institutionelle Ausgestaltung der Mitbestimmung unter dem Gesichtspunkt der Wahrung bzw. Ausweitung individueller Teilhabe und individueller Verwirklichungschancen. Aus dieser Perspektive sind Institutionen sowohl bezüglich ihres Potentials zur Ermöglichung von Teilhabe als auch empirisch mit Blick auf deren Verwirklichung zu prüfen. Dieser Ansatz soll in unserem Projekt für die betriebliche Mitbestimmung fruchtbar gemacht werden.

Literaturverzeichnis

Alewell, D. 2006. Zeitarbeit und Interimsmanagement in Deutschland – Ein empirischer und institutioneller Vergleich. In: *Schmalenbachs Zeitschrift für betriebswirtschaftliche Forschung (zfbf)* 58 (8): 990–1013.

Alt, R., Legner, C., und H. Österle. 2005. Virtuelle Organisation – Konzept, Realität und Umsetzung. *HMD-Praxis der Wirtschaftsinformatik*, 42 (242): 7–20.

Artus, Ingrid. 2014. Mitbestimmung und Leiharbeit. In: *WSI-Mitteilungen*, 67 (2): 113–121.

Artus, Ingrid, Röbenack, Silke und Clemens Kraetsch. 2014. Gründungsmotive. In: *Mitbestimmung* Heft 3: 27–29.

Atkinson, J. und N. Meager. 1986. *New forms of work organisation*. Institute of Manpower Studies.

Bach, N. 2009. *Effizienz der Führungsorganisation deutscher Konzerne*. Wiesbaden: Gabler Verlag.

Behrens, M. 2011. *Das Paradox der Arbeitgeberverbände. Von der Schwierigkeit durchsetzungsstarke Unternehmensinteressen kollektiv zu vertreten*. Berlin: Edition Sigma.

Behrens, M. und H. Dribbusch. 2014. Arbeitgebermaßnahmen gegen Betriebsräte: Angriffe auf die betriebliche Mitbestimmung. In: *WSI-Mitteilungen* 67 (2): 140–148.

Bellmann, L., Ellguth, P. und H. Seifert. 1998. Weiße Flecken in der Tarif-und Mitbestimmungslandschaft. *Die Mitbestimmung* 44 (11): 61–62.

Bialeck, N. und H. Hanau. 2018. Entgrenzung und Entbetrieblichung von Arbeitsverhältnissen als Herausforderung für die betriebliche Mitbestimmung. In: Redlich, T., Moritz, M. und J. P. Wulfsberg (Hrsg.) *Interdisziplinäre Perspektiven zur Zukunft der Wertschöpfung*. Wiesbaden: Springer Gabler, 177–193.

BMBF/TNS Infratest (Bilger, F. und B. von Rosenbaldt). 2011. *Weiterbildungsverhalten in Deutschland: AES 2010 Trendbericht*. Bonn, Berlin: BMBF.

Bosch, G. 2018. Die Debatte um Industrie 4.0 und Arbeit 4.0 in Deutschland. In: Fietze, S., Holtmann, D. und F. Schramm (Hrsg.) *Zwischen Provinzen und Metropolen – Stationen einer sozio-ökonomischen Reise*. Augsburg, München: Hampp, 233–242.

Brenke, K. 2011. *Solo-Selbständige in Deutschland – Strukturen und Erwerbsverläufe*. Forschungsbericht Nr. 423. Berlin: BMAS.

Bühner, Rolf. 1992. *Management-Holding*. Landsberg/Lech: Verl. Moderne Industrie.

Bühner, Rolf. 1996. *Gestaltung von Konzernzentralen*. Wiesbaden: Gabler.

Busch, C. und T. Vahle-Hinz. 2019. Gesundheit und Wohlbefinden in einer Arbeitswelt im Wandel: Aufrechterhaltung von Standards guter Arbeit bei multikulturellen Belegschaften und flexibler Arbeit. In: Alewell, Dorothea und Wenzel Matiaske (Hrsg.) *Standards Guter Arbeit – disziplinäre Positionen und interdisziplinäre Perspektiven*. Baden-Baden: Nomos: 39–61.

Coleman, J. S. 1990. *Foundations of Social Theory*. Cambridge: Belknap.

Däubler, W. und T. Klebe. 2015. Crowdwork: Die neue Form der Arbeit – Arbeitgeber auf der Flucht? In: *NZA* 2015 (17): 1032–1041.

Deinert, O. 2014. Kernbelegschaften – Randbelegschaften – Fremdbelegschaften. Herausforderungen für das Arbeitsrecht durch Reduzierung von Stammbelegschaften. In: *RdA* 2014 (2): 65–77.

Destatis (2017): *Weiterbildung*. Wiesbaden: Statistisches Bundesamt.

Deutscher Bundestag. 2001. *Entwurf eines Gesetzes zur Reform des Betriebsverfassungsgesetzes (BetrVerf-Reformgesetz)*. Drucksache 14/5741.

Dietl, H., Royer, S., und U. Stratmann. 2009. Value creation architectures and competitive advantage: lessons from the European automobile industry. In: *California Management Review* 51 (3): 24–48.

Dilger, A. 2002. *Ökonomik betrieblicher Mitbestimmung*. München/Mering: Hampp.

Dirlewanger, W. 1992. Outsourcing — Quell der Hoffnung? In: *Zeitschrift für Kommunikations- und EDV-Sicherheit* 8 (3): 187–195.

Drumm, H. J. 1996. Das Paradigma der Neuen Dezentralisation. In: *Die Betriebswirtschaft* 56 (1): 7–20.

Dunn, M. H. 1998: *Die Unternehmung als ein soziales System. Ein sozialwissenschaftlicher Beitrag zur Neuen Mikroökonomie*. Berlin: Duncker & Humblot.

Dütsch, M. und O. Struck. 2010. *Interne und externe Flexibilität: eine Analyse von Personalanpassungsformen anhand des IAB-Betriebspanels 2007*. Working Paper No. 2. Universität Bamberg.

Ellguth, P. 2018. Die betriebliche Mitbestimmung verliert an Boden. In: *IAB-Forum*. 24. Mai 2018. Onlinenachweis: https://www.iab-forum.de/die-betriebliche-mitbestimmung-verliert-an-boden/. Abrufdatum: 22. August 2018.

Ellguth, P. und S. Kohaut. 2010. Auf der Flucht? Tarifaustritte und die Rolle von Öffnungsklauseln. In: *Industrielle Beziehungen* 17 (4): 345–371.

Ellguth, P. und R. Trinczek. 2016. Erosion der betrieblichen Mitbestimmung – Welche Rolle spielt der Strukturwandel? In: *WSI-Mitteilungen* 69 (3): 172–182.

Ellguth, P. und S. Kohaut. 2016. Tarifbindung und betriebliche Interessenvertretung: Ergebnisse aus dem IAB-Betriebspanel 2015. In: *WSI-Mitteilungen* 69 (4): 283–291.

Ellguth, P. und S. Kohaut 2018. Tarifbindung und betriebliche Interessenvertretung: Ergebnisse aus dem IAB-Betriebspanel 2017. In: *WSI-Mitteilungen* 71 (4): 299–306.

Franzen, M. (2016). Folgen von Industrie 4.0 für die Betriebsverfassung – Betriebsbegriff und Vereinbarungen nach § 3 BetrVG. In: *Industrie 4.0 als Herausforderung des Arbeitsrechts*. München: ZAAR-Verlag. 107–126.

Frick, B. und D. Sadowski. 1995. Works councils, unions, and firm performance. The impact of workers' participation in Germany. In: Buttler, F., Franz, W., Schettkat, R. und D. Soskice (Hrsg.) *Institutional frameworks and labor market performance: comparative views on the U.S. and German economies*. London/New York, 46–81.

Gerlach, F. 2013. *Innovation und Mitbestimmung. Empirische Untersuchungen und Literaturstudien*. 2. korr. Aufl., Düsseldorf: Hans-Böckler-Stiftung.

Green, F. 2007. *Demanding Work The Paradox of Job Quality in the Affluent Economy*. Princeton: Princeton Univ. Press.

Greifenstein, R., Kißler, L. und H. Lange. 2017. *Trendreport Betriebsratswahlen 2014*. Study, Düsseldorf: Hans-Böckler-Stiftung.

Günther, J. und M. Böglmüller. 2015. Arbeitsrecht 4.0 – Arbeitsrechtliche Herausforderungen in der vierten industriellen Revolution. In: *NZA* 2015 (17): 1025–1031.

Haipeter T. 2017. Variety of Strategies. Arbeitgeberverbände ohne Tarifbindung in Deutschland. In: Sack D. und C. Strünck (Hrsg.) *Verbände unter Druck*. Zeitschrift für Politikwissenschaft – Sonderheft. Wiesbaden: Springer VS.

Hanau, H. 2016. Schöne digitale Arbeitswelt? In: *Neue juristische Wochenschrift (NJW)* 69 (36): 2613–2617.

Hanau, H. 2018. Arbeitskraftunternehmer 4.0. In: Fietze, S., Holtmann, D. und F. Schramm (Hrsg.) *Zwischen Provinzen und Metropolen – Stationen einer sozioökonomischen Reise*. Augsburg, München: Hampp, 299–304.

Hassel, A. 1999. The erosion of the German system of industrial relations. In: *British Journal of Industrial Relations* 37 (3): 483–505.

Heidemann, W. 2015. Trendbericht: Betriebliche Weiterbildung: Betriebs- und Dienstvereinbarungen. 2. aktualisierte Ausgabe. Düsseldorf: Hans-Böckler-Stiftung. *Report Nr. 9*.

Helfen, M., Nicklich, M. und J. Sydow. 2016. Interorganisationale Netzwerke und tarifpolitische Fragmentierung: Hebt Mehr-Arbeitgeber-Beschäftigung die Tarifeinheit aus den Angeln? In: *Industrielle Beziehungen* 23 (3): 280–308.

Hirschman, A. O. 1974: *Abwanderung und Widerspruch*. Tübingen: Mohr (Siebeck).

Homp, C. und W. Krüger. 1997. *Kernkompetenz-Management*. Wiesbaden: Gabler.

Huchler, N. 2017. Mitbestimmung 4.0: Innovation durch Partizipation und basisdemokratische Prozesse im Betrieb? In: *NZA-Beilage* 2017 (1): 121–125.

Jansen, C. 2018. *Regulierung der Arbeitsbeziehungen in Freien Berufen am Beispiel rechts-, wirtschafts- und steuerberatender Unternehmen*. München: Hampp.

Jirjahn, U. 2011. Ökonomische Wirkungen der Mitbestimmung: Ein Update. In: *Schmollers Jahrbuch* 131 (1): 3–57.

Kalleberg, A. 2001. Organizing flexibility: the flexible firm in a new century. In: *British Journal of Industrial Relations* 39 (4): 479–504.

Kania, T. und C. Klemm. 2006. Möglichkeiten und Grenzen der Schaffung anderer Arbeitnehmervertretungsstrukturen nach § 3 Abs. 1 Nr. 3 BetrVG. In: *RdA* 2006 (1): 22–27.

Keller, B. 2008. *Einführung in die Arbeitspolitik – Arbeitsbeziehungen und Arbeitsmarkt in sozialwissenschaftlicher Perspektive*. München, Wien: Oldenbourg.

Keller, B. 2018. Regulierung atypischer Beschäftigungsverhältnisse. In: Baron, D. und P. B. Hill (Hrsg.) *Atypische Beschäftigung und ihre sozialen Konsequenzen*. Wiesbaden: Springer VS, 215–245.

Keller, B. und H. Seifert (Hrsg.). 2013. *Atypische Beschäftigung zwischen Prekarität und Normalität.* Berlin: edition sigma.

Keller, B. und M. Wilkesmann. 2014. Untypisch atypisch Beschäftigte. Honorarärzte zwischen Befristung, Leiharbeit und (Solo-) Selbstständigkeit, Industrielle Beziehungen. In: *Zeitschrift für Arbeit, Organisation und Management* 21 (1): 99–125.

Kieser, A. 1996. Moden & Mythen des Organisierens. *Die Betriebswirtschaft: DBW* 56 (1): 21–39.

Koch, U. 2017. BetrVG § 1 Errichtung von Betriebsräten. In: Müller-Glöge, R. & Preis, U. und I. Schmidt (Hrsg.) *Erfurter Kommentar zum Arbeitsrecht.* (16. Aufl.). München: C.H. Beck.

Köhler, H.-D. 1999. Auf dem Weg zum Netzwerkunternehmen? Anmerkungen zu einem problematischen Konzept am Beispiel der deutschen Automobilkonzerne. In: *Industrielle Beziehungen* 6 (1): 36–51.

Kohaut, Susanne. 2018. Tarifbindung – der Abwärtstrend hält an. In: *IAB-Forum.* 24. Mai 2018. Onlinenachweis: https://www.iab-forum.de/tarifbindung-der-abwaerts trend-haelt-an/. Abrufdatum: 22. August 2018.

Kotthoff, H. 1981. *Betriebsräte und betriebliche Herrschaft. Eine Typologie von Partizipationsmustern im Industriebetrieb.* Frankfurt am Main.

Kotthoff, H. 1994. *Betriebsräte und Bürgerstatus. Wandel und Kontinuität betrieblicher Mitbestimmung.* München, Mering: Hampp.

Kraft, Kornelius und Jörg Stank. 2004. Die Auswirkungen der gesetzlichen Mitbestimmung auf die Innovationsaktivität deutscher Unternehmen. In: *Schmollers Jahrbuch* 124 (3): 421–449.

Krause, R. 2016. Digitalisierung der Arbeitswelt – Herausforderungen und Regelungsbedarf. In: *Verhandlungen des 71. Deutschen Juristentages.* Essen 2016. Bd. I. Gutachten. B. München: C. H. Beck.

Krebber, S. 2005. *Unternehmensübergreifende Arbeitsabläufe im Arbeitsrecht.* München: C. H. Beck.

Kullak, F. 1995. *Personalstrategien in Klein-und Mittelbetrieben: Eine transaktionskostentheoretisch fundierte empirische Analyse.* München, Mering: Hampp.

Lange, K. W. 1998. *Das Recht der Netzwerke: Moderne Formen der Zusammenarbeit in Produktion und Vertrieb.* Heidelberg: Verlag Recht und Wirtschaft.

Leßmann, O. 2013. Empirische Studien zum Capability Ansatz auf der Grundlage von Befragungen. In: Graf, G., Kapferer, E. und C. Sedmak (Hrsg.) *Der Capability Approach und seine Anwendung.* Wiesbaden: Springer VS, 25–61.

Martin, A. und S. Bartscher-Finzer. 2015. *Personal: Sozialisation – Integration – Kontrolle.* Stuttgart: Kohlhammer.

Matiaske, W. 1992. *Wertorientierungen und Führungsstil.* Frankfurt M. Bern: Lang.

Matiaske, W. 2004. Pourquoi pas? Rational Choice as Basic Theory for the Human Resources Management. In: *management revue* 15 (2): 249–263.

Matiaske, W. 2018. Das Arbeitsrecht als »Geschäftsgrundlage« der Personalwirtschaft? Kommentar zum Beitrag von Florian Schramm. In: Matiaske, W. und W.

Weber (Hrsg.) *Ideengeschichte der BWL: ABWL, Organisation, Personal, Rechnungswesen und Steuern.* Wiesbaden: Springer-Gabler, 503–507.

Matiaske, W. und T. Mellewigt. 2002. Motive, Erfolge und Risiken des Outsourcings – Befunde und Defizite der empirischen Outsourcing-Forschung. *Zeitschrift für Betriebswirtschaft* 72 (6): 641–659.

Mayer, J. 2000. *Veränderung und Angleichung tarifvertraglich geregelter Arbeitsbedingungen nach Betriebsübergang.* Hamburg: Diplomica Verlag.

Mefebue, A. B. 2013. *Die soziale Konstruktion des impliziten Arbeitsvertrages. Entwicklung und sozioökonomische Bedingungen.* Göttingen. Universitätsverlag Göttingen.

Mellewigt, T. und W. Matiaske. 2000. Strategische Konzernführung: Stand der empirischen betriebswirtschaftlichen Forschung. In: *Zeitschrift für Betriebswirtschaft* 70 (5): 611–631.

Moldaschl, M. und G. G. Voß (Hrsg.). 2003. *Subjektivierung von Arbeit.* München, Mering: Hampp.

Mückenberger, U. 1985. Die Krise des Normalarbeitsverhältnisses. Hat das Arbeitsrecht noch Zukunft? In: *Zeitschrift für Sozialreform* 31 (7): 415–434.

Mückenberger, U. 1985. Die Krise des Normalarbeitsverhältnisses. Hat das Arbeitsrecht noch Zukunft? In: *Zeitschrift für Sozialreform* 31 (8): 457–475.

Müller-Jentsch, W. 1995. From Collective Voice to Co-management. In: Rogers, J. und W. Streeck (Hrsg.) *Works Councils. Consultation, Representation, and Cooperation in Industrial Relations.* Chicago: Univ. of Chicago Press, 53–78.

Müller-Jentsch, W. 2008. Industrial Democracy: Historical Development and Current Challenges. In: *management revue* 19 (4): 260–273.

Müller-Jentsch, W. 2018. Seven decades of industrial relations in Germany: Stability and change through joint learning processes. In: *Employee Relations* 40 (4): 634–653.

Müller, Steffen. 2018. Warum gibt es Widerstand gegen Betriebsräte? In: *Wirtschaft im Wandel* 24 (2): 23–25.

Nienhüser, W., Glück, E. und H. Hoßfeld. 2016. Einstellungen zur Mitbestimmung der Arbeitnehmer – Welchen Einfluss haben Mitbestimmungserfahrungen? In: *WSI-Mitteilungen* 69 (3): 162–171.

Nienhüser, W. 1998. Macht bestimmt die Personalpolitik! Erklärung der betrieblichen Arbeitsbeziehungen aus macht- und austauschtheoretischer Perspektive. In: Martin, A. und W. Nienhüser (Hrsg.) *Personalpolitik. Wissenschaftliche Erklärung der Personalpolitik.* München, Mering: Hampp, 239–264.

Nienhüser, W. (2007). Betriebliche Beschäftigungsstrategien und atypische Arbeitsverhältnisse. Eine Erklärungsskizze aus Sicht einer politischen Personalökonomik. In: Keller, Berndt und Hartmut Seifert (Hrsg.) *Atypische Beschäftigung – Flexibilisierung und soziale Risiken.* Berlin: Sigma, 45–66.

Nienhüser, W. 2014. Works Councils. In: Wilkinson, A., Donaghey, J., Dundon, T. und R. B. Freeman (Hrsg.) *Handbook of Research on Employee Voice.* Cheltenham: Edward Elgar Press, 247–263.

Nienhüser, W. und W. Matiaske. 2006. Effects of the `Principle of Non-Discrimination´ on Temporary Agency Work in 15 European Countries. In: *Industrial Relations Journal* (37) 1: 64–77.

Nussbaum, M. 1999. *Gerechtigkeit oder das gute Leben*. Frankfurt a. M.: Suhrkamp.

Oehring, G. 1994. *FAG Kugelfischer überträgt Informationsverarbeitung an IBM.* In: Computerwoche.

Oetker, H. 2016. Digitalisierung der Arbeitswelt – Herausforderungen und Regelungsbedarf. In: *JZ* 71 (17): 817–824.

Pfeffer, J. 1996. *Competitive Advantage Through People: Unleashing the Power of the Work Force*. Boston: Harvard Business School Press.

Pfeiffer, S. 2014. Innovation und Mitbestimmung. Sammelrezension. In: *Industrielle Beziehungen – Zeitschrift für Arbeit, Organisation und Management* 21 (4): 390–404.

Pfeiffer, S. 2016. Soziale Technikgestaltung in der Industrie 4.0. In: Bundesministerium für Arbeit und Soziales (Hrsg.) *Werkheft 01 – Digitalisierung der Arbeitswelt*: 47–51. Onlinenachweis: https://www.arbeitenviernull.de/dialogprozess/werkhefte/erstes-werkheft.html. Abrufdatum: 30. September 2018.

Picot, A., Reichwald, R. und R. T. Wigand. 1996. *Die grenzenlose Unternehmung: Information, Organisation und Management*. 1. Aufl., Wiesbaden: Gabler.

Pongratz, H. J. und G. G. Voß. 2003. *Arbeitskraftunternehmer – Erwerbsorientierungen in entgrenzten Arbeitsformen*. Berlin: edition sigma.

Prahalad, C. K. und G. Hamel. 1990. The Core Competence of the Corporation. In: *Harvard Business Review* 68 (3): 79–91.

Promberger, M. 2012. *Topographie der Leiharbeit. Flexibilität und Prekarität einer atypischen Beschäftigungsform*. Berlin: edition sigma.

Rehder, B. und B. Vogel. 2015. Arbeit – Politik – Recht: Das Rechts(system) als Forschungsdesiderat in den Arbeitsbeziehungen. In: *Industrielle Beziehungen* 22 (1): 8–12.

Reinhart, G., Schack, R. und H. Ferstl. 2008. Organisationsanpassungen – von der Digitalen Fabrik zum Digitalen Unternehmensnetzwerk. In: *ZWF Zeitschrift für wirtschaftlichen Fabrikbetrieb* 103 (1–2): 17–22.

Richter, R. und E. Furubotn. 1996. *Neue Institutionenökonomik. Eine Einführung und kritische Würdigung*. Tübingen: Mohr (Siebeck).

Rieble, V. 2014. Mitbestimmung in komplexen Betriebs- und Unternehmensstrukturen. In: *NZA-Beilage* 2014 (1): 28–30.

Rohe, M. 1998. *Netzverträge*. Tübingen: Mohr Siebeck.

Rousseau, D. M. 1995. *Psychological Contracts in Organizations. Understanding Written and Unwritten Agreements*. Thousand Oaks: Sage Publ.

Schmidt, R. und R. Trinczek. 1999. Der Betriebsrat als Akteur der industriellen Beziehungen. In: Müller-Jentsch, W. (Hrsg.) *Konfliktpartnerschaft. Akteure und Institutionen der industriellen Beziehungen*. 3., überarbeitete und erweiterte Auflage. München/Mering: Hampp, 103–128.

Schnabel, C. 2005. Gewerkschaften und Arbeitgeberverbände: Organisationsgrade, Tarifbindung und Einflüsse auf Löhne und Beschäftigung. In: *Zeitschrift für Arbeitsmarktforschung (Journal for Labour Market Research)* 38 (2,3): 181–196.

Schnabel, C. 2016. Gewerkschaften auf dem Rückzug? Mythen, Fakten und Herausforderungen. In: *Wirtschaftsdienst* 96 (6): 426–432.

Schneider, Helena und Sandra Vogel. 2018. Tarifbindung der Beschäftigten in Deutschland – Eine Auswertung des Sozioökonomischen Panels. In *IW-Report*. Nr. 15/2018. Köln: Institut der deutschen Wirtschaft.

Schramm, F. 2018. Von Arbeitsrecht nur Spurenelemente? Zum Verhältnis von Personalwirtschaft und Arbeitsrecht. In: Matiaske, W. und W. Weber (Hrsg.) *Ideengeschichte der BWL: ABWL, Organisation, Personal, Rechnungswesen und Steuern*. Wiesbaden: Springer-Gabler, 495–502.

Schuler-Harms, Margarete und Katharina Goldberg. 2019. Soziale Absicherung von alter und neuer Selbständigkeit als Herausforderung für das Sozialrecht. In: Alewell, Dorothea und Wenzel Matiaske (Hrsg.) *Standards Guter Arbeit – disziplinäre Positionen und interdisziplinäre Perspektiven*. Baden-Baden: Nomos, 189–212.

Seifert, H. 2002. Betriebliche Bündnisse für Arbeit – Beschäftigen statt entlassen. In: Seifert, H. (Hrsg.) *Betriebliche Bündnisse für Arbeit*. Berlin: edition sigma, 65–85.

Sen, A. 2005. Human Rights and Capabilities. In: *Journal of Human Development* 6 (2): 151–166.

Sen, A. und M. Nussbaum (Hrsg.). 1993. *The Quality of Life*. Oxford: Clarendon Press.

Sennett, R. 1998. *The Corrosion of Character: The Personal Consequences of Work in the New Capitalism*. New York: Norton.

Stadlbauer, F. 2007. *Zwischenbetriebliche Anwendungsintegration: IT-Management in Unternehmensnetzwerken*. Wiesbaden: Springer.

Stettes, O. 2007. *Effiziente Mitbestimmung: Eine ökonomische Analyse*. Köln: Deutscher Instituts-Verlag.

Stettes, Oliver. 2015. Betriebsratswahlen 2014. Ein Rückblick auf Basis der IW-Betriebsratswahlbefragung. In: *IW-Trends* 42 (1): 3–20.

Sydow, J. und C. Wirth (Hrsg.). 1999. *Arbeit, Personal und Mitbestimmung in Unternehmungsnetzwerken*. München, Mering: Hampp.

Wassermann, W. und W. Rudolph. 2007. *Leiharbeit als Gegenstand betrieblicher Mitbestimmung*. Arbeitspapier (148), Düsseldorf: Hans-Böckler-Stiftung.

Wehner, M. C., Kabst, R. und M. Meifert. 2017. HR im internationalen Vergleich. In: *Personalmagazin* 2017 (2): 14–19.

Weitbrecht, H. 2017. Arbeitgeberverbände in der Tarifpolitik und im tarifpolitischen System der Bundesrepublik. In: Schroeder, W. und B. Weßels (Hrsg.) *Handbuch Arbeitgeber- und Wirtschaftsverbände in Deutschland*. Wiesbaden: Springer, 316–341.

Whyte, William H. 1956. *The Organization Man*. Harmondsworth, Penguin.

Wilkesmann, M., Ruiner, C. und B. Apitzsch. 2016. Hochqualifizierte Solo-Selbstständige im operativen Kern – Auswirkungen des Einsatzes von Honorarärzten auf die Professionsorganisation Krankenhaus. In: Matiaske, W. und A. Czaya (Hrsg.) *Periphere Arbeit im Zentrum*. Baden-Baden: Nomos, 95–117.

Williamson, O. E. 1984. Efficient labour organization. In: Stephen, F. H. (Hrsg.) *Firms, Organization and Labour. Approaches to the economics of work Organization*. London: Palgrave Macmillan, 87–146.

Wisskirchen, G. und J. Block. 2017. Auf der Suche nach dem Arbeitgeber: Mitbestimmung in komplexen Organisationsformen: oder et hät noch immer joot jejange!. In: *NZA-Beilage* 2017 (1): 90–95.

Zumkeller, A. R. 2015. Arbeitsrecht 4.0: Mittendrin statt nur dabei! In: *BB* 2015 (30): 1.

Zu den Autorinnen und Autoren

Dorothea Alewell ist Professorin für Betriebswirtschaft mit Schwerpunkt Personalwirtschaft an der Universität Hamburg. Ihre Forschungsschwerpunkte liegen im Bereich Personalwirtschaft und der ökonomischen Analyse des Arbeitsrechts.

Christine Busch ist Postdoc der Arbeits- und Organisationspsychologie an der Universität Hamburg. Sie leitet das BMBF-Verbundprojekt »e-RegioWerk« und ein Teilprojekt im Landes-Verbundprojekt »Standards Guter Arbeit«. Ihr Forschungsschwerpunkt ist Betriebliches Gesundheitsmanagement.

Jörg Felfe ist Professor für Arbeits- Organisations- & Wirtschaftspsychologie an der Helmut-Schmidt-Universität/Uni Bw Hamburg. Seine Forschungsschwerpunkte sind Führung, Mitarbeiterbindung, Betriebliches Gesundheitsmanagement.

Katharina Goldberg ist wissenschaftliche Mitarbeiterin am Lehrstuhl für Öffentliches Recht, insbes. Öffentliches Wirtschafts- und Umweltrecht an der Helmut-Schmidt-Universität. Ihre Forschungsschwerpunkte liegen im internationalen Steuerrecht und der Rechtstheorie. Sie beschäftigt sich zudem mit dem digitalen Fortschritt und dem Wandel von Rechtsnormen.

Hans Hanau ist Professor für Bürgerliches Recht, Handels-, Wirtschaft- und Arbeitsrecht an der Helmut-Schmidt-Universität/Universität der Bundeswehr Hamburg. Seine Forschungsschwerpunkte liegen im deutschen und europäischen individuellen und kollektiven Arbeitsrecht, insbesondere im Betriebsverfassungs- und Tarifrecht.

Sven Hauff leitet die Professur für Arbeit, Personal und Organisation an der Helmut-Schmidt-Universität/Universität der Bundeswehr Hamburg. In seinen Forschungsarbeiten setzt er sich insbesondere mit der Gestaltung des Human Resource Managements und den Wirkungen auf die Beschäftigten und den Unternehmenserfolg auseinander.

Ines Kanngießer ist wissenschaftliche Mitarbeiterin an der Professur für Betriebswirtschaftslehre mit dem Schwerpunkt Personalwirtschaft an der Fakultät Wirtschafts- und Sozialwissenschaften der Universität Hamburg. Forschungsgebiet ist die personalwirtschaftliche Analyse des Arbeitsrechts.

Katharina Klug ist Post Doc an der Professur für Arbeits- Organisations- & Wirtschaftspsychologie der Helmut-Schmidt-Universität/Uni Bw Hamburg. Ihre Forschungsschwerpunkte sind Arbeitsplatzunsicherheit, die Flexibilisierung der Arbeitswelt, sowie Führung und Gesundheit.

Wenzel Matiaske ist Professor für Betriebswirtschaftslehre am Institut für Personal und Arbeit der Helmut-Schmidt-Universität/Uni BW Hamburg und Research Fellow des Deutschen Instituts für Wirtschaftsforschung Berlin.

Tobias Moll ist wissenschaftlicher Mitarbeiter am Lehrstuhl für Personalwirtschaft an der Universität Hamburg. Er promoviert zum Themenkomplex Religion, Religiosität und Spiritualität am Arbeitsplatz.

Barbara Müller ist Professorin für Kirchengeschichte am Fachbereich Evangelische Theologie der Universität Hamburg.

Daniela Rastetter ist Professorin für Personal und Gender im Fachbereich Sozialökonomie an der Fakultät Wirtschafts- und Sozialwissenschaften der Universität Hamburg; Arbeitsbereiche: Frauen in Führungspositionen, Emotionsarbeit im Dienstleistungsbereich, Mikropolitik, Geschlechterverhältnisse in Organisationen und Diversity Management.

Florian Schramm ist Professor für Betriebswirtschaftslehre mit dem Schwerpunkt Personalwirtschaft an der Fakultät Wirtschafts- und Sozialwissenschaften der Universität Hamburg. Forschungsgebiete sind die Karriereforschung, die Qualität des Arbeitslebens sowie die personalwirtschaftliche Analyse des Arbeitsrechts.

Margarete Schuler-Harms ist Professorin für Öffentliches Recht, ins-bes. Öffentliches Wirtschafts- und Umweltrecht an der Helmut-Schmidt-Universität/Universität der Bundeswehr Hamburg. Sie forscht schwerpunktmäßig zum Medienrecht und zum Sozial- und im Gesundheitsrecht.

Christoph Seibert ist Professor für Systematische Theologie am Fachbereich Evangelische Theologie der Universität Hamburg.

Tim Vahle-Hinz ist wissenschaftlicher Mitarbeiter am Lehrstuhl für Occupational Health Psychology der Humboldt-Universität zu Berlin. Er forscht zum Themenschwerpunkt Arbeit und Gesundheit, unter anderem mit einer Fokussierung auf flexible Beschäftigungsverhältnisse.

Oliver Vornfeld, B.A. in Soziologie, Student der Evangelischen Theologie an der Universität Hamburg, studentische Hilfskraft beim Teilprojekt »Areit und Sinn« des interdisziplinären Forschungsverbundes »Standards guter Arbeit«